ALTERNATIVE
POLITICAL
ECONOMY
MODELS OF
TRANSITION

This book is dedicated to my family:

My parents, Spiros and Georgia

My brothers, Christos, Vangelis and sister Alexandra

My wife, Eleni, and daughter, Jorgia-Ariana.

ALTERNATIVE
POLITICAL
ECONOMY
MODELS OF
TRANSITION

JOHN **MARANGOS**

Routledge
Taylor & Francis Group

LONDON AND NEW YORK

First published 2009 by Transaction Publishers

Published 2017 by Routledge
4 Park Square, Milton Park, Abingdon, Oxon OX14 4RN
605 Third Avenue, New York, NY 10017

Routledge is an imprint of the Taylor & Francis Group, an informa business

Library of Congress Catalog Number: 2007033909

Library of Congress Cataloging-in-Publication Data

Marangos, John, 1962-
    Alternative political economy models of transition : the Russian and East European perspective / John Marangos ; with a new introduction by the author.
        p. cm.
    Rev. ed. of: Alternative economic models of transition, c2004.
    Includes bibliographical references and index.
    ISBN 978-1-4128-0696-1 (alk. paper)
    1. Comparative economics. 2. Europe, Eastern—Economic poli-cy—1989- 3. Former Soviet republics—Economic policy. 4. Europe, Eastern—Politics and government—1989- 5. Former Soviet republics—Politics and government. I. Marangos, John, 1962- Alternative economic models of transition. II. Title.

HB90.M359 2008
330.947'0009049--dc22

2007033909

ISBN 13: 978-1-4128-0696-1 (pbk)

Contents

List of Figures and Tables   vii

Foreword   ix

Acknowledgements   xi

Introduction to the Transaction Edition   xiii

PART I: COMPARATIVE MODELS OF TRANSITION

Chapter 1   The Collapse of the Stalinist Economic System   3

Chapter 2   The Analytical Framework   27

Chapter 3   The Cost of Transition   67

PART II: CASE STUDIES IN TRANSITION ECONOMIES

Chapter 4   The Shock Therapy Model of Transition   73

Chapter 5   The Neoclassical Gradualist Model of Transition   111
Preventive Therapy

Chapter 6   The Post Keynesian Model of Transition: 137
Developing a Civilized Society

Chapter 7   The Pluralistic Market Socialist Model of Transition   169

Chapter 8   The Non-Pluralistic Model of Market Socialism: 205
The Chinese Approach

PART III: CONCLUSIONS

Chapter 9   Was There an Optimal Model of Transition?   239

Appendix   251

Bibliography   267

Index   311

List of Figures and Tables

Figure 1   31

Figure 2   31

Table 1:   Alternative Models of Transition Based on Primary Elements   50

Table 2:   Secondary Elements of Transition Models   63

Table 3:   The Shock Therapy Process of Transition   98

Table 4:   Shock Therapy and Level of International Foreign Aid   106

Table 5:   The Neoclassical Gradualist Process of Transition   133

Table 6:   The Post Keynesian Process of Transition   164

Table 7:   The Market Socialist Process of Transition   197

Table 8:   The Chinese Process of Transition   231

Table 9:   Ranking of Alternative Models of Transition   238
       on the Basis of Elements of Cost of Transition

Table 10: Cost Indices of Alternative Models of Transition   239

Table 11: Ranking of Alternative Models of Transition   241
       on the Basis of Total Cost of Transition

Foreword

The collapse of Stalinism at the end of the 1980s surprised almost every-one, whatever their political perspective, and subsequent developments have continued to amaze, and often to disappoint, us. Anti-Stalinist Marxists – the great majority, by 1989 – hoped that the overthrow of the bureaucratic dictator-ship would allow the creation of decentralised, democratic socialist societies throughout Eastern Europe and, perhaps, eventually also in China. The exiled Czech economist Ota Šik had proposed a "Third Way' of this type after Soviet tanks demolished the Prague Spring of 1968. It soon became apparent, however, that there was absolutely no prospect of such a development in the 1990s.

Western liberals had great expectations of a quite different sort. Given the overwhelming advantages offered by private property and a full market economy, they anticipated a seamless adaptation to capitalism. A brief and very rapid tran-sition process, they believed, would permit the former victims of Stalinism to catch up with the West, probably within a generation. Their hopes, too, were soon dashed. Instead of the anticipated rapid growth and painless adjustment, serious problems emerged in all the transition economies, even in those most favourably placed, like the former East Germany. In most areas of Eastern Europe living standards plunged, and in some of them the majority of the population are still much less well off, in 2003, than they had been fifteen years earlier.

It is now a commonplace that institutions matter: not just organisational infrastructure such as the services of accountants, lawyers, bankers, public officials and regulators, but also more intangible (and much more important) questions of codes of behaviour, honesty and trust that determine the size of transactions costs – and indeed whether profitable transactions are possible in the first place. Where these institutions developed rapidly, building on what was there in 1989 and in some cases on a cultural heritage dating back to 1939, the transition process really was fast and relatively painless: Hungary, Poland and the Czech republic are prime examples. Where they failed to emerge the result was disaster, with economic decline compounded by political disorder, large-scale crime and pervasive corruption: Albania, Serbia, the Ukraine, above all Russia are cases in point.

All this, to repeat, is by now so obvious as to sound almost banal, but it was much less obvious to mainstream economists at the time, and many of them are still not quite sure what to make of it. The great merit of John Marangos's book

ix

is that he puts all these questions into a coherent theoretical framework, taking a political economy approach that integrates economics and politics with the social and ideological context in order to comprehend the failures (and also the successes) of the transition process. Marangos constructs five models of transition, which can be thought of as Weberian ideal types. Two of them are neoclassical: the shock therapy or 'big bang' model and the gradualist approach. The third is a Post Keynesian model, and the remaining two are forms of market socialism, with and without political democracy. The five models are articulated in six dimensions: formal economic analysis; competing notions of what constitutes a good society; beliefs concerning the feasible speed of adjustment; the relevant political structures; ideology; and the importance of initial conditions.

Marangos's analysis is too detailed and subtle to summarise here. Note, however, the importance of macroeconomics, emphasised especially in the Post Keynesian model but largely ignored in the neoclassical shock therapy model with its implicit assumption of full employment in the (rapidly-attainable) long run. Consider, also, the relative importance attributed in the five models to the goals of individual freedom, equality, community and material welfare, and the extent to which they are thought to be in conflict with each other. Ponder the quite different assumptions made in each model about the speed at which institutions, organisations, values and patterns of behaviour can realistically be expected to change. Consider the role that political democracy plays in each model, and the role of path-dependence (or hysteresis) in highlighting the significance of initial conditions. These are just a few of the issues that arise from Marangos's analysis, which is scholarly and comprehensive in its scope and nature.

His models can used in two ways. They certainly offer a means of interpreting the transition as a historical (though still continuing) process, but they also provide a framework for conducting a fascinating thought-experiment: how *should* the transition have been carried out? Was there an optimal model of transition? Could things have been done better? Or, as Marangos puts it in his concluding chapter: which model, if adopted, would have minimised the costs of transition? He distinguishes the economic, political and ideological costs borne by the citizens of the transition economies themselves, and adds to them what he terms 'international costs' of aid and direct investment incurred by foreigners. He then ranks each model, in each dimension, and assigns numerical values to the costs associated with each one. It is a highly original and distinctive method of analysis, and Marangos's conclusion will attract considerable controversy. The neoclassical gradualist model, he argues, offered the lowest cost of transition, followed by the shock therapy, authoritarian (Chinese) market socialist, democratic market socialist, and Post Keynesian models, in that order. Many readers will disagree with this ranking; I do myself. Many will quarrel with the methods used to obtain it. But no-one can deny the importance of the issues that Marangos raises.

J. E. King

Acknowledgements

This book is the result of a PhD thesis, 'Alternative Models of Transition for the Russian and Eastern European Economies', that I pursued at LaTrobe University, Melbourne, Australia. I received the assistance of a number of people in the preparation and completion of this book. First of all, I am grateful to John King who supervised my research and for writing the Foreword. His advice, guidance and understanding were valuable and greatly appreciated. I am thankful to Alicia Glenane and Sandra Bucovaz for proofreading the document and to Trisha Baker for formatting the document. I would also like to thank the anonymous referees for their constructive ideas, which transformed my PhD thesis into a book. Lastly, but not least, I am indebted to my wife, Eleni Petrousis, and my daughter, Jorgia-Ariana, for their support, encouragement, understanding and persistence.

Introduction to the Transaction Edition

Dear Reader,

It gives me great pleasure that you are holding in your hands *Alternative Political Economy Models of Transition*, published by Transaction. As we are approaching two decades of transition experience, I would argue the book more than maintains its relevance. The transition process has been associated with unemployment, inflation, inequality of income and wealth and a reduction in the standards of living for the average citizen in Russia, Eastern Europe, the former Soviet Union republics and Asia. The advice from international financial institutions (mainly the IMF and World Bank) and mature market economies to privatize state enterprises, minimize government intervention and liberalize international trade was essential, in their view, to stabilize the transition economies and create an environment conducive to 'creative destruction'. The emphasis during transition on economic variables ignoring politics, institutions, ideology, culture and generally the initial conditions is a reflection of the dominance around the world of the neo-liberal conceptualization of economic theory. As the citizens of the transition and developing economies are searching for alternatives to the Washington Consensus, the book attempts to provide workable processes towards alternative goals of transition. Hence, I emphasize the significance of the methodology adopted in this book.

Alternative Political Economy Models of Transition explicitly deals, from a political economy perspective, with transition issues that have been ignored by traditional economic theory. The book examines the prevailing consensus on transition and, as such, illustrates alternative processes to the ongoing transformation of these societies. The transition was, and is, a holistic, historical, dynamic and comparative process in nature. Political economy stresses that making economic sense and understanding economic relationships is not feasible without explicit awareness of power, institutions and values. The book analyzes issues in ways that go beyond traditional economic theories. Its focus is on alternative processes, politics, institutions, ideology-culture, inequality and corruption during transition. Meanwhile, with the entry to the EU, for most commentators the transition process has been completed. But social development, what the goal of transition should have been, is a never-ending undertaking. Hence, again, this highlights the relevance of the book.

The book made it to the bestsellers list in economics while published by Ashgate. My interpretation of the book reviews reveals that the book was a welcomed addition to the literature. John Hall (2005, p. 290) writes that '... I would like to applaud Marangos for his undertaking and for introducing a clear, useful, detailed, and operational approach to this complex subject' and 'He [Marangos] has generated a well-formulated, well-thought-out, and well-intended contribution to an important topic'. Alfred Oehlers (2004, pp. 311-312) writes 'it provides a clear exposition of the different ways the transition process may be conceived utilizing different and contending approaches within economics... This is couched within a rich tapestry providing an appreciation of the wider economic, social and political aspects involved, to present a comprehensive and holistic view of an economic system and the process of transition' and 'Marangos makes a useful contribution. The blend of theoretical and empirical material makes for an interesting approach to the subject'. Vliegenthart (2007, p. 477) writes that 'The differences between the various models are not well discussed in most of the literature on the process of economic transformation. It is here that Marangos makes an important contribution' and 'Overall, Marangos' book provides a well-informed state of the art on the economic debates that were held in the postsocialist countries in the last fifteen years. It contains useful insights in the different roads that could be taken in the economic transformation towards a market economy. Here the author demonstrates thorough knowledge of the different models'.

The main criticisms that the book received had to do with the evaluation and the ranking of the models in Chapter 9 without any resort to empirical evidence. John King in his Forward anticipated that 'the conclusion reached by Marangos will attract considerable controversy. The neoclassical gradualist model, he argues, offered the lowest cost of transition, followed by the shock therapy, authoritarian (Chinese) market socialist, democratic market socialist, and Post Keynesian models, in that order. Many readers will disagree with this ranking; I do myself. Many will quarrel with the methods used to obtain it'.

In my defense, I stated in the beginning of Chapter 9 that 'Consequently, my ambition is modest: to provide some insights to this important problem' of identifying an optimum model of transition. Also, I attempted to expand the comparison to incorporate the initial conditions and institutions revealing different results. I stated in p. 30 that 'The book is restricted to the development of theoretical and conceptual models of transition' and 'As such, empirical evidence will be incorporated selectively' (p. 31). Today, as we approach two decades of transition, the questions posed by the reviewers require answers; I do not deny that. Hopefully, the publication of *Alternative Political Economy Models of Transition* will stimulate such research.

I am indebted to my wife, Eleni, and my daughter, Jorgia-Ariana, for their understanding and patience. I would like to thank Transaction Publishers, especially Mary Curtis, for their willingness to make my book accessible to a wider audience. Lastly, I would like to thank my friends Aris and Xenia Bitzenis, they have proved to be "true" friends.

May your reading be challenging and why not troubling,

John Marangos
August 2007

References

Hall, J. (2005), Book Review: Alternative Economic Models of Transition, *Journal of Economic Issues*, March Vol. 39, No. 1, pp. 288-91.

Oehlers, A. (2004), Book Review: Alternative Economic Models of Transition, *Global Business and Economic Review*, Vol. 6, No. 2, pp. 310-2.

Vliegenthrat, A. (2007), Book Review: Alternative Economic Models of Transition, *Review of Radical Political Economy*, Vol. 39, No. 3, pp. 476-9.

Part I

Comparative Models of Transition

Chapter 1

The Collapse of the Stalinist Economic System

1 Introduction

The Central European, Eastern European, and Soviet Union economies, up to their collapse, were still functioning on the basic principles of the Stalinist economic system. Although changes took place, like the 1965 Liberman-Kosygin reform in the Soviet Union, they did not alter the economic system significantly. Thus, an analysis of the Stalinist economic system produces a useful approximation of the economic, political, and ideological structures of the Central, Eastern European, and Soviet Union (CEESU) up to its collapse. The reasons for the collapse of the Stalinist economic system have been analyzed extensively, for example by Nove (1983, 1989a), Desai (1989), Kornai (1992a), and Easterly and Fisher (1994). The dominant way of thinking shown in the literature concentrates on identifying the reasons for the collapse of the Stalinist economic system based only on economic relationships. This is a very simplistic analysis, which shows an incomplete understanding of the interaction of economic relations with other elements of society, especially with the political structure and ideology.

Krugman (1994, p. 63) asserted that economic growth based on the expansion of inputs could not be sustained forever. While I accept that the sources of extensive growth are finite, this alone was inadequate to explain the ultimate collapse. The Stalinist economic system, like any other system of economic development, was not restricted to the economic field. It was accompanied by political and ideological structures: 'the processes of the creation and realization of economic value are seen to depend at every moment on the concatenation of forces – economic as well as non economic – that combine to produce a unique effect, whether that be the money form of value, capital, surplus-value, and so forth' (Amariglio and Ruccio, 1994 p. 27). The political and ideological aspects of the society are fundamental: indeed economic systems cannot be understood or assessed in narrow economic terms. That is because the state has a monopoly of the legitimate use of force as a means of imposing restrictions

3

on individual behaviour, and the prevailing ideology releases the appropriate directives, moral standards, and values to motivate people to behave in certain predictable ways. The purpose of this analysis is to redress this neglect of the political and ideological elements by examining the economic, political, and ideological structures in an analytical framework in which they are all internalized. In addition, the aim of this chapter is to analyze the elements of the Stalinist system to identify which, if any, elements of centrally administered socialism should be retained during the transition process.

If we are to understand the Stalinist economic system, or any other economic system, it is essential to view it in a broad social science context. To understand the collapse of the Stalinist economic system, it is imperative to analyze all the relationships that influence economic choices. Whereas the economic structure of the Stalinist system did not encourage reform, the political and ideological structures were potential sources of reform; consequently, the collapse of the Stalinist system could have been avoided. Thus, we must examine the structure of the political authorities and the roles of the state as well as the prevailing ideology, which all impinge on the making of economic choices. By contrast, traditional economic analysis rests on the assumption of the supremacy of economic relationships, ignoring the influence of politics and ideology on economic outcomes.

Economic analysis and policy have to be seen from the broad social science perspective, since the economic structure of a society does not exist in a vacuum. Societies are not organized only on the basis of economic relationships. Engels (1977, p. 75) argues in a letter sent to J. Bloch on 21–22 September 1870 that 'according to the materialist conception of history, the ultimately determining element in history is the production and reproduction of real life. Neither Marx nor I have ever asserted more than this. Therefore if somebody twists this into saying that the economic factor is the only determining one, he is transforming that proposition into a meaningless, abstract, absurd phrase.'

No less important than economic factors are political institutions and ideology. It should be noted that the political and ideological structures could foster reform, which would have an impact on the whole system, as well as upon economic relations. That is because there is an intimate connection between these aspects, and societies are kept unified by the balanced development of the economic, political, and ideological structures. As with every economic system, the Stalinist economic system is governed by the need of balanced development of the economic, political, and ideological structures.

In this chapter I attempt to develop an analytical framework to aid understanding the relationship between the economic, political, and ideological structures. Whilst these different elements can be combined in different ways, in reality only certain combinations are possible, thus giving rise to certain economic systems. I argue that, while the economic, political, and ideological structures are interconnected, they must be consistent. It is stressed that the establishment of a consistent economic system requires: consistency within the economic structure; consistency between the political and economic structures; and, finally, consistency between the prevailing ideology and the politico-economic structure. Consistency, however, is not enough; a consistent economic system must be flexible and able to adapt to changes in social reality, thus making possible its survival over time. In other words, it must be viable (Ward, 1990a, p. 47). Thus, the economic system, in its broad social science context, must be both consistent and viable. In this way we are able to internalize the political and ideological structures.

Through these two concepts, we are able to view the economic system in its totality. Our focus, then, is not on narrow economic relationships but rather on the basis of economic–politico–ideological relationships. A consequence of viewing the economic system in this way is that it becomes apparent that changes in one structure must be accompanied by changes in the other structures; this is necessary in order to maintain consistency. Each structure being internalized within the economic system has the ability to stimulate reforms when social reality changes, consequently avoiding bottlenecks. However, the ultimate aim of any change should be not only the achievement of consistency but also of viability – the establishment of an economic system that has the capacity to change under changing conditions.

The method developed in this chapter is applied to an examination of the interrelationship between the economic, political, and ideological structures of the Stalinist economic system. Using the concepts of consistency and viability as analytical tools, we examine the system from a new and enlightening perspective. I will argue that the Stalinist economic system was once a consistent economic system: the economic–political–ideological structures were developed in such a way as to give rise to an economic system which facilitated the economic development of the Soviet Union in the 1930s and 1940s. Consistency made possible the survival of the Stalinist system in the short run. However, it did not facilitate internal change with the changing economic conditions; not only the economic structure but also the political and ideological structures were unable to foster reform. In consequence, the Stalinist economic system became inconsistent under the new economic conditions, rendering impossible the development of an economic system that would survive in the long run – that is, a viable economic system. Attention is now turned to the development of the analytical framework that will be used in the context of this work. Unlike the dominant way of thinking – as reflected in the work of Easterly and Fisher (1994), for example – the methodology developed here internalizes the impact of political structure and ideology which also contributed to the collapse of the Stalinist system.

2 Consistency and Viability

The ultimate survival of a society depends on whether or not the interrelationships between its institutions and its members are consistent with each other. History reveals a plethora of examples of societies being able to survive and advance because their structures brought people together in a productive fashion. On the other hand, there are examples of societies that did not survive because of a lack of consistency in the different elements within the society. As Giersh (1989, p. 1) argues, 'the economic order must correspond to the social order and the philosophy of the state. If these various components of underlying philosophy are compatible, then the system is stable.'

Societies have adopted various mechanisms to structure their politico-economic spheres. Among the most important are authority (central administration) and exchange, assuming that tradition is not relevant. The role of ideology is to justify the claims of control or autonomy, to induce personality transformation towards the claims, and to attempt to solve the free rider problem. The achievement of individual goals depends on the decisions and actions of the other members of the society. This makes the achievement of individual goals uncertain (Kemp, 1988, p. 9). Through authority, the pursuit of power or control, or through autonomy, the pursuit of freedom or independence, people try to reduce the uncertainty of achieving their goals.

However, societies need from time to time to restructure the internal relationships of their members. A consistent economic system needs to be flexible and adapt to changes. Changes in the way societies are structured are necessary because the goals that members pursue and the constraints they encounter cannot be taken as fixed. People change the content and the relative priority of their goals and values over time, so the system needs to introduce new mechanisms that facilitate their achievement. War, famine, or natural disaster may also result in a radical change of constraints, goals, and behavior, thus initiating internal changes. A particularly influential factor is competition with other societies. This puts pressure on each society to advance; otherwise, it will be seen to be falling behind, particularly in a world of international competition.

Thus, the survival of a particular economic-politico-ideological structure depends on its ability to introduce necessary reforms. Failure to adapt to the new conditions will result in the ultimate collapse of that particular structure. The outdated relationships give way to the new, either through a process of evolution or through command. However, the ultimate aim of reforms should be the balanced development of each aspect of the society – political, economic and ideological – as to achieve consistency. Otherwise, the whole reform will be doomed to failure. It is argued that the historical development of societies is the result of an endless struggle for consistency.

To understand and assess the Stalinist economic system, we need first of all to ask whether the system achieves consistency. This means that the system should aim at establishing consistency within the economic structure. Once the society has chosen its economic structure, its choice would ultimately have consequences for the political structure – requiring the establishment of consistency between the political and economic structures. For the system to function adequately, the establishment of a consistent politico-economic structure demands an ideology consistent with the society's economic and political structures. In what follows, we look in turn at each of these aspects.

2.1 Establishing Consistency Within the Economic Structure

An economic structure consists of three elements: property relations, organizational relations, and motivational relations. In terms of property relations, ownership of property results in property rights: the right to exclude other members from the appropriation of the resource, the right to use as well as the right to appropriate the surplus earned. Property is the result of scarcity and is a means by which the members of society are stratified into social classes. Organizational relations specify how economic units are coordinated so they can achieve their goals. The economic units are central authorities, households, and enterprises. With respect to organizational relations between economic units, information plays a critical role. Ward (1988, p. 4) outlines the role of information in determining the nature of objectives and how they can be achieved; the achievement of balance (the quantity demanded being equal to quantity supplied); and the nature of feedback or rectification in the event of an imbalance. Information to activate economic units can be distributed by tradition, by central administration or by markets. Motivational relations specify the incentives used to motivate economic units to pursue their goals. They can take a material or a non-material form. This depends on whether or not there is a perceived link between the actions of an economic unit and an increased claim on output produced. Consistency among property, organizational, and motivational relations is essential if a consistent and viable economic system is to be achieved.

2.2 Establishing Consistency Between the Political and Economic Structures

Once a society has chosen its economic structure, this has consequences for the decision-making process, especially for the structure and functioning of the central authorities. For example, if in the economic structure the units are coordinated through the commands of central administration, this has implications for the nature of the political structure. A non-pluralistic form of economic coordination of specialized economic units therefore requires, for consistency, a non-pluralistic political structure. Pluralism refers to a structure that recognizes, respects, and tolerates more than one view (Petrenko, 1989, p. 18). The political structure has to function in the same way, otherwise the power of the central authority will be questioned and undermined. On the other hand, if the economic structure encourages autonomy, an appropriate political structure has to be in place. If such a structure is lacking, authority will not last for long since individuals who experience the benefits of autonomy in the economic structure are likely to require the same in the political structure. Individuals participating in the market would ultimately require political pluralism. That is because market relations encourage the development of important qualities for personality development. The qualities gained through the market process can be used in other aspects of life, especially in the political process, thus influencing the nature of the political structure. Individuals developing their personality require political freedom as a means to achieve an internally consistent personality to guide internal consistent actions. Thus, the restriction of political freedom can only exist in the short run. In the long run, individuals develop qualities of cognitive complexity, autonomy, and sociocentricity – attitudes towards self and identification with moral values which would result in questioning and undermining the authoritarian political process, resulting in a political structure based on political pluralism (Marangos, 1997, p. 167).

2.3   Establishing an Ideology Consistent With the Economic and Political Structures

Ideology refers to a cohesive set of values and beliefs about others, the world, and ourselves. It promotes a particular pattern of social relationships and arrangements, and determines the goals of human activities and the moral standards of human behavior. Thus, we should regard ideology as a set of directives for activity, and the means for rationalizing human behavior, as well as an attempt to solve the free-rider problem. Its objective is to justify a particular organization, which its supporters seek to promote, realize, pursue, or maintain (Breth and Ward, 1982, p. 12). Ideology should not be considered as something unchanging and concrete. We need to point out that it can easily become a tool for reform, justifying changes in relations. However, while ideology may be flexible, its effectiveness is not totally unconstrained. There is always resistance to changes by those who have vested interests in maintaining the status quo and who use ideology to justify their conservative approach. Ideology must be consistent with the established consistency between economic and political structures, when these are not undergoing change. It must reinforce and justify the economic and political structures, so the system can function adequately. Ideology must release the appropriate directives, moral standards, and values to motivate people to behave in a certain predictable way determined by the system. It should be stressed, however, that while consistency is a necessary condition for the maintenance of a viable system, it is not sufficient. 'A system is considered to be viable if it is able to sustain itself, with adjustments, over long term' (Ward, 1990a, p. 47). For a viable economic system to exist, general economic laws must be respected – laws that operate more or less on all levels of development of the economy under all social and economic conditions (Sik, 1967, p. 107).

An important consequence of the general economic laws is that a viable economic system must be designed to facilitate intensive, rather than extensive, growth. Extensive growth strategy emphasizes the expansion of production primarily with the use of additional resources and capital investment, and/or increasing the labor force. Extensive growth cannot be sustained forever, since all the sources of extensive growth – such as natural resources, land, employment, and the rate of savings – are finite. Intensive growth strategy is achieved as a result of an improvement in the use of all means of production, especially better organization of labor and a sustained increase in its productivity. It is unlikely that any system will prove to be viable unless it is able to sustain a high rate of increase in labor productivity. This is reinforced by the long-term trend of labor to become the scarcer factor in production (Davies, 1969, p. 264). Thus, the economy must increasingly come to rely on higher labor productivity encouraged by rapid technological change. As Trotsky (1967, pp. 47–8) correctly stated, 'the strength and stability of regimes are determined in the long run by the relative productivity of labor'. Hence viability requires that the economic system achieve economic efficiency through intensive growth.

We turn now to the analysis of the Stalinist system in terms of consistency and viability, in order to reveal important interrelationships that can help us understand and evaluate the system and, of course, explain its collapse.

3 The Economic Structure of Stalinism

The rise of Stalinism, the command system of centrally planning the economy, was the result of many factors. Marx wrote very little on the economic structure of socialism. He implied, in general terms, that it would be a simple process to replace the law of value and the market with the control of production and distribution by the 'associated producers' because capitalism itself was already doomed to collapse. Stalin interpreted Marx's writings as requesting that the economy be structured on a command basis. Central administration in its Stalinist form enabled the authority to concentrate resources according to its priorities without being affected by considerations of profitability, private capital interests or public opinion.

The model was associated with a development strategy of extensive growth. Extensive growth provides the means for rapid industrialization, which, Stalin stressed, was necessary for the survival of socialism. Extensive growth is appropriate to economies, which normally possess a basic infrastructure, some form of educated elite and a pool of unskilled or untrained labor (Dyker, 1987, p. 127). In other words, extensive growth is suitable to an underdeveloped economy where centralization of decision-making may be the most appropriate way to economies on the relatively scarce resources.

With respect to property relations, under the Stalinist system all non-labor means of production were non-privately owned. Virtually all capital, land, and natural resources were state-owned. Collective property was allowed in the form of collective farms and some retail outlets. Private property took the form only of the private plot, the produce of which could be sold in 'spontaneous' markets. These were special markets in the cities where prices were determined by forces of demand and supply rather than by the central authorities.

The Stalinist economic system has also been described as a 'command economy'. That is because the model relies upon a centrally administered or bureaucratic form of organization in which the market is largely replaced by a set of commands or directives issued to the enterprises by the central administration. These commands were set in such a way as to achieve balance (quantity supplied equals quantity demanded) and the allocation of resources desired by the central planners. It should be pointed out that, while the central planning authority was the instrument for the implementation of policy objectives, it did not formulate policies. That was the responsibility of the party. The party was a 'leading role' party, i.e. it had the monopoly of power. It was also a 'correct line' party. The party claimed that by using the Marxist–Leninist paradigm it could scientifically derive the correct perception of things and make decisions through democratic centralism, which allowed debate before the decision was made and bound all members after this time. The party decided such things as the desired rate of growth of the economy, the allocation of the national product between consumption and investment, the allocation of resources to investment projects, the areas of potential technological change and the structure of final and intermediate demand; all this reflects the non-pluralistic nature of economic decisions. The state, through the State Planning Board and its Ministries, undertook all planning and administrative functions, with the aim of converting the policy decisions into concrete results.

The policy decisions took the form of five-year plans, which set targets in both physical and monetary terms. The central targets were then disaggregated and, through the state apparatus, reached each enterprise in the form of specific directives concerning the level of gross output, the increase in labor productivity, the amount paid in wages, where and when the output must be delivered, etc. Central planners concentrated their efforts on trying to avoid excess demand and excess supply of commodities rather than achieving an optimum outcome, satisfying effective demand and producing at minimum cost. They tried to include as many commodities as possible in the plan. While the capitalist system is criticized by Marxists on the basis of 'commodity fetishism' – the obsession of economic actors with commodities instead of social relations – in the Stalinist system this is transformed to 'plan fetishism' – the obsession of planners to include the greatest possible quantity of commodities in the plan, instead of achieving optimality.

However, it was impossible to plan a huge and complex economy such as the Soviet Union's with limited information and techniques. 'Mathematicians have calculated that in order to draft an accurate and fully integrated plan for material supply just for the Ukraine for one year, requires the labor of the entire world's population for 10 million years' (Nove, 1983, p. 33). That was one reason why, from the 1930s, heavy industry was developed at the expense of industries satisfying consumer needs. Up to 1988 the practice still remained much the same. As Gorbachev (19th All-Union conference of CPSU, 1988, p. 15) put it: 'Most of the enterprises that come under USSR ministries and departments and that are expected to produce durables for market, consider this as a secondary assignment and go to all lengths to side-step it.'

The recipient of the targets was the enterprise manager, who was a salaried employee and assumed full responsibility for the implementation of the enterprise's plan. The enterprise was run on the basis of 'one-man management'. The Soviet managerial system was authoritarian in that the central authorities appointed the manager and he/she was not accountable to his/her own workforce. For most of the time there was no direct participation of workers in the running of the enterprise, which took place with the agreement of the trade unions. Workers' rights disappeared in 1929, when it was decreed that all manager's orders were to be 'unconditionally binding on his subordinate administrative staff and on all workers' (Binns et. al., 1987, p. 15). The manager's responsibility was to fulfill the plans at any cost. To ensure that the centrally determined targets were met, a system of penalties and rewards was used, depending on whether targets were over-fulfilled, fulfilled of under-fulfilled. Thus the enterprise manager operating in the command economy found the most important constraints on his decision-making power were not market constraints. These non-market constraints ensured that enterprise managers had little effective decision-making power, as the major task of the manager was to achieve the targets of the central plans, which in turn were determined by the central authorities. Hence enterprise managers in a centrally administered system, in contrast to their counterparts in the market system, played an insignificant role in the determination of enterprise objectives.

Limited market relations exist in the model. For the Stalinist economic system, the presence or absence of market relations is linked to the property structure. Market relations are allowed in the model if they satisfy the condition set by the two-property thesis (Stalin, 1972, p. 1–29). This thesis requires that market relations are only justifiable if an exchange of property occurs between the participants involved in the transaction. Between state-owned enterprises there is no exchange of property in any transaction. Thus market relations are not permissible. Relations between state-owned enterprises must be centrally administered. Outputs are not exchanged between buyer and seller, but transferred from one state enterprise to another as a result of commands. When a transaction involves an exchange of property, such as between state and groups (e.g. collective farms) or state and individuals, then market relations are permitted. Thus market relations could be used to coordinate the peasantry when they exchange their produce, as they are organized in a collective farm.

Consumers were able to choose from whatever goods and services were available. It should be remembered that the 'correct line party' and the state determined the composition of final output collectively. There was consumer choice but no consumer sovereignty. Thus Stalin broke the unity between consumer choice and sovereignty that exists, as most economists argue, in capitalism. The breakdown between consumer choice and sovereignty in the Stalinist model reflects the non-pluralistic character of the economic structure. The 'leading role, correct line' party largely determines preferences. The state planners must draw up plans, which are consistent with the party preference function. Prices are centrally determined and are often set below the market-clearing level, with queues used to ration deficient supply. Because the supply of goods increased modestly while at the same time wages increased exces-sively, in a market system price increases would have accompanied the wage increases. However, the centralization of prices did not allow any price increase thus resulting in an increase in shortages, longer queues and substantial increase in prices in the black market. There was no link between the wage rate and living standards. Actually there was a reverse relationship between real wages and living standards. The higher the real wage, the more intense the shortages and the longer the queues, lowering labor productivity by reducing work and leisure time (Lipton and Sachs, 1992, p. 220–1). Keynes (1920, p. 240) stressed the consequences of such price structure: 'a system of compelling the exchange of commodities at what is not their relative value not only relaxes production, but leads finally to waste and inefficiency of barter.'

Market relations also existed in the form of 'spontaneous markets' for certain types of goods, particularly food. Each household in the group and the state farm sector was entitled to cultivate a private plot after fulfillment of its collective obligations. The produce of the plot and intermediate goods could be sold in special 'spontaneous markets' in the cities, where prices were determined by the forces of demand and supply. Even though the private plot was insignificant as a percentage of the total area cultivated, it played an important role. In 1978 it provided over 26 per cent of agricultural production, even though only 3 per cent of the land was privately cultivated (Nove, 1983, p. 89). In this area of the economy there was private property and coordination by market relations.

Most of the time workers had decision-making power as to their occupa-tion and its location. The system relied predominantly on material rather than moral incentives. Wages are centrally set and usually reflect the skill, seniority and service record of the worker involved and are justified on the basis of the socialist principle of distribution that says 'to each according to one's work' (Marx, 1966, p. 80). However, wages are set so as to distribute workers among enterprises and industries in accordance with demand, which is determined collectively by the central authorities. Because of administration costs and the adverse costs of changing planning indices, wages tend to be stable with respect to changing economic conditions (Breth and Ward, 1982, p. 160). This is not vastly different from the wage structure under capitalism. In 1931 Stalin attacked 'petty-bourgeois egalitarianism', demanding a substantial increase in wage differentials and increases in pay for managers and officials. The result was a new wage scale that made the difference between the least skilled and the highly skilled worker 3.7:1 (Nove, 1989a, p. 200). The 'party maximum', the rule that no party member was to receive a salary higher than that of a skilled worker, was abolished. This can be justified in terms of incentives, as human skills were in short supply and rewards were needed to encourage their acquisition. However, privileges for party officials and top managers resulted in inequalities, which created a hostile environment between the officials and the workers. Material incentives were supplemented by non-material incentives such as various forms of special approval (badges, banners, etc.), slogans, and a variety of forms of mobilization, such as the achievement of the targets of the five-year plan in four years or to 'save the motherland'.

Hence the Stalinist economic structure functions on a 'command basis'. Within the economic structure the Stalinist model achieves a degree of internal consistency through state property, central administration, and mainly material incentives. The command structure of the economy refers to the vertical structure of the system, which is associated with extensive growth and the rapid rise in the material technical base.

4 The Political Structure of Stalinism

With reference to the political structure, a division of decision-making power between the party and the state characterizes the Stalinist model. The party, which is a 'leading role party' (it has the monopoly of power), adopts a 'leading position' (its views determine most decisions) acting as a vanguard on behalf of the working class in the establishment and development of a socialist society and has 'a correct line' (the party scientifically derives the correct perception and solutions to problems).

The party was organized on the basis of the Leninist principle of democratic centralism. Thus any decision made by the party, which was seen as representing the 'correct line', was automatically binding on its members. 'The combination of these two concepts, democracy and centralism, is not at least contradictory' (Trotsky, 1967, p. 94). This was is true in some respects, since the Bolshevik party was until 1924 was a party with lively debates, freedom of criticism, intellectual struggle of factions and internal democracy. However, in the name of democratic centralism Stalin transformed the Leninist party into an authoritarian party. He believed in the existence of one answer, the correct answer to any question (Sakwa, 1989, p. 57). The 'correct line' was based on scientifically derived conclusions; therefore to disagree was to dissent from a true position. For Stalin, the party leadership decided what was correct; to disagree led to self-criticism, expulsion, to be identified as a dissident, or even much worse.

The recruitment policy of the party was based on the idea that party members represent the best of the population, the most dedicated and conscious, who are willing to sacrifice their time and effort to achieve the goals determined by the party hierarchy. In theory, party membership was not the result of a particular social position or a family tradition, since the personal qualities of the applicant were also important. However, in reality the party was a selective organization in that it was open only to a relatively small group of people who were expected to meet certain requirements. Certain social groups, such as men with higher education, and national groups, especially Russians, discovered that it was easier for them to join the party than for others. In addition, some senior posts were confined only to party members (Desai, 1989, p. 127). Party members were easily commanded and pressurized because party membership brings privileges. If party members dared to disagree, they could be denied their party membership card. An effective threat of expulsion meant the end of one's career and privileges.

Among the functions of the party were the determination of policy objectives; alteration of the prevailing ideology; guidance of mass organizations such as trade unions; and generally to act as a caretaker of the state apparatus. While the party defines the political objectives it does not directly organize the economy. It has no economic establishments under its command, since these are all legally and organizationally under government ministries. The rules of the Communist Party of the Soviet Union (Gill, 1988, p. 248, Article 60) determine that party organizations must not 'substitute themselves for Soviet, trade union, co-operative and other public organizations and they do not allow either merging of the functions of the Party and other organs'. Consequently, the party does not aspire to administer but to guide and to influence industrial organizations controlled by the government. In reality the party totally controlled the governmental functions.

The state, which was viewed, in ideological terms, as an instrument of the working class, was a large centrally administered organization, which performed statistical, planning, owning, and administrative functions. The state was structured primarily on the basis of the sectoral principle. This means that the functions of the state were partitioned on the basis of specialization of economic decision-making. Ministries usually control these sectors. Economic decision-making power was highly concentrated at the national territorial level, with very little discretionary power given to lower levels. However, during the history of the Soviet Union there were continual oscillations in the degree of regionalization and decentralization. For example, during the Khrushchev era, there was an increase in the degree regionalization and decentralization, which later on was rejected by Brezhnev. State institutions had formal, not real power. For example, none of the five-year plans and none of the sharp turns in foreign policy were even discussed by the supposedly supreme organ of the government, the Supreme Soviet, until after they had been implemented. Furthermore, elections to each political institution were held with only one candidate, nominated by the Communist Party (Binns et. al., 1987, p. 76). It should be pointed out that with growth of the economy, the role of the state increases, as state ownership increases with the growing socialization of production. Then, since state property increases the role of markets is reduced and the role of central administration grows, based on the two-property thesis, market relations are only justifiable if an exchange of property occurs between the participants involved in the transaction.

Decision-making power rested significantly with those with expertise, which was linked to one's economic and/or administrative role. This gave rise to a new elite group, which exercised power and enjoyed privileges. This group, the bureaucracy, acted in accordance with its own self-interests, presented as general interests and imposed upon society. As Marx (1975, p. 108) argued, 'the bureaucracy holds the state, the spiritual essence of society, in thrall, as its private property. The universal spirit of bureaucracy is secrecy, it is mystery preserved within itself by means of the hierarchical structure and appearing to the outside world as a self-contained corporation'. In the Stalinist system, it was not a bureaucracy in the narrow sense of hierarchy of officials only, but included also those in the state and the party who enjoyed a privileged position. It should be remembered that power rests with the party, but, since the party dominates the state, there is a dual structure of power: those in the party who exercise power via the party organs, and those in the party who exercise power via the state organs, which exploited workers throughout the entire history of the Soviet Union (Resnick and Wolff, 2002, p. 157). State ownership plus planning is not itself sufficient to prevent the emergence of a new ruling class. Members of the bureaucracy were the ones who objectively control the state and the means of production.

Mass organizations such as trade unions were totally controlled by the party and their character was changed so that they could function as an element of the state. This again reveals the non-pluralistic character of the economic and political structure of Stalinism. Independent trade unions representing the interests of the worker were transformed into administrative organs of the state, acting to ensure rapid industrialization. The primary functions of the trade unions revolved around increasing labor productivity through the enforcement of work discipline and conducting emulation campaigns (Nove, 1983, p. 84–5). Thus, with respect to the political structure, the command nature of the system is revealed through the 'representation' of the working class by the state and the party, which are both highly centralized, and whose decisions bind all members of the society.

5 The Ideological Structure of Stalinism

The ideology of Stalinism reinforced the 'command' nature of the economic and political structures. The individual did not exercise any power; rather the

Stalinist model sees the working class exercising its power through the party, the state, and the trade unions. It rejected the idea of worker self-management as well as pluralistic independent trade unions directly representing the worker's interests. In a society where the party represents the working class, and without any other mutually hostile classes, there is room for only one party (Nove, 1986, p. 11–12, 35). For Stalin, socialism is established when the state as a representative of the whole population has socialized property and substituted private market transactions with state planning (Resnick and Wolff, 2002, p.xi).

The Stalinist model accepts the Marxist analysis of social change based on class struggle, as well as the Marxist concept of socialism as a historical stage between capitalism and communism. The leading role party justifies the non-pluralistic economic and political structures on the basis of tutelage. The historical role of the party is through supervision and direction to develop the pre-conditions of communism. However Stalin, using the concept of tutelage, produced a theoretical justification for the use of repressive measures. The state could not wither away in a hostile capitalist environment. On the contrary, as the country gets closer to socialism the character of the class struggle sharpens, as desperate enemies seek to destroy the Soviet Union. Therefore, what was needed was more authority. In other words, 'for the state to wither away its power must first be maximized' (Nove, 1989a, p. 63). However, I believe that the problem with tutelage is that it will never wither away, because it is linked with the privileges of the bureaucracy. The bureaucracy will resist its own dissolution and as such tutelage will continue.

The model is strongly collectivist in nature. Social – particularly state – property and central administration are seen as essential to the development of socialism. The Marxist-Leninist productivity principle of distribution and a material incentive form of motivation were seen to be required in a society where scarcity continues due to the lack of technological development and inner individual self-regulation of wants. Abundance of goods will only be possible in communism, where inner self-regulation of wants exists and technological growth, which benefits the whole society, is not restricted by the profit motive. Thus, in the ideological sphere, the 'correct line', which is derived scientifically and is adopted by the state, reinforces the command nature of the Stalinist system.

6 Consistency of the Stalinist Economic System

A high degree of consistency within the economic structure and between the economic, political, and ideological structures was achieved in the Stalinist economic system by functioning on a 'command' basis. The society was organized on a hierarchical basis. Authority was the means by which the structure was developed. Authority ensured that what had to be done was done. Hence consistency between the economic structure (state property, central administration), the political structure (leading role, correct line and democratic centralist party), and the ideological structure (with plans reflecting the correct line derived by the party and imposed on enterprises and households) was achieved. Resnick and Wolff (2002) argued that the Soviet Union and subsequently Eastern Europe represented, across their entire history, essentially a state form of capitalism.

The survival of Stalinism depended on the ability of the system to sustain itself, with adjustments, over the long term. This required the introduction of necessary reforms when the economic conditions changed. In a world of increasing international awareness and competitiveness, this requires an adequate rate of material progress. Of course, also from a Marxist socialist viewpoint, expanding material production is essential (Marx, 1966, p. 81). There can be no doubt that the Stalinist system, in spite of its shortcomings, worked for some time as a vehicle of rapid economic growth, particularly in industry. The achievements of the non-pluralistic system were noted around the world during the 1930s, 1940s, and early 1950s. While the system was inappropriate for achieving even modest increases in labor productivity in the long run, a rapid increase in material production was possible as long as the sources of extensive growth existed. Once they were exhausted, the rate of growth of material production inevitably declined and since immaterial production was always discounted, inconsistencies developed.

Thus economic growth in the Stalinist model was based on the successful utilization of the sources of extensive growth. Without this, a high rate of growth of material production was not possible. The elimination of the sources of extensive growth and the development of inconsistencies would inevitably result in Stalinism collapsing if the system lacked internal forces making possible the shift from extensive to intensive growth. Thus the question that needs to be answered is whether the Stalinist economic system could facilitate the shift from extensive to intensive growth when the sources of extensive growth were exhausted. It should be pointed out that by viewing the economic system from a social science perspective this shift can be encouraged from either the economic, political, or ideological structure. That is because a change in one structure must be accompanied by changes in the other structures. In this way we can explain the collapse of the Stalinist system not just in terms of economic relations, which is the traditional way of thinking, but rather on the basis of the whole economic-politico-ideological spectrum. Our objective is to discuss whether these spheres facilitate or inhibit the development of the material base, resulting in a thorough and comprehensive study of the reasons for the collapse of the Stalinist economic system. In what follows we critically assesses the economic, political, and ideological structure of Stalinism.

7 A Critique of the Economic Structure of Stalinism

With respect to the economic structure there is a requirement that the society's property, organizational and motivational relations do not represent an inhibiting factor to economic growth as a consequence of its high level of inefficiency and lack of creativity in the use of resources. Thus there is a need to examine whether a significant level of waste is a consequence of reliance on the Stalinist economic model.

When the sources of extensive growth are diminishing, or in the absence of large sources of extensive growth, sustained increases in material production require increasing levels of economic efficiency. This requires a structure that will generate accurate information and appropriate motivation. A rejection of the market mechanism in production, as in the the Stalinist model, will place the burden of a non-wasteful allocation of resources on the central authorities. It is an enormously complex task, which grows with the expanded diversity and complexity of material production and the increasing importance of immaterial production. That is because the central authorities require a vast amount of accurate information, which is difficult to obtain, as well as their inability to solve the computation question. An important contradiction stems from the simple fact that the center cannot know in full detail what in fact was needed by the society, and yet the entire logic of the Stalinist system rests upon the proposition that it is the duty of all subordinate management to obey instructions from the center. That is because they supposedly embody the needs of the society (Nove, 1983, p. 73). This is the result of the non-pluralistic 'correct line' nature of the economic structure.

Even if it were possible for a centrally administered form of organization to provide adequate information, it would take a considerable period of time to adjust to the continually changing conditions associated with a dynamic process. As a result, central administration lacks the flexibility of market relations. In addition enterprises were faced with a soft budget constraint (Kornai, 1992a, p. 140–5). If a state enterprise's spending exceeded its revenue, it received assistance to cover its debt, in the form of a subsidy, a reduction in taxes, an increase in credit, or an increase in the administered prices of the goods sold. In this way the enterprise will always be bailed out in difficult situations. Planners, in contrast to enterprises in the market system, are under less pressure to adjust to changing economic conditions or rather they adjust in differed ways.

A further source of waste stems from the existence of conflicting objectives between the central authorities and the enterprises, which result in inconsistent actions. Managers demand the greatest possible volume of investments, large quantities of labor, material and machinery, and easy targets, and they are interested in maintaining a sort of routine – a quiet life, avoiding any changes. There is an incentive to hoard materials in order to ensure that future output targets could be met, given the unreliability of supplies. If the supplies dry up, the managers can depend on the 'tolkachi' (= pusher), middlemen with special connections, who are able to cut through the bureaucracy and arrange by any means, almost invariably illegal, the needed supplies (Desai, 1989, p. 12). Managers tended to mislead or even falsify data relating to the performance of the enterprise. They understated their potentialities and overstated their needs. This had disastrous consequences for the economy, which lost one of the important means of functioning properly – objective information about needs, reserves and potentialities. Managers tried to make plan fulfillment as easy as possible. They had an interest in narrowing down the range of goods produced, avoiding the production of new products and innovations, and they preferred to produce goods that used large quantities of material at the expense of quality.

On the other hand, the central authorities tried to reduce and limit the demands for investments, for human labor power and materials, and to push for higher targets. Because the central planning body knew the likely behavior pattern of management, the planners tended to proceed on the basis of past reported performance. This, in turn, led cautious managers to avoid 'excessive' improvements in performance, which would cause them to be given greater tasks in the next plan period. In the end a compromise subjective command emerged, which was in the interests of both parties but probably not in the interests of the economy (Sik, 1967, p. 8). These sources of waste were aggravated by the potential arbitrariness of the central authorities in a system where relations between enterprises and the state were not governed by enforceable legal procedures. The central planning body was able to change plans during the planning period without the enterprise having any legal right of redress. This discouraged initiative and dedication if, in the light of a slightly improved performance, the planning body raised the required targets in some arbitrary fashion.

The magnitude of the resources of personnel and equipment engaged by the central authorities to operate such a form of organization inhibited the development of the economy. It was not simply the task of obtaining information and drawing up plans but, in addition, the need to supervise and assess managerial performance, which required such a vast amount of resources to be tied up in what was essentially an unproductive activity. With this vast machinery it was not likely that decisions would be made quickly and/or would reflect local conditions. Furthermore, as the diversity and complexity of material production and the importance of immaterial production increases, so does the level of conflict and waste, due to the magnified information problems. The enterprise ceased for all practical purposes to function as an independent decision-making economic unit. Prices, their movements and relationships, did not influence the enterprises in selecting the line of production, in cutting production costs and in meeting market demand. Morcover, divorcing the domestic from the international market means that an important potential source of pressure to reduce costs and improve quality had little or no effect on enterprises. The Stalinist system discouraged creativity. In particular, it was unable to stimulate the development of new products or new methods of production. Managers of enterprises were interested in achieving short-term goals, which worked against creativity. The job of the manager was to fulfill the plan at any cost. Stalin encouraged this:

'The victors are not judged' (Nove, 1989a, p. 79). In other words, achieve the plan using all means, even illegal ones.

Enterprises would receive the amount of wages and resources provided they fulfilled the planning targets. Managers were reluctant to adopt new techniques, because it made it more difficult to achieve their output targets in the short run, the adoption of new techniques requires some interruption of production. It was also in the interest of the manager to preserve the internal structure of the enterprise so as to maintain the targets at the same level (determined by past performance). Products did not need to satisfy the market test, but only the planners' test. In this way, increasing quantities of unecessary production were forced on consumers. Yet the enterprises continued to produce such products as long as they achieved the planned gross output targets. In the absence of the market test, what the state was willing to accept was paramount, and it was irrelevant whether or not the consumers desired the goods. The basic inter-relationship between consumer choice and consumer sovereignty was broken down by Stalin's two-property thesis.

A country like the Soviet Union, which is favored with immense natural resources, can maintain extensive growth for a while by constantly expanding plant capacity and employing more and more labor. There was in 1929 much unemployed labor, voluntary and involuntary as well as under-employed and unused natural resources. There was uncontrollable consumption of raw materials, which the Stalinist system encourages due to the high level of investment and the systematic under-valuation of natural inputs. This results in a rapidly growing demand for raw materials; enterprises are not interested in producing goods at as low as possible material cost as there is no disincentive to using all the allocated inputs. However, the sources of extensive growth are finite – in particular, labor and natural resources. The time must come when growing material production requires the exploitation of intensive sources of growth, such as increases in labor productivity.

Furthermore, there are production processes that by their nature are de-pendent upon the initiative and involvement of the worker. These cannot be completely controlled from above. In agriculture, the initiative and commitment of the individual worker is central (Sik, 1967, p. 209). Agricultural planning is complicated by the infinite variety of land and the need for flexible deci-sion-making, depending on the weather, making unworkable the imposition of centrally administered constraints on farms. The Stalinist model overestimated the economies of scale in agriculture, and underestimated the diseconomies of scale. It forced collectivization and bureaucratic methods of administration, which led to a decline in agricultural production.

These difficulties were likely to become more obvious and more severe as the economy became more complex and sophisticated, where interrelationships between economic units became great in magnitude. It was expected that the accumulated problems of a distorted industrial structure, an ageing or obsolete production base, low labor productivity and the wasteful utilization of production resources, would result in a sharply decreasing rate of economic growth. The average annual growth rate between 1975 and 1985 was 2 per cent and from 1979 to 1982 there was no growth at all (Laquer, 1989, p. 198). Between 1981 and 1985 production declined in 40 per cent of industrial sectors, including agriculture and transport. The standard of living to two-thirds of the population started to fall (Aganbegyan, 1988, p. 16).

Summing up the negative characteristics of the Stalinist non-pluralistic system of economic development, we observe: rapid industrialization, which was prompted at the expense of the development of all other productive sectors of the economy, especially agriculture and services; inefficiency in all branches of production; failure to modernize production technology; and a relatively very high consumption of raw materials. In addition, when the sources of extensive growth were exhausted a shortage of labor appeared and, as a consequence, there was a slowing down in the rate of material production. Thus, in the face of an absence of a variety of consumer goods, and since moral incentives are never adequate, a breakdown appeared in the incentive system. Terror became the natural alternative for the central authority to be able to enforce its decisions.

Hence it appears that the Stalinist economic structure does not facilitate, but rather inhibits, the shift from extensive to intensive growth. There was no incentive from the central planning board to encourage the shift, since this would result in a substantial reduction in its decision-making power in favor of increasing that of the enterprise, effectively making itself obsolete. The shift would not be encouraged either by the managers or the workers, since this would require the removal of the 'soft budget constraint' and a radical change in managerial and worker responsibilities. In addition, reform within the structure of the enterprise was unlikely. The individual worker could not question managerial authority, and was therefore unable to encourage reform. The trade union has been denied the right of active representation, being transformed into an administrative organization. The managers did not encourage a reform in the internal structure of the enterprise, which would facilitate intensive growth, because this meant that their managerial responsibility would be subject to a radical change. An intensive growth system of development will not mean the achievement of specific targets; rather it will require the constant need to update equipment, the need to be efficient and to meet the market test. Thus the manager's position and authority becomes vulnerable, and this strategy is therefore very risky. For these reasons the Stalinist economic structure lacked the internal forces, which make possible the shift from extensive to intensive growth. Even though the sources of extensive growth, such as labor and natural resources, had been exhausted, extensive growth was linked with the interests of the central planning board, the managers, and even the workers. We also need to add the interests of the military sector, which, while it was exposed to effective international competition, also resisted any change. A shift to intensive growth will result in competition for resources, thus making fewer resources available and controlled by the military sector; thus reducing its importance and undermining its power. Hence, there was no incentive by any economic actors to change the *status quo*.

While change was not facilitated in the economic sphere, a possible source of reform is in the political structure. It should be noted that, if the political sphere were able to respond and adjust to the new economic-political conditions, this would have eventual consequences for the economic structure, according to the hypothesis of consistency. If, on the other hand, the political structure also lacks internal forces of change, this will only inhibit the possibility of change. A thorough analysis of the political structure of Stalinism, in this respect, is needed to explain its ultimate collapse.

8   A Critique of the Political Structure of Stalinism

In the Stalinist system, as already mentioned, workers are 'represented' by the party, state and trade unions; this is a reflection of the non-pluralistic nature of the system. Thus we do not expect the system to provide democratic channels by which the individuals can participate and debate. This can be seen even within the enterprise, which is run on the basis of one-man management, with no direct participation of workers in the decision-making process. Indeed the very nature of central administration works against effective workers' participation in decision-making, as it requires a single point of responsibility and power, the manager, for enterprise performance to be judged. The enterprise is structured so as to ensure managerial authority. The trade union is preoccupied with a number of administrative functions instead of representing the interests of the workers.

The Stalinist system used specific methods of central control over statewide and local politics. They included the recommendation of candidates for local office, the control of potential appointees for these offices through the nomenclature system (a hierarchical system of ordering of party members based on seniority and loyalty), the use of party discipline to remove officials who no longer serve the center effectively, and the dispatch of high ranking 'instructors' to supervise local meetings to make sure that the center's choices were implemented (Sakwa, 1989, p. 55–59).

The rulers of the Soviet Union formed a class, which for lack of a better term we call the bureaucracy apparatus, the sum total of all those who participate in the monopoly of power administration at whatever level of the society (Laquer, 1989, p. 278–283). The monopoly in the exercise of power entailed important material social privileges. In Marxian terms, the bureaucrats were unproductive labor; the bureaucracy produced no surplus and lived off a large portion of the workers' produced surplus (Resnick and Wolff, 2002, p. 240). The bureaucrats were quite conscious of their specific material interests and defended them against all adversaries. The elimination of the 'party maximum' and the campaign against 'petty-bourgeois egalitarianism' meant that the privileges of high officialdom could not be publicly criticized, and the very existence of such privileges was made a state secret. This could be successfully achieved in the absence of openness. On 13 February 1986, under the regime of *glasnost*, *Pravda* wrote: 'When considering social justice, it is impossible to close one's eyes to the fact that party, soviet, trade union, economic, and even Komsomol leaders sometimes objectively intensify social inequality by their enjoyment of all kinds of special buffets, special shops, special hospitals, and so on' (Sakwa, 1989, p. 226).

The means of production were state property; control of the state by the bureaucracy made the bureaucracy the real administrator and decision-making body of the society without being accountable to anyone. The bureaucracy as a class 'owned' the state as its private property. In its pursuit of power and privilege, this apparatus acted to perpetuate and expand itself into a new form of social stratification, some of the characteristics were the dominance of the state at the expense of direct control by the workers in the factories and councils, the end of any independent trade unions, and the transformation of the party into a non-democratic, non-pluralistic party, which imposed the interests of this elite group upon the people rather than acting as a vanguard of the people. In addition to this, there was the absence of elected officials who are subject to recall by the people if they abuse their position, thus making the bureaucrats non-accountable; the end of free debate, discussion and the expression of conflicting views in favor of a 'correct line' where all party members must adopt the view of the elite or face the consequences; and, finally, the appropriation of the surplus produced by the workers, which was used by the bureaucracy in its own self-interest. This was reflected in wide wage differentials, high bonuses for members of the bureaucracy, the production of luxury consumer goods, exclusive shops, special advantages for their children and in allocating 12 per cent of GNP to military expenditure (Walker, 1986, p. 125).

The command system of administration, with its tight control over planning and the allocation of supplies, and its counter-productive and distorting initiatives, had become the insurmountable obstacle to any structural reform. Any change in the organization of the system in the economic sphere involved a loss of power for the bureaucracy itself. This meant that the bureaucracy itself would not initiate any significant reform. The bureaucracy will only accept reforms if they serve the interests of at least the majority of the bureaucratic class. In addition, the bureaucracy could use its power to sabotage any changes, needed to realize new goals under the new politico-economic conditions. Thus the bureaucracy did not initiate changes, which would question its place in society; rather it resisted policies, which might disturb its position, and acted as a repressive force against anyone that might challenge its position. Even if the top bureaucracy initiated reforms, the middle and lower ranks had the power to frustrate any changes.

An analysis of the political structure of Stalinism reveals that the bureaucracy cannot initiate significant reform, since this would undermine its power. This is a reflection of the non-democratic, non-pluralistic and non-accountable nature of the system. It means that the much-desired shift from extensive to intensive growth will not be initiated by the political structure and, if not encouraged by the ideological structure, this would result in the ultimate collapse of Stalinism.

9   A Critique of the Ideological Structure of Stalinism

Marx stressed that a rapid increase in the material technical base is a necessary pre-condition for a society to move towards communism (Marx, 1966, p. 81). This was also an essential element of the Stalinist ideology. It had the aim of justifying the existing economic and political structure as the only possible 'socialist' structure, which can achieve this goal. However, with the exhaustion of the sources of extensive growth, which results in falling rates of growth, this can be resolved only by a revolutionary change in ideology. Ideology should not be viewed as a constraint but rather as a flexible instrument of reform. An analysis of the Stalinist ideology is required to reveal whether it can facilitate the shift towards intensive growth, thus avoiding the system's ultimate collapse.

The Stalinist system enforced its ideology through the 'correct line' doctrine. The party scientifically derived the correct perception of things, which was binding on all party members and, since the party adopts a leading position, its views determined most decisions. The party, through the economic, political, and ideological mechanisms, which it controlled, ensured that the 'correct' perception prevails. This extends to deriving what is or is not 'correct knowledge'. For example neoclassical economics was seen to be incorrect because it is capitalist knowledge. Such a distinction between capitalist and socialist knowledge had disastrous consequences for scientific development and its application. Capitalist knowledge was considered anathema; however, the criteria that constituted capitalist knowledge were never stated precisely, thus allowing the central authority to effectively determine 'correct knowledge'. In this way, the Stalinist non-pluralistic system of economic development did not foster self-expression and the development of new ideas, thus inhibiting reform. The necessary pre-condition for significant reform, a critical perspective, was eliminated. A tendency towards conservatism was a logical consequence. To this we need to add that while the official ideology condemned attitudes such as status-seeking, elitism, careerism and a conservative mentality, which were perceived as anti-socialist, they were widely practiced (Breth and Ward, 1982, p. 57). This resulted in the moral and ideological confusion of individuals.

10   Conclusion: Was The Stalinist Economic System Viable?

There can be no doubt that for a time the Stalinist system worked as a vehicle of rapid growth. In spite of its shortcomings, it enjoyed a measure of success.

However, we should not confuse achievements with viability. Bottlenecks arose when the sources of extensive growth were exhausted. If a high rate of economic growth cannot be achieved, Stalinism will collapse, as its ideology is based on a rapid increase in material production and, in particular, the superiority of socialism to capitalism. As Varga (1939, p. 15) claimed, a 'socialist planned economy thus leads to a rapid improvement of the material and cultural situation of the working people in the Soviet Union, while capitalist anarchy leads to the growing material, cultural and moral decline of the masses of working people'. However, the collapse of the Stalinist system could have been avoided if the political authorities had facilitated reform. This implies changes in the political structure and ideology. However, in the political sphere, the system gave rise to a concentration of power and wealth in the hands of a non-accountable bureaucracy, which did not allow changes that reduced its privileges. In the ideological sphere, the correct line restricted individual thinking and development, turning citizens into passive and apolitical beings. The necessary plurality of ideas was unable to develop, and without it reform is not possible.

Thus the Stalinist system does not provide the mechanism of reform, and was not able to adjust itself when the conditions changed. The foundation of the Stalinist ideology, that through the concept of tutelage, a viable socialist economic system could start with non-pluralism and move over time to pluralism is not valid. This is due to the fact that the political and ideological structure inhibits the transformation. It should be noted that for Resnick and Wolff (2002) the communist and socialist alternative to capitalism never prevailed in the Soviet Union and Eastern Europe.

The analysis of the Stalinist economic system and the reasons for its collapse is useful in identifying the starting point of the transition process. In addition, knowledge of how the system facilitated the making of economic choices, the outcome of these choices and the implications of alternative economic policies, as outlined in this chapter, is essential. This analysis would assist us in determining what, if any, elements of the system should be retained during and after the completion of the transition process. This question forms one of the parameters of the transition problem and is incorporated in the analytical framework developed in Chapter 2. Attention is now turned to the development of the analytical framework, which will be used in developing alternative political economy models of transition.

Chapter 2

The Analytical Framework

1 Introduction

Economists have provided arguments that the centrally administered economies of the Soviet Union and Eastern Europe, due to their highly bureaucratic structure, were inefficient and lacked creativity and, thus, inhibited progress. For these reasons, as it was demonstrated in Chapter 1, it was not difficult to predict the ultimate collapse of the centrally administered economies. However, while there was widespread belief among economists that these economies were not viable, this was not formalized by developing models that would facilitate the transition from a centrally administered to a market economy. Whereas there was a vast amount of literature on how to transform capitalist economies into socialist economies, nothing appeared to offer advice on how to change centrally administered socialism into a market economy. This could have been attributed to the difficulty associated in predicting the timing of the collapse.

During the transition process, elements of centrally administered socialism and embryonic market relations co-existed. This made traditional economic theory irrelevant; thus, the transition processes 'had to be conceived and implemented largely in the dark' (Sestanovich, 1992, p.vii). While the collapse of centrally administered economies did not surprise economists, the transition process did. The transition process in Central Europe, Eastern Europe, and the former Soviet Union (CEEFSU) was one of the most dramatic non-marginal adjustments in economic systems ever experienced. The complexities involved did not have any historical parallels and the general desire for quick results caught economists unprepared. Consequently, the transition process turned out to be far more complex than initially hoped and 'created new challenges for everyone', since transition economies 'traveled into uncharted waters' (Porket, 1998, p. 163; Yergin, 1999, p.xi; Parker, Tritt and Woo, 1997, p. 3; Urban and Fish, 1998, p. 178).

Economic science responded by developing an appropriate body of economic analysis to facilitate and provide some form of direction for the transition process. The movement from a centrally administered to a market-based economy was commonly referred to as the 'transition problem'. While the word 'transition' – the passage from one state to another, in this case from a centrally administered to a market-based economy – might seem appropriate, it did not explicitly capture all the complexities involved. The word 'transition' or 'reform' was a misnomer for what was occurring; 'revolution is more fitting' (Murrell, 1991b, pp. 3–4). The transition process entailed superseding the essential properties of the centrally administered economy, consequently destabilizing the economic system and replacing it with a market economy. In order to solve the transition problem, several key issues had to be addressed. These were:

- *What form should the end-state take?* While most economists agreed on the introduction of market relations in the CEEFSU economies, the market as such was not a homogeneous entity.
- *What process should be used to achieve the desirable end-state?* Important factors to be considered in reform implementation were the speed and the sequencing of the reforms.
- *What means should be used to induce the reforms?* The choice of policy instruments had a significant impact.
- *What elements, if any, of the existing structure of the centrally administered economy should remain?* It was necessary to determine whether any aspects of the centrally administered economy were consistent with, and desirable in, a market economy.

The answers to these questions could not have been derived by using economic analysis alone, but also depended on the perception of social reality and ethical issues. Based on assumptions about economic behavior, the following questions arose. How does the economic system function and respond to change? Also, what is a good society? The answer inevitably reflected the observer's personal assessment of each economic and non-economic performance dimension as well as the significance assigned to those performance dimensions. In addition, alternative and often conflicting economic theories used different criteria for determining how society and the economy functioned and how society should distribute responsibilities between the market and the government. Thus, different views on 'social reality' and 'what is a good society?' were associated with distinct methodologies and a particular set of social values, which have implications for economic policy formulae. This gives rise to alternative models of transition, based on different assumptions, different methods of analysis and different goals. The 'battle of ideas' in the transition case focused on which model was most realistic, feasible, desirable and appropriate for the process in question. Awareness of such a background facilitates the interpretation of the less clear sources of disagreement between economists and of the overall complexities involved.

The collapse of the centrally administered economies cleared the way for the development of economies based on market relations. The use of market relations was proposed in terms of information and motivation. It was argued that the market was a superior form of organization, resulting in a superior outcome compared with central administration, and even with the presence of market failure. With the introduction of market relations in CEEFSU issues, which were previously deemed hitherto irrelevant, became extremely important. Concepts such as prices, credit, unemployment, money supply, interest rates and reserve ratios had never been part of discussions in centrally administered economies. Consequently, the hegemony of the market process among economists implied a transformation in the economic system. Non-market alternatives will not be considered in this book.

Nevertheless, the transition process was not restricted to the economic field, so the debate was not solely about the superiority of market relations over central administration. Market relations are not independent of other social relations. It would seem that the political and ideological aspects of the transition were fundamental. Indeed, economic reforms cannot be understood or assessed in narrow economic terms. To understand and form an opinion about the transition, it is essential to view the process in a broader social science context, incorporating political and economic relations as well as ideology. To understand changes in an economic system, it is essential to analyze all the relationships that influence economic choices. In addition to economic relationships, the structure of the political authorities and the state, and the prevailing ideology, must be examined, as well as the external environment. All have an influence on economic choices. That is because the state has a monopoly over the legitimate use of force as a means of imposing restrictions on individual behavior. The prevailing ideology releases the appropriate directives, moral standards, and values to motivate people to behave in a certain predictable way. All these elements give rise to different market-based economic systems and this diversity cannot be adequately conceptualized as simply mixtures of capitalism and socialism. That is why Horne (1995, p. 391) wrongly concluded that 'perhaps the main lesson learnt from the experiences of transition economies is how little is understood of the process of systemic economic transformation and the factors that explain apparent success or failure'. Murrell (1995, p. 175) argued, 'I am inclined to think that the surprise at the course of events [in transition economies] is mostly an accurate reflection of the state of our knowledge of the processes of system-wide change. This simply says that there is much to learn'. I strongly believe that such confusion and supposed ignorance can only be avoided when economic analysis and policy are viewed from the broad perspective of social science. Often the confusion in economics stems from obedience to a particular theoretical school.

A social science perspective 'involves recognition that, as well as "the market" which is the primary focus of orthodox economists, state, class, gender, race, and ideology are key elements in shaping the social order of modern capitalism' (Argyrous and Stilwell, 1996b, p.xi). Within this framework, economic relationships are perceived as interconnected and interdependent with non-economic structures. Consequently, the development of a strategy for the transition process reminds us of the statement by Hirshleifer (1996, p. 91) that 'ultimately, good economics [in our case good transition economics] will also have to be good anthropology and sociology and political science and psychology'.

Hence, the success of the transition process depended not only on specifying the necessary economic conditions, but also on whether certain conditions were satisfied with respect to the non-economic elements. Differences in historical background, national culture, economic and political structures, and international aspirations can affect growth patterns. For this reason, the analysis adopted in this book is in the tradition of 'political economy', which incorporates within the framework of economic relationships the interaction between political institutions, social consciousness, and ideas. Consequently, the analysis of the transition process was consistent with the tradition of political economy, as neoclassical economics alone is not enough. The transition is a holistic, historical, dynamic, and comparative process in nature and, as such, a political economy approach would seem appropriate. 'Political economy is necessarily procedural, human, institutional and environmental in its scope' (O'Hara, 1999, p. 128). Political economy stresses that making economic sense and understanding economic relationships is not feasible without explicit awareness of power, institutions, and values. In particular, political economy maintains that politics and economics are not reducible to one another. Aslund (1995, p. 12), one of the architects of the shock therapy approach, argued that 'to a considerable extent, therefore, my interest focuses on political economy'. However, a political economy approach eventuates in disagreement and in alternative transition models. Different 'views on social reality' and 'what is a good society?' give rise to alternative models of transition.

The aim of this book is to develop an analytical framework to model the transition process. As Woo, Parker and Sachs (1997b, p.xi) reasoned, the focus was 'on developing a systematic understanding of the economic and institutional dynamics underlying the transformations from centrally planned to market economies'. A hypothesis is developed that the elements of the transition process were equally important and must be interconnected and, thus, consistent. Viewing the transition process in its totality, the terms of this analysis are not narrow, economic 'independent' variables but, rather, encompassing the whole politico-economic-ideological spectrum. Nevertheless, this hypothesis does not dismiss developing transition models on the basis of different priorities and sequencing of the elements of the reform program.

The aim of this book is to consider alternative political economy models of transition, based on three different methods of economic analysis, different views of 'what is a good society?' and different speeds of implementing the transition policies. As a result five alternative models of transition are developed: The Shock Therapy model of transition, the Neoclassical Gradualist model of transition, the Post Keynesian model of transition, the Pluralistic Market Socialist model of transition, and the Non-Pluralistic Market Socialist model of transition (The Chinese model of transition).

The book is restricted to the development of theoretical and conceptual models of transition. Each model is a construction based on the values and beliefs that most economists of the particular model subscribe to. Each model is a stylized version of the view of how the economy operates, with reference to the transition from a centrally administered to market economy, suggested by the economic theory in question. As such, empirical evidence will be incorporated selectively. The analytical framework developed, which proposes different models of transition, makes it possible to understand the transition process from a new and more enlightened perspective. It provides a better understanding of the complexities involved in the transition process and the differing opinions between economists. That is because the differences between economic models result from differences in political, philosophical, cultural, and moral arguments and values. All models have their own ideologies and sets of values, based on which models are defined.

To my knowledge, there have been no attempts to develop and compare alternative models of transition. In addition, there is very little literature available on the transition process based on the tradition of political economy. An exception is Radice (1993, p. 13), who distinguished between three alternative transformation paths: the neoliberal path (which aims to achieve a rapid and comprehensive commodification of economic life), the protectionist path (which aims to develop a viable national economy), and the state-development path (which aims to develop a national strategy to compete effectively in international markets). His analysis was limited, and focused on government strategies and practices relating to foreign capital investment. As a result, his analysis did not encompass all the elements of the transition in the tradition of political economy.

2   The Primary Elements of the Transition Models

Exposition of the transition problem in economic literature appears to over-simplify the complexities involved. In most cases, economists writing on transition have reduced it to an isolated variable of the economic sphere. The transition problem was 'pigeon-holed' into thematic subcategories like pricing policy, government expenditure, investment policy, and unemployment, thus ignoring the interrelated nature of economic policies, institutions and behavior. Alternatively, economists provided a solution to the problem by sometimes explicitly, but mainly implicitly, assuming specific behavioral assumptions and/or economic relationships. These assumptions resulted in a pre-determined position, which was presented and defended as the only feasible one. Thus, modeling of the transition process was highly subjective and based on value judgments. Comparisons, which ignored these aspects, were meaningless.

To avoid these problems the parameters of the transition problem firstly required to be specified. This requires the establishment of a process by which elements of the transition problem will be identified and included in each model. The elements of the developmental process of transition modeling are:

- *A view of social reality or what exists (existed):* This refers to the type of economic system that existed in CEEFSU – centrally administered socialism – and how it facilitated the making of economic choices, the outcome of these choices and the implications of alternative economic policies, which was outlined in Chapter 1. This analysis is necessary to identify what, if any, elements of the centrally administered economic system should be retained.
- *A view about what constitutes a good society:* This refers to the desirable end-state. An attempt to solve the transition problem required a specification of an acceptable, desirable, and feasible economic system. The aim of the transition process was to initiate changes that would ultimately bring about an economic system consisting of elements and outcomes that were considered acceptable, desirable, and feasible. A view of a good society is concerned with the assessment of each economic and non-economic performance dimension in conjunction with the significance assigned to these performance dimensions. Such views reflect values, not social reality. As such, a view of a good society is influenced by normative rather than positive analysis. Thus, it cannot be rejected purely by an appeal to facts. However, it is important to note that facts are always relevant to ethical judgments.
- *Desired changes:* The transition to a market economy required the exposition not only of the desirable end-state but also of a process by which this could be achieved. The comparison of social reality and what is a good society produced, on the one hand, a judgment about the outcomes of the existing system and, on the other hand, a view concerning the unavoidable changes that had to be introduced to stimulate the development of the appropriate outcomes; that is, a good society.
- *Means of initiating the desired changes:* What remained was the development of an appropriate mechanism by which the desirable economic system could be achieved. This referred to the policy instruments that would be used to encourage the desired changes. It should be remembered that this mechanism should use only policy instruments consistent with the economic analysis in question and the desirable and feasible economic system. As such, the model in question would be based on a specific body of economic analysis, thus determining the behavioral assumptions and the economic relationships.

A schematic presentation of the developmental process of transition modeling is presented in Figure 2.1. The schematic presentation reveals that the aim of the modeling process is to identify the policy instruments to achieve the ultimate goal of a good society. This is achieved by initiating desired changes in social reality, as shown in Figure 2.2.

Figure 2.1
Developmental Process of Transition Modeling

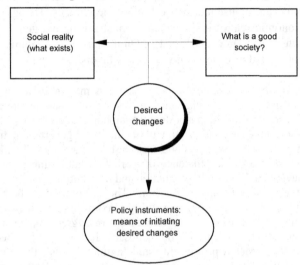

Figure 2.2
The Aim of the Process of Transition Modeling

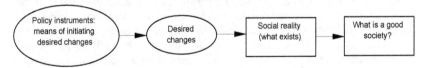

The contrasting of social reality and what is a good society produces the desired changes, which would determine the policy instruments necessary to bring about the wanted changes.

The aim of the modeling process is to identify the policy instruments to achieve the ultimate goal of a good society by initiating desired changes in social reality.

After identifying the process of transition modeling, the next question that needs to be addressed concerns the basis on which different models are distinguished from each other. The aim is to detect what I call the 'primary elements' that differentiate transition models. The primary elements of each model are distinct to, and characteristic of, a specific model. The primary elements are: (1) Economic Analysis, (2) What is a Good Society? (3) Speed, (4) Political Structure, (5) Ideological Structure, and (6) Initial Conditions. The primary elements of each transition model are analyzed below.

2.1   Economic Analysis

Economic analysis involves the application of a social scientific method to the making, and consequences, of economic choices. Using economic analysis, economic reality is described by abstracting and generalizing its basic characteristics (Dow, 2002, p. 19). On the basis of economic analysis, three alternative bodies of methodologies can be distinguished:

- *Neoclassical Economic Analysis:* Employs marginalist economics, in which individuals are characterized by rational maximizing behavior. Prices are determined in a perfectly competitive economy by supply and demand curves in equilibrium without market or government discretionary power. Neoclassical economics is based on the Jevons//Walras model, which stipulates the efficiency of markets in allocating resources and achieving equilibrium in production and distribution.
- *Post Keynesian Economic Analysis:* The assumption of the neoclassical model that individuals are utility maximisers and firms maximize profits is questioned. Using the concept of aggregate demand, where consumption is determined by disposable income and planned investment by expected profitability and 'animal spirits', there would be persistent labor market disequilibrium. Prices are determined within an oligopolistic environment by cost-plus pricing with the presence of market power.
- *Marxist Economic Analysis:* Power is an essential characteristic of the market economy and results in exploitation and alienation. In addition, the malfunctions of the capitalist system are inherent and fundamental rather than the imperfections of an otherwise harmonious economic mechanism. Marxist economics predicts that the capitalist system will suffer crises, which become increasingly severe and ultimately lead to its collapse, facilitating the development of a socialist system.

2.2   What is a Good Society?

The three possible bodies of economic analysis above may be combined with three possible different views of 'what is a good society?' since 'the choice of economic system is profoundly ideological' (Aslund, 1995, p. 5). The three alternatives are:

2.2.1 Competitive Capitalism. The neoclassical model of transition encompasses an approximation of competitive capitalism as a vision of a good society. Market power is a consequence of the use of discretionary power by the state. Without the discretionary power of the state, individuals will behave 'as if' they are in competitive capitalism, thus eliminating all forms of discretionary power. The state should play a minimal role, and should be allowed to act only where there is market failure. The presence of market failure does not imply state action; private solutions should be sought first. That is because by definition government failure results in worse outcomes than market failure; thus private hands are preferable even in the case that they might be imperfect. It should also provide a 'safety net' to avoid physical deprivation. Justice means equal treatment by the state for all citizens. The state should not be involved in redistribution of income and wealth. The market outcome is the just outcome; thus, there are no discretionary income and wealth redistribution policies.

For the neoclassical economists, the establishment of a free market was imperative. That is because that due to individualism associated with a free market process people have an explicit and complete set of priorities. They express their preferences through the market process, which in turn is a reflection of their values. There is no distinction between individual preferences and society's values. Consequently, economics is neutral in the choice between values. Society's choice is the sum of individual choices. The market outcome is just and acceptable to all market participants. Both parties in an economic transaction should benefit, provided the transaction is voluntary and informed. Otherwise, the transaction will not take place. In this way, through the market process everyone is able to escape coercion by one buyer or seller by going to another. The market prevents one person from interfering with another; no one individual can influence or direct the actions of another, allowing a high degree of autonomy. In addition, society is able to harvest the benefits of the division of labor and specialization of function. Society is able to cope with complexity in an effective way.

2.2.2 Social-Democratic Capitalism. The Post Keynesians favor a social-democratic capitalist system. Post Keynesians seek as much freedom as is compatible with a socially desirable outcome, thereby justifying a series of interventions by the state. Post Keynesians in no way discredit the primacy of individual values, the principle of private ownership or the advantages of the market. They stress the importance of the right combination of the above elements with the common good, state property and planning. The welfare state is the expression of the common good, the means of achieving the objectives of society, especially those of minorities and the disadvantaged. The negative outcomes of the capitalist system are not inherent and can be avoided. Market power is not the result of the actions of government, but rather of technology, economies of scale and industrialization. However, the discretionary power of the government can improve the outcome of the economic system and stimulate the development of a civilized society.

The ultimate goal of transition economies should be the establishment of a 'civilized society' based on the principles outlined in Davidson and Davidson (1996) and Marangos (2000–1). Post Keynesians argue that neoclassical economics is based on individual behavior motivated by greed, disregarding the cost to society. For neoclassical economists loyalty, responsibility, the pursuit of excellence, love and compassion are all goods with a price that can be traded freely in the market. Based on such assumptions, whatever the market outcome, that was what people preferred. Meanwhile, individual behavior motivated by civic values benefits the whole society. In some circumstances there might not be any individual benefit at all due to deliberate non-self-interest behavior. In contrast to Post Keynesians the neoclassical economists would consider this to be irrational. Actually, civic values were essential in the transition process: 'Without civil society, capitalism will not create a civil economy' (Fish, 1994, p. 41). It could be argued that the absence of a civil society in transition economies might have been an advantage for the neoclassical model. Policy could be implemented without the constraints of autonomous voluntary organizations typical in a civilized society. Post Keynesians argued, however, that once civil values had been eroded in transition economies it would be extremely difficult to re-establish them. That was why the transition process could not be based on the simple rules of the ahistorical neoclassical economic model. Because 'without civic values in economics – our chief tool of government – we will never be able to achieve justice, domestic tranquility, a secure national defense, prosperity or the blessings of liberty' (Davidson and Davidson, 1996, p. 59). Post Keynesians would expand the role of government intervention in order to drive the market closer to civic values.

2.2.3 Market Socialism. As the name of the model implies, this is a combination of a market system with socialist principles. The market socialist model is concerned with the optimal combination of centralization and decentralization, of markets and planning, of individualism and the common good, and of public and private property. A market socialist model is distinct from other models due to its different goals, which are to prevent exploitation, reduce alienation, achieve greater equality of income, wealth, status, and power and to satisfy basic needs. These can only be realized through the establishment of a socialist economic system, according to market socialists, as the negative outcomes of the capitalist system are inherent and, cannot be avoided merely by using the discretionary power of the state.

Market socialists focus as much on the organization of power as on the distribution of resources. Both neoclassical and Post Keynesian economists have ignored the issue of power. The impact of power in the transition economies was extremely important because those without the protection of powerful interest groups suffered. Market economies varied widely in their patterns of power and privilege, and depended heavily on the way in which the market economy was established. The initial distribution of property gave rise to inequalities, which were exaggerated by the market process and therefore resulted in an unequal distribution of power. The ex-communists enjoyed advantages in the transition economy because of their preferential access to financial capital held in local government banks and credit co-operatives. In a world of scarce financial capital this access gave rise to substantial economic and political power. The market socialist assertion was that it was possible for power in the transition economies to be equally distributed and decentralized. In such an environment, people were serious about their rights of voluntary and effective participation in self-government. Ultimately, the goal of socialism in the transition economies was to extend self-government in all aspects of the society, especially in the economic sphere. 'Socialism does not mean state control of the economy; it means social, democratic control of the economy' (Noonan, 2000, p. 33). Socialist democracy represents an extension of capitalist democracy. A corollary of this is that the economy would need to be drawn more closely under popular control if the government was ever to become genuinely democratic, greatly facilitating political consensus.

In China, in early 1982, the vice chairman of the Communist Party, Chan Yun, announced that China would develop an economic system that he called the bird in a cage: the market mechanism, like a bird, would be allowed to fly freely within the cage of central planning. The plan would be 'primary' and the market would be 'secondary'. In 1992 the 14th Party Congress decided to establish the goal of creating a 'socialist market economy' in China. In 1993 the constitution was amended to acknowledge that China was operating in the 'primary stage of socialism' that its immediate goal was to build a 'socialist market economy' which effectively required 'opening to the outside world'. Socialism was identified with combining individual incentives with limitations on asset accumulation by individuals and with providing 'fair' opportunities to those in less advantageous socio-economic positions. However, the nature of the Chinese economic reforms – gradual and evolutionary – necessitated a hard, strong, efficient, and flexible non-pluralistic state to precisely allow a more controlled, slower transition process. China's non-pluralistic leaders did not need to be troubled about a loss of political legitimacy rather they were anxious about political stability. The reform process in China had maintained political stability and, on the whole, control of the macro economy.

2.3 Speed

The movement towards a market economy may take two forms: the 'shock therapy' or 'big bang' approach, and the 'gradualist' or 'evolutionary' approach. Campbell (1991, p. 7) queried 'whether the socialist reformers can "create" these markets or whether they must grow organically'. This addresses the issue of human consciousness and perceptions when a dramatic change in behavior is required, such as the transition from central administration to markets. The opposing views, with regard to speed, reflected the different beliefs about individual responses, which can either be rapid or time-consuming. The distinction with regard to speed was relevant only for the neoclassical model, since both Post Keynesians and market socialists were in favor of a gradual approach. They agreed with the neoclassical gradualist economists that change had to be slow since institutions organizations and patterns of behavior and thinking could not be changed immediately.

2.3.1 Shock Therapy. The shock therapy (or big bang) approach was characterized by a rapid implementation of reforms, minimization of time intervals between measures, and fast correction of policy mistakes. 'The main issue is to cross the rising river as fast as possible in order to reach the other shore and establish a firm foundation for the construction of a new economic system based on the market' (Aslund, 1992a, p. 87). The shock therapy approach assumed that the transition process did not necessarily imply a reduction in output: important reforms in economic structures were not necessarily associated with a reduction in living standards. Thus, it was argued that the stabilization program and the institutional reforms should have taken place at the same time. Lipton and Sachs (1990, p. 100) quoted Bolivia's former Planning Minister, Gonzalo Sanchez de Losada, who in 1986–89 administered the reform process in his country and stated that, 'if you are going to chop off a cat's tail, do it in one stroke, not bit by bit'. Getting the prices right from the beginning would encourage entrepreneurship under hard budget constraints. The underlying assumption was that individuals would always respond quickly to the incentives provided, even when dramatically new behavior was required.

For the shock therapy supporters, the speed of reform was the imperative issue. A shock therapy approach to transition was the most effective way to salvage the economy for the people because it did not provide the privileged classes with enough time to extract a large share of the resources. Deterioration in short-term output and the rise of unemployment, a common development in all transition economies, was not necessarily a negative sign. They mirrored a systematic and structural change due to the misallocation of resources under the previous centrally administered regime. Unemployment, however, was not linked to the speed of transition, or the resoluteness of stabilization, but rather to wage inflexibility and the creation of new jobs. A gradual process of transition was undesirable because it ignored the links between reforms, increased transition costs, damaged the credibility of the process, restricted individual behavior, and allowed the formation of special interest groups. The gradualist approach would curtail economic transformation, since the dynamism of 'creative destruction' – that is, the replacement of non-viable enterprises with modern and efficient ones – would be subdued. A gradual process would have been highly uncertain because reformers would only have known the first step or piece of the whole process; it would be a piecemeal approach. The transition economies, which lacked the endurance to implement a shock therapy process, suffered the higher economic and social costs associated with gradualism, which resulted in unequal redistribution of wealth and astounding rent seeking.

2.3.2 Gradualism. Neoclassical economists who were in favor of the gradualist approach, along with the Post Keynesians and the market socialists, argued that the changes in the economic system, which were needed to complement the introduction of market relations, could not be introduced rapidly: these changes inherently take time. There was need for gradual change, since institutions, organizations and patterns of behavior and thinking would not change immediately. These elements could only take shape and function after an 'organic historical development' (Kornai, 1990, p. 52). So the process of change had to be slow. It could be speeded up, but nevertheless had to be slow. Otherwise 'artificial transplants hastily forced upon these societies will be rejected by their living organisms' (Kornai, 1990, p. 20).

For the neoclassical gradualist supporters, a gradual process of transition was preferable to a shock therapy approach because it allowed time for adjustment, reduced transition costs, gained political support, and created the condition for the reform process not to be reversed. The market economy required adequate institutions and massive new legislation and legal codes, which could not be achieved by the shock therapy process. The revolutionary character of the collapse did not result in an immediate change in individual behavior. Under the new economic conditions, individuals to be effective market participants had to acquire the necessary personal and practical knowledge. Personal and practical knowledge is that inarticulate knowledge required in the effective performance of any activity. This type of knowledge can only be acquired by direct acquaintance with the activity and it is inherently specific to particular contexts; thus, knowledge acquired under centrally administered socialism was irrelevant. If learning is to persist, solving market problems while important it is not sufficient. Individuals must also look inward. Individuals need to reflect critically on their own behavior, identify the way they often inadvertently contribute to wrong solutions and then change how they act. In particular, they must learn regarding the way they go about defining and solving problems can be a source of problems in its own right. It is argued that if individuals were able to experience an inconsistency in their actions, they would correct it. But if the error was of a magnitude to produce mistrust rather than trust, correcting it was not straightforward. In order to produce trust, individuals must entrust themselves to others. Thus, individuals learning how to reason about their behavior in new and more effective ways break down the defenses that block learning. The transition process required systemic change in learning, knowledge, perspective, and motivation.

For the Post Keynesians, the necessary reforms towards a market economy could only be determined on a case-by-case basis, incorporating the specificity of each case and concurrently developing the principles and objectives of transition. This was only possible through a gradual process of transition. The gradualist procedure accepted the coexistence of elements of the old and new structures of organization during the transition process. As the process gathered momentum the role of the old elements would diminish while the role of the new ones would increase. This required active state intervention. The successful introduction of the market mechanism in a formally centrally planned economy was only possible after a change in attitudes, thinking, and culture appropriate to the market process. This behavioral pattern was not innate; it must be learned. In mature market economies information and learning were important ingredients to inform economic actors what was expected from them and to encourage appropriate responses and behavior. Consequently, the development of market relations was the result of a historical process, which takes time.

For the pluralistic market socialists, the transformation of social relations into entirely different settings that were non-centrally administered and non-capitalist could only take place through a gradual process. Progress would be evolutionary, incrementalist, a succession of small forward steps. There is always a fear of change and innovation in any society. People and institutions can only be changed slowly. The level of conservatism in the transition economies, however, was justified not only on the basis of fear but also on the basis of huge vested interests in the status quo. Every reform, especially economic ones, had to be approved by conflicting interest groups that were committed to the existing regime. Thus, there was a need for a type of strategy through which the transition would be implemented. The wrong process and speed of reform would have endangered the whole reform. Such considerations might help explain the market socialists' initial emphasis on substantive immediate non-economic reforms, particularly in the areas of openness, political democratization, and ideology–education, accompanied by only gradual economic reforms. These changes created a context within which more difficult economic reforms could be initiated, and differentiated the model from Stalinism.

The Chinese approach to reform was characterized by being piecemeal, partial, incremental, bottom-up, experimental, and adaptive through learning, and was marked by frequent shifts of direction and ad hoc responses to unanticipated outcomes. The experience in transition economies demonstrated that no transition unfolded in a precise predictable way. China was no exception. Through the protracted interplay of politics and economics, China's transition experience was as messy and unpredictable. However, by luck and design, the fact remained that certain economic–political–institutional forces shaped a chaotic and inconsistent set of policies into coherent process. China's experience raised the possibility that 'growing out of plan' was a feasible alternative to creative destruction (Rawski, 1992, p. 16). Thus, the Chinese experience offers a strong counterexample to the sweeping claim, made in support of shock therapy that the gradual reforms must fail.

2.4   Political Structure

It was important to recognize that 'politics denote the activities and institutions that determine authoritative public decisions for society as a whole' (Caporaso and Levine, 1993, p. 20). Consequently, the transition process also depended on developments in the political structure. 'In the transition, the liberalization of political markets is often as important as the liberalization of economic markets' (Parish and Michelson, 1996, p. 1043). That is because market reforms initiated 'modern' civil societies, stimulating the emergence of autonomous interest groups, political parties, independent media, and opportunities to participate in political processes. Political legitimacy and cohesion were essential elements of the reform process, which was so extensive and radical.

The political structure determines the decision-making process in society, and this has consequences for the structure and function of the central authorities. It also determines the bureaucratic constraints, that is, formal and informal orders or prohibitions enforced through pressures or threats upon the individual by the bureaucracy. Political decisions would influence market structures. There is a link between economic and political structures. Once a society has chosen its economic structure, this will have consequences for the decision-making processes, and especially for the structures and functioning of the central authorities. In terms of political structure, there are three different types of transitional models:

2.4.1 Political Pluralism: A transitional model with political pluralism introduces fundamental changes with consent, debate and discussion, agreement and compromise. With pluralism there is recognition that antagonism and conflicting interests exist in society, based on the diversity of human beings. There is no single correct line, no sole and invariably correct perception of issues. It means that the common good will not be laid down in an authoritarian or totalitarian manner by the state, but is determined through a plethora of different opinions which are freely discussed (Bracher, 1989, pp. 231–44). Most importantly, pluralism does not involve discretionary power; individuals have to follow rules.

2.4.2 Democracy: Democracy is the continuing responsiveness of the top authority to the preferences of the members of the society, through a structurally defined procedure like elections. Within a democratic system all members are considered as political equals. Democracies generate and sustain the right of participation in the choice of government, in the process of legislation and in the control of administration. Democracies require the existence of political parties that compete to win office within defined periods of time. In a democratic political system there is a combination of rules and the government exercises discretionary power.

2.4.3 Non-Pluralism: This is where the transition to a market economy is characterized by a non-pluralistic process, based on a party that is a leading role party (with a monopoly of power), which adopts a leading position (its views determine most decisions) and a correct line (the party scientifically derives the correct understanding of things). An example of this is the Chinese model of transition.

While there was a need for changes in the political structure in transitional societies, these changes did not necessarily involve democracy. Some neoclassical economists argued that what a market economy needed was a 'light' government, not necessarily a democratic one. These neoclassical economists would have preferred a pluralistic non-elected government, which did not exercise discretionary power, to one which was democratic but intervened, distorting the market (Walters, 1992, p. 101; Intriligator, 1998, p. 241). Rausser (1992, p. 317) disagreed, arguing that, 'sustaining economic success in the long run, in fact, may require democracy'. Braguinsky (1998, p. 237) argued that democracies emerged in transition economies spontaneously.

The shock therapy approach was consistent with pluralism and not democracy. That is because radical economic reform had to go ahead, based on some simple and specific principles, which did not require the input of the people in determining economic policy. Actually, democracy and the electoral process posed a threat to the radical reform program. Within the democratic process, the ultimate aim of any government is to survive the political competition with alternative political parties. This would certainly result in the governments pursuing shock therapy to succumb to the pressure of popular opinion to reduce the necessary short-term negative outcomes of shock therapy; distorting in this way the whole reform program. Hence there should not be any political interference with shock therapy and it should be implemented independently of the political process. Consequently for the shock therapy supporters the establishment of an effective democratic system to enhance accountability was not a top priority; speed was the top priority and the speedy establishment of markets enhanced accountability.

For the neoclassical gradualist supporters, democracy was not an obstacle to reform but, rather, an essential element of the overall transition program. The absence of any broad political consensus made it extremely difficult to confront the transition problems. The nature of the neoclassical gradualist process required the maintenance of centrally administered elements in the economy, which would enable the bureaucracy to exploit their power. At this time, reformist governments faced an increasingly broad and aggressive array of interests some of which strongly opposed the reform program; political, economic, and financial interests influence the drafting of economic policy. Within a democratic environment, abuse of power would be scrutinized by the mass media and by voluntary and spontaneous associations that citizens formed to apply political pressure on a variety of issues. The neoclassical gradualist approach faced with the aggressive array of interests tried to design the sequencing of reforms so as to build, through the democratic process at each stage of transition, constituencies for further reform.

For the Post Keynesians democracy was extremely important for transition economies since democracy results in consensus building to create effective anti-inflationary and employment policies. Democracies generate and sustain the right of participation in the choice of government, the process of legislation, and the control of administration. Policy-making is a continuous process of proposing, utilizing, assessing and modifying policy, reflecting the variety of preferences and interests of the members of society. Society's choice is not simply a matter of adding up individual choices; society's choice is the result of the participation by concerned individuals in the decision-making process. Macroeconomic policies are, in fact, political decisions. The common will is not laid down in an authoritarian or totalitarian manner but determined through a plethora of different opinions freely discussed. Providing there is majority support, they could be put into effect. For Post Keynesians, in contrast to shock therapy, pluralism gives rise to political parties and representation, and thus to democracy.

According the market socialists a reform of the basic relations in the economic structure would not prove to be effective unless combined with significant reforms in the political structure. An essential prerequisite of economic and social development under market socialism in transition economies was the introduction of a modern pluralistic political structure, that is, democracy. Multi-party politics was also essential in the transition economies in order to put under the microscope policies and plans and initiate changes. Otherwise, the people would lose interest in work and politics, as had happened in the past, making the construction of democratic market socialism impossible. Through democratization the market socialists sought to achieve an effective form of public control. This can only take place when people have equal, easy access to complete and truthful information on achievements and impediments. In market socialism, the sectoral and spatial distribution of investment would be subject to both political as well as economic pluralism. The national five-year plan would be based primarily on the plans of the enterprises, which themselves were derived from projected market demand. In addition to taking into account the interdependence associated with investment decisions, the planning process would be a process of debate. Even the greatest precision in the economic calculus will never eliminate the necessity for making political decisions in drawing up plans of development. It follows that the optimization of economic decisions embodied not only the system and techniques of economic calculus but also a corresponding political mechanism within which conflicting interests could be clarified and compromised. The democratic process itself could help to educate voters as to the real alternatives they faced and to engage their cooperation rather than their resistance to required measures. All would participate in the decision-making so that the decisions taken in the name of society were as close as possible to real social preferences.

However, the adoption of democracy would also result in changes in the economic model that reformers strive to introduce. The transition process, based on democracy may influence the model itself. Such changes may be of a minor nature and could be incorporated without altering significantly the basic model. For example, the acceptance of multi-party politics, the concessions for private property and hiring labor were not included in the original Gorbachev market socialist model, but were added at a latter stage. However, pluralism exacerbated the difficult situation of transition in the Union of Soviet Socialist Republics (USSR) by allowing the people to show their dissatisfaction. The attempt to keep the union together in a political pluralistic environment resulted in large concessions to the republics, which ultimately resulted in the break-up of the Soviet Union. It was a 'cost' that the reformers had to pay if pluralism was to be an essential precondition for the implementation of the model.

Those in favor of a non-pluralistic process, the non-pluralistic market social-ists in China, argued that the implementation of such radical reforms required a politically stable and powerful government which had enough authority to implement the reforms, independent of public opinion and vested interests. For example, 'the possession of such a hard state has been the single most important advantage enjoyed by the East Asian tigers over the major Latin American coun-tries' (Unger and Cui, 1994, p. 85). In this way, the government would be able to concentrate on the reform process and avoid any problems associated with the political process, thus formulating unconstrained economic policy. The achieve-ment of efficiency does not require parliamentary democracy. Authoritarian rule may likewise be capable of achieving a dynamic improvement in the standards of living. A transition process based on non-pluralism would have avoided the problems that Gorbachev had to face, according to non-pluralistic socialists in China. The choice between democracy and non-pluralism effectively had to do with the nature of economic and political power and whether the central authority was willing to relinquish some of its power in favor of participation by the people through pluralism. Accordingly, it depended on whether the reformers were willing to accept the input of the people in the development of the transition program, at the cost of altering the model significantly. In the case of China reformers followed Mao who supported 'putting politics in command' (Weil, 1996, pp. 218, 219).

2.5   Ideological Structure

Ideology refers to a cohesive set of values and beliefs about others, the world, and ourselves. It embodies a distinct 'world view' as to how society and, thus, the economic system function. 'Ideas and ideologies shape the subjec-tive mental constructs that individuals use to interpret the world around them and make choices' (North, 1990, p. 111). The introduction of market relations in the former centrally administered economies unavoidably eventuated in a change in ideology. This was because human behavior takes place within a given ideological framework, with its specific values, beliefs, and worldview. Ideology assists in overcoming the free-rider problem.

Ideology advocates a particular pattern of social relationships and arrangements, and determines the goals of human activities and the moral standards of human behavior. Ideology determines and creates human personality, which influences the identity of a society. Thus, we should regard ideology as a set of directives for activity as well as the means for rationalizing human behavior: 'The purpose of ideology is not to mystify but to clarify' (Heilbroner, 1996b, p. 32). It is used to justify a specific economic structure, which its supporters seek to promote, realize, pursue, or maintain. The economic, political, legal, moral, and religious institutions are what they are because they facilitate and uphold the ideological framework of the society: 'For economic terms to mean anything, they must be related to other terms, to their cultural context' (Dugger, 1996, p. 35).

However, while ideology was flexible, the innovator was not totally unconstrained. The introduction of market relations into a centrally administered economy required a different set of behavior, values, and norms. The existing 'cultural frames' and conceptions of control were irrelevant. There was a need for an ideology to encourage individuality, instead of individuals being submissive and showing no initiative. Otherwise market relations would become unworkable. Old patterns of behavior, non-competitive culture and conduct and old expectations were very difficult to change. Not only was a change in institutions required, but also adjustments in thinking, although the law could not establish the latter. Voting in the Parliament, for example, would not create the market. A change in ideology was necessary to remove the stigma associated with initiative and self-help. This then enabled appropriate encouragement, moral standards, and values to motivate people to behave in appropriate ways determined by the market system. However, conformity to the old ways of behavior may suppress the formulation of new values and norms and become a barrier to the entry of efficient methods of behavior appropriate to the market process. The transformation would only occur if the benefits from traversing from one to another exceeded the costs. Due to switching costs it may be more economical to remain with the old pattern of behavior rather than change.

Ideology can encourage within a market system:

2.5.1 Self-Interest. With respect to the ideological structure, market economies have developed an ideology that emphasizes and encourages self-interest and self-help based on Adam Smith's (1986 [1776], p. 119) famous arguments. Neoclassical economists stress that in order to be able to understand social phenomena we need to understand individual actions. Individuals are allowed, within defined limits, to follow their own values and convictions rather than somebody else's, and individuals should not be subject to coercion. The neoclassical model would be in favor of stimulating a self-interest ideology.

2.5.2 Common Good. The question arose whether there was a need to bring together the goals of the individual and society. Should there be any restriction on individual behavior in a market system in the name of the common good? If the answer were yes, then how would the common good be determined? Perhaps by an open pluralistic/democratic process where individuals come together to plan for the common good, or through a leading-role, leading-position, and correct-line party? The answer needs to be incorporated in each transition model. The Post Keynesian model combines a self-interest ideology with the common good within a democratic political environment.

2.5.3 Participation. The decision-making process does not only involve the formulation of the common good, but may also involve the breakdown of hierarchical relations within the enterprise and society. The question then arises whether the transition model will allow the effective participation of the workforce in the decision-making process of the enterprise. The market socialist model integrates self-interest, the common good, and participation. While the pluralistic market socialist model would encourage participation in all aspects of decision-making, the non-pluralistic Chinese model encourages participation only through the party mechanism.

Both shock therapy and neoclassical gradualist economists stressed that there is no other way of understanding social phenomena than through an understanding of individual actions. Individuals should be allowed, within narrowly defined limits, to follow their own values and convictions rather than somebody else's, and individuals should not be subject to coercion by anyone. The need to strive for a better economic position, to accumulate wealth and competition are inherent in human behavior and thus cannot be eliminated. They can be suppressed, but not eliminated. However, there was a significant danger associated with the development of the ideological structure, and in particular with nationalism. The role of nationalism, which is part of ideology, should not be underestimated, especially. Neoclassical economists are totally hostile to the pursuit of policies that promote economic nationalism. As the economies of CEEFSU proceeded towards a market economy, nationalism did not encourage the maintenance of cultural diversity, inclusiveness, and heterogeneity, but rather favored social and cultural distinctiveness, exclusivity, and purification. This would probably have resulted in justifying discretionary measures in the name of 'protecting the nation', effectively withholding the attainment of a free market system. A national policy based on isolationism and xenophobia would have resulted in distortions of economic behavior. Reformers in the transition economies pursed a large number of policies such as increasing tariffs, economic planning, and discouraging foreign investment and multinationals, supposedly to achieve economic and thus political independence. Reformers advocating these policies were out of touch with the interdependent world economy, which ensured their failure. Hence, appeals to nationalism and distinctive national identity and culture could only be used as excuses to stop and reverse the reform.

For the Post Keynesians, market values had to be blended with local cultural traditions. The implementation of the neoclassical transition model resulted in a cultural and ideological vacuum. This led to the development of ideological structures foreign to the market process, such as neo-communism, national chauvinism, militarism, and authoritarianism (Poirot, 1997, p. 236) instead of a civilized society. Hence the Post Keynesians recommended the development of an ideology consistent with a civilized society. Individualism should be combined with the common good, necessitating government intervention.

The pluralistic market socialists argued that the people in transition economies had been 'misled, fooled and bamboozled' and had been blinded to both their own financial self-interest and the higher social interest. 'People's capitalism' has been a grossly distorted misrepresentation of reality (Yunker, 1997, p. 97). The probability that a given individual, who did not anticipate a substantial inheritance, would nevertheless become a wealthy capitalist, was almost nonexistent, nor was this probability significantly enhanced by such worthy and worthwhile human endeavors as hard work, entrepreneurship and risk taking. Pluralistic market socialists did not underrate the socio-cultural, moral, and psychological incentives and the spiritual development of the personality of each citizen. The most complex questions concerned the transition of people's thinking and consciousness. This was because the consequence of transition in thinking and consciousness defined the way people would work towards the transformation of the society. This could hardly be achieved through slogans, appeals and good decisions alone, all of which had been tried before. Black markets, speculation, and unequal rights under Stalinism and immature market capitalism in CEEFSU all humiliated the ordinary worker. The worker who was humiliated and offended is not a productive worker. Only a worker who was respected could be a good worker and a true citizen. In the existing economic climate in transition economies, there was a need for a new type of worker, not in terms of general education and professional training, but with a more responsible attitude to work and with higher organizational ability combined with discipline, creativity, and initiative. No transition problem could be solved without using the intellectual potential of the people. Pluralistic market socialism was characterized by a concern for general principles rather than specific goals, and recognition of the unpredictability of the contingencies involved in socialist construction. Although market socialists expressed confidence in the inevitability of humanity's advance to communism, this advance was characterized by unevenness, complexity, and contradictions. A further aspect of the

ideological reform was to identify mistakes and correct them. It was not possible any longer to forbid the revelation of the truth. Information had been kept
as a state secret, and news about shortcomings and failures reached the people
by rumor and in a distorted way. The actual facts eventually filtered across the
countries concerned. In an international environment of global communications,
media, travel and transnational economies, it was no longer possible to insulate
countries which thoroughly discredited party propaganda.

According to the Chinese reformers, truth should still be sought from facts,
but only within the fence of Four Cardinal Principles: China would continue
to follow a 'socialist road', it would be governed by a 'dictatorship of the
proletariat', it would be led by the Communist Party, and it would be guided
by Marxist-Leninist-Maoist thought. In contrast, to CEEFSU were a product
of transition process was the rise of nationalism and the break up of nations,
China's national policy-makers repeatedly made it clear that attempts to break
away from rule by Peking would be repressed.

2.6   Initial Conditions

The transition process was characterized by uncertainty and the absence of
any historical paradigms. Hence, the *Economist's* (Anonymous, 1990, p. 18)
metaphor about the transition process was that there was no known recipe for
unmaking an omelet. However, models are the result of abstractions and do
not include all the elements observed in reality. The same applies to the transition process. The transition process was a set of heterogeneous phenomena. In
other words, while the CEEFSU economies were structured on the basis of a
central administration, this did not mean that these economies were identical.
The need for change was recognized long ago and the political authorities in
these countries had experimented, to varying degrees, with reform. In addition
to each country's initial economic structures and economic conditions, there was
a need to incorporate their own political, cultural, and ideological elements, the
institutional elements, power relationships and the role of the state. All these
elements were unique to each country.

However, there was disagreement on whether the transition process should
have taken into account the historical and cultural factors which underlay the
unique features of each country, or whether there were analogies between different
countries in similar states of their economic, political, and social development. Few
economists attempted to approximate the initial conditions of centrally administered economies with the stabilization programs initiated in the mature market
economies. For example, Sachs (1993a, p. 3) argued that the prototypical case was
Spain; Edwards (1992, p. 131) argued that it was Latin America, while Aslund
(1992a, p. 26) argued for Central and Eastern Europe after World War I.

The attempt to approximate any of the initial conditions of the centrally
administered economies with the experience of any mature market economy

was, in my view, unwise. The stabilization programs initiated in mature market economies assumed a well-functioning market with developed institutions and the dominance of private property, inflexible prices, and wages in the short run, and forward-looking economic actors motivated by individual material incentives. The initial conditions of centrally administered economies – such as dominance of state property, central control of the whole economy and the encouragement of non-material incentives – did not approximate the conditions of any mature market economy. Therefore, the question arose: 'what is the impact of strategy and policy, and sequencing, as opposed to country-specific initial conditions such as politics, pattern of industrialization, or institutional structure?' (Parker, Tritt, and Woo, 1997, p. 3). Herr and Westphall (1991, p. 323), Share (1995, p. 577), Kagarlitsky (1993, p. 88), Barratt-Brown (1995, p. 169) and Frydman, Rapaczynski and Turkewitz (1997, p. 44) argued that the efficiency and feasibility of any transition strategy depended on the specific conditions prevailing in the individual countries. In contrast, Sutela (1992, p. 87) argued that experience had revealed that the basic elements of a market economy could have been adapted to different historical and cultural environments. Recognizing the distinctiveness of each country as well as the limitations of economic models makes us aware of the need for a balance between specificity and generalization.

The shock therapy supporters argued that the transition program they proposed had general application across economies with immensely different initial conditions and political environments. Initial social factors did not substantially influence economic growth in transition economies rather it was openness and investment. Cultural differences were not an obstacle to the introduction of market relations and the shock therapy model could be implemented independent of any specific economic-political-ideological conditions. Consequently, the shock therapy approach did not show any concern about the initial conditions of each county in the transition economies.

The neoclassical gradualist economists showed some concern for the initial conditions since they shaped the gradual transformation of the society. Policy instruments and goals needed to reflect the specific economic conditions of the time and change accordingly. This required constant reassessment of the specific economic situation and active government participation in economic affairs. The dynamics of reforms differed between transition economies because the starting points were varied. The starting point required clarification. It was not accidental the Central, Eastern Europe and the Baltic states are performing much better than the Commonwealth of Independent States, since centrally administered socialism was established a lot later in these regions. In addition, Hungary was at a relatively advantageous position in the start of the transition process – the gradual reform process started in 1968 with the New Economic Mechanism – and as such the ability to avoid hyperinflation should also be contributed to the advantageous initial conditions. However, neoclassical gradualist supporters argued that this should not have been used as a pretext to substantially delay the reforms and distort the achievement of a free market.

The Post Keynesians considered culture and ideology and, in general, the initial conditions, were important. Institutions and social practices and are founded on customs, traditions, and habits which are deeply ingrained and only slowly deserted and replaced by others. For example, prices are determined in a social market, not just an economic market, by custom, power, and competition. As normal cost is quite constant, mark-ups are established in the short run by custom, convention, and reasonableness and in long run by competitive pressures and market power. The transition process was a heterogeneous phenomenon. It was not possible to copy existing market models, contrary to what the supporters of shock therapy argued. Post Keynesians argue that economic development is a path-dependent process. Economic processes, most importantly the transition process, 'are generally to be seen as path-dependent, and as such, any outcome whether equilibrium or not, depends on the route followed ... in other words, current developments depend on past events as reflected in expectations, beliefs, institutions, etc.' (Arestis and Sawyer, 1993, p. 9). Consequently, the transition process was a path-dependent process that relied on the initial conditions, the policies initiated and the external environment. While the initial conditions may exhibit some commonalties there were definite differences as well. The economy, history, politics, and government intervention were inextricably linked in the development of a market system. Thus the transition process depended on historical, political cultural and ideological conditions prevailing in the country. Reform strategists should not, Post Keynesians argued, ignore these factors.

For the market socialists, initial conditions were extremely important in shaping socialism, because of the hostile capitalist world the transition countries would be surrounded by, if they chose the socialist path. Pluralistic market socialists insisted that the construction of socialism in each country, including transition economies, would have to take into account the specific idiosyncrasies and uniqueness of each nation's experience. Transition economies could be transformed only within the limits of their own traditions and possibilities. Chinese reformers agreed by defining the official of the goal of China's economic reforms as 'a socialist market economy with Chinese characteristics'.

The distinguishing features of the different transition models, based on each set of unique primary elements, are summarized in Table 2.1.

In sum, shock therapy emphasises speed; neoclassical gradualism emphasises democracy; Post Keynesianism emphasises democracy, the common good and initial conditions; pluralistic market socialism emphasises effective democracy (eliminating power), common good and initial conditions; and Chinese reform emphasises political stability achieved through non-pluralism and initial conditions.

3 The Secondary Elements of the Transition Models

After identifying the primary elements unique to each transition model, the next step is to identify the elements of each model with respect to the desirable reforms. The following aspect of the developmental process of transition modeling involves an analysis of the secondary elements. Each model has to answer questions relating to: i) Price Liberalisation-Stabilisation; ii) Privatization; iii) Institutional Structure; iv) Monetary Policy and Financial System; v) Fiscal Policy; vi) International Trade and Foreign Aid and vii) Social Policy.

Table 2.1
Alternative Models of Transition Based on Primary Elements

	MODELS OF TRANSITION				
Primary Elements	Shock Therapy	Neo-classical Gradualism	Post Keynesian	Market Socialism	
Economic Analysis	Neoclassical		Post Keynesian	Marxism	Marxism Maoism
What is a Good Society?	Competitive Capitalism		Social Democratic Capitalism	Market Socialism	Market Socialism With Chinese Characteristics
Speed	Shock Therapy	Gradualism	Gradualism	Gradualism	Gradualism Two Track System
Political Structure	Pluralism	Democracy	Democracy	Effective Democracy	Non Pluralism
Ideological Structure	Self-Interest		Self -Interest Common Good	Self-Interest Common Good Participation	Self-Interest Common Good Participation Through the Party
Initial Conditions	Irrelevant	Some Concern	Important	Extremely Important	Special Chinese Initial Conditions

3.1   Price Liberalisation-Stabilisation

The transition models implied alternative processes of price liberalization. The shock therapy supporters advocated immediate price liberalization and, thus, the removal of any restrictions on prices. Advocates of the remaining models supported price controls and the gradual removal of administrative controls over prices. Stabilization means the elimination of inflationary pressures, whether open or repressed under the guise of monetary overhang. Monetary overhang is the amount of money consumers have kept on hand because there has been nothing to buy with it. In an environment of price liberalization, inflationary pressures had to be dealt with effectively.

In addition, it was extremely important to determine the role of the state within the stabilization process: 'The redefinition of the state's role in Eastern Europe is thus only very imperfectly captured by the metaphor of "withdrawal"' (Frydman, Rapaczynski and Turkewitz, 1997, p. 42). State intervention can take a variety of forms. Firstly, the state could have a minimal role in the market process, which neoclassical economists favor. In this case, there would be no need for state intervention; it would be inactive in terms of the market outcome, except in cases of market failure, and the market would function freely. Secondly, state intervention could be in the form of industry policy designed to assist enterprises in confronting competitive forces through the provision of information, tax concessions, and tariff protection. Industry policy encourages enterprises indirectly, through market incentives, to reach a market outcome that is desirable from a societal point of view. Thirdly, state intervention could be through regulation, which restricts enterprise choice. Post Keynesians are in favor of using both industry policy and regulation. Industry policy was essential, Post Keynesians argued, due to the inability of the market system to pick winners. However, market socialists argued that industry policy and regulation were totally ineffective in a capitalist system because the state did not have the power to enforce its decisions. Power resides with the owners of capital. Private owners would refuse any attempt to influence their decision-making process, especially if these decisions contradicted their goals such as profit maximization. Consequently, in order to succeed, state intervention, which used society's benefit as a yardstick, required the elimination of the sources of power; that is, private property. This could only be achieved in a socialist system, the market socialists argued. State intervention in a market socialist system takes the form of market planning. Meanwhile, the non-pluralistic market socialists would implement, in addition to market planning, non-market instruments to allocate resources through central directives.

3.2   Privatization

Most economists identified the privatization of state enterprises as the most pressing issue to be solved: 'The success of privatization will be decisive for the Russian reform program' (Chubais and Vishnevskaya, 1997, p. 76). Private property is the foundation of market economies: without private ownership the market cannot exist, and vice-versa. However, the establishment of private property did not exclude the development of other forms of property. Whether a majority or minority of property should be privately owned depended on what was deemed to be a good society.

Nevertheless, establishing effective private ownership was an essential pre-requisite for the creation of a market economy. This faith in private property is based on the incentives it produces, which always guarantee the efficient use of resources and eliminate shortages. Privatization should be a pluralistic process and, as such, analogous to the political process. This was because most govern-ments were ignorant of the real capital stock of their economies. A pluralistic privatization process would be time-consuming. However, due to transparency it would not allow collusion between individuals with goals that were against the public interest. In addition, a pluralistic process would be translated into political support and would be a means to overcome any inevitable setbacks on the way to a market economy. Again, 'there is a trade-off that must be resolved between, on the one hand, the speed and cost of the transition and, on the other, the "quality" of the resulting process' (Rausser and Simon, 1992, p. 268). For Kornai (1990, p. 54) 'embourgeoisement is a lengthy historical process'. In contrast to this view, Fischer (1992, p. 238) argued with respect to privatiza-tion that there was a trade-off between speed and equity. For him speed was the paramount concern.

The privatization of state property had additional objectives, such as provid-ing revenue to the government, stimulating the restructuring process and enticing foreign investors to became active participants. There was no historical experi-ence of privatization starting from a centrally administered economy without private property and a capitalist class. The lack of any historical parallels gave rise to a new set of problems, such as whom to sell to, how and what to sell, and whether considerations of equity and fairness should be taken into account. The answers to these questions were linked to the following alternative ways in which privatization could take place:

3.2.1 Restitution. There was a legal requirement for the property to be returned to the rightful owners, where former owners existed and could prove their past ownership before the state expropriated their property, or for the provision of compensation. The success of the restitution process depended on the existence of the past owners, of the appropriate documentation and political judgment about which acts of expropriation to redress. For example, in Bulgaria there were 1.7 million claims for the restitution of agricultural land. By 1993, 23 per cent of the land had been returned to the rightful owners (Brada, 1996, p. 69). By June 1992, Latvia had privatized 17 per cent of its farms through restitution (Aslund, 1992a, p. 77).

3.2.2 Sale of State Property. Kornai (1990, p. 83) and Chubais and Vishnevs-kaya (1997, p. 74) argued strongly that the transformation of state property into private property could only take place by auctioning state enterprises and selling them to the highest bidder. In this way all individuals would have the opportunity to become owners at real market prices. Foreigners would also have the ability to participate so long as some guidelines were imposed to protect the nation's interests, which, of course, depended on what was considered to be a good society. This national policy, however, should not be based on isolationism or xenophobia. An obstacle that needed to be overcome was that the financial assets of the people were not adequate to purchase state enterprises. This problem could be solved by the state providing loans to finance purchasing of state enterprises.

3.2.3 Financial Intermediaries. This involved the transfer of ownership of enterprises to financial intermediaries whose ownership structure may consist of pension funds, worker and/or management funds, citizen funds, or private financial institutions such as banks and government agencies. The advantage of this method was that it was fast and could be viewed as equitable. However, there was a loss of government revenue involved. There was also a shortage of experienced financial managers operating in a market environment who could administer these financial intermediaries efficiently.

3.2.4 Distribution of Vouchers. Under this scheme, every adult member of the society was supplied with vouchers that could be used to buy shares in the enterprise in which they worked or at a share auction, to subscribe to invest-ment funds, or sold for cash. This was privatization through free distribution of shares to the whole population because all citizens had contributed to the development of state enterprises through their taxes. This type of scheme was adopted in Russia, Czechoslovakia, Lithuania, Mongolia, Poland, Romania, and Latvia. Free distribution could be justified on the basis of equity, since those who were otherwise able to purchase property were likely to have accumu-lated wealth either illegitimately or by abusing their power under the previous regime. The advantages of this method were speed, relative transparency, and the creation of an instant capital market, less political opposition from insiders and popular support for the reform process. In addition, it helped develop a share-holding culture. The scheme was also difficult for a future government to reverse. 'From both the equity and the efficiency viewpoints, championing the public is a very wise privatization strategy' (Shleifer and Boycko, 1993, p. 51). A counter-argument was that property acquired for nothing might not be treated seriously. However, the market process would be able to solve this problem, since those who were not intending to use their shares productively would sell them to those who would. The free distribution of shares would be an unattractive solution, however, if the goal of privatization were to increase government revenue.

3.2.5 Combination of Free Distribution With the Participation of Financial Intermediaries. The free distribution of shares might be accompanied by the development of holding companies quoted on the stock market, which played the role of core shareholders, with a clear mandate to restructure the firms and divest themselves of the firms in their portfolio at some time. However, there was confusion in that these holding companies were supposed to be part of the private sector, but were established and more or less controlled by the government.

3.2.6 Spontaneous Privatization. The collapse of the centrally administered system conveyed power to the enterprise management and provided managers with the ability to appropriate state enterprises for their own benefit. In other words, those who managed state enterprises took possession of the enterprise's assets and transformed them into a joint-stock company, thereby effectively becoming owners of the enterprise. This was an easy way out of tackling the complexities involved with privatization and also could be implemented very fast. However, it violated the principles of equity, since managers became owners by, in effect, confiscating the enterprise. In addition, there was a high probability that efficiency might not increase when people who formally managed these enterprises poorly now owned them. Managerial self-interest motivated spontaneous privatization and there was an inclination for managers to lower, as much as possible, the value of the assets, consequently being able to secure the enterprise at a very low price. It was a selective privatization process without pluralism, consultation, or debate, an auto-appropriation process by the few well-informed individuals in a position of power.

3.2.7 Labor-Managed Firms. Another alternative was to transfer the ownership of the enterprises from state to the workforce, creating operative-managed/co-operative firms. This had the advantage of very low administration costs and it could be implemented extremely rapidly. In addition, managed-managed firms had a useful role to play, since they would be able to fill the gaps left by the private and state sectors. Unsuccessful state enterprises might become managed-managed firms/co-operatives.

Under this structure, ownership and control were exercised by all members of the co-operative in the form of group property. All members of the co-operative had equal rights to participate in the decision-making process. The fundamental characteristic of the managed-managed firm was that it was democratically administered. The decision-making process in managed-managed firms was based on the democratic principle of one vote per person, rather than on one vote per share. It is the standard that the International Co-operative Alliance requires its members to embrace, and it is also the rule assumed in the theoretical literature.

In capitalist firms, management employs labor and has the ultimate decision-making power, whereas in managed-managed firms, labor employs management and ultimate decision-making power remains with the labor collective. In small managed-managed firms the labor collective is able to carry out all managerial functions. However, as the size of the firm increases the complexity of organization increases also. Large managed-managed firms need some delegation of authority; that is, the appointment of managers. Using their specialized skills, which labor does not possess, managers assist in the formulation of decision-making by the collective; however, decision-making power still resides with the workers. Hence, managers are hired and dismissed by labor. Whereas in capitalist firms managers are ultimately accountable to shareholders, in managed-managed firms managers are ultimately account-able to the work collective.

The co-operative firm requires from its members loyalty, self-monitoring solidarity and commitment to the firm and to the ideas of labor management. As a result, the managed-managed firm does not need to dedicate so many resources to monitoring. Bowles and Gintis (1996, p. 320) and Doucouliagos (1995, p. 90) argued that the proposition that managed-managed firms were inherently inefficient was not accurate. Participation in decision-making and productivity are positively related. Managed-managed firms can be as efficient as capitalist firms. Managed-managed firms do not suffer the problems associated with investment, monitoring and incentives, or face higher transaction costs, as stated in the traditional literature (Ward, 1958; Vanek 1970; Meade 1972; Alchian and Demsetz, 1972; Jensen and Meckling, 1979; Furubotn 1976; Frank 1985; Williamson, 1985; Eswaran and Kotwal, 1989; Pejovich 1976, 1987). As such, the dominance of capitalist firms in mature market economies and the relative scarcity of the managed-managed firms are independent of efficiency considerations. Institutional bias, credit rationing, path-dependent behavior, and the impact of the forces of conformity contribute to managed-managed firms being out-numbered in mature market economics. In mature market economies the prevailing institutions, and not market oscillations, reinforce the duplica-tion of capitalist firms. Therefore, managed-managed firms were considered an alternative to private property for economies in transition, since the institutional structure was in a process of unfolding. The course of events might have evolved towards an institutional structure that facilitated the development of managed-managed firms. Since it was not efficiency considerations that undermined the development of managed-managed firms, the role of the co-operatives was determined by the view of a good society. Meanwhile, only Post Keynesians and market socialists encouraged the development of labor-managed firms.

3.2.8 Leasing. For some state assets, where privatization was not desirable or not possible due to the high risks involved, privatization could take the form of leasing state property to individuals. As long as the lease or rent was market-determined this would result in the productive exploitation of resources, as well as the creation of the preconditions for transforming these assets into private property. Pluralistic market socialists were in favor of leasing land and capital equipment, while the Chinese reforms introduced only the leasing of land.

In my view, it was very likely that those transition programs that employed a combination of the different methods of privatization, depending on the circumstances of the particular enterprises, had the greatest possibility of success. Nevertheless, the dominant method of privatization depends on value judgments with regard to equity and speed. The shock therapy model was in favor of the immediate privatization of state enterprises through restitution, auctions, and free distribution of vouchers. Conversely, neoclassical gradualists were in favor of a slower pace of privatization though auctions. Post Keynesian economists were in favor of a gradual privatization process, which would involve restitution, the free distribution of vouchers, and the transferring of ownership to financial intermediaries that were state controlled. A combination of the free distribution of vouchers and the transferring of ownership to state financial intermediaries, and labor-managed firms, was also favored. Pluralistic market socialists favored transferring ownership to the workers and, thus, encouraging the development of labor-managed firms to enhance participation and retain a large percentage of state-owned enterprises together with leasing land and capital equipment and the privatization of small enterprises. However, non-pluralistic socialists suggested the retention of state enterprises and encouraged the development of co-operatives in the form of township and village enterprises and private enterprises in special economic zones together with the leasing of land.

3.3 Institutional structure

A radical change such as moving towards a market economy required reform in the institutional structure consistent with the institutional arrangements that were fundamental for the proper functioning of a market economy. The transition economies, without the heritage of a market economy and democracy, had to provide a hospitable foundation for the establishment of institutions for a market economy. An institutional arrangement can be formal or informal.

The role of economic institutions is to make individuals responsive to the economic environment and make the economic environment responsive to individual actions. The institutional structure determines the rules of the game in a society, which are humanly devised restrictions that mould human interaction. It identifies the constraints within which rational economic actors comprehend, plan and use to achieve their goals. Institutions encourage competitive or co-operative behavior, reduce or increase transaction costs and provide the organizational foundation for production and exchange. In addition, each society's interests are embedded in the institutional structure and institutions change in accordance with customs, regulation, and ideology and ad hoc decisions by those who hold power. 'Indeed, the market cannot properly be understood separately from the economic, social and political institutions necessary for its functioning and its legitimacy' (Stilwell, 1996, p. 95). Hence, under the new economic conditions of emerging markets, economic actors struggle to establish institutions to facilitate competition, and to serve their interests through both informal arrangements and formal institutions.

The market process requires 'complex institutional arrangements' (Frydman, Rapaczynski and Turkewitz, 1997, p. 46). The institutional structure embodies property rights and organizational relations. The most important of these are the state, human and civil rights, property laws, habits and other unwritten conventions. Institutions have an important role in reducing uncertainty, as Keynes (1936), Lin (1989, p. 3) and North (1990, p. 6) stressed. While uncertainty may have a stimulating effect on the one hand, on the other it discourages action. Institutions introduce, to a certain degree, regularity, predictability, and appropriate responses to unforeseeable changes in the economic environment, in this way facilitating individual decision-making especially with respect to investment decisions. Developing an appropriate institutional structure was essential if the newly formed market economies were to obtain the potential benefits of market relations. This was because 'exchange presupposes clear boundaries which the system must generate. Without clear boundaries exchange communication may lead to socially and economically intolerable consequences' (Dietz, 1992, p. 34). In addition, the purpose of the institutional structure is to minimize transaction costs associated with economic actors controlling and rendering precise their property rights and exercising these associated rights. The foremost aim of the institutional structure was the establishment of a 'system of well-defined property rights which forms the basis for the rationality of behavior of economic agents and, therefore, the basis for affluence and prosperity' (Klaus, 1995, p. 45).

The question that needed to be answered by the transition modeling process was how would an appropriate institutional structure be developed in the transition economies? Would it involve government action? As Lin (1989, p. 4) and Kregel, Matzner and Grabher (1992, p. 28) argued, institutions often emerge spontaneously and through repeated social interaction, however, in most cases they have to be made by conscious state action, a statement with which the Post Keynesians and the pluralistic market socialists would agree. However, Rapaczynski (1996, p. 87) and Dietz (1992, p. 34) disagreed with this argument, stressing that institutions are largely the product of market forces, rather than the result of government action. The neoclassical model would follow this argument.

Informal constraints such as trust also have an important role to play in a market economy. Informal constraints cannot be as precisely defined as formal rules. They are extensions, elaborations, and qualifications of rules that 'solve' innumerable exchange problems not completely covered by formal rules and, in consequence, have tenacious survival ability. Routines, customs, traditions, and culture are words we use to denote the persistence of informal constraints. Consequently, path dependence, again, is a major factor in constraining our ability to alter performance for the better in the short run. For fear of social opprobrium and ostracism, an individual may be reluctant to violate the informal arrangements, even if the material gains from this violation appear to be very large. As a consequence, informal institutions play a role in shaping the formal rules. Hence, institutional development in transition economies did not only involve the development of formal but also informal institutions. The development of informal institutions could only be gradual. Strangely enough, the Chinese process of transition placed emphasis on informal institutions, in contrast to CEEFSU, which emphasized the formal institutions of private property rights.

3.4 Monetary Policy and Financial System

In addition to privatization and the development of institutions there was a need to develop specific institutions, to enforce hard budget constraints. This would be achieved by reforming the banking system, dividing its functions between a central bank and commercial banks. Enterprise restructuring and privatization could not be meaningful without reform in the banking sector. The enforcement of a hard budget constraint was required by commercial banks, operating under bankruptcy laws. The budget constraint is the sum of financial resources available to the decision-maker that places a constraint on spending. However, firms under central administration encountered a soft budget constraint, instead of the hard one faced by capitalist firms. Whenever a socialist firm was in the red, the central authority would bail it out with financial assistance in the form of subsidies, reduced taxation, provision of credit, or increased administered prices (Kornai, 1992a, pp. 140, 145). In this way, the banking system could deal with enterprises on the basis of commercial principles. They would lend only to creditworthy borrowers for specific purposes, allowing entrepreneurs to finance their long-term economic projects and plan their production and trading activities.

The role of the central bank was a controversial issue. Should the central bank be independent and pursue monetary policy with the aim of achieving a pre-determined target rate of inflation? This question was inexorably linked with the perception of whether the money supply was exogenously determined and, thus, controlled by the central bank, or endogenous. Neoclassical economists highlight the danger associated with the prerogative of commercial banks to create money, which, if excessive, will cause excess demand and place pressure on prices. Consequently, there is a need for regulation by the central bank through the imposition of liquidity constraints. The prime aim of the central bank, in the neoclassical view, should be to control the money supply to avoid inflation. 'Inflation is not a natural disaster; it is created by government or the political powers behind them, and only the governments and political powers can put an end to it' (Kornai, 1990, p. 106). For the neoclassical economists, the development of a privately owned, competitive and stable financial sector was essential to the operation of a market economy, as it was the center for the mobilization and distribution of financial resources and the pricing and allocation of risk.

Meanwhile, 'Post Keynesians rank the supportive responsibilities of the central banks above their control duties' (Moore, 1979, p. 126), indicating the need for a state-controlled central bank and a combination of a privately and state-owned banking system. Marxists highlight the need to eliminate the power of the financial establishment so that the government can control the money supply and be able to use it as an effective instrument of discretionary policy. This implies a government-controlled central bank and only state-owned commercial banks.

The role of the IMF and World Bank in influencing the establishment of an efficient financial infrastructure and financial intermediaries in transition economies is very important in this context and requires explanation. Whereas the IMF is concerned with creating the macroeconomic conditions for growth, the World Bank is concerned with the promotion and financing of economic growth. Both international financial institutions impose and maintain policy conditionality on recipient governments and also provide technical assistance. The recipients of the IMF funds are central banks, not governments or enterprises, because the primary purpose of such loans is to strengthen the external position of a country during the adjustment period. The IMF insists on bank privatization, often with the participation of foreign financial institutions. The IMF stresses sound regulation and supervision of banks, bank consolidation, improving capital adequacy requirements and the strengthening in bankruptcy procedures. The World Bank's support of financial sector reform in transition economies includes: improvements in the legal and regulatory systems, especially in the areas of banking legislation and supervision; modernization of payments systems; restructuring and or privatizing state banks; support for the emergence of core of efficient commercial banks; provision of extensive training in banking services, credit operation, accounting and auditing and phasing out direct credit and non-budgetary interest rate subsidies. Both institutions assume that by the use of standard demand management tools, such as central bank credit, interest rates, expansion of the banking system's assets and limiting fiscal deficits, it is possible to force the necessary adjustment of structural imbalances in transition economies. The starting point of the IMF's macroeconomic program is achieving the targeted price path, specified in terms of the monthly inflation rate. The conditionality imposed by both international financial institutions is based on an idealized view of the efficiency of markets, which is consistent with the neoclassical notion that impediments created by the state are the single most important factor inhibiting the expansion of the private sector. Both institutions embody a certain ideological agenda that mirrors the conventional concepts of neo-classical economics; consequently the programs are often divorced from the recipient countries' initial conditions.

Conditionality imposed by the IMF and World Bank – imposition of a numerous of conditions, some often political in nature, as a precondition for assistance – did not work; it did not lead to better policies or to faster growth. Countries that perceive that reforms have been imposed on them do not really feel invested in and committed to such reforms. Stiglitz (2002, p. 242) argues that conditionality should be replaced by selectivity: giving aid to countries with a proven track record, allowing them to choose for themselves their own development strategies. Participation by recipient countries in program for-mulation is very important. To be successful, policies and programs had to be owned by the recipient countries. Consensus-building that resulted in policies and development strategies that were adapted to the situation in the particular country was essential.

3.5 Fiscal Policy

Each transition model had to identify the role of budgetary policy and specify whether there was a link between government expansionary policies and inflation. Further considerations were whether the taxation system should be neutral, attempting to minimize dead weight losses, or whether the govern-ment should use its discretionary power to tax people differently, perhaps based on ability to pay.

On the one hand, the neoclassical economists argued that the tax system should be neutral and the budget balanced. Accordingly, the government should not use the tax system as a means to encourage or discourage certain behavior because this would create distortions, except where market failures arose as in the cases of public goods and externalities. It was essential to abolish all sub-sidies and establish a hard budget constraint, since subsidies distort the market, increase the budget deficit and encourage waste. Instead of subsidies, loans from commercial or other institutions, or even from other enterprises would become part of the normal financial life of each enterprise.

On the other hand, Post Keynesians favored the use of the government's dis-cretionary power to implement fiscal policies to achieve full employment. Post Keynesians believed that the labor market does not automatically equilibrate independently of the budget. Market socialists argued that the discretionary fiscal policies of the government proposed by the Post Keynesians were totally inef-fective. According to market socialists, power was the natural result of private property, which was able to neutralize government fiscal policy. Consequently, there was a need, together with discretionary fiscal policies, to have the majority of property in a social form.

3.6   International Trade and Foreign Aid

Foreign trade was an important ingredient in the development of markets and in fostering structural change and economic growth. The liberalization of foreign trade was an essential part of the transition process. The dispute with regard to foreign trade between alternative models was about whether a uniform and convertible exchange rate, with imports and exports moving freely between borders, contributed to economic welfare, as the theory of comparative advantage argued.

The shock therapy supporters favored the immediate establishment of free trade and a fully convertible exchange rate. They argued that a fully convertible currency would restore faith in the currency, reduce inflationary expectations, and stimulate foreign trade. A fully convertible exchange rate would make it possible to attract foreign investment, which was essential to overcome stagnation, since foreign investment provided resources, technology, and expertise. Some allowance needed to be made to protect infant industries; consequently the state would be able to raise a certain amount of revenue from tariffs. The neoclassical gradualist economists were in favor of a gradual process of achieving full convertibility through a payments union. The Post Keynesians were in favor of maintaining tariffs through a permanent clearing union. They argued that the principle of comparative advantage was valid only in the ideal world of full employment. Thus tariffs and a discretionary exchange rate policy were essential. Market socialists were in favor of maintaining tariff and non-tariff barriers through a socialist customs union. The non-pluralistic socialists in China, on the other hand, maintained tariffs and non-tariff barriers and implemented a discretionary exchange rate policy.

All schools of thought recognized that foreign aid and credits could have assisted in avoiding a crisis in transition economies. Sachs (1993a, p. 6) stated that 'the West cannot escape responsibility for the changes ahead'. Neoclassical and Post Keynesian economists highlighted the need for conditional foreign aid to assist with the transition process, while market socialists were suspicious of the terms and conditions associated with the provision of foreign aid. For the market socialists, only non-conditional foreign aid could be accepted. However, capitalist market economies and international organizations dominated by a capitalist free market approach were not willing to assist in the development of a market socialist system.

3.7   Social Policy

The development of a social policy was urgently required to avoid hardship due to the transition process. Social policies during the transition consisted of interventions by the state designed to sustain or enhance the welfare of poor and vulnerable groups. As a result, in Russia and Eastern Europe, social programs were an indispensable part of the transition program. Most importantly, social policy played a political, as well as social welfare role, by helping to protect large numbers of unemployed people from major declines in their standards of living and, at the same time, maintain support for the reform program. Thus, the transition and social program required transparency and participation from the disadvantaged, so that this group was not marginalized.

For the neoclassical economists, the introduction of welfare benefits had to be non-discriminatory and available for a limited period, to discourage dependence. The social program was only a 'safety net'. In this context, neoclassical gradualist economists argued that discretionary measures were necessary as long as a gradual transition process was taking place, which, hopefully, would only endure for a short period of time. For the Post Keynesians, the welfare state, which was an expression of the common good and the result of government discretionary power, was the means of attaining the equity objective of society. The market socialists were very critical of the effectiveness of the welfare state, particularly because capitalists always avoided tax payments, thereby creating a fiscal crisis for the government. An effective welfare state required the elimination of power in society and the establishment of a basic-livable income for all, independent of individual economic conditions. For the Chinese model of non-pluralistic market socialism, welfare provision took the form of the enterprise funded 'iron rice bowl'.

A schematic representation of the secondary elements of the transition models appears in Table 2.2.

4   The Process of Transition

The adoption of a gradual process of transition would not only involve specifying the required policies of a successful transition but would also entail a process: a sequence by which the reforms should be introduced. There was a need for a strategy by which the reform program would be implemented, stipulating the order of reforms based on the interconnectedness of transition policies. Consequently, a gradual process of transition necessitated a process of the sequencing of reforms: at least a rough sketch of possible routes, if not a precise map (Roemer, 1994a, p. 126). This would make the transition process more complex, because the modeling process involved a judgment not only with regard to the program of reform, but also in relation to the priority of necessary reforms. Supposedly, the shock therapy approach to transition avoided this problem since all the reforms were introduced in one shot. In fact, even the shock therapy model required a sequence of reforms, since some of the elements of the model had to be introduced gradually. The time framework for the completion of the transition process was a disputed issue. Mihalyi (1993, p. 90) argued for a three to five-year, Abel and Bonin (1993, p. 330) for a twenty-year and Csaba (1995, p. 88) for a twenty to twenty-five year transition process.

Table 2.2
Secondary Elements of Transition Models

MODELS OF TRANSITION					
Secondary elements	Shock Therapy	Neo-classical Gradualist	Post Keynesian	Pluralistic Market Socialism	Non-pluralistic Market Socialism Chinese Model
Price Liberalization Stabilization	Immediate price liberalization No state intervention	Gradual price liberalization Gradual removal of sources of state intervention	Gradual price liberalization Industry policy and regulation	Gradual price liberalization Market planning	Gradual price liberalization Market planning and directives
Privatization	Restitution, auctions and free distribution of vouchers	Auctions	Restitution, free distribution of vouchers, state financial intermediaries, a combination of free distribution of vouchers and state financial intermediaries, labor managed firms	Appropriation of firm by workers (labor managed firms). Leasing of land and capital equipment, privatization of small enterprises	Development of TVEs and private firms in special economic zones. Leasing of land
Property Relations	Minimum state	Minimum state	Majority private with some social property	Majority social with some private property	Majority social with some private property
Institutions	Formal and Informal institutions product of market forces	Formal and Informal institutions product of market forces	Formal institutions product of state action and informal product of market forces	Formal institutions product of state action and informal product of market forces	Informal Institutions product of market forces
Monetary Policy Financial System	Independent central bank and privately owned banks	Gradual establishment of independent central bank and privately owned banks	State-controlled central bank and privately and state-owned banks	State-controlled central bank and state-owned banks	State-controlled central bank and state-owned banks

Table 2.2 (cont.)

MODELS OF TRANSITION					
Secondary elements	Shock Therapy	Neo-classical Gradualist	Post Keynesian	Pluralistic Market Socialism	Non-pluralistic Market Socialism Chinese Model
Fiscal Policy	Neutral taxing system and balanced budget	Gradual neutral taxation system and gradual balanced budget	Discretionary taxation system and discretionary fiscal policy	Discretionary taxation system and discretionary fiscal policy	Discretionary taxation system and discretionary fiscal policy
Inter-national Trade	Free trade, fully convertible currency	Payments union	Clearing union	Socialist customs union	Tariffs and non-tariffs barriers, discretionary exchange rate policy
Foreign Aid	Conditional foreign aid	Conditional foreign aid	Conditional foreign aid	Non-conditional foreign aid	Non-conditional foreign aid
Social Policy	Safety Net	Gradual Safety Net	Welfare State	Welfare state guaranteed employment; Guaranteed basic-livable income	Enterprise funded Iron Rice Bowl

The time framework adopted in this book is for phasing the transition over a ten-year period. This is consistent with Fischer and Gelb (1991) and Fischer and Sahay (2000) even though ten years is really a very short period to turn an economy around (Kolodko, 1999b, p. 253). As such the time framework is not important, but rather the sequencing.

5 Conclusion

The analytical framework presented in this chapter based on a political economy approach results in alternative models of transition as a result of a distinct set of primary and secondary elements and a different process of transition. In addition, alternative models of transition would give rise to a different level of cost associated with the transition process. The next chapter focuses on identifying the cost of transition.

Chapter 3

The Cost of Transition

The aim of the transition process, independently of the model implemented, was first and foremost to increase social welfare in transition economies by the adoption of market relations (non-market alternatives are not considered in this book). The problem of social choice in transition economies was to derive social preferences with regard to alternative models of transition based on the preferences of individuals, which required a minimum level of pluralism/democracy within the society or within the party. The presumption was that the governments in transition economies, responding to social preferences, party preferences or international pressures, would or should pursue social optimality that is the maximization of social welfare. An attempt is now made to formulate propositions by which we can determine whether the social welfare that could be achieved by a transition model was higher or lower than that associated with another transition model. Effectively, the goal is to formulate propositions by which we can rank, on the scale of better to worse (or from worse to better), alternative transition models open to the societies of CEEFSU. The level of social welfare associated with each model would be equal to the Net Benefits of Transition:

Social Welfare of Transition = Net Benefits of Transition =
= Benefits of Transition - Costs of Transition.

Whether a transition process would have increased or decreased social welfare depended both on the effects on the objective world (a change in income and wealth distribution, more or less output, more or less positive and negative externalities, a change in output mix, etc.) and its effects on the subjective world (changes in knowledge, beliefs, aspirations, and the like). The benefits of transition were associated with the implementation of the model of transition achieving the ultimate goal, a 'Good Society', on the assumption that within a 10-year period, the transition process would have been completed and a market economy would be achieved on the basis of the values and trade-offs that each transition model subscribed to. It has been demonstrated that what is seen to constitute a 'Good Society' is based on value judgments – that is, on normative analysis. A good society that is regarded as optimal according to one set of values may rank very low according to another set of values, and as such, comparisons were meaningless without taking into account the value system. Consequently, disagreement on 'What is a good society?', what ought to be done in CEEFSU, was a matter of different value judgments. However, if we define the benefits of transition in some positive sense and confine ourselves to the study of factors affecting the net benefits of alternative models of transition, then we can derive a positive study of the benefits of alternative models of transition.

The objective of all models of transition was the establishment of a market economy; all models of transition aspired to achieve a higher social welfare associated with the benefits of a market economy. The advantages of market relations over central administration has been highlighted throughout the book, but as pointed out, the exploitation of those advantages depended on geographical, historical and cultural differences. Nevertheless, by arguing that all transition models aspired to achieve a market economy, we are not committing ourselves to value judgments behind the objective common goal of all transition models. Therefore, one way out of the dilemma of reducing the difficulty of measuring the benefits of alternative models of transition is to argue that the benefits of all transition models were the product of the establishment of a market economy, ignoring the type of market economy.

In other words, in the absence of better information and specific evidence to the contrary, we may disregard the value judgments of alternative market economies and concentrate on the objective goal of the establishment of a market economy. Consequently, the transition from central administration to markets as the dominant form of organisation would result in the achievement of a minimum level of benefits independently of the transition model implemented, due to the intrinsic nature of market relations being superior to central administration. Further exploitation of the benefits of market relations depended on the geographical, historical, cultural pre-existing factors or the initial conditions. By ignoring these initial conditions associated with the further exploitation of the advantages of market relations, a minimum set of benefits would have materialized, common to all transition models. Thus, each transition model achieves a minimum level of benefits of transition by the mere fact that all transition models aimed to maximize social welfare by the adoption of market relations. By restricting ourselves to the minimum level of benefits associated with market relations, the question of the measurability of the benefits of transition is answered by assuming, the minimum level of benefits coincided for all transition models.

Therefore the maximization of social welfare, the maximization of the net benefits of transition, can be interpreted as minimization of the cost of transition. An optimal model of transition should minimize the cost of transition, on the assumption that the benefits of transition for all models equal the common minimum level of benefits, as a result of the establishment of a market economy. The cost of transition is the opportunity cost of implementing a model of transition. The implementation of a transition model involved an opportunity cost, the value of the best alternative forgone. In our case the best value alternative forgone is interpreted as the alternative transition model forgone. The measurement of the cost of transition does not need, for our analysis, to be cardinally measurable: ordinal measurability is adequate. Ordinal measurability involves the ability to rank. With ordinal measurability one can say that the cost of transition for model X is higher or the same than that of model Y, but cannot say how many times higher, nor can one compare differences in the cost of transition.

The implementation of a transition model, independently of the nature of the model, confronted a set of objective constraints. These constraints were associated with the domestic and external environment within which the transition process was unfolding. Reforms that satisfied the constraints could be implemented with a lower cost than reforms that conflicted with the constraints, giving rise to a higher cost. It should be taken as given that the people in CEEFSU strongly desired the implementation of the necessary reforms to establish a market economy with the lowest possible cost, interpreted as economic and ideological-behavioral cost. People were able to show their approval or dissatisfaction with the reforms by exercising there newly established democratic rights, giving rise to a political cost associated with the reform process. With regard to the external environment, governments in transition economies faced a set of constraints regarding financial aid and foreign direct investment. Mature market economies and international financial organizations were only willing to provide financial aid to transition economies which pursued a shock therapy approach, giving rise to a financial aid cost associated with the transition model implemented. As well, multinationals were only willing to invest in transition economies which allowed a high degree of economic freedom in decision-making consistent with the free market approach, giving rise to a direct foreign investment cost.

The cost of transition consisted of the Economic Cost, Political Cost and International Cost. International cost consisted of International Financial Aid Cost and Foreign Direct Investment Cost.

- *Economic cost:* associated with the reduction in output and employment, increases in inflation and balance of trade deficit that each model recommended.
- *Political cost:* associated with the maintenance of political support for the reforms each transition model recommended.
- *Ideological cost:* associated with necessary change in the ideological and cultural foundations of individual behavior required by the chosen model.

- *International Cost:* associated with the external environment in response to the model implemented. International cost can be distinguished between the following two elements:
    - *(a) International Financial Aid Cost:* associated with the provision of international financial aid by international financial institutions and mature market economies in response to the model implemented.
    - *(b) Foreign Direct Investment Cost:* associated with the voluntary movement of financial capital to the transition economies in response to the transition model implemented.

The next step is to analyze each model by using the primary and secondary elements developed within the analytical framework to determine the recommended process of transition and to attempt to give preliminary indication of the costs of transition associated with each model. The schematic presentation of Table 2 indicates that my goal is to analyze the setting of the policy instruments of each transition model. It must be stressed that the development of each transition model will be based on a set of ideas to which individual economists would subscribe. The primary and secondary elements give rise to alternative models of transition. The aim of the next chapter is to develop the shock therapy model, incorporating both primary and secondary elements, and to identify the reasons for its short-lived implementation. A chronological summary of what actually occurred across CEEFSU appears in the Appendix.

Part II

Case Studies in Transition Economies

Chapter 4

The Shock Therapy Model of Transition

1 Introduction

The shock therapy model derived its name from Poland's stabilization and liberalization program, initiated on 1 January 1990, which became known as 'shock therapy' or 'big bang'. The countries that followed with the shock therapy approach were Czechoslovakia (starting January 1991), Bulgaria (February 1991), Russia (February 1992), Albania (July 1992), Estonia (September 1992), and Latvia (June 1993). Jeffrey Sachs was an adviser to the Polish government and both he and Anders Aslund advised the Russian government and guided its shock therapy reform process. Aslund was, in fact, an economic adviser to the Russian government from November 1991 to January 1994. Both Sachs and Aslund shared the belief that the transition economies were in such a terrible mess that a radical and comprehensive program was required to introduce any kind of rational order. There was no smooth transition, and no 'soft landing' appeared possible: there was only a need for harsh medicine.

The supporters of the shock therapy model argued that the elements of the model would have ensured growth at full employment with low inflation and stability. In summary, the shock therapy model was a neoclassical model of transition advocating the immediate implementation of the necessary reforms to establish a free market process. The transition process demanded the introduction of a package of measures, containing the required reforms, which needed to be approved by the political process and introduced immediately. Correspondingly, the reform process was not only an economic, but also a political, challenge. The government had to prove its commitment to capitalism by initiating a credible reform program, so as to win the people's support.

The implementation of the shock therapy model was short-lived. Despite the substantial initial support for governments initiating the process in transition economies, considerable undesirable outcomes resulted, such as unemployment and inflation. This led to the unpopularity of the governments. High inflation and unemployment caused social and political instability and threatened the fragile democratic governments. The risk was substantially increased by the adoption of proportional representation as the basis for parliamentary representation, which resulted in multi-party coalitions that were weak, fragile and easily pressured. As Boycko (1991, p. 44) argued, 'no matter how strong the purely economic case for "big bang" price decontrol is, this measure cannot be recommended to a politically weak government whose primary objective is to stay in power'. Transition governments suffered head-on confrontations with the powerful political and economic blocks, which resulted in populism together with a public disillusioned with the shock therapy process. Intrinsically, these governments did not have the power to pursue the policies required by the shock therapy platform. In a democratic environment, the substantial reduction in output and employment associated with shock therapy resulted in the ultimate downfall of these governments through the electoral process. The threat to the shock therapy process from the electoral process was recognized by Woo (1997, p. 311).

The reasons why the shock therapy process of reform did not deliver all the aforementioned benefits were recognized to some degree by Sachs (1995b) and Aslund (1994a, p. 24). For the shock therapy supporters, there was nothing wrong with the fundamental elements of the reform strategy, but rather with the inadequate response by the mature economies and the international financial institutions in assisting the transition economies. Among mature market economies and international organizations, 'there was no intellectual understanding of what to do' (Sachs, 1995b, p. 61), there was an unwillingness to make any substantial commitment, and there was no political will. Mature market economies and international organizations neglected to observe that the frail governments that supported and implemented the shock therapy process would have been unable to survive without substantial international financial support. Governments of the transition economies were unable to provide adequate social expenditure programs to reduce the transition costs and, thus, maintain support for the shock therapy reforms. The International Monetary Fund (IMF) and World Bank particularly failed to provide the necessary financial resources to help offset the necessary budget deficits.

2   Primary Elements of the Shock Therapy Model

2.1   Economic Analysis

The shock therapy model is based on neoclassical marginalist economic analysis. Individuals are characterized by rational maximizing behavior based on self-interested behavior represented by demand functions with exogenous preferences, and prices are determined in a perfectly competitive market by supply and demand curves, in equilibrium, without market power. The behavioral assumptions used do not imply that everybody's behavior is consistent with rational choice. However, competitive forces will see that those who behave in a rational manner will survive, and those who do not will fail. Neoclassical economics is based on microeconomic foundations, inquiring into conditions of static equilibrium. The economy can be viewed as being in equilibrium. The macroeconomic variables are the result of aggregating microeconomic relationships. Savings determine investment, and equilibrium is achieved at full employment by an adjustment in wages. Consequently, as long as there are no impediments to the operation of the market process, allocative and productive efficiency is always achieved. The neoclassical dichotomy maintains that nominal variables cannot affect the long-run equilibrium real variables such as employment. The state should only provide for 'truly' public goods (Aslund, 1994c, pp. 181–2).

2.2 What Is a Good Society?

Neoclassical economists view the history of civilized societies as a timeless effort to enhance freedom. This effort is concentrated on structuring all spheres of life and developing institutions that help achieve freedom for the individual in all aspects of life. Anything that reduces freedom in one aspect of life is likely to reduce it in other areas as well. Individual autonomy and sovereignty are of the highest priority for free people. Restrictions on individual behavior by general interests and/or state interests are not accepted. It is argued that the intrinsic motivation behind human actions is based on the human need to be self-determining and self-reliant. This is expressed by pursuing and accomplishing goals that are optimal from the individual's point of view.

The market as an economic institution is the expression of economic freedom. The market, in the absence of any form of discretionary power, is an institutional process in which individuals interact with each other in the pursuit of their economic objectives. Planning and markets are not compatible coordination mechanisms that can be harmoniously combined in any proportions. Indeed, planning can only eventually lead to coercion. However, economic freedom cannot be absolute. The philosophy underlying economic freedom is not the crude self-interested behavior of getting what is desired by whatever means. Rather, the means must be within defined rules. To facilitate freedom, free societies have developed appropriate laws and institutions, which include defined property rights and procedures guaranteeing the execution of contracts.

Private property is the foundation of economic freedom and an essential ingredient for the efficient operation of the market. 'An economy with a predominantly state ownership is unbalanced by definition and is also inflation prone' (Winieski, 1992, p. 274). Confidence in private property is based on the incentives that it produces, incentives that guarantee the efficient use of resources and eliminate shortages. State involvement should be reduced to a minimum. In the event of market failure, government action is not automatically required. Priority should be given to private alternatives, with minimal use of state property. That is because 'government-political failures' are in fact more serious and inevitable than 'market failures'. In the absence of government and market failure, the operation of a competitive market results in efficient scarcity prices, which are indispensable to the operation of the market system.

The market, as a means to economic freedom, promotes political freedom because it separates economic power from political power. Using the spontaneous forces of society results in using as little coercion as possible. The market is a means by which the organisation of economic activity is removed from the control of the political authority. By enabling people to co-operate with one another without coercion; it reduces the scope of political power. Furthermore, the market serves as a source of potential opposition to the misuse of political power, a form of accountability. Hence, neoclassical economists, either as shock therapy supporters or gradualists, were in favor of an economic system based on private property, free market relations and individual material incentives. As such, an approximation of competitive capitalism in which there were fewer opportunities for corruption and rent seeking, was feasible and desirable.

2.3   Speed

The shock therapy model highlights the interdependence and mutually supportive and interactive character of economic relationships, implying that reforms should be introduced simultaneously. Fragmented changes would have been ineffective. As one Polish economist argued 'you don't try to cross a chasm in two jumps' (Sachs, 1990, p. 19). The program has been described as a 'leap to a market economy' (Sachs and Lipton, 1990, p. 48) and a 'jump to a market economy' (Sachs, 1993a).

According to the shock therapy model, restructuring could not have taken place without an effective pricing system, and an effective pricing system could not have existed without a convertible currency. In turn, a convertible currency was impossible without opening the economy to international competition, and international competition could not have been effective without restructuring. The idea that there was a choice between doing one radical measure or another was simply misleading. There was no trade-off, but on the contrary, complementarity. Countries such as the transition economies, experiencing such severe macroeconomic imbalances, could not have afforded to implement their reform policies slowly: 'They need a strong dose of medicine quickly' (Thomas and Wang, 1997, p. 223). Both the economic and political situation required a rapid and comprehensive reform: 'if a house is on fire, you do not tell the fire brigade to pour water slowly' (Aslund, 1994a, p. 37). 'Shock therapy, on the other hand, means a person who, while putting in his first leg, cannot wait to put in his second one' (Woo, 1994, p. 281). 'Bitter medicine is easier to take in one dose than in a prolonged series of doses' (Balcerowicz, 1994, p. 87).

Hence, it was preferable to employ one shock instead of a series of shocks over a prolonged period.

However, the implementation of microeconomic liberalization without macroeconomic stabilization would have been a shock without therapy. Thus macroeconomic and microeconomic reforms had to be concurrent. This was why the reform program needed to be sweeping and expedient. Jeffrey Sachs (1990, p. 19) stated that 'Poland's goal is to establish the economic, legal and institutional basis for a private-sector market economy in just one year'. The negative consequences associated with the transition program, such as reduced living standards and the rise in unemployment, could have been minimized as long as the reform program was comprehensive and consistent. The transition countries should have borne the necessary recession and endured the radical reform because in the long run economic growth prospects were guaranteed. Otherwise, however, the period of output reduction would have been extended unnecessarily. The speed of the transition process would have been negatively correlated with the continuance of output decline and positively correlated with the intensity of output recovery. Official data tended to overstate the decline in output and failed to recognize the benefits associated with increased quality of products and the eradication of queues. The negative outcomes were not the result of the reform process as such; rather they were due to the inconsistencies inherited from centrally administered socialism. 'This mistaken attribution results in an overstatement of the "costs" of the reforms, and therefore an undue pessimism about the reform policies themselves' (Lipton and Sachs, 1992, p. 214). There was no foundation for criticism of the shock therapy process, which was 'politically motivated rather than analytically sound' (Lipton and Sachs, 1992, p. 214). In fact, more radical reforms would have resulted in a smaller fall in output, *ceteris paribus*.

Maintaining distorted prices and entry barriers, as the gradualists recommended, would only have encouraged activities such as speculation, diversion of state supplies, and corruption. Gradualism would have resulted in an environment of ill-defined property rights, badly operated markets, distorted investment, an uneven distribution of wealth, reduced social welfare, a closed economy, high inflation, shortages, recession, social dissatisfaction, and possibly unrest. Regulation, which was really what a gradual process involved, would only have resulted in corruption by politicians and bureaucrats. Once regulation is in place it keeps expanding to repair the perceived damage caused by the original regulatory framework. Thus self-interested groups should not have been allowed the necessary time to coordinate and change the course of the reform. The shock therapy process was believed to be the only efficient course, as it provided benefits quickly, with minimum private and social costs. Gradualism has not been confirmed as superior to the shock therapy approach. Importantly, the longer the transition process, the more the time available for self-interest pressure groups to regroup and use their monopoly and political power to oppose the reforms. For example, the bureaucracy in Russia resisted with all means the implementation of any real reform. In summary, a gradual process would have substantially undermined the credibility of the reforms. 'Move too slowly and the consensus that supports the reform can collapse. It is uncertainty, not speed, that endangers a reform program and casts doubt on the government's credibility to carry it out' (Macesich, 1991, p.x). Only comprehensive programs implemented rapidly and vigorously had any chance of succeeding. Fedorov (1992, p. 108), who initially supported a gradual approach, changed his mind and argued that a gradual reform was politically unacceptable. He became one of the most important supporters of applying shock therapy in Russia.

Most importantly, a gradual process would have resulted in the wastage of the precious reserve of political capital developed after the collapse of centrally administered socialism. At the time, people were willing to accept radical solutions to the difficult economic problems they faced. A gradual process would have resulted in political competition between parties based on self-interest and, thus, disillusionment of the public. Balcerowicz, Blaszczyk and Dabrowski (1997, p. 135) argued that, according to social psychology, people are more willing to adjust their behavior in an environment that is going through a radical change than during a gradual one. People conceive that the initial crisis is less significant as long as there is a positive outlook for early benefits in the future. In contrast, the longer it takes to implement the necessary reforms, the more the public's psychology changes, influenced by the possible social costs. Thus, if people had been properly informed and prepared psychologically, they would have accepted the hardships with relative ease and people were willing to accept suffering if they were convinced of the benefits associated with the radical solution. Consequently, 'under the circumstances prevailing in Russia in late 1991, it would have been lethal to hesitate or move more slowly' (Aslund, 1995, p. 11). In reality, the gradualists were not gradualists at all but rather 'obstructionists' (Rostowski, 1993, p. 101).

The transition process was mostly a political problem rather than a social or even an economic one. It was political weakness that undermined the radical transformation and not the undesirable short-term economic and social outcomes essential for restructuring. Therefore, since the political credit available to the transition government would last only for a limited time, this called for a shock therapy approach.

2.4   Political Structure

Shock therapy supporters favored a democratic process of decision-making. Thus, 'the market revolution has gone hand-in-hand with a democratic revolution' (Sachs, 1995b, p. 50). The justification was that democratization was essential for the transition process, since it immobilized the transitional rent seeking of the old elite by establishing new institutions to eliminate their power and, at the same time, rendered new policies credible. Otherwise, without democratization, civil society would have been weak and the power of the substantial old elite would have compromised the reform process and transferred power to the anti-democratic establishment. Therefore, democracy and economic reform were complements in transition economies. Correspondingly, the goal of the transition economies should have been to establish a democratic society as rapidly as possible.

In my view, however, a democratic political process was inconsistent with the shock therapy process of transition. That is because democracy requires the continuous responsiveness of the government to the preferences of the members of society. The common will is not laid down in an authoritarian or totalitarian manner by the state but is determined through a plethora of different opinions, which are freely discussed. Provided they find majority support they can be put into effect. The shock therapy model of transition to a market economy can only be consistent with a 'light' government, not a democratic one. Woo (1994, p. 288) revealed that the literature about the experience of the transition economies demonstrated 'that political openness prevents sustained economic reforms'.

The government could not have relied on requests for faith, patience, and calm. Radical shock therapy economic reform had to go ahead, based on some simple and specific principles. It did not require input by the members of society. The electoral process also posed the most severe threat to the reform process, since politicians with illusory promises could easily have hijacked voters. Within the democratic process, the ultimate aim of any government is to survive in political competition with alternative political parties. This certainly would have resulted in the newly formed governments in transition economies succumbing to the pressure of political opinion to reduce the necessary negative outcomes of the reform program. Hence, consistent with shock therapy, there should have been no political interference, and the reform process should have been implemented independently of the political process. The program must be implemented consistently in spite of criticism and without favoring anyone: everybody must follow the basic rules. This could only have taken place by stripping the government of its discretionary power and assigning it the responsibility of maintaining the rules written in the constitution in accordance with the shock therapy process of transition, in the tradition of Hayek (1986) Buchanan (1986) and Friedman (1980). As Hayek (1979, p. 35) pointed out:

> Although there is good reason for preferring limited democratic government to a non-democratic one, I must confess to preferring non-democratic government under the law to unlimited (and therefore essentially lawless) democratic government. Government under the law seems to me to be the higher value ...

Consequently, the shock therapy model is consistent only with a non-elected government, which does not exercise discretionary power, instead of one, which was democratic but intervened in the market, preventing attainment of a free market economy. Shock therapy supporters were implicitly in agreement with Walters (1992, p. 101) when he stated, referring to the transition economies, that 'we should not claim democracy as either sufficient or even necessary for a liberal society with a market economy', since 'democracy is neither necessary nor sufficient for good economic performance' (Intriligator, 1998, p. 241). Consistently applied, shock therapy was deeply anti-democratic.

Therefore, since the political structure could not be democratic, should it have been pluralistic? I am in agreement with Woo (1994, p. 290) that 'sustained economic reforms do not require Stalinist-style political repression'. It is my view, first of all, that there had to be consistency between the economic structure and political structure, since authoritarian political structures cannot exist alongside free markets in the long-term. Furthermore, the political prerequisites of the transition process demanded the establishment of a political structure that constrained the employment of political power in the market, regardless of who exercised it. A written constitution specifying the minimal role of the government, the removal of its discretionary power and the establishment of political freedom necessitated a pluralistic political process. All individuals were obliged to be involved in the formulation of the constitution, motivated by self-interest, not coercion. The constitution influences all individuals, so it was beneficial for them to participate in the process of its development. Meanwhile it was in the interests of the transition government to encourage such participation through a pluralistic process, because only then would individuals have been willing to comply with the restrictions on economic and political behavior that ensured the elimination of discretionary power. The development of a 'good constitution' (Aslund, 1994c, p. 190) did not require democracy, only pluralism.

I agree with the ideas of Woo (1994, p. 289): 'we think that it is wrong, or at least premature, to claim that political liberalization undermines economic reforms'. Political pluralism did not undermine the shock therapy program; democracy did, as experience demonstrated. The implicit 'assumption is that correct economic theory must subordinate democracy' (Glasman, 1994, p. 79). Correspondingly, 'the processes of liberalization and democratization in the society will survive only if they are completed by a strong executive power that exerts control over the entire Russian Federation. I believe that this power is not only desirable, but inevitable' (Mau, 1992, p. 273). Woo (1994, p. 306) also concluded his paper with the statement that 'the effective one-party rule in Japan, Korea, Singapore, Malaysia, Indonesia, and Taiwan are testimonies to the compatibility of a market economy with many political forms'. This implied that Woo preferred one-party rule, which was consistent with the shock therapy approach. Aslund (1997e, p. 191), citing China as an example, argued that in the end a developing economy could function sufficiently without democracy.

2.5 Ideological Structure

With respect to the ideological structure, neoclassical economists have developed an ideology that emphasizes political and economic freedom and encourages self-interest and self-help, as presented by Adam Smith (1986 [1776], p. 119). Market power results from the state's use of its discretionary power. Without discretionary power, individuals would behave 'as if' they were in competitive capitalism. Hence, the state's role should be minimal; it should be a 'minimal state' and the constitution should allow it to act only where there is market failure. It should also provide a 'safety net'. Justice does not mean equality of income distribution, but rather justice means equal treatment by the state. That is, everyone is entitled to basic human rights and equality before the law, together with rejection of all privileges based on class, color, religion, or gender. Hayek viewed human nature as primordially socialistic, which he conflated with dependency, and civilization had the effect of creating institutions that encouraged people to be more individualistic.

An ideological foundation for the development of a market system already existed in CEEFSU, based on the values and the deeply rooted individualism and rationality of the people. Competition and the need to strive for a better economic position and to accumulate wealth are inherent in human behavior, and thus cannot be eliminated. They can be suppressed, not eliminated. These values could have fostered an effective market system as long as all impediments to individual behavior were removed. The people in transitions economies were 'troubled, restive, and impatient' (Sachs, 1991a, p. 26). The argument that people in transition economies would not have been able to respond immediately to market opportunities due to the suppression of the entrepreneurial spirit did not have any substance. On the contrary, 'it seems that the deadening decades of communism did not dull the acquisitive spirit, but rather sharpened it' (Sachs, 1993a, p.xiii). Consumers in transition economies reacted positively to the market reforms, and their behavior was consistent with and predicted by neoclassical economic theory. The number of private enterprises increased dramatically as entrepreneurship was oppressed but still alive and self-interest and self-help was replacing paternalism and statism. The slogan: 'Towards the market at the expense of the state, not the citizens' was very popular in Russia (Kosmarskii, 1992, p. 31). Thus the acquisitive spirit increased in CEEFSU. 'All over Eastern Europe, the entrepreneurial spirit has turned out to be excellent' (Aslund, 1994a, p. 35). Correspondingly, 'the cultural barrier had evidently been exaggerated' (Aslund, 1995, p. 271).

2.6 Initial Conditions

While the problems associated with the transition process might have been serious and complex, they were not unparalleled. The transition process, for the shock therapy supporters, was not peculiar, complicated, or enigmatic. 'In fact in many ways it is a well-trodden path' (Sachs, 1993a, p. 2) and had been tried out with success in many places around the world. The problems faced had to be solved by ordinary means and the 'uniqueness' of the situation required unhesitating and determined action. 'Everything in this setting pointed to the need for a hard and rough stabilization policy' (Aslund, 1997d, p. 186). Many elements of the transition program did have general application across economies with immensely different initial economic and political environments. Initial social factors did not substantially influence economic growth in transition economies; rather openness and investment. Thus, 'in principle the tasks and instruments of macroeconomic stabilization are the same in Russia as elsewhere' (Aslund, 1995, p. 181).

3   Secondary Elements of the Shock Therapy Model

3.1   Price Liberalization-Stabilization

Price liberalization and stabilization were preconditions for a successful reform process. Price liberalization was also required for the establishment of a hard budget constraint. Reform of the price mechanism was necessary to allow prices to reach their equilibrium values. Impersonal market forces determined prices, not the government, which was influenced by political considerations. In this way the increased prices reduced real money balances to the appropriate level for monetary equilibrium. Given the lack of a scarcity-based price system it was infeasible to develop an effective stabilization program. The price system had been so distorted under centrally administered socialism that it was impossible to determine which enterprises should have closed or continued operation. Furthermore, the valuation of enterprises could not have taken place without knowing the prices of inputs: this necessitated market competition. Higher prices were in the interests of society because they eliminated shortages and queuing; induced greater availability and quality of goods; facilitated lower prices than on the black market; and eliminated corruption. It was better to face a single increase in prices than high and persistent inflation, since there was nothing beneficial associated with high inflation and its accompanying corruption. In fact, prices were often lower than on the black market, even though the official inflation rate had increased.

The shock therapy economists were in favor of an adjustment approach that involved an immediate jump in the price level. This was necessary so that investment decisions were not distorted by transitional prices. It also required the abolition of subsidies, which would have resulted in higher prices. However, this would also have made budget resources available to finance social programs. Any restrictions on prices were undesirable because they disrupted the market process. Higher prices would have encouraged the development of new enterprises and competition, as under these conditions it would have been profitable to operate. This involved freeing prices, declaring exchange convertibility, and encouraging devaluation. In this way the monetary overhang would have been eliminated. For competition to be effective the inefficient enterprises had to go into bankruptcy. Permanent 'rehabilitation' of bankrupt companies by the government would have made a market economy impossible. The introduction of competition would also have resulted in positive externalities throughout the state sector, since competition encouraged restructuring in this sector. The experience of the Polish economy, with full economic recovery and annual GDP growth rates of four per cent, 'is testimony to the power of macroeconomic policy to induce structural adjustment' (Berg, 1994, p. 377).

Naturally, output would have been reduced. It was an inevitable 'natural cost' for the development of market relations. It was pointed out that the goal of the transition process was 'economic transformation, and not instant growth' (Aslund, 1994a, p. 32). However, the statistical evidence was misleading because it failed to demonstrate the real transformation in output. Improvements in quality, the elimination of queues and forced substitution cannot be reflected in statistical data. Taking into account these qualitative transformations, it was argued that living standards were not substantially reduced.

An efficiently functioning labor market was a principal prerequisite for a successful transition. The widespread indexation of wages and the large percentage of the labor force employed in state enterprises were obstacles to the achievement of stabilization. Thus wages should also have been market-determined, giving rise to unemployment, which was part of the remedy. Furthermore, market-determined wages, complementing private ownership of enterprises, would have ensured job creation. It should have been remembered, as Schumpeter states, that the fundamental aspect of economic development is 'creative destruction'. Consequently, the transition process would have necessarily involved some 'destruction'. However, at the beginning of the reform program, to avoid a wage-price spiral due to hyperinflation, Sachs and Lipton (1990, p. 56) recommended a tax-based wage policy to encourage wage rises below the increases in inflation. For example, the Polish government initiated penalties on wage increases, the so-called *popiwek* (Balcerowicz, Blaszcyzk and Dabrowski, 1997, p. 138), under which wages were to increase by 30 per cent of the monthly inflation rate in January 1990 and 20 per cent thereafter. Enterprises conceding wage increases above the norm were heavily taxed.

Data have revealed that unemployment was not a substantial problem in the shock therapy process, and private sector development was able to increase employment. Nevertheless, in market economies inflation can only be contained with some unemployment. Inflation was totally undesirable and has been labeled the most serious problem of transition. Inflation distorted the economic functions of prices and all other economic institutions, having a negative impact on economic growth. As long as high inflation prevailed, and the more hesitant the reform, the larger would be the total fall in output. The fight against infla-tion had to take place immediately. Postponing any action, with the excuse that other elements of the economic system had to be in place, 'would be like abandoning a fire to try and rebuild a house while it was still burning. Similarly, attempting to eliminate galloping inflation gradually would be like trying to put out the fire slowly' (Balcerowicz, Blaszcyzyk and Dabrowski, 1997, p. 135). Consequently, there was only one viable alternative: 'a money-based orthodox program' (Dabrowski, 1997, p. 50).

Shock therapy economists argued that inflation was caused by irresponsible governments that increased the money supply to finance budget deficits and/or the result of pressure groups that used their discretionary power to force the government to offer preferential treatment in the form of tax concessions and subsidies. Most importantly, in the transition economies, inflation was the result of rent seeking by the old elite that exploited the weakness of the state. Thus, the only way to eliminate inflation was by reducing the role of the government and requiring it to follow specific rules. Due to the lack of experience and information in the transition process, there was no bank of knowledge from which to draw to fine-tune the economy. The state administration inherited by the command economy was incapable of making any informed decisions. Consequently, the functions of the state needed to be minimized, especially during the initial stages of the transition. To assign the responsibility to bureaucrats and then expect suc-cess was impossible. 'An important conclusion to draw from this experience is that the costs of such an economic transition are inevitably high; but if inflation is allowed to rise, they will be even higher' (Aslund, 1995, p. 177).

'In short, there is no plausible social argument for so-called soft stabilization policies' (Aslund, 1995, p. 176). It has been claimed that empirical evidence was conclusive in indicating that only shock therapy was effectual in repressing inflation. While price liberalization was not irreversible, it would have ensured that a return to the previous state of affairs would have been extremely costly. Essential supplementary policies for stabilization were a stable exchange rate, an appropriate institutional environment and an independent central bank and, of course, privatization.

3.2   Privatization

The industrial structure under the command system was inefficient, since state enterprises were inefficient and inclined towards financial crisis. This was because of internal rent seeking and the imposition of non-economic goals by governments upon state enterprises, which were used as instruments to serve personal goals. Thus privatization aimed to reduce political interference in the economy: 'whatever else privatization is supposed to accomplish, it will fail unless it succeeds in this objective' (Frydman, Rapaczynski and Turkewitz, 1997, p. 85). The undesirable functioning of state enterprises was due not only to soft budget constraints but also to the principal-agent problem. Marketization without privatization was not considered a viable alternative. The experience of CEEFSU and China revealed that marketization without privatization destabilized the economy, increased inflation and the likelihood of corruption and did not heighten efficiency. There was a need for a radical change in the property structure by reducing, restructuring, modernizing and privatizing state enterprises. Consequently, 'until privatization has been accomplished, the economic crisis is likely to persist' (Aslund, 1992a, p. 87).

The dominant form of ownership had to be private. Private ownership of enterprises constituted the ultimate form of decentralized property rights because individuals owned their equity, which was freely transferable. Without private property, effective market relations could not have existed: 'When there are no capitalists there is nobody to represent the interests of capital' (Sachs, 1993a, p. 29). When there was a dominance of state ownership, it was impossible to maintain financial discipline under a soft budget constraint. In this context, private ownership of unprofitable firms was still desirable. However, a market economy did not prohibit other forms of property, as long as they survived the market test. 'A pluralistic ownership is a precondition of political democracy' (Aslund, 1992a, p. 71).

In addition, privatization was a means of increasing popular support for the whole reform program. Political support for the reform program reduced the power of opponents, altering the balance of political power. For example, in Russia the populist character of the voucher system of privatization preserved the whole privatization program. Political support for privatization resulted in a positive externality in facilitating reforms in other areas. In addition, immediate privatization could have produced the goods that consumers wanted. Privatization of state enterprises was a means of reducing the budget deficit, even in the case of a non-sale of state enterprises such as the transfer of state enterprises to pension funds, in this way reducing the budget obligations for social security payments.

Not all firms had to be liquidated, provided there was appropriate restructuring as a result of privatization, the development of new enterprises and the opening the economy to international competition. The proposal to prepare state enterprises for privatization through corporatization, under the direction of the government, a popular 'transition measure' in mature capitalist economies, was not acceptable to shock therapy supporters. It was considered to be undesirable and an unnecessarily time-consuming process that would have resulted in an extremely slow privatization process. The government had to focus on establishing a framework for privatization and not be actively involved in the restructuring of state enterprises. The government did not have the knowledge or the ability to restructure enterprises. That was the responsibility of the private owners: 'winners and losers cannot be selected, *a priori* from among Poland's 7,800 industrial enterprises in the state sector' (Sachs and Lipton, 1990, p. 53).

Enterprises had to be privatized first and then restructured under private owner-ship. The private owners possessed a great deal more information and incentive to restructure the enterprise in an efficient manner. Moreover, the proposition of developing necessary measures to ensure that 'perfect owners' acquired the enterprise was senseless. The market alone could have selected the perfect owners, by using the objective yardstick of efficiency; therefore there would have been no need to use any discretion. 'Only a sufficiently pluralistic market can generate sound owners' (Aslund, 1992a, p. 75).

Labor-managed firms were out of the question. 'It is a method to be avoided ... [and] threatens to discredit the very idea of privatization among the popula-tion' (Chubais and Vishnevskaya, 1997, p. 69). This was based on the traditional efficiency objections to labor-managed firms. It was even less proper to transfer ownership to the management, which constituted an even smaller percentage of the workforce in the enterprise. It appeared that spontaneous privatization was faster and less time-consuming. However, the problems associated with spontaneous privatization were not only economic but also political. The ap-propriation of state enterprises by managers, through spontaneous privatiza-tion, resulted in social unrest, which questioned the political legitimacy of the government. Hence there was a need to develop a suitable legal framework, especially 'conflict of interest' laws to prohibit spontaneous privatization and discourage labor-managed firms. In addition, the transitional measure of trans-forming state enterprises into state holding companies was undesirable, as this was likely to become a permanent mechanism and state enterprises would, thus, not have been privatized.

'Without question the Achilles Heel of the economic reform program in Eastern Europe is the state industrial sector' (Sachs, 1991a, p. 28). This was due to the employment in state enterprises of a large percentage of the labor force in CEEFSU, and the consequent emergence of a powerful pressure group. At the end, shock therapy supporters conceded that giving a share of ownership to workers and managers was an important strategic move. It was not based on ideology or justice, but rather on the need to facilitate rapid privatization. In this way, both workers and managers were transformed into supporters of privatization. Meanwhile, workers and management in small and medium en-terprises received corporatization with evident eagerness in Russia (Boycko, Shleifer and Vishny, 1993, p. 154).

The privatization process had to be initiated concurrently for all enterprises, using across-the-board mechanisms: 'the great conundrum is how to privatize such an array, in a manner that is equitable, swift, politically viable and likely to create an effective structure of corporate control' (Sachs, 1990, p. 22). Thus privatization should have taken place through a combination of different methods: sales, free distribution or other means, but preferably through free distribution (Sachs, 1991b, p. 67). Boycko, Sheifer and Vishny (1993, p. 148) argued that the voucher auctions in Russia were a notable success in initiating enterprises into the private sector. By April 1995 three-quarters of Russian industry was privately owned (Boone and Fedorov, 1997, p. 180). The shock therapy supporters argued that the government should not allow unreasonable claims to frustrate the process, which had to be rapid and transparent. To achieve a fast privatization process, the authorities had to avoid the lengthy, laborious, and costly task of case-by-case privatization. For example, retail shops could have been privatized immediately by auctioning them under the supervision of municipal governments. The privatization of land was relatively painless and high economic advantages were associated with family farms. Such actions would have helped facilitate the establishment of a market economy, reduced shortages, improved the quality of goods and provided the privatization process with a more positive image.

In this context, shock therapy supporters argued that the development of new firms, as a means of stimulating growth, should not have been underestimated. Since the efficiency gains of privatized firms would have taken some time to materialize, any improvement in economic conditions in the short run would have come from the establishment of new firms. Actually, the birth of a private ownership market economy would have been the result of two mechanisms: 'bottom-up privatization', whereby new firms are formed, and 'top-down' privatization in which state enterprises are privatized. The main effect of introducing market relations was the origination of new firms, which could be used as a measure of success. The increase of competition due to new firms had a major influence in depoliticising state firms. However, economic welfare could only have been maximized if state enterprises were privatized. The development of new private firms was not a substitute for restructuring and/or privatizing state enterprises. This was because the private sector did not develop in a vacuum: the restructuring and reduction of the state sector was crucial for the genesis of the private sector.

Privatization and financial restructuring manifested the greatest intellectual and political complexities of the entire transition program. This was due to privatization being driven by many conflicting objectives. Firstly, there were issues of fairness, compensation, restitution, enterprise efficiency, budgetary revenues, and employment concerns. Secondly, it was based on previously unknown methods such as vouchers, management acquisitions, and worker buyouts, which were characterized by administrative complexity as there were thousands of small, medium and large enterprises that operated within a legal vacuum, incomplete markets, and were fraught with the possibility of corruption.

I believe that the concerns and reservations that shock therapy economists had about the privatization process were unfounded. The aim of the shock therapy process was to develop an economy based on market relations without the presence of discretionary power. In such an environment it did not matter who the initial private owners were, because ultimately the only firms that could have survived were those employing efficient management practices. Therefore, whether the privatization process gave ownership of state enterprises to the workers or management, or to members of the society, they would only have been able to retain their ownership rights if they used their property productively by satisfying market demand at minimum cost. If they used their ownership for non-market purposes it would have increased the costs of production. In the long run, in a competitive environment, this would have resulted in a substantial fall in consumer demand for the goods produced by the enterprise, endangering the viability of this enterprise. For example, if labor-managed firms increased wages instead of repaying their loans, it would have resulted in bankruptcy or take-over and the removal of their ownership rights and possibly their employment. Labor-managed firms would have survived in a free market environment if, and only if, they satisfied market demand at minimum cost, similar to the way private firms did. These firms would have lost the characteristics that made them labor-managed. Nee (1996, p. 913) argued that, due to market competition, collective ownership in China had led to behavior by the collective owners similar to that of the owners of private firms. Hence, in a competitive market, which was the ultimate goal of shock therapy supporters, only efficient owners and efficient behavior would have been able to survive, independently of how the initial distribution of ownership took place. The establishment of competitive market conditions ensures that managers serve the interests of the enterprise. In addition, the development of small and medium-sized enterprises, and the spread of entrepreneurial motives, helped force enterprises to behave in an appropriate manner. Aslund (1995, p. 247) justified 'irregular privatization' in terms of avoiding the obstruction of privatization by interest groups. In a free market process, as long as 'irregular privatization' did not institute discretionary power, it was desirable. Consequently, the development of a free market process would have derived an efficient ownership structure, making the method of privatization unimportant as long as the privatization process was rapid. Ownership of property by the Mafia was not desirable because they did not respect the rules of a competitive market.

3.3   Institutional Structure

The aim of shock therapy was not only to eliminate the unreasonable distortions of the central allocation of resources, but also to establish the appropriate institutions in organizing the new market mechanism for allocating resources. The transition economies did not have any capitalist institutions. In direct contrast they were command economies. Participation in the market process, as the shock therapy supporters argued, was not based on the crude self-interested behavior of getting what you want with whatever means; rather, the means you use to get what you want must be within defined rules. Thus the transition economies required the development of an independent judiciary and an executive subject to the rule of law. This was in sharp contrast to the traditions of autocratic rule under the Tsarist regime and centrally administered socialism. The move towards a market economy required the destruction of the legal and political processes of the past. Transition economies had to develop appropriate laws and institutions, which included defined property rights and well-enforced rules of contract, which were essential if they were to be able to obtain the benefits associated with the market process. 'Without law, there can be no property rights and without these there can be no real economic stabilization or development' (Aslund, 1997c, p. 14). In addition, the institutional structure would also have guaranteed that there would be no return to the status quo. Consequently, the reforms could not have prospered until authorities and individuals developed respect for the law and legal processes.

The institutional structure was one of the most challenging aspects of the transition modeling process. The development of institutions appropriate to the market process, although essential, was extremely complex and time-consuming and, once operative, was very difficult to change. This raised doubts regarding the feasibility of the shock therapy approach. Actually, these doubts were unwarranted. Property rights and the institutional structure, like any other good, were the result of consumer sovereignty; consumers determine not only the composition of output but also the composition of institutions. 'Contrary to the common economist's assumption that a system of property rights is a precondition of a market economy, the development of market institutions is often a prerequisite for a viable private property regime' (Rapaczynski, 1996, p. 102). Thus the development of market relations did not need to be postponed until an appropriate institutional structure was in place, since the emergence of markets did not require a sophisticated institutional structure. A simple economy did not need an advanced judicially enforced system of property rights: 'Little economic or legislative sophistication is required' (Aslund, 1992a, p. 11). Some simple rules would have been adequate; as the markets evolved so too would have the legal system and enforcement mechanisms simultaneously. 'Thus institutional structure was a necessary but not a sufficient condition for the needed reforms' (Klaus, 1995, p. 46). While government initiation may have developed the necessary institutions, market-produced institutions frequently appeared and were operative beforehand.

Hence, while prescribing an immediate transition to a market economy, the shock therapy supporters believed that only the market could have delivered operative institutions. Effectively, and paradoxically, the shock therapy approach recommended the gradual development of market institutions. The imperative of not using government intervention in the market resulted in a contradiction in the shock therapy model. Shock therapy supporters required the immediate destruction of the institutions of central administration, which implied the establishment of market institutions by the government, thus minimizing the time necessary to create these institutions. In contrast, the shock therapy economists were willing to sacrifice speed in the context of institutional development, in order to avoid government intervention, which they regarded as totally undesirable.

Efficient institutions could not have been intentionally designed. Governments and individuals did not have the knowledge base, because past experiences were inadequate and, in the case of centrally administered socialism, irrelevant. No one was able to predetermine the market outcome; thus there could not have been any prescription to develop market institutions. The development of the institutional structure was path-independent, which implied that the development of the necessary institutions was not culturally embedded. Institutional change comes as a result of free market relations, which would have delivered, in due course, the best outcome in response to the need for structural change based on the universal principles of self-interested behavior. Fundamental changes in relative prices are the most important source of institutional change by altering norms, which subsequently creates incentives to construct more efficient institutions.

Individuals participate in the market process based on an evident set of rules. The culture of respect for property rights in mature market economies is not the result of habits, convictions, religious beliefs or the rule of law. These could not have sustained complicated and innovative behavioral patens; rather it would have been the result of a self-enforcing process initiated by spontaneous market behavior. 'The reason why most people perform their contractual obligations, for example, is not that they are afraid of remorse or state coercion, but that in the extended context in which they are expected to conduct business, a breach would be against their best interests' (Rapaczynski, 1996, p. 89). These self-enforcing mechanisms would not have preceded the emergence of market relations. Likewise, they would not have been the result of government action. The development of the institutional structure was a very elaborate procedure, which the government did not have the knowledge to implement. These institutions were 'nearly never created by conscious design' (Frydman, Rapaczynski and Turkewitz, 1997, p. 42).

In this context, since people were rational and made efficient choices using market relations, the market outcome was always an efficient one. Capitalist institutions, the result of the market process, could only be efficient institutions. That is because 'exchange is the basic communicative element from which all other modern economic institutions (prices, money, private property, organizations and so on) emanate' (Dietz, 1992, p. 37). Government supervisory bodies are inherently inefficient in providing an effective overseeing mechanism. Accordingly, any interference from the state would only have subverted enterprise ethics, and should have been avoided. Subsequently, institutional change was a derivative. The most important goal was the spontaneous development of market relations through the removal of most restrictions on individual activity. While the new market relations served to aid the development of the institutional structure, the institutional structure often served to strengthen the new market relations. 'Indeed, the legal responses are often only effective against a background of self-enforcing market mechanisms' (Rapaczynski, 1996, p. 102).

All the transition economies experienced the negative phenomenon of corruption, and with it a rise in crime. This compromised the economic reform program and led to inflation, inequalities, and disillusionment with the transition goals in the eyes of the people. This was because civil society was weak and disorganized. Of course corruption was not something new. The members of the party under the previous state of affairs used their political power for their own betterment by exploiting the country's resources, which 'were nominally owned by the state and thus by nobody' (Sachs, 1995a, p. 22). However, with the establishment of political pluralism, corruption could not have been hidden under the party shield of protection. The origins of corruption remained the same: the old guard, using the positions of power it had inherited, was able to build wealth illegally. Nevertheless, corruption was the result of a gradual process instead of a shock therapy approach. For example, Boone and Fedorov (1997, p. 186) argued that there was no doubt that the gradual and ill-defined process of reform in Russia was induced and, often, motivated by corruption. The ill-defined laws and legal procedures, the piecemeal removal of price controls, the subsidies provided by the government, the maintenance of trade barriers and the inconsistent regulations, were all the result of a gradual approach which led to the growth of corruption at every level of government. In reality, there was no reliable legal system. The only way to avoid becoming a Mafia economy and to cure corruption and crime was, and still is, radical liberalization (Aslund, 1995, p. 170; Aslund, 1992a, p. 174).

In such an environment, spontaneous market relations were not operative. This would have resulted not only in the creation of inefficiencies in the operation of the market economy but also, more importantly, in this context, the institutional change that comes about as a result of free market relations would not have taken place. State enterprises were operating, in effect, without any market norms, and there was no hope that conditions would have improved as long as spontaneous market forces were inhibited in generating self-enforcing institutions. 'In Eastern Europe, there is no effective governance of managers, and as a result there are no clear incentives to manage the enterprises in an efficient manner' (Sachs, 1991a, pp. 28–9). The only possible way to encourage some form of business ethics for business managers was 'to hit them hard and break the ties through strict macroeconomic stabilization. The managers needed to undergo true economic shock therapy' (Aslund, 1995, p. 187). Therefore, the economic transition process involved a transition to profound new values.

3.4   Monetary Policy and the Financial System

Financial stabilization was extremely urgent because it 'is a prerequisite for social stability and for many other reforms' (Sachs, 1996a, p. 131). As a consequence, monetary policy was central in achieving stabilization and liberalization. The role of the central bank had to be redefined. It had to become an effective monetary authority: it could not have been the provider of a soft budget constraint. Most importantly, there had to be only one central bank to administer the effective instruments of monetary policy. It was essential to realize that the control of the money supply and credit required one independent central bank and not several independent regional banks with the power to issue money, as occurred, for example, in Russia with the republics, after the collapse of the Soviet Union. The new political environment produced a very unusual monetary system: a monetary union of fifteen independent states with fifteen independent central banks. Surprisingly, the IMF and the European Union recommended the maintenance of the rouble currency area, with 15 central banks responsible for printing roubles and coordinating monetary policy. The justification for this was that the non-Russian republics were not ready to manage their own currencies. Sachs and Lipton (1997, p. 80) emphasized that it was impossible to coordinate 15 independent central banks, which had the independent right to issue rouble credits and were not willing to co-operate with each other. This was because the several central banks competed with each other and were under extreme political pressure to provide credit in their specific regions, destabilizing the whole economy. There was an incentive to free ride by issuing rouble credits at the expense of the rest of the members. Due to the existence of the rouble zone, Russia was forced to offer credits to the non-Russian republics of about 10 per cent of GDP in 1992 (Sachs, 1997b, p. 128). 'It is a nearly self-evident proposition that a single currency area should have a single bank of issue' (Lipton and Sachs, 1992, p. 237). The IMF persistence in artificially maintaining the rouble zone ensured hyperinflation and the failure of stabilization policies in the non-Russian republics. Consequently, 'there should be one currency, one central bank, and one monetary policy in one currency area' (Aslund, 1992a, p. 61).

There had to be an unconditional ban on central bank financing of the budget. However, the government and the monetary authorities had been put under intense strain due to the necessary substantial reduction in production and living standards and the increase in unemployment. This resulted in concessions to pressure groups. As a result, the money supply had increased unnecessarily due to budget deficits, extra-budgetary non-economically sound expenditure, and loans from the state banking system. All this was due to the lack of central bank independence. Thus monetary policy had to be restricted, cheap credit to firms and government had to be abandoned and interest rates should have been market-determined. Consequently, a restrictive monetary policy was essential, as was the establishment of a positive real interest rate. Indeed inflation was more dangerous than unemployment.

The central bank had to establish credit targets to hold overall money growth to levels consistent with the rapid elimination of inflation. This was because inflation is a monetary phenomenon. The quantity theory of money states that the monthly rate of inflation is equal to the rate of growth of the money supply minus the rate of growth in output. Therefore, monetary policy should have followed a specific rule: that is, increasing the money supply in line with the increase in real output. In this way the danger of inflation would have been reduced. This was possible only by establishing an independent central bank with the aforementioned rule stated in its constitution. Independent central banks have recently emerged in Albania, Armenia, Bulgaria, the Czech Republic, Estonia, Hungary, Poland, and Romania (Grabel, 2000, p. 6). An empirical study of twelve transition economies found that countries with independent central banks experienced lower levels of inflation and greater macroeconomic stability than did countries with dependent central banks. As Aslund (1995, p. 220) concluded, 'the evidence is clear: the quantity theory of money is applicable in Russia, too'. Money indeed matters. All this was thought to be so obvious that Macesish (1991, p. 8) argued that money and monetary theory were ideologically neutral.

The privatization of the banking system was essential to facilitate the reallocation of resources. However, due to the large amount of bad debts accumulated by commercial banks in CEEFSU, it was socially undesirable for the banks to default. Thus the government had to take action in this respect. Otherwise, as long as the bad loans existed, the banking system would have been unstable. The government had to initiate bankruptcy procedures for state enterprises, whereby commercial banks transformed their loans into equity. As a result, the banks would have taken over and managed the enterprise or sold it, which would have produced an efficient and rapid privatization process, and stopped the continuation of credit loans to inefficient enterprises. The alternative of writing-off bad debts would have immediately made banks insolvent, losing any interest in their balance sheet.

3.5   Fiscal Policy

The reduction of large budget deficits was required in order to eliminate hyperinflation. As the budget deficit was the main source of money creation and, hence, inflation, the reduction of the budget deficit was at the top of the agenda for any economic reform plan. Contracting military expenditure, extinguishing subsidies, eliminating enterprise investment financed by government expenditure, and reducing state administration expenses could easily have reduced the budget deficit. In addition, the aim was to reduce the power of the bureaucracy to sabotage the reform, with no reductions in social expenditure being necessary. However, the reduction in the budget deficit would have resulted in a number of inefficient firms closing down, as the sources of their survival – government subsidies and inexpensive credit – were eliminated. A balanced budget, or even better, a surplus (Aslund, 1992a, p. 66), and fiscal responsibility were essential guarantees to new firms and foreign investors that the transition government was serious in putting its affairs in order. The budget deficit was directly linked to the inflation rate. The higher the budget as a percentage of GDP, *ceteris paribus*, the higher the inflation rate. Consequently, 'in this sense, the most important step towards monetary stabilization is, in most cases, not really monetary policy, but fiscal policy' (Sachs, 1997a, p. 249). This was why the IMF and other international organizations recommended that the transition economies substantially reduce their budget deficits. Meanwhile, the reduction in the budget deficit would have resulted in a substantial increase in the resources available to alleviate the 'short-term' negative consequences of the transition program, such as unemployment and reductions in the standards of living.

Sachs (1994, p. 6) argued that while reducing the budget deficit could reduce inflation, altering the way in which the deficit was financed could also decrease it. Inasmuch as the budget deficit was financed by foreign financial resources (such as foreign borrowing, grants, aid) or by domestic borrowing (by the creation of Treasury Bill market), it would not have resulted in inflation. The introduction of a Treasury Bill market would have allowed flexibility in fiscal and anti-inflationary policy by permitting the government to borrow from domestic investors rather than printing money. Consequently, it was possible to have low inflation and a small budget deficit, which could have financed the necessary social programs. A Treasury Bill market would also have absorbed the excessive savings due to the monetary overhang. The benefits of Treasury Bills were acknowledged by some transition economies, which established a Treasury Bill market.

The insistence of the IMF on budget cuts rather than deficit financing did not allow aid to be used to finance the budget deficit. In fact, IMF aid was conditional on reducing the budget deficit. For example, while the Russian government revealed that it would have liked to sell bonds to finance the budget deficit, the IMF showed no interest in its proposal. However, the loans provided by the IMF were very short-term in nature and were offered at commercial rates. These loans were used to finance government expenditure on imports. But 'such cuts are economically and politically unjustified' (Sachs, 1994, p. 7). There might have been some concern over financing the budget deficit with external resources because it would have increased public debt. However, there was an argument for the provision of grants rather than loans, as occurred for example with the Marshall Plan. Nevertheless, even if external financing were provided in the form of loans, the transition economies would have been able eventually to repay them. For example, the public debt of Russia as a percentage of GDP in 1993 was less than that of almost all OECD countries (Sachs, 1994, p. 8). The loans would have been managed productively and also used to fight inflation. 'There is therefore room to borrow now in support of stabilization and consolidation of the reforms' (Sachs, 1994, p. 8). In addition, privatizing state enterprises could have financed the budget deficit. This would have ended the responsibility to provide subsidies, creating a further positive impact on the budget.

With respect to the tax structure, there was a need for the introduction of new taxes consistent with the market processes such as value added and income taxes instead of taxes on the profits of state enterprises under the old regime. As a consequence of these changes to the tax system it appeared inevitable that the share of state revenues in GDP fell from almost 50 per cent to 40 per cent (Aslund, 1994c, p. 185). Consistent with this was the elimination of subsidies to state enterprises and the reduction of public investment spending.

3.6 International Trade and Foreign Aid

The mature market economies had an opportunity to consolidate capitalism as a global economic system, creating a law-bound and affluent international system by integrating the transition economies into the global market system. After a long period of self-imposed isolation the transition economies had the opportunity to be part of a highly integrated and interdependent global economy. The breakdown of COMECON resulted in a substantial decline or, even worse, a total collapse of trade, but it also forced enterprises to restructure. From the shock therapy perspective on transition, 'the collapse of the old intra-FSU trade flows was both inevitable and desirable' (Aslund, 1995, p. 112). The establishment of national currencies and free trade with free prices were essential to achieve stabilization. With the introduction of market relations the artificial nature of the old trade pattern was revealed. There was no incentive for firms to pursue international trade, as it was not profitable. Nevertheless, the rapid removal of trade barriers and implementation of policies that encouraged direct integration of the transition economies with the international economy would have brought large and immediate benefits and unleashed previously oppressed entrepreneurial activities. International trade was considered a means for encouraging efficiency, introducing competition into domestic markets and increasing the availability of goods. In fact, the transition process was a combination of the marketization and the internationalization of economic affairs.

The shock therapy supporters advocated complete liberalization of the international trade sector by currency devaluation to the black market level and the removal of trade barriers. Radical trade liberalization was an essential component of the successful trade performance of transition economies. It also seemed likely that free trade was the way to initiate competition. Trade liberalization would have created positive externalities by stimulating privatization, even though privatization was taking place slowly due to political pressures and sectoral interests. Transition economies would have been able to import a rational price system and benefit from the transfer of technology, which would have stimulated increases in productivity growth. This would also have permitted the reduction of environmental pollution, since foreign investors would have been able to modernize plant and equipment. Due to international integration, a substantial increase in exports would have taken place, with the mature market economies removing their previous dependence on the Soviet Union. This did not imply, however, inaction on the part of mature market economies: 'the greatest foreign policy misjudgment of our time would be to assume that such a system will automatically fall into place' (Sachs, 1995b, p. 50).

The liberalization of international trade and the establishment of a convertible currency were among the most important prerequisites for a successful transition to capitalism. Essentially, 'convertibility and external liberalization are natural bedfellows' (Sutela, 1992, p. 89). The exchange rate should have been liberalized at the same time as domestic prices, which would have reaffirmed both the complementary nature of economic policies and the need for a shock therapy approach. The traditional arguments that devaluation would not have stimulated exports but only increased the price of imports, that trade liberalization resulted in unemployment, and that protectionism had to remain, had no empirical basis. 'These arguments were false for Latin America, and they are false for Eastern Europe' (Sachs, 1991b, p. 67). Limitations on international trade, such as tariffs, trade licenses and quotas, should be eliminated.

The arguments that CEEFSU countries should not have opened their borders to free international trade, nor introduced a convertible currency, because enterprises were inefficient and could not have survived fierce international competition, were false. Ricardo argued that international trade was the product of comparative – not absolute – advantage. Any country could have engaged in free trade, and, similarly, any country could have had a convertible currency. Current account convertibility could have been introduced in one shot, as the experience of Poland indicated, which was in contrast to the experience of Western Europe in the 1950s (Balcerowicz, Blaszczyk and Dabrowski, 1997, p. 159). In any case, restrictions on capital account convertibility were ineffective due to modern market technology. It was fruitless to attempt to identify the firms or industries that had comparative advantage, because nobody, not even the government, had the knowledge to predict market outcomes. Hence a convertible currency was essential to achieve a reliable price system, competition, monetary discipline, make the comparative advantage principle workable, foster privatization, and create property rights. The policies recommended by the shock therapy supporters ensured that the liberalization of foreign trade was irreversible, as the Russian experience confirmed (Aven, 1997, p. 67).

A freely floating exchange rate would have adjusted to reduce inflation and stimulate competition. The achievement of a stable foreign exchange market was only possible by maintaining a restrictive monetary policy. The government might have wished to maintain a fixed exchange rate. I believe that both fixed and floating exchange rates are consistent with the shock therapy approach, since neither involves government intervention. Nevertheless, a fixed exchange rate eliminates the instability caused by a fluctuating exchange rate. Sachs (1996b, p. 149; 1997a, p. 249), Aslund (1995, p. 183), Fischer, Sahay and Vegh (1996, p. 62) and Sutela (1992, p. 92) were in favor of a pegged exchange rate at the start of the stabilization programs, and then a more flexible rate after one or two years. The international experience revealed that the most successful stabilization programs were based on a pegged exchange rate, such as Bolivia in 1985, Israel in 1985 and Mexico in 1987 (Sachs, 1997a, p. 251). In the transition economies, the early peggers – Czech Republic, Estonia, Hungary, Poland and Slovakia – performed much better than the floaters in reducing inflation. The peggers achieved inflation below 100 per cent per year by 1994 (Sachs, 1996b, p. 149). It was the intention of the Gaidar government in Russia to peg the exchange rate. However, the necessary financial resources required for the stabilization fund – six billion dollars – did not exist. Again, this highlighted the urgency and the importance of foreign aid. Nonetheless, the IMF was not willing to establish a stabilization fund as long as the exchange rate was not stabilized. But if the exchange rate had been stabilized there would not have been a need for the stabilization fund.

The restoration of trade between transition countries through the so-called 'free trade arrangements' in any form suggested by the other models was not desirable. This was because limited administrative resources would have been diverted away from the main goal of integration into the international economy. Wang (1996, p. 23), Fischer, (1993, p. 350) and Eichengreen (1993, p. 345) argued that the creation of a regional trading block such as a payments union would have been a fruitless exercise. Such arguments were drawn from estimates that showed most of the international trade generated for transition economies would have taken place with mature market economies and not between transition economies. There were very few analogies between the former Soviet Union and post-war Western Europe to justify the establishment of a payments union. Post-war Western Europe would have been in a better economic situation if convertibility had taken place earlier (Aslund, 1992a, p. 27; Fischer, 1993, p. 349). Consequently, the only sensible alternative was the establishment of independent convertible national currencies. This had distinct advantages over a payments union because it created the preconditions for stabilization and, also, there would have been a monetary authority responsible for monetary policy. The financing and liquidity problems for interstate transactions would have been solved easily. Mistrust would have been removed, since enterprises would have been dealing directly and making payments straight to each other. 'Convertibility would naturally render trade and payments multilateral and was by no means unattainable' (Aslund, 1995, p. 113).

Foreign direct investment should be encouraged as long as the traditional conditions existed: political stability, free markets, an appropriate legal environment and a stable and convertible currency. These conditions could only have been achieved by using the market mechanism. As already argued, the development of an institutional structure based on self-enforcing mechanisms would have been able to attract foreign investment. Protectionism was inconsistent with the shock therapy model. Moreover, protectionism by mature market economies 'could undermine the economic logic of reform and eat away the political and social consensus of the reform program' (Sachs, 1993a, p. 102). However, there might have been some justification for a low tariff in the initial stages of transition, of about 10 to 15 per cent, to protect domestic industries for a very short time and to raise state revenues (Aslund, 1992a, p. 48).

The shock therapy model presupposed debt cancellations, international transfers, balance of payments, and budgetary support as a means of overcoming stagnation and maintaining political support for the reform program. 'No country this century has undertaken radical market reforms without sizeable foreign aid' (Sachs, 1995a, p. 22). Without relief from the large debt problem, the much-needed capital inflow would have been restricted, removing a major source of economic growth. All external debt should have been frozen and rescheduled to ease the burden and allow the transition economies to start afresh. It was the responsibility of the mature economies to assist the transition economies as much as possible because 'the world has much to gain from the emerging system, and much to lose if we fail to act decisively to put it in place' (Sachs, 1995b, p. 50). If this assistance was not forthcoming it was possible that there might have been a rise in xenophobia, jeopardizing the vast opportunities associated with the opening of the CEEFSU market to international trade. Importantly, foreign aid and borrowing would have reduced the need for the monetary financing of the budget deficit. The budget deficit and the necessary social programs could have been financed by foreign aid and borrowing from international organizations without increasing the domestic money supply. Consequently, 'this money could help to make a democratic and economic transformation feasible which otherwise would not be feasible' (Sachs, 1992b, p. 210).

According to the Economic Commission for Europe (ECE, 1994) in its Economic Survey of Europe for 1993–1994, there was a 'slow disbursement' of financial assistance to transition economies. The IMF and World Bank funds were only released to countries that demonstrated their commitment to economic programs for standby credit or showed progress towards Systemic Transformation Facilities (STF). According to the Commission, most countries failed to adopt an economic program approved by the IMF, were unable to meet periodic performance criteria for the release of scheduled tranches, or could not have satisfied development bank conditions. As a result, the World Bank's funding to Eastern Europe declined in 1993 (ECE, 1994, p. 133). The Commission attested it was not certain whether the inability of these countries to access these funds contributed to their inadequate economic performance and, thus, their failure to meet the conditions set by the financial institutions. However, I believe the IMF's and World Bank's stringent conditions could not have been met and that foreign assistance was not forthcoming, leaving the shock therapy governments to flounder along their own paths of political demise. 'All Western countries were ruled by weak and shortsighted political leaders. No one showed international leadership' (Aslund, 1995, p. 220).

3.7   Social Policy

The development of an appropriate safety net was one of the most challenging aspects of the reform program, aiming to ensure that those disadvantaged by the initial development of the market process were not trapped in poverty, subject to unequal opportunities or low standards of living. The transition process involved transforming disguised unemployment into open unemployment, creating discontent. A suitable safety net would have done away with panic, disillusionment and resistance by the people. As such, the safety net would have required an increase in social spending. A well-targeted safety net for the Soviet Union in 1991 would have required only 2.4 per cent of Gross National Product (Aslund, 1995, p. 239). The administration of social programs had to take place using private sector management methods – transparency and isolation from political influence – to be effective.

Yet the provision of these benefits, associated with the social policy, was substantially restricted by the severe limitations of financial resources available to transition governments. To be able to fund large social transfers, transition economies had to impose high taxes, which would have resulted in distortions, capital outflow, tax evasion and illegal economic activity through the black market. It must be added that an adequate social policy was not only associated with the provision of equal opportunities to the citizens of transition economies and the elimination of poverty traps but, more importantly, it would also translate into political support for the economic reforms. Accordingly, providing adequate social benefits was politically more important than reducing the budget deficit (Aslund, 1997c, p. 17). As such, it was essential for mature market economies and international organizations to support the transition program with the indispensable financial resources to fund the social policy. 'Financial assistance from the West for a strengthened social welfare system is surely needed' (Sachs, 1991a, p. 28). Graham (1997, p. 336) stressed that 'no level of external support or resources can substitute for domestic political commitment (and allocation of resources) to addressing the social cost of reform'. However, political commitment alone was not enough to finance the necessary social programs. Consequently, the generosity of the mature market economies and of the international organizations was essential. It should be remembered that the safety net programs had to enhance the political sustainability of the economic reforms.

Income inequality did not increase substantially, as the critics of shock therapy argued. In Russia in April 1993, income inequality was no greater than in the UK, and a lot less than in the USA (Illarionov, Layard and Orszag, 1997, p. 142). Shock therapy economists were not surprised by the link between the speed of the reform process and the reduction in life expectancy. While changes in life expectancy varied between transition countries, they were inversely related to the speed and depth of reforms (Sachs, 1996a, p.

131). In the Czech Republic, Poland and Slovakia, which all introduced a shock therapy approach, life expectancy rates continued to increase during the transition period. However, it was a different scenario in countries that took a gradual approach, such as Hungary, where life expectancy was reduced, and the Ukraine, where it plunged (Sachs, 1996a, p. 131). The inflation caused and maintained by the gradual approach increased stress, making life unpredictable, and more people were confronted with difficulties they could not have managed (Aslund, 1995, p. 288). Before the transition process started it was predicted that a social disaster would take place due to the extremely high social costs involved. But this did not come about. The transition economies had the means to overcome a social disaster. However, they did not have the means to maintain the shock therapy process.

4   Process of Transition

Even though the shock therapy process implied an immediate liberalization of markets, as we can see from Table 4.1, there were some elements of the transition program that had to be introduced gradually. As such, the necessary institutional structures, both formal and informal, could only have been developed gradually. In addition, a balanced budget could only have been achieved after the maintenance of budget deficits funded by foreign aid. A fully convertible exchange rate could only have been implemented after maintaining the pegged exchange rate and tariffs for a short period of time. An incomes policy had to be maintained throughout the transition process.

5   The Cost of Transition

Using the cost criteria of the transition process identified in Chapter 3, it can be argued the implementation of the shock therapy approach in transition economies would result in the highest economic cost comparing with the remaining models of transition. This was due to the large reduction in output and employment, large increase in inflation and the large balance of trade deficit. Shock therapy supporters recognized the high economic cost of their approach but viewed these negative outcomes as necessary and short term. With regard to the political cost the shock therapy approach had initially high political support but as the negative outcomes of the process started to hurt the majority of the population, political support was reduced and all governments that implemented shock therapy lost power after the first term in office, as demonstrated in the following section. With regard to the ideological cost the people in CEEFSU placed the shock therapy model at the lower-end of ideological cost since the approach was consistent with the desire to establish a capitalist economic system.

With regard to the International Financial cost the international financial institutions and governments in mature market economies were willing to pro-

Table 4.1
The Shock Therapy Process of Transition

	Years	1	2	3	4	5	6	7	8	9	10
Price Liberalization Stabilization	Price Deregulation										
	Incomes Policy										
Privatization	Privatization of Small Enterprises										
	Privatization of Large Enterprises										
Institutional Structure	Formal Institutions										
	Informal Institutions										
Monetary Policy and the Financial System	Hard Budget Constraint										
	Independent Central Bank										
Fiscal Policy	Budget Deficit										
	Tax Structure										
International Trade and Foreign Aid	Pegged Exchange Rate										
	Floating Exchange Rate										
	Tariffs										
	Conditional Foreign Aid										
Social Policy	Safety Net										
	Private Welfare Providers										
	Years	1	2	3	4	5	6	7	8	9	10

vide funding to the transition economies, which implemented shock therapy placing the model at the lowest end of the cost. Lastly, with regard to the Foreign Direct Investment Cost, multinationals were deterred to some degree from finance projects in transition economies that implemented shock therapy due to the instability caused by the process. The dominant method of privatization was through the free distribution of vouchers, which effectively prohibited foreign participation.

6   Conclusion

While it was easy to become discouraged with the transition process, Sachs (1991a, p. 26; 1996a, pp. 132–3) was confident that the experience of transition revealed the ability of the centrally administered economies of CEEFSU to transform rapidly into market economies. In essence, the shock therapy model was an orthodox macroeconomic stabilization program, emphasizing price liberalization and strict budgetary policy. The aim of the shock therapy model was to remove social obstacles driven by anti-social self-interest. The result would have been a free market that, as the supporters of the model argued, in the long run guaranteed full employment, stability and growth. With regard to the associated costs of the reform process, these costs were exaggerated. The implementation of the shock therapy approach was a success (Balcerowicz, Blaszczyk and Dabrowski, 1997, pp. 131, 156–7; Aslund, 1995, p. 3; Samonis and Hunyadi, 1993, p. 18; Porket, 1998, p. 195). The radical reforms of shock therapy did not increase unemployment, halt the development of the private sector or hinder the evolution of institutional structures. The countries performed better, even though they suffered a decline in output in the beginning of transition. They were the first ones to achieve positive economic growth (Aslund, Boone and Johnson, 1996, p. 226).

The course of economic development initiated by the shock therapy process could have been considered radical in a historical context, since the experience of mature market economies demonstrated gradualism as the appropriate procedure (Rosati, 1994, p. 429; Polanyi, 1944; Bardhan and Roemer, 1993, p. 16; Xiaoqiang, 1992, p. 61; Murrell, 1992b, p. 80). As discussed, the case for the implementation of the shock therapy process went further than the benefits associated with the free market economies. Transition economies were surrounded by the mature market economies and, thus, a dominant world ideology of free markets. Transition economies, entering economic development at a later stage, were influenced by the current strategy of economic growth adopted by mature market economies.

The implementation of the shock therapy approach can be interpreted as a voluntary decision made by the transition economies. The argument developed by Gerschenkron (1962; 1968) is relevant here. He suggested economic development was determined by differences in historical background, national culture, economic and political systems and the degree of lateness in fostering economic development. A distinction can be made between leaders and followers, where latecomers face different sets of internal and external environments in fostering economic growth. Actually the conditions of the latecomers differ in many respects from those in the more advanced countries at the time that they entered economic development. The mere fact of the existence of advanced countries also changed the environment of the followers, so that it was likely that they would take a different course of development than the one followed by the early starters. Gerschenkron's (1962; 1968) argument was applied to the experiences of the developing countries in the 1960s when Keynesian ideas strongly influenced economic policy. State property, government intervention, discretionary fiscal and monetary policies and restrictions on trade resulted in low unemployment and inflation and economic stability and security. This period between 1950 and 1973 was considered to be the Golden Age of Keynesianism, with capitalism's strongest growth performance. The latecomers during this period aspired to narrow the income gap and sought to do so as quickly as possible and at any cost. This was extremely difficult, due to the pre-existence of poor economic conditions, which constrained their growth potential. There appeared to be a contradiction between the available resources and the ultimate goal of economic development, which resulted in tensions. The more backward the country was at the starting-point, the higher the level of tensions. Tensions resulted in impatience, and impatience resulted in extreme, radical and rapid reforms. Thus the latecomers in economic development, viewing the benefits associated with Keynesianism during the 1960s and being impatient to achieve the living standards of developed countries, took Keynesian policies to the extreme. The dominance of state property, and the distorted market due to discretionary measures and restrictions on trade, were among the key characteristics. Interestingly, the advantage to latecomers was that they could have borrowed technologies from the mature market economies without needing to 'reinvent the wheel'. However, it was not adequate simply to purchase technology: it had to be exploited. More important, it was not without cost; it required financial commitment.

By the 1990s, the perception of economic policy had changed radically from that of the 1960s. The dominant worldview was that of a free market: deregulation, privatization and free trade. The latecomers, the transition economies of CEEFSU, aspired to narrow the income gap as quickly as possible and at any cost; this necessitated the shock therapy process. As discussed, this was because tensions resulted in impatience and this impatience led to extreme, more radical and more rapid reforms, such as the shock therapy process, than those used by the mature market economies when they started their economic development. 'Haste, impatience, and radical action translate into a high time preference, a high discount rate for future benefits for the sake of short-term achievements' (Ofer, 1987, p. 1799). Hence the shock therapy process of transition can be interpreted as reflecting the need of the transition economies as latecomers to achieve the standard of living of advanced economies. This resulted in the hasty introduction of reforms in the hope of immediate benefits. It was a sad reminder of the past because it seemed similar to the strategy of Stalin's famous call in 1931: 'We are 50 or 100 years behind the advanced countries. We must make good the distance in ten years. Either we do it or they crush us' (Berliner, 1988, p. 161).

While Gerschenkron's (1962; 1968) argument helps to explain the voluntary decision of the transition economies to implement the shock therapy approach, it is equally possible to argue that the strategy was in fact forced upon transition economies. Transition economies had to satisfy conditions imposed by the IMF, World Bank and mature market economies in order to secure funding for their reform processes. Funding was conditioned upon the implementation of the shock therapy approach. Effectively this left the transition economies with no real choice. For example, IMF and World Bank loans to Romania were stopped because the privatization strategy that was adopted limited foreign ownership (Gowan, 1995, p. 34). How then can the implementation of a gradualist approach by a few countries be explained? The promises of substantial funding never materialized, as the shock therapy supporters noted. As a result, few of the transition governments ignored the recipe for shock therapy and chose to follow their own gradual course.

The shock therapy model assumed large debt cancellations and large financial assistance in the form of grants and long-term loans. Instead, foreign aid was substantially below the necessary amounts and took the form of export credits. Meanwhile, financial support by mature market economies was modest, if not totally inadequate. It was estimated that the Soviet Union had required about $30 billion annually in the first two years of the reform process and then $20 to $25 billion in the third and fourth years, respectively (Sachs, 1992b, p. 215). In 1995, Russia received roughly $380 million in aid from the USA; that is, one-sixth of the aid to Egypt (Sachs, 1995b, p. 57). Mature market economies and international financial organizations gave more financial support to Gorbachev than to supporting the transition process (Aslund, 1995, p. 282). Meanwhile, Russia never had the possibility of stabilizing without 'massive foreign assistance' (Layard, 1993, p. 32). The IMF and the World Bank, the only real financiers of the transition process, 'have proven to be largely inefficient' (Sachs, 1995b, p. 61). Financial assistance has been very small and financial aid totally inflexible. Sachs (1994, p. 5) insisted there was a need for a change in the timing and character of foreign aid for the transition economies. Financial assistance should have taken the form of grants, not loans. The IMF had refused to support the establishment of a stabilization fund. Even when it announced in 1995 the possibility of the establishment of stabilization funds, the IMF continued to inform transition economies that these funds would be available only after inflation had been reduced (Sachs, 1996b, p. 150), in other words, when they were no longer required. In addition, the European Union's response was far from desirable in assuring full membership at a future date and opening the European market to East European products (Sachs, 1991a, p. 32). Unfortunately, 'the international community had not woken up' (Aslund, 1995, p. 99).

Sachs (1991a, p. 31) was adamant with regard to the need for financial aid provided externally:

Passing through the valley of tears requires first and foremost, political leadership, and second, enough social consensus to sustain a stable set of policies. But even Moses and the Israelites would not have made it through the wilderness without some manna from heaven. External assistance can be vital in the perilous first years of change. And Moses did not face re-election for forty years (though he certainly faced a leadership challenge at the base of Mt. Sinai).

Sachs (1991a, p. 31) argued that the reform program could be achieved 'only if the reforms are given the time to work'. In reality, 'Russia and the West have never missed an opportunity to miss an opportunity ... . Unfortunately, the West failed miserably to speed the needed reforms' (Sachs, 1997b, p. 127). Lipton and Sachs (1992, p. 216) were well aware of the necessary conditions for the shock therapy process to succeed: 'in our view, the social basis for the reforms exist. The real test will be in the area of political reform and in the extent of Western support'.

Advocates of the shock therapy approach were less concerned with ex ante than with ex post political constraints. With respect to ex ante political constraints, the basic idea was that there was a window of opportunity, a grace period. So, ex ante political constraints did not exist initially but constraints may have been present later. Therefore, it was necessary to be quick and decisive in making all the major decisions on transition. Accordingly, there was an internal contradiction in the reform program: the shock therapy process, while rapid, required some unspecified time to be operative, depending on fragile coalition governments based on a democratic process of decision-making. Under these circumstances it was impossible for a reform program of this magnitude and social cost to survive a democratic decision-making process; economic reforms result in severe social costs immediately, but produce benefits only gradually. On the one hand, Balcerowicz, (1994, p. 75) argued that 'this "visibility effect", absent in classical democratizations, was likely to encourage unfavorable assessments of the whole transition and, consequently, to influence electoral outcomes and the subsequent direction or pace of the economic transition'. On the other hand, Balcerowicz (1994, p. 87) argued that it was not necessary to assume that the discontent under shock therapy would have been greater than with a gradual approach, citing Romania as an example. The discontent over the shock therapy process was reflected in the electoral process, in which radical reform governments were replaced in favor of governments that championed a gradual approach. Fedorov (1997, p. 126) recognized the electoral danger associated with the rapid transition process, arguing that 'only a much faster reform movement can save the situation from deterioration which could be politically dangerous'. In contrast, the Polish experience showed that 'severe stabilization measures are not easily forgiven' (Bim, 1992, p. 189). As Gaidar argued at the time, we 'looked into the abyss and pulled back' (Arnot, 1998, p. 229).

I have argued that a democratic political process was inconsistent with shock therapy. The shock therapy supporters hoped that this inconsistency could have been avoided by the visionary actions of the leaders of mature market economies and the responsibility assigned to the international financial institutions to stabilize the emerging market economies. It has already been pointed out that the problems associated with the reform process were political, not economic. Thus, economic aid was mainly required to support the frail governments that implemented the shock therapy process in a democratic environment. The purpose of foreign aid was to reduce the costs to individuals in continuing to apply shock therapy and, at the same time, maintain support for the government. Support for the governments implementing the shock therapy process was very high initially but started to deteriorate when the social cost increased. The result was that governments which implemented shock therapy lost power after only one term in office, leaving the reform process in disgrace. The new governments, dominated usually by ex-communists, reversed the course of reform and proceeded with a gradualist transition approach (Weisskopf, 1996, p. 281; Graham, 1997, p. 339; Jin and Haynes, 1997, pp. 93, 94). Hence, as a political strategy, shock therapy turned out to be suicidal for the governments that launched it. Actually the transition governments that pursued shock therapy did not have a mandate from the people to introduce the radical reforms, as in the Polish and Russian cases.

Parker, Tritt and Woo (1997, p. 8) and Boone and Fedorov (1997) recommended a better political management of the reform process in Russia. They argued, surprisingly, that in-depth political reforms would have improved the outcome and the credibility of economic reforms. Nevertheless, accepting an argument like this does not resolve the contradiction. The argument is tautological. By identifying reforms as unsuccessful, they are also being branded as non-credible (Ickes, 1996, p. 302). Could it be argued that a better political management of the market reform process, or more credible policy-makers, would have made possible the survival of the shock therapy model in a democratic environment without any substantial financial support? Unfortunately, for the shock therapy supporters, the answer is no. In contrast to my view, Boone and Fedorov (1997, p. 185) argued that 'these benefits must be contrasted with the Russian reality that very often foreign assistance has slowed reforms – because it allowed Gorbachev, and Russian president Boris Yeltsin, to temporarily postpone making needed policy changes'. However, as I have argued, the amount of foreign aid was so inadequate that it was unable to influence the political decision-making process. In the end, 'the problem is political' (Aslund, 1995, p. 312).

Aslund, Boone and Johnson (1996, p. 227) argued that the shock therapy process did not lead to public discontent. According to their interpretation of events, the public demanded faster reforms and the dissatisfaction with gradualism was greater than it was with shock therapy. As a result, gradualists were more likely to lose elections than shock therapy governments. However, where the shock therapists lost elections it was because they were less well organized than the former communists (Aslund, Boone and Johnson, 1996). In addition, it was not uncommon for incumbent governments to become unpopular irrespective of the economic outcomes (Roland, 1994b, p. 30). It is worth noting that while gradualist reform governments replaced shock therapy governments, a radical leadership never replaced the gradualists. Other gradualists always replaced gradualist reform governments.

The shift to gradualism took place in Poland on the 19 September 1993, in Russia on the 12 December 1993, in Bulgaria on 18 December 1994, in Estonia on 5 March 1995, in the Czech Republic on the 1 June 1996 and in Latvia on the 25 July 1997. In all cases, this occurred after unfavorable election results for the shock therapy governments. Table 4 demonstrates the link between the countries that implemented shock therapy and the foreign aid received during the same period. Latvia was an interesting case. Latvia was able to sustain the shock therapy process and the government managed to remain in power after the first term elections. The Latvian case highlighted the crucial role for foreign aid as well as authoritarian rule. The authoritarian style of the Skele leadership was able to maintain the shock therapy reforms in the face of strong opposition. In addition, Latvia benefited from a total of 153.9 million SDRs from the IMF while Estonia received 65 million SDRs and Albania, 62.4 million SDRs. In other words, Latvia received more financial assistance than Estonia and Albania combined, despite being similar to Estonia in terms of population, size and level of industrialization. The IMF justified the large amount of aid because it considered Latvia was a country displaying 'a remarkable degree of stability' (ECE, 1993, p. 233). This implied that both the Birkavs and Skele governments implemented a reform process consistent with IMF guidelines. As a result, Latvia was able to sustain the burden of the reforms because of the level of foreign assistance coupled with its authoritarian rule. In Latvia, foreign aid helped maintain the authoritarian rule for some time. However, authoritarian rule did not last for long and, in Latvia, the Skele government only lasted five months after the successful election results before it was forced to resign under serious accusations of corruption. This also highlighted the problem associated with the provision of ample financial assistance under authoritarianism to facilitate transition: it encouraged corruption. Thus, as of August 1997, when Skele's government resigned and Krasts's government took power, the economic reforms slowed dramatically.

Interestingly enough, at subsequent elections, 'radical' reformers returned to power, such as Mart Laar in Estonia and, Balcerowicz in Poland and 'radical' governments replaced gradualist ones in Bulgaria in 1996, in Romania in 1996 and in the Ukraine in 1999. However, the 'radical' reformers have implemented a gradual process. There are no examples in CEEFSU of a shock therapy process being implemented by the 'radical' reformers returning to government. The momentum was lost following the electoral defeats after their first term in office.

Not surprisingly, one could attempt to argue that 'real shock therapy' was never implemented. As Sachs (1997b, p. 127) claimed about Russia: 'Despite the uproar in recent years about 'shock therapy' in Russia, knowledgeable observers understand that it simply never occurred, an obvious point when one compares Russia's disorganized and partial stabilization efforts with the decisive actions in the Czech Republic, Estonia, or Poland'. In reality, in Russia 'real laissez faire for the benefit of the private sector persisted only for a period of three months, from February to April 1992' (Aslund, 1997e, p. 200). In addition, 'in Lithuania, Russia, and Hungary, radical reform never came close to being adopted' (Balcerowicz, 1994, p. 87). But this explanation begs the question and leaves a large gap between theory and practice in explaining the failure of the shock therapy approach. However, Aslund (1995, p. 312) stated: 'good theory has stood the test, whereas poor theory has proven faulty'. Indeed the failure of the shock therapy program to incorporate the political process, concentrating instead on economic relationships, led to the demise of the model. Despite these arguments, Aslund (1995, p. 316) was adamant: '...the case has nevertheless been made: Russia could (and did) reform, and it has become a market economy'. Wherever radical reform took place, the succeeding ex-communist governments continued the reform process (Aslund, Boone and Johnson, 1996, p. 273), but at a slower pace. As a result there might have been instability but not a total reversal of the reform (Fedorov, 1997, p. 126).

Table 4.2
Shock Therapy and Level of International Foreign Aid

Country	Transition Type	Reform Began	Gradual Shift	IMF Agreements Start	Financial Support End	Million SDRs
Poland	Shock therapy	1 Jan 1990	19 Sep 1993	18 April 1991	17 April 1994	1224.0
				8 Mar 1993 - standby	7 March 1994	476.0
Czecho-slovakia	Shock therapy	1 Jan 1991	Slovakia: 1 Jan 1993 (after the break up of Czechoslovakia Slovakia pursued a gradualist approach). Czech Rep: 1 Jun 1996 slow down of some economic reforms - mainly privatization of health system & railways	Slovakia 1 Jan 1993 (IMF quota total)		257.4
				22 July 1994 standby - STF		115.8
				Czech Rep.		64.5
				1 Jan 1993 (IMF quota total)		589.6
Bulgaria	Shock therapy concept slow imple-men-tation	1 Feb 1991	18 Dec 1994	17 April 1992 - standby	16 April 1993	155.0
				11 April 1994 - standby	11 April 1995	116.0
				- ESAF		69.7
Russia	Shock Therapy	2 Feb 1992	12 Dec 1993	5 Aug 1992	4 Jan 1993	719.0
				30 June 1993 - STFb		1078.3

Table 4.2 (cont.)

Country	Transition Type	Reform Began	Gradual Shift	IMF Agreements Start	Financial Support End	Million SDRs
Albania	Initially gradual then shock therapy	June 91 – gradual July 92 – shock therapy	19 June 1997	26 Aug 1992 – standby	25 Aug 1993	20.0
				14 July 1993 – ESAF[c]	13 July 1996	42.4
Estonia	Shock therapy	Sept 1992	5 Mar 1995	16 Sept 1992 – standby	15 Sept 1993	27.9
				27 Oct 1993 – standby and STF	26 Mar 1995	23.2
				12 April 1995		13.9
Latvia	Shock therapy	5 June 1993	25 July 1997	15 September 1992	15 September 1993	
				– STF	March 1995	54.9
				October 1993		11.6
				– standby	March 1994	11.6
				–STF		22.90
				December 1993		22.90
				standby		30.00
				– STF 24 May 1996		

[a] Standby credit

[b] STF: Less demanding than standby credit. New temporary IMF financing facility designed to provide assistance to member countries facing BOP difficulties

[c] ESAF: Enhanced Structural Adjustment Facility

Sources: Economic Survey of Europe 1993–1994, Economic Commission for Europe, 1994 pp. 138–139

Keesing's Record of World Events Vol. 40, No.7, July 1994, Longman, UK.

EIU Country Report, Slovakia, 2nd Quarter 1995, Economic Intelligence Unit, U.K. p. 29

Chapter 5

The Neoclassical Gradualist Model
of Transition: Preventive Therapy

1 Introduction

The fundamental basis of the neoclassical gradualist approach to transition was the need to establish economic, institutional, political, and ideological structures before any attempt at liberalization was undertaken. Without this minimum foundation, radical reforms would have inhibited the development of a competitive market capitalist system. This was because 'privatization, marketization, and the introduction of competition cannot be contemplated in an economy reduced to barter' (Carrington, 1992, p. 24). Moreover, the implementation of the reform program required minimum standards of living to foster a social consensus and, also, the transition process had to be guided by the principles of voluntariness and free choice.

The aim of the neoclassical gradualist transition process was to initiate profound and unique changes, a 'transformational recession' (Kornai, 1993a, pp. 182, 189; Kornai, 1994, p. 41), to overcome the 'shortageflation' syndrome (Kolodko, 1993, p. 21) by initiating 'preventive therapy' (Kornai, 1997a, p. 183). This was only possible by taking 'the longest road' (Abel and Bonin, 1993, p. 230), or 'rebuilding the boat in the open sea' the title of the Elster, Offe and Preuss (1997) book.

The introduction of market relations to the centrally administered economies was not a simple task. In the transition economies, the market was underdeveloped, the private sector was immature, and democratic institutions were weak. Institutions were changing rapidly and the behavior of individuals was constantly adjusting. As a result, 'a special kind of dynamic analysis is needed' (Kornai, 1994, p. 2). Given the nature of the neoclassical gradualist transition process it was impossible to solve the associated problems independently of the political and social aspects of the reform: 'so often, everything turns out to depend on everything else!' (Ridley, 1993, p. 352).

According to the neoclassical gradualist approach it was desirable to maintain a semi-centralized system, coupled with a combination of centralized markets.

The distinguishing feature in the neoclassical gradual transition process was that the ultimate goal of an approximation to competitive capitalism would have been achieved by the gradual elimination of centralization. The objective was to create a large class of people with interests in the former state sector, through a process of embourgeoisment that developed genuine Schumpeterian entrepreneurs.

The neoclassical gradualist transition process was implemented in a number of countries, including Romania, Hungary (which had a tradition of gradual transformation, starting in 1968 with the New Economic Mechanism) and Slovenia.

2   Primary Elements of the Neoclassical Gradualist Model of Transition

Based on the primary elements of the transition modeling process in Table 1, the two neoclassical models of transition were similar in terms of economic analysis (neoclassical): 'what is a good society?' (approximation to competitive capitalism); and ideological structure (self-interest). The goals of the gradualist process were quite similar to those of the shock therapists. However, the two neoclassical models differ in terms of their speed, political structure and the relevance of the initial conditions to these models. While these common elements were analyzed under the shock therapy model in Chapter 4, the present chapter focuses on the remaining different elements of speed, political structure and initial conditions.

2.1   Speed

A market capitalist system did not have to be imposed upon society. As long as the restrictions on self-interest and individual action were removed, albeit slowly, capitalism would have been the natural outcome. However, the neoclassical gradualist economists did not rule out the possibility of a 'minimum bang' for some aspects. Whenever immediate changes were needed, immediate action was required. The choice was between fast and costly restructuring versus slow but less expensive restructuring.

Based on the gradualist approach, an economy should not be fully liberalized until the country has achieved a reasonable level of macroeconomic stability and a competitive financial system of supervision, and firms are subject to hard budget constraints. The relocation of resources to satisfy the new and costly economic conditions would have been a lengthy process, with an unavoidable reduction in production. This would have resulted in severe reductions in real incomes and living standards. Individuals would not have been able to take advantage of the new opportunities the free market provided because they would have lacked the resources for effective participation. There would have been a need to restructure the bureaucracy and free prices and capital markets without suffering unemployment, so as to provide opportunities for everyone. Thus it would not have been possible immediately to remove shortages, inequities in the distribution of income, and the anti-social behavior that these negative outcomes of the transition process would have fostered. It would not have been in the interests of society to remove government control and enforce a hard budget constraint immediately, which would have been resisted by pressure groups. Consequently, for the neoclassical gradualist economists, 'the optimal path of reform would be one that conserves some of existing organizational capital in the early stages of transition' (Murrell, 1992a, p. 43). Thus, 'one must be under no illusion that this process will be anything but gradual' (Blanchard, et al., 1992, p.xvii).

The human learning process is complex and does not favor swift change. From the neoclassical gradualist perspective, people in CEEFSU would not have known how to act in a market economy. While small-scale trading could have been easily learnt, business ethics and the legal aspects of economic activity would have taken much longer. The interactive process of learning-by-monitoring, learning-by-doing and the acquisition of knowledge and new behavior are organic processes that last for several years. As a result, the productivity of small changes would have been greater than that of large changes. History does not move in leaps, but in marginal adjustments: small and gradual steps are easier to correct than sudden and major steps. Therefore, 'capitalism has never been introduced by design: it evolved organically' (Csaba, 1995, p. 99), similar to the 'nurturing of a greenhouse plant' (Svejnar, 1991, p. 131). Taking into account the social costs, sequencing, learning-by-doing, institution-building, structural adjustment, administrative capacity, behavioral change, informational asymmetry, lack of commitment, political constraints and the danger of the reversal of the reform, a long and very complex and multifaceted process was favored.

Based on gradualism, the reforms were not doctrinaire but evolutionary and pragmatic, and the changes were made in tiny, fragmented, concurrent, and consecutive stages. Compromises did not derail the reform. Indeed, they were critical to the reform's success by avoiding traumatic upheavals and contributing to the relatively calm political atmosphere, providing a foundation for a credible reform of policy. The need for 'patience, humanity and tact' (Kornai, 1995b, p. 13; 1996, p. 17) again justified a gradual approach.

A gradual neoclassical process of transition necessitated the sequencing of reforms: a gradual process required transition-by-design rather than transition-by-chance. Timing and sequencing of liberalization were imperative because poor timing would have resulted in prolonged stagnation. Not surprisingly, the concept of sequencing gave the impression to Aslund (1997c, p. 16) that sequencing meant proceeding in a linear fashion. This, however, was not necessarily the case. A gradual process did not exclude the concurrence of several transformation measures. Consequently, 'sequencing is not merely a major problem of transition but is synonymous with it' (Porket, 1998, p. 178). The shock therapists avoided sequencing by introducing the reforms immediately. Under a neoclassical gradualist process, the transition was more complex because of the attention to the order of introducing the necessary reforms and the 'painful trade-offs and choices between bad and worse' (Kornai, 1992b, p. 18). Adopting a suitable reform strategy was not simple, and success required 'a convincing, detailed, practical program whose implementation must begin at once' (Kornai, 1994, p. 59) to avoid corruption and 'crony capitalism'. As Csaba (1995, p. 15) stated: 'only the most vulgar or ignorant representatives of the economics profession could seriously be convinced of the feasibility of institutional quick fixes.'

The belief that the market could be initiated through shock therapy was 'wrong, and in several cases has caused more problems than it has solved' (Kolodko, 1999b, p. 233). The 100- or even 500-day approaches were not feasible, and were in fact disastrous. It was wrong to presume that a free market would have developed overnight, or that the transition economies could have jumped to a more sophisticated coordination mechanism once the infrastructure of central planning was eliminated. The severity of the unavoidable recession was increased substantially by the errors and mistakes of the transition governments, which mainly stemmed from their adoption of the shock therapy model. Their economic performance, to date, has been even worse than it was under centrally administered socialism (Olson, 1995, p. 437). The shock therapy approach resulted in anxiety, uncertainty, fear, despair, and a loss of hope. Unfortunately, it was the past failures of gradualism that had driven some of its former supporters to advocate 'shock therapy' types of solutions.

Gradualism enabled transition to start with reforms that were likely to have the best outcomes for the majority, whilst delaying the less attractive changes. This process increased the feasibility of the reforms by designing an optimal sequencing, from a political economic point of view, by building constituencies for further reform. Thus both economic and political constraints necessitated a gradual restructuring.

2.2   Political Structure

Kornai (1995e, p. 64; 1997a, p. 122) agreed with Sachs (1993a, p. xiii) and Lipton and Sachs (1992, p. 215) that the fundamental transition problem was political and not economic. This had often been ignored in economic policy analysis and recommendations were characterized by technocratic approaches. The failures of partial reforms in centrally administered socialism were associated with the exclusion of the political process (Wolf, 1991, p. 57). Politics is not an external factor for any economy, but an endogenous variable imposing constraints: ignoring politics is 'bad economics', and it was necessary to be 'respectful of politics' (Kornai, 1997a, pp. 151, 169; Olson and Kahkonen, 2000, p. 15; Roland, 1994b, p. 27; Furubotn, 2000, p. 120).

The adoption of democracy should have resulted in the formulation of a 'social contract', a 'developmental consensus' (Csaba, 1995, p. 90), among the variety of self-interest groups who were prepared to restrain their demands to help solve the transition problems. Without minimal political cooperation, even well developed economic programs would have failed. Kornai (1995c, p. 246) argued that the transition process resembled a prisoners' dilemma. Prisoners have to compromise because they achieve more collectively than they would through non-cooperative individualist behavior. An essential element in engineering such consensus was the construction of channels for ongoing consultation and negotiation between interest groups. The establishment of a consensus provided credibility for the reform process. For example, in Hungary the elections revealed that the majority of the population preferred parties with a more cautious approach to transition and, subsequently, gave the governing coalition a mandate to follow the policies of a 'calm force' (Andorka, 1994, p. 29). In Russia, however, no one enjoyed a mandate to launch the shock therapy program (Csaba, 1995, p. 221; Kornai, 1997a, p. 127). A democratic political structure was an absolute condition of the gradualist approach to successfully change an economic system, in contrast to the shock therapy approach.

The process of gradual reform – the priorities and trade-offs, the minimization of social cost and the implementation of 'true reforms' (Kolodko, 1999b, p. 247) that serve the interests of society and not the few in power – could only have been decided by the participation of the people through a democratic process. This was essential to achieve social and political stability and avoid confrontation. Broadly speaking, political rules in place lead to economic rules, and good economic performance is directly linked with democracy, though the causality runs both ways. Kornai (1995d, p. 150; 1995e, pp. 62, 159, 220; 1997a, p. 178; 1993b, p. 333) elevated the achievement of a democratic political structure to be the number one goal of transition: 'If it comes to a conflict between efficiency and the cause of democracy, I am sure that defence of the institutions of democracy is the supreme task.' Democracy should not be sacrificed, even for efficiency. Active state participation was required, consolidated by the political process, to correct the imperfections of the market caused by self-interested lobbying and informal elements such as organized crime. Commitment to reforms was counterproductive. Given the immense amount of learning that had to take place, initially, the chosen policies would have been unsatisfactory and the ability to change extremely important.

The implementation of the shock therapy model – which resulted in disillusionment, massive unemployment, inequality of wealth and corruption – endangered the fledgling institutions of democracy and inhibited meaningful economic reforms. This judgment is consistent with my assessment of the political structure of the shock therapy model. The shock therapy model was in harmony with political pluralism, not democracy. For the neoclassical gradualist supporters, democracy was not an obstacle to reform but, rather, an essential element of the overall transition program. The shock therapy approach highlighted how speed could constrain a government, whereas the gradualist approach tried to design the sequencing of reforms so as to build, through the democratic process at each stage of transition, constituencies for further reform.

2.3   Initial Conditions

The neoclassical gradualist process was inconsistent with rigid thinking and, as in the case of the shock therapy model, the implementation of the reform program independently of the initial conditions. 'Sensible economics' required the incorporation of the initial conditions in the transition process (Murrell, 1995, p. 165). Policy instruments and goals needed to reflect the specific economic conditions of the time and to change accordingly. For example, Russia, Eastern Europe, and China had different sequencing for their reforms due to their different circumstances (Ickes, 1996, p. 302; Roland, 1994b, p. 37).

In terms of economic development, the socialist experiment was a temporary aberration in the course of historical events. However, the initial conditions of each ex-socialist country determined both the output response during marketization and the speed and sequencing of transition policies. The different initial conditions made the situation quite unique and there was 'no ready-make recipe' (Kornai, 1995b, p. 34), 'no single detailed road map' (Fischer and Gelb, 1991, p. 91).

Incorporating the initial conditions in the transition process justified a gradual approach. This was because the level of a society's civilization, history, culture, size, efficiency and the degree of social satisfaction were related to what actually occurred in the economy. As a result, the dynamics and the speed of reform differed between transition economies because the starting points were varied. The starting-point required clarification, and there could not be a uniform line – thus, governments could not have undertaken liberalizing measures simultaneously. Instead, there was an 'optimal' order of economic liberalization, depending on the initial conditions (McKinnon, 1993b, p. 4; Csaba, 1995, p. 17).

Murrell (1995, p. 173) was critical of the shock therapy views that market economic systems were the same everywhere, whether in 'Russia of 1913 or the OECD of 1994'. Top-down reforms resulted and were a sad reminder of the past, when the central authority designed such reforms. Foreign economists, mainly from America, designed the shock therapy reforms. In the case of Russia, Jeffrey Sachs admitted he felt like a surgeon who had sliced open a patient only to discover that nothing was supposed to be there! Kingston-Mann (1999, p. 41) added: 'the surgeon not only had the wrong diagnosis but mistook the patient for someone else, because the patient's history was so unfamiliar to the surgeon. At the end, Aslund (1994c, p. 189) agreed that: 'it might be appropriate to differentiate for various formerly communist countries with regard to their preconditions ... Hungary may get away with much more interventionist policy than Russia would be able to do.'

3 Secondary Primary Elements of the Neoclassical Gradualist Model

3.1   Price Liberalization and Stabilization

The adjustment of the quantities to the new prices had to be gradual. Stable domestic price-level permitted greater domestic financial deepening and higher real deposit rates, reducing risks and greatly simplifying the liberalization and stabilization of the real exchange rate. Meanwhile, the absence of designed price controls and policies resulted in inflationary pressures without eliminating shortages. The price controls were not a fruitless exercise, as the shock therapy supporters insisted. The price controls and policies facilitated the transition and reduced the associated costs to the people. There was a real trade off between the short-term quantitative anti-recessionary gains and the long-term qualitative benefits of economic growth. The efficiency gains from price liberalization were uncertain. Prices could not be liberalized immediately: there had to be transitional pricing, whereby prices of basic foodstuffs, energy products, and utilities were controlled. For example, an agricultural price support system, similar to the European Union's agricultural policy, could have been introduced temporarily, with tariffs on imported food. Prices would have reached their equilibrium values through a gradual process, because prices and the real exchange rate are endogenous variables. Furthermore, such controls would have served as a partial substitute for the otherwise underdeveloped social safety net.

The shock therapy argument for total price decontrol was flawed and extremely destructive. While central administration had been removed, price signals did not immediately replace the role of directives since individuals were not yet competent to evaluate and utilize this new type of information. As long as state enterprises were bidding for scarce resources with soft budget constraints no meaningful equilibrium could have existed, and their unconstrained bidding caused the price level to increase indefinitely. Indeed, that was a 'shock without therapy' (Kolodko, 1999a, p. 33); thus 'prices should not be liberalized on their own' (Csaba, 1995, p. 71) until the consumer goods market was satiated at the controlled prices. Price liberalization would not have been sufficient to develop competitive markets.

Based on the neoclassical gradualist approach, the government retained some 'relaxed' price controls while permitting the remaining prices to be freely market-determined. Despite the subsequent surpluses and shortages this was a characteristic of every market economy. During the period of price stability, the interest rate had to be controlled to achieve real financial growth without undue risk of major financial panic and collapse. Importantly, while neoclassical economists highlighted the urgent need to reduce inflation, neoclassical gradualist economists were willing to accept inflation to reduce social hardship, especially in terms of unemployment.

Inflation was 'the constant public enemy number one of the transforming countries' (Csaba, 1995, p. 69). However, in Hungary, due to the gradualist approach there was no hyperinflation to halt. Kornai (1996, p. 2; 1995e, p. 149; 1993b, p. 323) argued that increasing unemployment could have reduced inflation and increased efficiency. Improvements in efficiency required the rejection of full employment and job security, and the wearing down of social security provided freely by the enterprise. However, it would have been ill advised, 'to impose an urgent and radical curb on inflation at the expense of all other tasks' (Kornai, 1997a, p. 213). High unemployment imposed serious financial burdens on the state and, indirectly, on the whole economy. More importantly, unemployment created social dissatisfaction, which posed the most immediate threat to the maintenance of the whole reform program. An extended recession was expected, resulting in several years of high unemployment that without state intervention would only have gone higher.

While the objective should have been market-determined wages, it was in the interests of society in the transition phase to maintain some control over wages and try to avoid the wage-price spiral. This was because inflation is a dynamic process, generated and sustained by price and wage increases. Deregulating wages in an environment of weak profit motive, soft budget constraints, and unemployment would not have helped the transition process. Moreover, wage increases should not have been fuelled by rises in the price of imports due to devaluation. The government had to set guidelines for the determination of wages, which were strengthened by tax incentives: that is an Incomes Policy. Progressive taxation above the pre-determined norm would have acted as a disincentive to excessive wage increases and the partial, not automatic, indexation of wages. This would have maintained industrial peace and reduced inflation. It was a transitional measure that could have speeded up the reform process. The shock therapy supporters and the Post Keynesians were in agreement on this.

The development of market relations in CEEFSU was 'path-dependent', like most economic phenomena. The role of the state in economic policy was among the most debated theoretical and practical aspects of the transition. The state sector was too big to be 'left alone', while the private sector was growing and 'likely to become a political and economic time bomb that would undermine the whole reform process' (Frydman, Rapaczynski and Turkewitz, 1997, p. 83). During the transition period the economy was like 'no man's land' (Kornai, 1994, p. 47) and it was the responsibility of the government to exert some influence. The transition process involved a protracted and increasing social cost. This could not have been reduced without state intervention, and if the results were disappointing confidence in the government would have been eroded. However, as Kornai (1995b, pp. 26, 27) stated, the government does not 'start up' growth, it only influences growth.

According to Kornai (1994, p. 62) 'there is no chance of determining theoretically, once and for all, the optimum degree of state activity'. In the transition process the government had shared responsibility for the development of the market economy. 'Honeymoons end, and so does the opportunity to blame hard times on the old system' (Nelson, 1994, p. 54). Not doing anything was unacceptable: 'it does not help much to say that if the government sticks to its guns, the economic agents will have to change their behavior' (Frydman, Rapaczynski and Turkewitz, 1997, p. 45).

The role of the state in the transition economies was two-fold and essential. On the one hand, state activity was determined according to the free market concept: developing, implementing and enforcing the rules and only acting to correct market failure. On the other hand, state activity, beyond the traditional notion of the state, was determined by the idiosyncrasies of the transition process. The state had to initiate and actively assist the development of the new institutions required by a market economy, the establishment of certain organizations and abolition of others, and the transformation of property relations. In contrast to the shock therapy model, and due to the gradualist nature of the reforms, an activist-strong state was extremely important. This activist-strong state was solid but democratically controlled. As the experience of the Ukraine, Romania, and Russia demonstrated, a weak government was not in a position to bring about stabilization (Csaba, 1995, p. 83). Meanwhile, it should have been remembered that 'socialism and serfdom go hand in hand' (Carrington, 1992, p. 23), and 'people are irritated by the state interfering in their private lives and harassing individuals' (Kornai, 1992a, p. 16); thus a minimal state should have been the ultimate goal (Gustafson, 1999, p. 213). The political authorities and the citizens must ensure, through a democratic process, that attempts to return to centralism and bureaucratic decision-making were neutralized. Once the transition was completed, state intervention in the economy would not have been necessary. As markets developed and the pace of reforms (institutional, structural and financial) gained momentum, the role of the state would have been reduced, and with it any remaining discretionary power.

3.2 Privatization

A competitive market capitalist system required a dominance of private property because 'there cannot be capitalism without capitalists' (Gustafson, 1999, p. 26) and 'common property is nobody's property' (Carrington, 1992, p. 23). However, the efficiency virtues associated with privatization – the main instrument of overcoming the recession and stimulating growth and employment – were 'a simplified misconception of the real relationship' (Kornai, 1994, p. 50) and policies were aimed at artificially accelerating the privatization process. Both privatization and liberalization were simply instruments of economic policy, not targets, and privatization of state enterprises was very painful. This was because politicians would not have given up their control of state enterprises so easily. Meanwhile, 'state-owned enterprises have become dependent on the paternalist helping hand of the state and the constant availability of a bail-out, just as many weaker-willed individuals become addicted to the relief of smoking, alcohol or drugs' (Kornai, 1995d, p. 148).

Based on the gradualist approach, growth would have resulted from the development of new enterprises in the short term. In the long run, growth would have resulted from the privatization of state enterprises and the enforcement of hard budget constraints. In contrast, the shock therapy supporters argued that growth in the short run would have been the result of privatization. The shock therapy economists were 'stuck on the theme that one is to create the new economy by privatizing the old' (Leijonhufvud, 1993, p. 124). Immediate privatization resulted in a reduction in output, increased unemployment and a reduction in aggregate demand. Considerations of growth were not given due attention; there was a negative relationship between the speed of privatization and economic performance. By implementing a gradualist approach to privatization, it was the responsibility of the government to ensure that an appropriate balance was achieved between short-term, anti-recessionary goals and long-term growth goals. Consequently, the immediate privatization of state enterprises was not necessary, since theoretical and empirical evidence indicated that rapid privatization was clearly utopian and misplaced in the transition process. The gradual process of transition required not only a slow process of privatization but also, more importantly, its postponement. The neoclassical gradualist economists favored 'deferred privatization', and even though Kornai (1992c, p. 174) claimed that he was a 'believer in the process of privatization proceeding as fast as possible', he did not think it could have been 'accelerated by some artful trick'.

Consequently, by approaching the privatization issue from this point of view, the question was not how to privatize state enterprises but rather how to develop the appropriate conditions to stimulate the development of new enterprises. A suitable legal environment and an appropriate institutional structure were essential. The privatization process consumed most of the already scarce resources, thereby hindering the growth of new enterprises. There was an inverse relationship between the amount of privatization and the rate of growth of new enterprises (Murrell, 1992a, p. 46). In addition, the experience of developing countries showed that growth had taken place through the development of new enterprises and not by adapting the existing ones (Krueger, 1992, p. 221). Thus it was argued that instead of speculating on the speed and the type of privatization, reformers should have concentrated on the development of new enterprises, restricting the development of monopolies and developing an appropriate institutional framework. This would have resulted in a set of conditions where the speed and the type of privatization process would not have been significant. Consequently, while privatization attracted headlines, it was often argued 'that the privatization issue deserves somewhat less – and the institutional requirements of a market economy much more – priority than in the past' (Olson, 1992, p.x).

Privatization and the establishment of legal institutions could not be part of shock therapy policies because they could not be achieved within a short period of time. The speed of privatization was determined by institutional factors. 'In fact, the simple-minded notion that "privatization" is all that is needed to set faltering and failed economies on the path to growth is a travesty of institutional reasoning that reflects the primitive understanding of most economists about the nature of institutions' (North, 1997, p. 12). Successful privatization and the development of market infrastructure must be nurtured from small beginnings, whereby a sorting process eventually identifies viable enterprises. Consequently, 'the resulting spontaneous order is best grown from the bottom up' (McKinnon, 1992a, p. 35).

The interests of society would not have been served by immediate privatization, since the tax agency would not have been efficient in collecting tax revenue. Gradualists were in favor of firstly restructuring and corporatizing state enterprises, and privatizing these organizations later. The experience of the transition economies revealed that terminating soft budget constraints and liberalizing prices, foreign trade and commercial activity encouraged enterprise restructuring independently of ownership. Thus, the 'ownership structure and the modus operandi cannot be changed overnight by legislative "gunpowder"' (McKinnon, 1992a, p. 35). In actual fact, privatization of any variety was a political issue, which might result in the re-nationalization and deferment of privatization. Consequently, in a democratic society, neither the sequencing nor the speed of privatization could have been planned, since it determined 'who will eventually get to the sunny or the shady side of this evolving capitalist paradise' (Jarai, 1993, p. 78).

Kornai (1990, p. 83) argued that the transformation of state property into private property could only have taken place by auctioning state enterprises and selling them to the highest bidder. Privatization could have helped to increase state revenue through the proceeds of selling enterprises. The Hungarian government was in agreement with Kornai that privatization had to result in 'real owners' or 'strong owners' rather than artificial recipients of state assets (Frydman, Rapaczynski and Turkewitz, 1997, p. 87; Samonis and Hunyadi, 1993, p. 31; Mihalyi, 1993, pp. 90, 106). Privatization revenues had to fund the budget deficit and reduce public debt. This was considered a major advantage of the sales strategy over the free distribution of shares.

Kornai (1992c, p. 157) did not show any enthusiasm for compensating the original owners of enterprises. In Hungary, original owners were eligible for compensation vouchers (Samonis and Hunyadi, 1993, pp. 35, 36; Mihalyi, 1993, p. 92). Due to the auctioning of state enterprises, all individuals would have had the opportunity to become owners at real market prices. The frequent argument against privatization by sale was that the accumulated public savings were too small to buy the state enterprises. Experience revealed that this was not the real bottleneck in the privatization process (Kornai, 1997a, p. 159). The deferment of privatization allowed the development of a domestic entrepreneurial class with proven managerial expertise to accumulate sufficient capital to buy state-owned industrial assets.

Foreigners would also have had the ability to participate, so long as some guidelines were imposed to protect the nation's interests. The national policy, however, should not have been based on isolationism or xenophobia. The government would have had to regulate the participation of foreigners. Through the privatization process, most property should have remained 'in national hands, because they are indispensable to sovereignty' (Kornai, 1992c, p. 174). In other words, 'capitalism should strike root primarily in domestic soil' (Kornai, 1992c, p. 174) so as to foster the development of domestic entrepreneurs. In Hungary, foreigners dominated the purchase of state assets. In 1991, 85 per cent of the 40.1 billion forint of privatization revenue came from foreign investors (Samonis and Hunyadi, 1993, p. 38; Jarai, 1993, p. 80).

There were no problems associated with the managers of the state enterprises who were capable of buying the firm purchasing the organisation, as long as it was done legally, even though most of the new owners were from the old economic elite of the Communist Party. Kornai (1999, p. 166; 1997a, p. 152) did not show any concern as long as the new owners' behavior was consistent with market behavior. Thus issues related to the fairness and equality of the privatization program would not have been a concern. In Hungary, the government initially opposed 'spontaneous privatization' but eventually realized that it was the best solution to the problems of privatization. It consequently adopted spontaneous privatization, but under the guises of 'enterprise-initiated' privatization.

The neoclassical gradualist economists did not favor the privatization of state enterprises through the free distribution of vouchers or through financial intermediaries. Kornai considered it curious 'to turn all citizens into shareholders overnight by a free distribution of shares' (Kornai, 1992c, p. 172). With shares distributed so widely, the monitoring problem was not solved. In Hungary, officials contemptuously dismissed free distribution schemes as dangerous experiments, incapable of producing 'real owners' (Frydman, Rapaczynski and Turkewitz, 1997, p. 95; Samonis and Hunyadi, 1993, p. 31). There was no justification for the distribution of free gifts beyond the discount price of share purchases by employees and the distribution of property to pension funds and non-profit organizations.

In conclusion, the neoclassical gradualist economists did not favor immediate privatization in the transition process: there was a 'real economic cost' (Murrell and Wang, 1993, p. 387) associated with immediate privatization. The democratically elected government had initially to gain control of state enterprises and make managers accountable prior to privatization. Ironically, large state enterprises had to be re-nationalized before they could be privatized, and even then the gradual neoclassical approach would not have been gradual. Instead of a gradual process of privatization, enterprises were put up for auction. Hence, the gradualist privatization process was more a 'deferred big bang privatization' process. The only difference between the gradualists and the shock therapy supporters was the proposed timing of privatization, not its speed.

3.3   Institutional Structure

A proper institutional structure was 'the Achilles heel' (Svejnar, 1991, p. 134) of transition, because 'institutions matter' (Bardhan, 2000, p. 245). Private property and the building of institutions are fundamental to a free market. While macroeconomic stability was a necessary, but not a sufficient, condition for transition into a market economy, institutions were necessary and sufficient. A credible transition process could only be achieved by getting the institution 'right' in terms of an institutional structure that could direct and channel economic activity to achieve sustainable and equitable long-term growth. The evolutionary paradigm of institutional development was also used to justify a gradualist approach to reform as 'the resulting spontaneous order can indeed spread rapidly' (McKinnon, 1992a, p. 35). As Coase (1992, p. 714) advised: 'without the appropriate institutions no market economy of any significance is possible'. Gradualist neoclassical economists realized that the overall institutional environment greatly restricted the options available to policymakers.

Neoclassical gradualist economists accepted Coase's theorem that clear property rights, preferably private property rights, were essential for a well-functioning market economy in CEEFSU. For market capitalism to consolidate and function efficiently, it was imperative that the institutional structure protected private property, enforced contracts, imposed financial discipline, and generally created a stable legal environment. Having market-oriented institutions in place while old institutions were torn down was crucial for reforms to be effective. Apparently, institutional changes would have been initiated by the market process, albeit slowly.

Gradualist economists argued that the transition to a market economy had to be facilitated by an institutional structure. It was preferable that the development of this structure was gradual, natural, organic, and voluntary, as opposed to the constructivist, state-directed establishment of institutions. A gradual process allowed time to clarify the institutional principles and to test institutional adjustment. Institutional development was a complex evolutionary process, causing the ineffective institutions to wither away and choosing as survivors the ones truly fit for the task. Market-supporting institutions aimed to make the transition more effective and harder to reverse.

The development of market institutions takes time, which was one reason why the transition recession in CEEFSU was persistent. Appropriate government initiatives would have hastened the development and helped reduce the length of the recession. The institution of private property cannot exist without government (Olson, 2000, p. 131). However, recent history has demonstrated that transition governments had 'committed many sins of omission in this respect' (Kornai, 1993a, p. 200; 1994, p. 49). The collapse of centrally administered socialism did not leave the society in an institutional vacuum. Accordingly, the practices and habits, informal arrangements, organizational structures and social norms of society were slowly transformed into the basis for the establishment of credible commitments: people would have rationally adopted the new conventions as they emerged. The pre-existence of an institutional structure, even though contradictory and segmented, provided the basis for 'rebuilding organizations and institutions not on the ruins but with the ruins of communism as they [economic actors] redeploy available resources in response to their immediate practical dilemmas' (Stark, 1996, p. 995). Change, even revolutionary change, such as the transition process, was the result of adjusting to the new uncertainties, by adapting the previous norms to the new economic conditions. This new institutional structure 'is not replacement but recombination' (Stark, 1996, p. 995).

The shock therapy approach to institutional development was vague, inconsistent, and toothless. 'Instant people's capitalism' was not possible and was distinctly 'un-Hayekian', since spontaneous markets based on common law best evolved from existing commercial practices. The failure of transition economies to stimulate growth after the implementation of the shock therapy process was attributed to the neglect of the institutional structure and the destruction of existing arrangements and information processes. While institutions change slowly, they have a strong influence on economic performance and stabilization.

Governments had an important role in supporting the ever-changing market with the appropriate institutional structure. Otherwise 'trade relations are destroyed by the absence of market institutions' (Kornai, 1994, p. 47) and 'laissez faire is not optimal' (Thomas and Wang, 1997, p. 218). Essentially, the success of the privatization process depended on how rapidly the market legal frameworks and supervisory institutions developed, how promptly the bankruptcy proceedings and liquidation processes were in place, and on the reliability of the free transfer of property rights. Institutional change was imperative to divorce tax collection by various levels of government from the ownership of firms.

The transition economies that relied on the spontaneous appearance of the necessary institutional structure, without any government initiation, were unable to manage the transition process adequately. Nevertheless, governments should not have been expected to replace the spontaneous, decentralized, organic growth processes of institutions, as often social arrangements might have been more powerful than government in establishing the rules: fewer rules usually have advantages over more regulation.

The implementation of the shock therapy process without any institutional fundamentals in place resulted in 'bandit capitalism' in the transition economies (Kolodko, 1999b, p. 249). The rise of criminal activity and Mafia methods of imposing financial discipline were 'alarming and intolerable' (Kornai, 1995e, p. 153; 1993b, p. 327). These harmful side effects can partly be explained as a result of a healthy process, namely the abolition of the police state. It would have taken some time to develop the necessary legal infrastructure for property and contract rights to become secure in the long run. At the same time, the establishment of democracy and markets opened the curtains and made crime more visible. It revealed an unexpected amount of official corruption and Mafia-style crime, which was not compatible with a mature market economy. The increase in crime was the result of weak institutional arrangements. According to a recent World Bank study, half the Russian economy is now in the hands of the Mafia (Kingston-Mann, 1999, p. 35).

Private enterprises would have changed their behavior and followed the road of legality if the legal structure had offered them protection of their property rights and guaranteed contracts. All necessary incentives should have been used to encourage a law-abiding and tax-paying enterprise, with the possible use of a stick-and-carrot approach. 'A system where "only the stupid pay taxes", the contracts are not executed as agreed, or the payments are not made on time, is hardly a market economy. It is rather chaos stemming from institutional disintegration' (Kolodko, 1999b, p. 249). Mature market economies have demonstrated that individual self-interest, based on 'buyers beware' and firms with clearly delineated property rights, foster crime prevention, lawful behavior, and law enforcement: these governments did not need to pour financial resources into combating fraud. Consequently, the creation and advancement of a legal framework for the market economy should have been much higher on the agenda of international financial organizations. Once in place, it would have provided a secure base for growth through liberalization and privatization. Thus it was the responsibility of the newly formed governments to initiate a pluralistic process for the development of an appropriate institutional structure consistent with the political, historical and cultural traditions prevailing in the country.

In summary, the development of the institutional structure for the shock therapy and the neoclassical gradualist process approaches appear to be quite similar. However, it is my view that while both argued that market institutions can only result from market forces, the proposal of the neoclassical gradualist economists allowed institutions to develop concurrently with market relations. For shock therapy supporters, the first goal was the development of market relations, on the assumption that the institutions would have followed in due time. The neoclassical gradualist argument suffered from the same flaws. Neoclassical gradualist writings failed to offer a concrete process of institutional development. They simply left the end-state to be determined by the market, assuming that the most efficient institutions would have emerged. The neoclassical gradualist break with shock therapy was far less complete than it appeared to be.

3.4   Monetary Policy and the Financial System

The imposition of hard budget constraints on enterprises, in the context of macroeconomic stabilization, was the driving force of adjustment. Monetary policy was the fundamental lever in achieving monetary stability, a necessary condition for growth. The soft budget constraint resulted in inefficiency, breakdown of consumer sovereignty and distorted investment decisions. Thus reform of the financial system had to be a high priority. The lack of substantial progress in institutional reforms, particularly in privatization and the financial sector, had not prevented major structural adjustment and efficiency gains as a result of hard budget constraints. Meanwhile, as with all the elements of the transition program, monetary stability could only have evolved gradually as, for example, in Hungary.

The governments in transition economies should not have been pressured to provide cheap credit and subsidies and to finance investment projects. Firms had to learn that a bank was not an institution for distributing money on orders from above or friendly recommendations from politicians. Firms had to follow the rules of financial discipline strictly. There had to be credibility with respect to a 'no bail-out' commitment. Kornai (1993b, p. 330; 1995e, p. 156) compared the behavior of firms with that of animals and stated that: 'observations of animals provide firm evidence that habits acquired in the initial, particularly sensitive stage of life have an extremely strong influence. They become impressed deeply and almost irreversibly in the memory, and prompt the animal concerned to repeat the experience.'

While hard budget constraints would have resulted in unemployment, Kornai (1992a, p. 10) was convinced that it was better to have accepted the serious problem of unemployment openly than artificially to sustain terminally ill firms. The imposition of the hard budget constraint was essentially a political issue, and it required a broad social consensus, public support and a credible government that would not succumb to pressure. Only the gradual establishment of an independent central bank could have achieved this. The governments should not have had to follow the monetary rule nor introduce restrictive monetary policy (Kornai, 1995c, pp. 240, 241).

The neoclassical gradualist economists argued that premature attempts to transform the banking system would have worsened the overall situation by losing control over monetary policy. For example, in the 1980s, China, Hungary, the Soviet Union, and Poland undertook the premature decentralization of the banking system, which resulted in increased inflation and lost control over credit (McKinnon, 1993b, p. 7). Institution building must first be sufficiently advanced, and stabilization ought to be consolidated into stability. Only then should financial markets have been liberalized in a gradual manner. Consequently, 'consolidation of financial discipline is a lengthy process of evolution that extends over several years' (Kornai, 1995d, p. 150; 1995e, p. 159). Partial deregulation of interest rates generally comes first, accompanied or followed by the development of commercial banking and non-bank institutions. Development of a securities market takes longer, as it requires further institution building and the establishment of a legal infrastructure.

In the short run, successful macroeconomic stabilization in the transition economies would have required a major re-centralization of the government's control over money and credit and the elimination of 'wildcat banks'. Prices had to be re-centralized as part of the stabilization package. However, this would have presented an unfortunate policy dilemma. In order to secure macroeconomic stabilization in the short run, important banking and commodity pricing policies had to move counter to the ultimate goal for long-term liberalization. It would have been necessary to re-regulate the financial system as well as the state enterprises (Kolodko, 1999b, p. 236; McKinnon, 1995a, p. 106; 1995c, p. 70; Stark, 1990, p. 376). In the initial stages of liberalization, licensing a mass of new domestic or foreign banks to enable entry into the newly opened domestic capital market would have been a mistake (McKinnon, 1993b, p. 53).

The banks were burdened with non-performing loans. One approach, suggested by Blommenstein and Marrese (1991, pp. 103–4, 105), would have been for the government to 'purchase' the banks' bad loans with long-term bonds paying an interest rate. The banks' capital would have grown due to the elimination of bad loans and from income accruing from the government bonds. In contrast, Dittus (1994, p. 338) and Csaba (1995, p. 111) argued that bygones should be treated as bygones.

The reduction of enterprise lending was the result of more prudent behavior by the banks and the constraints and incentives under the new economic and legal environment. Moreover, the reduction in enterprise lending was also the result of the inability of the banks to evaluate risks and monitor borrowers. 'Building up those skills will take time' (Dittus, 1994, p. 359), again necessitating a gradual transition process. Another reason for reduced bank lending was the government's budget deficit. To finance their budget deficits, transition governments issued Treasury Bills with high interest rates, which were very attractive to banks and individuals. Crowding-out took place, and it reduced lending to enterprises. In addition, the level of uncertainty was unusually high for a market economy. McKinnon (1991, p. 118; 1992b, p. 108; 1993b, pp. 53, 139; 1995c, p. 68) noted that, in the initial stages of the transition to a more open capital market, reliance on self-financing was the preferred and simplest technique for imposing financial restraint on liberalized enterprises. Thus in the optimum order of financial liberalization the development of ordinary commercial banking had to be deferred until monetary and fiscal control was achieved and the price level stabilized. Thus the immediate imposition of the hard budget constraint, the reliance on self-financing, the gradual establishment of an independent central bank and partial control over interest rates created the pre-conditions for the development of a market-based financial system and for interest rates to be liberalized.

3.5   Fiscal Policy

Balancing the budget was a long-term concern but, in order to avoid further inflationary explosions, 'effective fiscal reforms must come much earlier in their transitions' (McKinnon, 1995a, p. 96). While every effort had to be made to reduce the budget deficit – or ideally to produce a surplus – any reductions were unlikely in the first years of transition. It would have been dangerous to reduce the deficit too drastically or too quickly. Rapid and drastic cuts in government expenditure would have suddenly reduced aggregate demand and caused deeper recession. As a result, the need for growth did not require an immediate reduction in the budget deficit. However, a fiscal stimulus entailed an inflationary outcome and crowding out. There was a need to restructure government expenditure so that the reduced demand from government consumption was replaced by investment demand.

The timely task of stimulating growth might have been the only way to eliminate the budget deficit and it may have required increasing government debt to finance the deficit. Kornai, (1995b, p. 9; 1995c, p. 243; 1996, p. 12) did not see this as a problem, as long as the loans were used for promoting growth, since they would have created their own resources for repayment. Surprisingly, Kornai (1996, p. 36) was willing to stimulate investment projects by providing tax concessions.

A drastic improvement in the transition governments' ability to collect tax revenue was necessary both for macroeconomic stabilization and to support longer-term market-oriented and institutional reforms. While institutions for tracking and collecting personal income taxes would have taken some years to put in place, tax reform and systematic changes needed to be implemented simultaneously to avoid distortions. There could not have been welfare reform without a profound, considered reform of taxation and vice versa (Kornai, 1997c, p. 1185). Stabilization required a simple taxation system. Successful implementation would have required major new administrative bureaucracies to collect the taxes and achieve the necessary political consensus, which was undoubtedly difficult. Nevertheless, the reformers had no choice. Such a comprehensive new tax system was simply a necessary condition for reforms to succeed.

Taxes in transition economies were already high, due to the premature welfare state (Kornai, 1996, p. 16). A broad flat tax or even a poll tax would have been preferable to increasing marginal income tax rates. There would have been no need for a progressive tax system that penalized those who increased their income and/or savings. With respect to the tax structure, Kornai (1990, pp. 127–132) recommended a linear consumption tax in the form of a value added tax (VAT), which was best suited to enterprise taxation. There would have been some progressive element in differentiated VAT rates to satisfy the requirement of fairness in distribution and meet the criteria for joining the European Union. The tax rate should have been the same for all firms: a single, linear non-progressive payroll tax and a single, linear non-progressive profit tax. However, Kornai (1992a, p. 14) argued that 'regrettably, I cannot rule out the possibility of the process being protracted and, thus, plagued with severe fiscal problems caused by loss of budget revenue in the meantime'. The transition governments were weak and unable to collect taxes, not because of the legacy from the past, but owing to an ill-advised free market approach and poorly orchestrated deregulation and privatization. It was difficult to bring tax collection under the control of the sovereign state, because of the mismanagement of liberalization and the manner in which institutional redesign took place. However, by giving up control of state property, the government, in effect, gave up its tax base. 'Enterprises can no longer so easily serve as cash cows or as vehicles for indirectly taxing households' (McKinnon, 1995c, p. 44). Privatization should have been postponed until the institutional basis of tax collection had been set up and became operational, bringing government finances under control: 'if there is any fiscal gain in privatization, it is in the future rather than immediately' (Csaba, 1995, p. 115). When tax morality improved and the tax base expanded, tax rates could have been lowered.

3.6   International Trade and Foreign Aid

A sustained movement towards free trade was crucial for the successful transition to a market economy, to promote the growth of exports, curb the rise in imports and improve the trade balance and the balance of payments. Neoclassical gradualist economists argued that since the economies in transition had inherited obsolete production methods, participation in international competition was very difficult. While the collapse of COMECON trade had a serious impact, COMECON itself was fraught with problems because it was influenced by political decisions. It was expected that transition economies would have had current account deficits, which were temporarily tolerable (Kornai, 1993a, p. 218). There was an argument for maintaining a moderate level of tariffs and transforming quantitative restrictions into tariffs. This would have provided protection and given time for the firms to adjust, while also providing the government with an income. Temporary protection for some domestic industries had to be determined on the basis of economic rationality, not pressure from lobby groups, and to be in line with the prescriptions of WTO so that it did not lead to protectionist retaliation by foreign trading partners. International trade would have also contributed to the process of creative destruction.

Convertibility would have required an appropriate exchange rate, which would have needed to depreciate heavily to adjust to the new economic conditions. The progress toward complete current account convertibility could only have been gradual, as in Hungary. A devaluation of the currency would have stimulated exports and reduced imports. The premature elimination of exchange controls would have facilitated unwarranted capital flight, increased foreign indebtedness, or both. 'Free foreign exchange convertibility on capital account is usually the last stage in the optimal order of economic liberalization as we shall see' (McKinnon, 1993b, pp. 10, 117). Without direct government participation, the foreign exchange market was highly unstable. There was a lively debate about the advantages and drawbacks of various exchange rate regimes. The regime that was chosen by Hungary's financial authorities, the pre-announced 'crawling peg', had certain advantages. It made the intentions of the policy-makers clear, maintained commitment, reduced speculation and also tied the hands of the monetary authorities and reduced their room to maneuver.

It might have been in the interests of transition economies, especially the former republics of the Soviet Union, to have co-coordinated price liberalization, budgetary and credit reforms. Williamson (1991a, pp. 11–14; 1992, pp. 29–31), Van Brabant (1991b, pp. 63–95), Kregel et al. (1992, pp. 102–3), Fischer and Frenkel (1992, p. 40) and Dornbusch (1993, pp. 107–8) recommended the establishment of a 'Payments Union' between transition economies. An organisation similar to the European Payments Union (EPU), which operated from mid-1950 to 1958, was suggested because the convertibility of the currency would not otherwise have been sustainable, due to the inelasticity of import and export demand. Permanent current account deficits would have encouraged depreciation and detracted from the gains in international competitiveness due to the inflexibility of wages. Most European countries suffered monetary overhangs and repressed inflation. International financial markets were controlled heavily and capital account currency exchanges were only allowed in exceptional circumstances. If convertibility had been initiated immediately, rather than the EPU, European incomes would have been reduced by one to two per cent, which was the same as the contribution made by the USA under the Marshall plan. This was an all-too-familiar scenario among the transition economies. Through the Payments Union, transition economies would have been able to establish current account convertibility more rapidly between member states and the rest of the world and avoid large depreciation. The Union would have achieved currency convertibility, intra-regional economic collaboration, exploitation of comparative advantage, structural adjustment, reduction in the social costs of transition, the development of rational trade and prices, and have prepared transition economies for participation in international trade. The Payments Union was a stage in the gradual transition process to reduce the social costs and create the pre-conditions for full membership in the European Union. The Payments Union did not require the removal of financial or fiscal policies by the sovereign state. Van Brabant (1991a, p. 64) argued that 'I see such a facility as an indispensable instrument of the reform process'.

The participation of the mature market economies in designing, guaranteeing and administering the Payments Union was essential. The European Payments Union required a set of institutions – such as the Organisation for European Economic Cooperation and the Bank of International Settlement – with the ability to monitor compliance and impose penalties. The financial commitment for setting up and maintaining a Payments Union would have been quite small and would have attracted financial assistance from mature market economies and international organizations. It would not have distorted economic incentives. 'It is difficult to think of a more productive form of aid than endowing a capital fund for an Eastern Payments Union that could prevent the collapse of inter-republic trade' (Williamson, 1991a, p. 14). However, the idea was rejected (Williamson, 1991a, p. 12). The international organizations did not permit this idea to flourish, probably because the newly formed ex-Soviet republics and Central and Eastern Europe had to depend on trade with Russia for a substantial number of years. Such a union might have provided a mechanism to impose centralization of trade and restrictions on the free movement of capital. In addition, the EPU was associated with extended institutions and agreements that had the short-term goal of economic union. The long-term goal was political union. CEEFSU, encouraged by mature market economies and international organizations, were moving against these links and the degree of economic and political commonality was rather shallow.

The role of foreign aid was considerable for the transition economies, since it was intended to speed and increase the likelihood of the success of the transition reforms. 'I do not know if there has been a case of a country accomplishing this shift entirely out of its own resources' (Kornai, 1995b, pp. 30, 31). This, of course, was in the interest of mature market economies. Partial debt forgiveness was necessary which was anathema to the IMF and World Bank. The World Bank's technical assistance and long-term project support would have remained invaluable, as well as the IMF's role as a short-term international crisis manager. However, they should not 'bribe a country into opening its trade accounts since capital injected at the time makes liberalization much harder to sustain' (McKinnon, 1993b, pp. 116–9). Unfortunately, however, Western aid did not have positive effects and there was excessive optimism and naïve hope placed in the scale of Western economic aid and its helpful stimulating impact on production. Had the transition economies followed the aforementioned optimum order of liberalization, their need for external capital would have been limited (McKinnon, 1993b, pp. 116–9).

3.7   Social Policy

The transition process was expected to improve the standard of living of the people: 'otherwise, the exercise would not make much sense' (Kolodko, 1999a, p. 34). However, the first taste of the market process was quite bitter for the majority of the population. For example, Russia's population now is older, poorer and sicker than in 1991 (Gustafson, 1999, pp. 173, 188; Bratkowski, 1993, p. 5; Van Brabant, 1993, p. 76). Lack of attention to the social safety net was not unusual in transition economies. Russia's budget expenditure on health was less than one per cent of GNP, and price reform was not accompanied by monetary compensation (Murrell, 1995, p. 166; Gustafson, 1999, p. 186; Alexeev, 1991, p. 388). However, improving the environment and the health, skills and mobility of the population were the keys to economic growth and the ultimate popular acceptance of market reforms. That was why 'nobody, not even an economist with rather strong laissez-faire principles, would go so far as to propose that the state abandon all its welfare functions' (Kornai, 1995b, p. 10; 1996, p. 14). A major deterioration in the economic and social well being of society endangered the transition process.

In addition, inequality was increasing, offering most opportunities to only a segment of the population. Inequality was unavoidable during the initial years of transition. However, beyond a certain limit, income disparities inhibit the expansion of economic activity, stunt economic growth and delay recovery: inequities hamper crucial institutional and structural reforms. Russia's Gini coefficient doubled in the first six years of transition, reaching the level of the Philippines, reflecting the corruption and 'crony capitalism' that were related to the continuing recession, growing inequality and spreading poverty.

The existing welfare provision could not have halted the decline, which presented one of the gravest of all the transition problems. There could not have been a 'shock therapy' of the welfare system, complete withdrawal by the state or a demolition of the welfare state. As with most elements of the transition process, welfare reform would have had to be gradual – the result of evolutionary change and natural selection – necessitating the maintenance of the budget deficit. There were 'no quick fixes' and welfare reforms should have been tactful and humane and introduced with 'great patience, compassion, and understanding' (Kornai, 1995c, p. 240). The aim was to establish sophisticated, reassuring, institutional forms of non-state voluntary insurance.

The transition economies had to create a safety net from scratch. A key task of the transition process was the radical reform of the pension and health care systems, and the provision of social assistance for children and the aged. In mature market economies, the demand for economic security is the major motivating force of savings. This type of savings had been stalled due to the paternalistic practices of the previous governments. This poses the familiar efficiency versus security argument. 'Support is one thing, but paternalism as a substitute for individual action is quite another' (Kornai, 1997a, p. 231). Kornai (1996, p. 15; 1997a, p. 95) defined social policy in Hungary under the Kaidar regime (1956–89) as a 'premature welfare state'. Although Hungary was much less developed than the Scandinavian countries, the welfare commitments were much greater. The premature welfare state adversely affected the development of the market sector and cast doubt on long-term prosperity.

The private sector had to be encouraged to provide welfare services in order to minimize the premature welfare state. It was envisaged that there would have been a minimal level of state-funded services provided for everyone and private-funded services in line with contributions to insurance policies. Individuals would have had a choice between welfare service providers which, in turn, would have created competition of prices and quality of service and also decentralization. Surveys in Hungary revealed support for welfare reforms because they would have encouraged the market mechanism and private enterprise in the provision of services, allowing choice. Voluntary organizations would have overseen the private providers and ensured high quality services by imposing rules. The government would have had to play an active part as initiator of the reform process. The welfare system, 'after decades of spoon-feeding and subservience to political whims, must be to bestow greater sovereignty on citizens' (Kornai, 1997c, p. 1186).

4 Process of the Transition

According to the neoclassical gradualist approach, as demonstrated in Table No. 5, the first priority was fiscal control, in conjunction with several other key initiatives. A tax department had to be established to collect taxes from households and firms and replace the traditional tax base of state-owned enterprises, which would have disappeared. At the same time, the institutional structure would have to have been overhauled, an incomes policy introduced, a payments union established and tariffs for non-Payment Union members maintained and gradually eliminated. A safety net would have to have been introduced simultaneously. Both formal and informal institutions would have been the result of market forces. Meanwhile, both prices and interest rates would have to have been controlled.

Once the initial reforms were in place, the budget constraints could have been hardened in Year 2, with the imposition of self-financing together with the development of an independent central bank. The privatization of small state enterprises could have been initiated in Year 2 and the restructuring and/or corporatization of large state enterprises could have started. Once the restructuring and/or corporatization of large state enterprises gained momentum in Year 7, price liberalization, and deregulation of the interest rates and the banking system could have been initiated. With the completion of restructuring and/or corporatization at the end of Year 8, large state enterprises could have been auctioned in Year 9. The vacuum in the provision of enterprise welfare services could have been filled by the gradual development of private welfare providers, which would start in Year 2.

Before the privatization of large enterprises, the payments union would have become redundant at the end of Year 8 after achieving convertibility, a floating exchange rate, and the elimination of tariffs to establish free trade. The budget deficit would have been funded by conditional foreign aid throughout the transition process.

5 The Cost of Transition

Using the cost criteria of the transition process identified in Chapter 3, it can be argued the implementation of the neoclassical gradualist approach in transition economies resulted in the lowest economic cost (as the Chinese model) comparing with the remaining models of transition, since it used as prototype the Chinese model of transition and maintained centrally administered directives. As well, the neoclassical gradualist approach had the lowest political cost, since it appears to be the model with stable political support. With regard to the ideological cost the people in CEEFSU placed the neoclassical model at the lowest ideological cost since the approach was consistent with the desire to establish a capitalist economic system and involved a less change in behavior compared with shock therapy. With regard to the International Financial cost the international financial institutions and governments in mature market economies were willing to provide funding to the transition economies, which implemented the neoclassical gradualist approach however to a lesser extent that those countries that implemented shock therapy placing the model at the lowest end of the cost but above shock therapy. Lastly, with regard to the Foreign Direct Investment Cost multinationals were willing to finance projects in transition economies that implemented neoclassical gradualist due to the stability offered by the process and the dominant method of privatization was through auctions, which effectively encouraged large foreign participation. The Financial Direct Investment cost places the model at the lowest transition cost together with the Chinese approach.

6 Conclusion

Gradualist transition supporters argued that the process clearly outperformed the shock therapy approach, rather than merely avoiding some of the obvious flaws (Csaba, 1995, p. 191). This was because it was naïve and premature to free prices, float the exchange rate, and privatize and decentralize decision-making before proper fiscal and monetary control over the economy had been established. Shock therapy failed and was wrong and dangerous: neither selective memory, statistical manipulation, nor elastic use of the notion of success could have shown that shock therapy was a triumph.

The neoclassical gradualist process of transition combined a democratic political structure with a market economy. In contrast to the shock therapy supporters, the policies of the neoclassical gradualist economists had to be approved by the democratic political process in order to facilitate transition. However, efficiency considerations should not have been at the expense of democracy. Meanwhile, a neoclassical gradualist approach entailed the maintenance of short-term inefficiencies. However, these priorities presented an unfortunate policy dilemma for the neoclassical gradualist economists. In order to secure macroeconomic stabilization in the short run, important pricing, enterprise, banking, interest rate and international trade policies had to move counter to the ultimate goal of long-run liberalization. Transition governments were encouraged by the neoclassical gradualist economists to seize the financial assets of enterprises, command outputs through state orders, and reinstitute price controls and other such devices. Consequently, the recommendations were for the re-regulation of the financial system, international trade, and state enterprises (Kolodko, 1999b, p. 236; McKinnon, 1995a, p. 106; 1995c, p. 70; Stark, 1990, p. 376).

If competitive capitalism were the ultimate goal of neoclassical gradualist economists, there was an apparent contradiction with the recommended strategy of transition. A competitive capitalist system required a government with no discretion. However, re-regulation and re-nationalization occurred during the transition period. The government's discretionary power was increased in the name of gaining control of economic affairs.

However, there was a direct link between increased government power and the interests of the bureaucracy and other lobby groups. The crucial question was: how could the economy, from a system of increasing government power during the transition period, be transformed into a free market system? The neoclassical gradualist economists failed to reveal how this would have been achieved. Strangely enough, the state was expected to 'wither away' (Csaba, 1995, p. 89; Abel and Bonin, 1993, p. 230). Stalin had advanced a similar argument: for the state to 'wither away', its power firstly had to be maximized (Nove, 1989a, p. 63). However, the state would never have 'withered away', as it was linked to the interests and privileges of the bureaucracy, and to other lobby groups and sectoral interests. These groups would have resisted their own dissolution, and state power and intervention would have continued. This argument was maintained by neoclassical economists to explain the lack of reform in the Stalinist system. Paradoxically, the same argument finds validity in the neoclassical gradualist process of transition.

Table 5.1
The Neoclassical Gradualist Process of Transition

	Years	1	2	3	4	5	6	7	8	9	10
1. Price Liberalization	Price Deregulation								■	■	
Stabilization	Incomes Policy	■	■	■	■	■	■	■			
2. Privatization	Privatization of Small Enterprises			■							
	Restructuring of Large Enterprises			■	■	■	■	■	■	■	
	Privatization of Large Enterprises										■
3. Institutional Stricture	Formal Institutions	■	■	■	■	■	■	■	■	■	■
	Informal Institutions	■	■	■	■	■	■	■	■	■	■
4. Monetary Policy	Hard Budget Constraint			■							
and the Financial System	Independent Central Bank			■							
5. Fiscal Policy	Budget Deficit	■	■	■	■	■	■	■	■	■	■
	Tax Structure	■									
6. International Trade and Foreign Aid	Payments Union	■	■	■	■	■	■	■	■		
	Tariffs	■	■	■	■	■	■	■	■		
	Floating Exchange Rate									■	
	Conditional Foreign Aid	■	■	■	■	■	■	■	■	■	■
7. Social Policy	Safety Net	■	■	■	■	■	■	■	■	■	■
	Private Welfare			■	■	■	■	■	■	■	■
	Years	1	2	3	4	5	6	7	8	9	10

Chapter 6

The Post Keynesian Model of Transition: Developing a Civilized Society

1 Introduction

The Post Keynesians argued against rapid, radical, and far-reaching economic reforms in transition economies. They argued that a stabilization package with gradual liberalization and active government intervention would have provided better results than the neoclassical models of transition. However, people in transition economies required not only better results but also expediency, because 'life is not long enough; human nature desires quick results ...' (Keynes, 1936, p. 157).

Herr and Westphall (1991, p. 308) argued that the movement towards a market economy required the formation of a hierarchy between coexisting organizational elements, in order to establish social coherence in the economy, in which market relations dominate. In other words, while market relations were unimportant under the previous structure, they now had to be elevated to the dominant mode in the economy. This ascent of the market process required, on the Post Keynesian view – a specific composition of political, economic, legal and cultural institutions in society to ensure the dominance of market relations. However, international financial institutions, mature market economies and governments in transition economies did look favourably on the Post Keynesians' propositions. The association of extensive government intervention with centrally administered socialism precluded the implementation of any of the Post Keynesians' policies as transitional measures.

2 Primary Elements of the Post Keynesian Model

2.1 Economic Analysis

Post Keynesianism is based on the writings of John Maynard Keynes, particularly *The General Theory of Employment, Interest and Money*, which has imperishable relevance to current economic and social problems. Keynes (1936, p. 372) argued that the most prominent failure of the market system was its inability to provide full employment. Keynes 'hated unemployment because it was stupid and poverty because it was ugly' (Robinson, 1974, p. 10). The differences between methods of economic analysis are not based on varying subject matter but, rather, on different views of economic life. In the case of the Post Keynesians, a different vision of 'what is a good society?' is offered, which requires an alternative economic theory.

Post Keynesians reject the three assumptions of orthodox economic theory: the neutrality of money (changes in money cannot influence real economic variables), gross substitution (everything is substitutable for everything else) and that the economic environment is ergodic (the future can be estimated from past statistical information). Post Keynesianism is a more general theory because it is based on fewer assumptions. The transition process was a non-ergodic process because neither the result nor the relevant probability distributions could have been deduced from the past. The transition was a unique process. Keynes (1936) declared that 'we simply do not know', which clearly was relevant for transition economies.

Post Keynesians are concerned with history, uncertainty, distributional issues and political and economic institutions – all of which, they believe, influence the determination of output and employment. The economic system is defined as an amalgamation of social institutions responsible for satisfying the material needs of the members of the society by producing and distributing the social surplus. Post Keynesians argue that their analysis is concerned with the dynamic behavior of the economic system and resource allocation. The economic system expands or contracts in time from an irrevocable past to an uncertain and statistically unpredictable future. The neoclassical concept that the economy moves to a unique and exogenously established equilibrium has no relevance for the real world. The capitalist economic system lacks any internal self-correcting mechanism for maintaining appropriate levels of aggregate demand, low levels of unemployment and stable prices. Thus government economic policy is essential in avoiding such market failures. Post Keynesians elevate the role of effective demand in a monetary economy as the engine for economic growth. The goal of economic policies and institutional arrangements is to encourage high levels of aggregate demand, with the aim of achieving and maintaining full employment.

For the Post Keynesians, the economy operates in historical time, which implies that its past is unchangeable and that the future is uncertain. Economic actors make decisions with partial ignorance, due to the fact that information does not exist and cannot be inferred from any existing data. Thus, 'history matters and agents are uncertain' (Dunn, 1999, p. 4). Once uncertainty is recognized as a deep attribute of real-world economies, the traditional concept of equilibrium is undermined and the simplistic propositions of laissez-faire are no longer relevant. That is because uncertainty about the future results in economic instability. In a world of rational expectations, the future is a statistical image of the past, while in a world of uncertainty, the current outcome cannot provide information about the future accurately; thus, free markets are not necessary efficient.

It could be argued that Post Keynesian policy recommendations would have been more relevant to the transition economies than neoclassical ones, as the process was characterized by uncertainty. In addition to the uncertainty associated with the normal functioning of the market, the transition process gave rise to 'transition uncertainty', due to institutional and systematic transformation, the behavioral inheritance of the past and political and social changes (Lah and Susjan, 1999, p. 591). The traditional notion of rationality (optimal positions are always calculable) was irrelevant. The procedural notion of rationality (the limited ability to process information) was relevant for transition economies due to the inability of individuals to process information accurately under transition uncertainty.

2.2   What is a Good Society?

The foundation of a good society can be traced to Keynes, since 'he indulged in an agreeable vision of a world where economics has ceased to be important and our grandchildren can begin to lead a civilized life' (Robinson, 1974, p. 10). Post Keynesians are in favor of a social-democratic capitalist system, which implies a variety of property forms and a market with state intervention within a democratic political system. Post Keynesians are seeking only as much freedom as is compatible with a socially desirable outcome. They are therefore prepared to trade freedom for other dimensions such as equality, stability, security, and social justice to bring about a novel synthesis. They disagree with the view that all governments can do is to produce oscillations from equilibrium positions and are unable to influence the long-run level of economic activity. The schism between equity and efficiency in the neoclassical model does not appear. Both equity and efficiency can be achieved as long as there is a redefinition of the concepts of freedom and efficiency. Efficiency does not designate maximization of output at minimum cost but, rather, the maximization of social welfare. This is due to the extensive nature of the externalities associated with production and consumption. 'If it is necessary to give up a bit of market efficiency or a bit of aggregate income, in order to contain democracy-threatening uncertainty, then so be it' (Minsky, 1996b, p. 364). Thus the aim of economic policy should be the development of an open, democratic, civilized society, which should not be sacrificed for narrow efficiency considerations.

Market behavior is consistent with non-self-interested behavior. In fact, self-interest does not adequately explain economic behavior. Individuals are motivated not only by self-interest but also by loyalty, love, compassion, responsibility, and the pursuit of excellence: individuals are also motivated by internalized moral values. Market participants require honesty, maturity and civility to finalize transactions. In the meantime, the economy itself requires ethical behavior by individuals so as to achieve efficiency: 'The difficulty is not getting ethics and history into economics but in imagining or crediting an economy that excludes them' (Brockway, 1998, p. 165). Hence, the exchange of goods and services in an economy is not simply the result of the aggregation of individuals' maximizing behavior, as assumed by neoclassical economists.

Davidson and Davidson (1996, p. 7) argued that this type of individual motivation is based on 'civic values'. It cannot be assumed that interests are well defined and obvious. Information costs, cognitive processes, and ideology are relevant in influencing individual behavior. Consequently, antagonists may have co-operated to achieve common goals – society's goals – based on civic values. The aim of the transition process should be to stimulate a 'reasonable economy' (Schlack, 1996), 'capitalism with a human face' (Minsky, 1996b, p. 358), 'open and humane "shared-prosperity" capitalism' (Minsky and Whalen, 1996–7, p. 161), and a 'civilized society' (Davidson and Davidson, 1996). A civilized society cannot prosper on the hardships of its members. Civic values are the result of a particular historical process, an amalgam of community, social and personal exchanges between members of the society. Consequently, 'the evaluation of public policies [in transition economies] can be very different once we adopt an alternative to the conventional perspective of human well-being' (Whalen, 1996c, p. 8).

Post Keynesians value the primacy of individual values, the principle of private property, and the advantages of the market, stressing their importance in conjunction with the common good, state property and planning. 'A prosperous civil society combines self-interest and civic values so that the citizens may reap the benefits of each' (Davidson and Davidson, 1996, p. 1). The private sector remains the employer of first resort, while the state is employer of last resort. By making full employment the main goal of economic policy, 'a full employment economy is supportive of democracy whereas an economy based on transfer payments supports resentment' (Minsky, 1996b, p. 367).

Discretionary economic management by the state is the means by which economic performance is linked with the community's values, objectives and trade-offs. The use of discretionary power by the central authorities guides individual choices towards social goals. To create the conditions for transition to a civilized society, Post Keynesians stress the importance of an active state in economic affairs. A weak state would be inconsistent with a prospering private sector, due to the fact that capitalism, based on free markets, is inherently cyclical and unstable. A weak state would not be able to hinder the abuse of monopoly power, which undermines the attainment of social goals and economic justice. What the neoclassical economists failed to recognize was that the transition process did not only involve the development of markets but also the development of the state. These two 'cannot be divorced from one another because much of state building is about market building' (Fligstein, 1996, p. 1080). Polanyi (1944, p. 140) revealed a paradox: 'the road to the free market was opened and kept open by an enormous increase in continuous, centrally organized, and controlled interventionism.'

Capitalism's institutional structure must incorporate citizens' limited tolerance for uncertainty and insecurity. When detrimental consequences arise from uncertainty, which cannot be covered by private insurance, it is the responsibility of society to intervene. Economic insecurity must be reduced to make possible prosperity for all the members of society. The welfare state is an expression of the common good – the means of attaining the objectives of society – especially those of minorities and disadvantaged groups. By assisting individual incomes with socially provided funds, 'civility and civic responsibility are promoted' (Minsky, 1996b, p. 364). Poverty in mature market economies is due to an unwillingness to tax and fund essential welfare programs.

Hence government intervention was essential, because the state was responsible for economic performance. State intervention ensured full employment, economic planning guaranteed the achievement of social goals, and state property avoided market failure. This was in total contrast to the neoclassical view, which was the dominant ideology imposed on CEEFSU: 'Everyone who tried to talk about the role of the state or industrial policy was branded a conservative or an institutionalist, unaware of basic truths of economic analysis at best' (Yavlinsky and Braguinsky, 1994, p. 114). The transition economies had the opportunity to establish the institutional prerequisites for market capitalism, which is naturally unstable. These were to provide full employment and economic growth, and reduce insecurity and increase high living standards for successful twenty first century capitalism.

2.3   Speed

For Post Keynesians, the movement towards a market economy could only have been gradual. Institutions, organizations, and patterns of behavior and thinking could not have been changed immediately. There could only have been a slow response by economic actors to the transition process. In addition, the transition program had to be flexible enough to be adapted to the changeable character of the socio-economic conditions. Gradualism allowed for changes and flexibility in the formation and implementation of the transition program. The reforms necessary for a market economy, and the principles and objectives of the transition, could only have been determined and developed on a country-by-country basis. As the process gained momentum, the gradualist procedure enabled elements from the old way of organizing to be slowly replaced by new methods. This required active state intervention. According to the Post Keynesians, the uncontrolled and 'rushed' shock therapy approach to the market process failed and caused a significant reduction in standards of living.

The market is a social institution, comprising a complex network of information, which has been cultivated over time by deliberate human actions. Market outcomes are influenced by past decisions, current conditions and future expectations. Markets operate within a framework of regulations, interpersonal relations and expectations. The superior performance of the market economies may be attributed to their institutional and behavioral structure. Indeed, creating a system of effective enforcement and of moral constraints on behavior is a long and slow process. The successful introduction of the market mechanism in a previously centrally planned economy was possible only after a change in attitudes, thinking, and culture. In mature market economies, information and learning were important to inform economic actors what was expected and to encourage appropriate responses and behavior. Consequently, the development of market relations was the result of a historical process, which takes time.

The emergence of entrepreneurs who were able and willing to take risks is an evolutionary process, not simply a result of free prices. However without a capitalist class to adopt the new opportunities for investment there is only 'destruction' without 'creation' (Csaba, 1995, p. 7). Such destruction would only result in the indefinite postponement of the development of a civilized capitalist class. The collapse of centrally administered socialism and the implementation of the shock therapy model resulted in an uncreative destruction, which encouraged black markets, speculation, unfair trading and illegal activities. As a result, the market system lacked many of the positive attributes that might have been achievable otherwise.

Post Keynesian economists argued that the behavior of economic actors could not have changed as rapidly as the neoclassical transition models assumed, since people would have resisted changes that reduced their living standards. The Polish experience revealed that it was a mistake to assume that state enterprises and banks would have adjusted immediately to market principles (Ellman, 1994, p. 2). The hyperinflation caused by the shock therapy approach created an environment that was not conducive to structural, institutional, and financial change. This not only made shock therapy unworkable, but also retarded substantially the development of a civilized society. Taylor (1994, p. 70) argued that the experience of developing countries had illustrated that it took decades for transitions of this type to materialize. 'In short, market economies cannot be shocked into existence' (Poirot, 1997, p. 237). The development of a civilized society required a gradual transition, implying an unavoidably long process for new market conventions to emerge. Also, it would have given economic actors time to adjust their behavior so as to be able to take advantage of the new opportunities offered.

2.4   Political Structure

The ultimate political process that the Post Keynesians perceived as generating political freedom was democracy. Democracy requires the continuing responsiveness of the ruling authority to the preferences of the members of society, through a structurally defined procedure such as elections. Democracy results in a consensus, which was extremely important for the newly formed market economies. It would allow reforms to take place in a peaceful manner, rather than in an authoritarian fashion. In this way, the government would have gained popular support. In a democratic environment 'societal support for the new regime tends to be conditional, not habitual. The government cannot take political compliance for granted – it must work for it' (Bigler, 1996, p. 220). As such, transitional governments that did not enjoy popular support were unable to create effective anti-inflationary policies. Wittman (1989) argued that democratic political markets were organized to encourage maximization of social welfare, were highly competitive, and politicians were rewarded for their efficient behavior. Indeed political markets possessed the same qualities as efficient economic markets. This does not imply that one is superior to the other.

Post Keynesians recognized that antagonism and conflicting interests exist in society, due to the diversity of human beings. There is no correct line, no correct perception. Once central control was removed in transition economies, political and economic bargaining among individuals and groups emerged. Developing and implementing economic policies in such an environment was a challenging task. Nevertheless, since individuals were not only motivated by self-interested behavior, the Post Keynesians argued, there was an implicit social agreement between members of the society that promoted tolerance and conveyed disagreement in such a way that did not destroy civic values (Davidson and Davidson, 1996, p. 17). Democracy and civic values are internally linked and each sustains and promotes the other. Political civility, tolerance, compromise, and mutual trust are necessary for effective democracy. Society's choice is not simply a matter of adding up individual choices. Rather, it reflects participation in the decision-making process by concerned individuals eager to derive the best knowledge available to make the appropriate choices. Self-interest and civic values all contribute to obtaining a desirable solution from society's point of view. 'Indeed, the experiences of former socialist countries show how inseparable political institutionalization is for the development of civil society' (Fish, 1994, p. 35).

In the transition economies, state intervention was necessary to alter the market outcome in a desirable way, but who would have devised the desirable outcomes and how? For example, an incomes policy could not have been imposed by an independent central bank, because independent monetary authorities were inconsistent with the democratic process. Income, financial and exchange rate policies have distributional effects influencing the whole of society. The political process provides a solution, with continuing policy decision-making, policy correcting and policy remaking based on participatory decision-making. Macroeconomic policies are, in fact, political decisions and, if not accompanied by a democratic process, remain despotic. Democracy in the transitional economies ensured that the process of decision-making reflected the preferences of individuals. Value judgments about economic performance in the name of the people could not have been structured without the same people participating, debating, and compromising. So economic planning would have been the crystallization of a variety of diverse opinions, ideas, and interests. Democracy in the transition economies has contributed to highlighting the civic responsibility of the reform process. The shock therapy insistence on the credibility of economic policy was essentially anti-pluralistic and anti-democratic (Grabel, 2000, p. 1). The credibility criterion discredited pluralism, rejected the value of disagreement, and obstructed the formation of consensus, which are all features of a civilized democratic society. The implementation of the shock therapy approach, which effectively ignored the political structure, did not allow optimism about the development of the civil political institutions, Post Keynesians argued.

2.5 Ideological Structure

The Post Keynesians developed an appropriate ideology to encourage an acceptable role for each economic actor based on civic values. Ideology was a means to justify state intervention in the name of society. Neoclassical transition models associated governments with bureaucracy, waste and corruption and markets with individualism. Post Keynesians did not share this concept. Actually, the implementation of the neoclassical transition model resulted in a cultural and ideological vacuum. While individualism, private property and the market were still dominant forces there was also a need to bring together the goals of individuals and society. Market power was not simply the result of the actions of the government. The market power of enterprises was due to economies of scale. The market power of unions was due to specialization and industrialization. However, the use of the discretionary power of the government could have improved the outcome of the economic system by reducing market power. The goals of economic policy would have been derived through the political process. The government should have used economic incentives to encourage individual behavior appropriate to the social goals. Regulations could have been used where individual motivation was lacking. Individualism should have been combined with the common good, necessitating government intervention.

2.6 Initial Conditions

The transition process took place in a specific dynamic cultural context, characterized by instability and unpredictability. There was no single strategy:

'it is extremely naive to expect simple copying to be the shortest way to heaven' (Csaba, 1995, p. 133). Ultimate success depended on whether or not sufficient non-economic conditions prevailed, and this included political, ideological, and cultural dimensions, as the Post Keynesians argued. CEEFSU were characterized by widely different civilizations, history, religion, and different levels of economic and political development. This strongly influenced the way transition problems were solved, since capitalism comes in many varieties.

However, introducing private property and markets could not have in any way delivered success, since the problems associated with the transition process involved the specific socio-economic conditions of the society in question. The neoclassical transition models 'ignore [d] the real environment in which the economy is located' (Rider, 1994a, p. 595). The shock therapy approach did not incorporate the differences between countries, even though they were recognized. 'Instead economic, political, and social differences across countries are treated as aberrations from the model's assumptions which will be ironed out over time with further market liberalization' (Smyth, 1998, pp. 386–7). For the neoclassical transition models, any endeavor to embody the non-economic factors would only have resulted in undermining the operation of the free market process. Although the characteristics of each transition economy differed, the neoclassical transition models did not think this important enough to justify a change in strategy. This was due to the fact that transition programs were devised by technical experts who were totally ignorant of the economic, political, cultural and history of the country in question. It was not accidental that Central, Eastern Europe and the Baltic states are performing much better than the former Soviet Union, since centrally administered socialism was established a lot later in these regions (Smyth, 1998, p. 368). Thus Post Keynesians disagreed with the neoclassical economists because they believed that culture and ideology and, in general, initial conditions were extremely important. Institutions and social practices function and are founded on customs, traditions, and habits which are deeply ingrained and only slowly deserted and replaced by others.

Economic processes are generally path-dependent (Arestis and Sawyer, 1993, p. 9). Consequently, the transition process was a path-dependent process that relied on the initial conditions, the policies initiated and the external environment. The economy, history, politics and government intervention were inextricably linked in the development of a market system. Reform strategists should not, Post Keynesians argued, have ignored these factors.

3 Secondary Elements of the Post Keynesian Model of Transition

3.1 Price Liberalisation-Stabilisation

The implementation of the neoclassical transition models was based on Say's Law: the level of production was the result of the supply side of the economy.

Thus it was essential to get the prices correct at the beginning of the transition process. 'Cutting wages and eliminating price distortions are the only means that the mainstream theory has in hand for driving the economy toward high employment' (Taylor, 1994, p. 72). What neoclassical economists failed to recognize was that the forces of aggregate demand, and not supply, determined the level of output and thus the level of employment. In the labor market, the rigidity of wages was not the cause of unemployment. Wage or price flexibility was neither a necessary nor a sufficient condition for full employment equilibrium. Also, the aggregate supply constraint was neither necessary nor sufficient to explain unemployment. Flexible wages increased uncertainty, without having an influence on employment; planning was made laborious. Decreasing money wages would have resulted in a reduction of profit expectations. The volume of employment depended on aggregate demand factors, not on wage rates. In a non-ergodic world the cause of involuntary unemployment is the existence of non-producible assets, such as money, which are held for liquidity purposes. In contrast to Friedman's point of view, producible goods are not substitutes for money: 'Paraphrasing Keynes one could say that liquidity preference has to do with an urge for inaction, rather than action' (Dequech, 1999, p. 415). The explanation of unemployment lies in the money market and not in the labor market. Unemployment is a natural outcome of a money-using laissez-faire economy. Neoclassical economists, by assuming that Say's Law holds, only solve the unemployment problem by assumption and not by economic analysis. In a non-monetary economy there is no rational explanation for the existence of unemployment. Keynes (1936, p. 192) argued that those orthodox economists who relied on rigidities to explain unemployment were 'weaker spirits ... [whose] ... common sense cannot help breaking in – with injury to their logical consistency'.

It was questionable whether the immediate freeing of prices in transition economies would have stimulated growth. The restructuring of the economy and the reallocation of resources takes some time. It was better to have enterprises operating, even though they were inefficient, and give them the opportunity to become efficient, rather than close them through immediate price liberalization. Freeing prices encouraged speculation, which did not stimulate increases in output and efficiency. Thus, in the presence of very rapid inflation, flexible prices would have been no better than fixed prices in achieving efficient resource allocation. Restructuring and reallocation of resources stimulated efficiency due to influential non-economic factors, such as expectations and political stability, as well as free price signals. The enterprises' response to shock therapy was very different from the neoclassical adjustment process. Enterprises reduced output, but did not improve their efficiency, and increased prices based on a mark-up pricing scheme (Kuznetsov, 1992, pp. 475, 476). In reality, due to the implementation of the shock therapy model, the mechanism of self-correction for the misallocation of resources was not created.

What the neoclassical transition models did not recognize was that prices are determined in a social market, not just an economic market, by custom, power, and competition. In particular, in oligopolistic and monopolistic market environments, prices are based on a mark-up principle. As normal cost is quite constant, mark-ups are established in the short run by custom, convention, and reasonableness, and in the long run by competitive pressures and market power. In this environment, firms may maintain prices by reducing profits in the face of the threat of new entrants. Prices are not a means of resource allocation but, rather, a way of generating funds for the expansion of the firm. Enterprises in mature market economies implement pricing procedures based on normal costs and target rates of return. Likewise, enterprises under central administration applied mark-up pricing. There was no reason for enterprises to change their pricing policy with the introduction of market relations. Flexibility in prices is achieved by flexibility in mark-ups. Whenever firms are required to increase investment and lack the internal funds, they increase prices by raising mark-ups. Profit maximization is not the ultimate goal; rather, firms aim to generate enough internal funds to finance planned investment, subject to some minimum profit constraints. Prices are not linked with current demand, but with future demand, which helps determine investment expenditure sufficient to satisfy such forecasts. All these factors could be summed up as the 'animal spirits' of the entrepreneurs. The institutional environment in which firms make decisions determines these animal spirits. Subjective and psychological elements also influence animal spirits, which are partially endogenous and in part exogenous. In such a world, it is an objective fact that the future is uncertain in a non-predictable way and, as such it is natural that investment would be volatile.

During the transition process, there should not have been a concern over 'equilibrium' prices, because reforms took place in a state of disequilibrium. Neoclassical transition models were based on an obsession with static efficiency, while the transition process was a dynamic phenomenon, making neoclassical economics irrelevant. 'Nothing stands still, the system moves on, and the future is always different from the past' (Peterson, 1996, p. 157). Due to uncertainty, investment was reduced in transition economies. This exaggerated reductions in aggregate demand that, in turn, reduced output and increased inflation and unemployment. There was a 'capital strike' (Taylor, 1994, p. 65). In such circumstances, it was the role of the government to intervene and stimulate the economy with public investment. Public investment would have also crowded in private investment by reducing production costs and creating a favorable investment climate. As a result, wage income would have grown, stimulating non-inflationary growth in consumption.

In the Kaleckian and Keynesian traditions, savings adjust to investment, rather than the reverse, which is assumed in neoclassical theory. Thus credit has to be created to finance investment ahead of the generation of the corresponding saving. Due to the endogenous nature of money, credit is created by the banking system. High proportions of profits are saved, and such profits form a substantial part of total savings. Hence there is a close link between profits, savings and investment. 'The investment market can become congested through a shortage of cash. It can never become congested through a shortage of savings' (Davidson, 1994, p. 132). Almost all corporate investment is financed out of retained corporate profits, while net household saving is close to zero and, in addition, households mainly lend to each other in aggregate (Palley, 1998a, p. 100; Asimakopulos, 1979, p. 64). In transition economies, the banking system was not familiar with the new economic conditions and was unable to create the necessary credit. Profits were not adequate to provide savings, due to substantial reductions in output. These profits were also spent on imports or deposited in foreign banks. Savings were not available from the previous generation because there had been no savings incentives under the previous governments. As a result, the government had to appropriate and direct savings into productive investment. Such mobilization of savings could only have taken place via the state-run development functions of the new government. This could have been part of an industry policy designed to stimulate demand and encourage access to capital, skill and infrastructure enhancement.

Inflation was an immediate problem faced by transition economies as a result of introducing market relations. The shock therapy approach favored liberalizing prices immediately, under conditions of macroeconomic disequilibrium, while still having effectively soft budget constraints and a monopolistic structure. The Post Keynesians argued that this could only have bred inflation. What neoclassical economists did not realize was that inflation was not necessarily the result of 'excess demand', but rather arose from a fundamental conflict over the distribution of income. Conventional instruments of fiscal and monetary policy *per se* could have not controlled inflation. 'The control of inflation requires something more than control of the stock of money (even assuming that such control were possible)' (Arestis, Dunn and Sawyer, 1999, p. 541). The shock therapy supporters recommended severe fiscal and monetary restraint. Aggregate demand reduction through inflationary wage cuts was an essential part of the shock therapy model. However, this only resulted in temporarily reducing inflation, and the social costs were high, with persistent unemployment, reduced capacity utilization, and low economic growth. In such circumstances, it was irrational to initiate immediate price liberalization. However, eventually, moderate levels of inflation increase income and the inflationary effects of expansionary policies do not substantially influence the long-run output level (Atesoglu, 1998, p. 491).

Post Keynesians favored an incomes policy together with price controls, increased imports, and a buffer stock policy for important resources and agricultural products to ensure adequate supply and price stability in the long term. A tax-based incomes policy is a 'clever' anti-inflationary policy (Davidson, 1994, p. 149). It is consistent with a civilized society, because it combines self-interest and civic values in the determination of wages. Under a tax-based incomes policy, firms that pay a wage increase above the socially acceptable non-inflationary level, based upon the average labor productivity growth, would be penalized by higher taxes. Davidson, (1994, pp. 150–1) compares the tax-based incomes policy to road regulations controlling driving behavior. While speed limits are set at a socially acceptable level, the magnitude of the limit is based on the driving conditions. A tax-based incomes policy is fundamentally linked with expansionary fiscal and monetary policies. As a result, 'planned recessions would be a thing of the past' (Davidson, 1994, p. 151). An incomes policy was essential for an effective anti-inflationary policy. Surprisingly, both neoclassical models also recommended an incomes policy.

For the development of market relations, according to the neoclassical transition model, it was enough to remove state control and economic planning from the economy and introduce private property. Market relations would only then have been the natural outcome, a necessary and sufficient condition for wealth creation. Post Keynesians disagreed, believing that markets did not grow organically; rather they must be created. As Polanyi (1944, p. 139) stated 'there is nothing natural about laissez-faire. Free markets could never have existed had things been left to take their course ... laissez-faire was created by the state'. The development of market relations could not have been the responsibility of the market; there was a need for government action.

3.2   Privatization

Large-scale privatization was not essential to overcome shortages as the neoclassical transition models stipulated. It appears that the soft budget constraint explained inflation rather than shortages (Ellman, 1994, p. 11). However, according to the Post Keynesians, selling state enterprises to the highest bidder, as recommended by neoclassical gradualist economists, violated equity principles. The amount of savings available in the transition economies was not enough to finance a large privatization drive. The only people who could have purchased firms were those who had benefited under the previous regime through black-market and illegal activities. The typical answer from mainstream economists – 'the firm is worth whatever someone is willing to pay for it' or 'let the market decide' – were problematic where there was not yet a market and where, in fact, the explicit motive for the sales was to create a market. There were political as well as equity reasons against auctioning firms, because there would have been a lack of support from the majority of the people: the true owners of state assets. Meanwhile, contrary to the neoclassical transition model, where culture did not matter, Stark (1992) argued that the privatization strategies pursed had a high degree of national path-dependence. This resulted in 'a complex mosaic of national and regional pathways' (Smith, 1996, p. 135).

The superiority of private property over state property, as a number of economists argued, should not be interpreted as implying that state property did not have a role. There was a role for state property in areas where private property did not function efficiently, that is, whenever there was market failure. The contentious issue is whether state property should be instituted beyond the areas of market failure. Post Keynesians would argue that there is a role for state property beyond market failure. In addition Post Keynesians claimed that market failure was extensive, encompassing, for example, market power and information. Their main contention, however, was that the majority of property should still remain in private hands.

Vickers and Yarrow (1991, pp. 113–8) argued that empirical evidence demonstrated that private property had efficiency advantages in competitive conditions, but was not superior when there was market power. Meanwhile, when state owned firms were subjected to competition similar to private firms, their performance was superior. It was not ownership that determined efficiency but environmental factors. Thus the development of competitive conditions and a regulatory framework should have been the goal, not ownership. The case for privatization in the transition economies became even less clear when the underdeveloped markets for capital, corporate control, and managerial labor were considered. The absence of a capital market where take-overs could be initiated, the lack of corporate control in the form of institutional norms and the substantial imperfections in the managerial labor market could only have promoted managerial failure. Under these conditions, enterprise managers did not behave in an 'optimal' way, as prescribed by the neoclassical model. This actually facilitated 'spontaneous privatization' – the transformation of state enterprises into joint-stock companies – whereby the managers became the new owners.

The Post Keynesians concluded that no form of ownership was perfect. Private firms suffered market failures, a divergence between private and social benefits and costs. Public enterprises experienced government failures, a divergence between political and social benefits and costs. Therefore private ownership with competitive and regulatory markets, while eliminating government failure, still gave rise to market failure. The more desirable ownership structure depended on the magnitude of the imperfections. For this reason Stark (1996, p. 1023) argued that 'it is not in finding the right mix of public and private but in finding the right organisation of diversity to yield both adaptability and accountability that post-socialist societies face their greatest challenge'. Consequently, there were no firm guidelines with respect to appropriate ownership structure. The experience of mature market economies demonstrated the variety of ownership structures in these economies and the changing character of ownership structure over time. As such, the framework of political and social institutions, traditions and history, and the state of economic growth of the particular country, had to be included in the analysis of the development of property relations. Consequently, there was no single ideal strategy with respect to privatization. It had to be done on a case-by-case basis, depending on the type of asset, the internal organizational structure, the level of technology, and the need for capital.

The implementation of the shock therapy model of privatization resulted in a cruel deception, in which many individuals colluded, a few profited, and the public at large was the great loser. Privatization, in an environment of hyperinflation and instability, could only have bred corruption. Instead of the development of an efficient private ownership structure, managers responded to the high level of uncertainty by breaking their firms into numerous joint stock and limited liability companies along divisional, factory, departmental and workshop lines. This gave rise to a new form of ownership, which Stark (1996, p. 1014) named 'recombinant property': 'recombinant property is a particular kind of portfolio management. It is an attempt to have a resource that can be justified or assessed by more than one standard'. In this way, managers and banks controlled and reaped the benefits of the most profitable parts of the enterprise, while the unprofitable, loss-making, and inefficient parts became the responsibility of the state. Recombinant property did not increase efficiency because, firstly, it did not reduce monopoly power, since the same management effectively still controlled the numerous break-ups. In addition, there was a loss of economies of scale. Rather than genuine restructuring, there was a transfer of the responsibility to state.

The initial distribution of private property was paramount for the Post Keynesians, in contrast to the shock therapy approach, since the initial distribution of property would have determined those members of society who would have started from an advantageous position. In an environment in which market power was permanent, due to the nature of technology and industrialization, the 'free' market process would not have been able to alleviate any of the arising inequalities. Rather, these inequalities would have increased in magnitude. In relation to whether restructuring should have preceded privatization, the answer was clear for the Post Keynesians. They believed it was the responsibility of the government to use discretionary measures to ensure the viability of enterprises before and after privatization. The government should assist and equip enterprises with the essential internal structures necessary to survive the competitive market process. Moreover, the maintenance of state enterprises facilitated the development of a civilized society, since the transition would not have necessarily involved a massive increase in unemployment. As Bucknall (1997, p. 12) proposed, 'the Russian experience suggests that privatization first is not the best way to proceed'.

In summary, for the Post Keynesians, there could have been a transition to a market economy without a substantial change in property ownership. This was because ownership, as such, was less important than competition, the incentive structure, and the nature of regulatory policies. There would have been no gain to society if state enterprises were replaced by private monopolies. Thus restructuring and the establishment of the regulatory framework needed to precede privatization. However, 'some critical minimum of property rights reform may have to be undertaken quickly, for democracy without a solid market economy is unthinkable' (Van Brabant, 1991a, p. 35). Post Keynesian methods of privatization would have incorporated restitution of state property to the rightful owners and liquidation of enterprises that could not have been revived. In addition, efficiency and equity would have guided the process and this would only have been possible through the distribution of free shares to the people. The government would have needed to retain a percentage of shares as a source of revenue, with the balance going to the workers, to pension funds, in order to finance retirement benefits, and the rest to the population. Such an exercise would have attracted political support from the people. In addition, free shares to the workers would have provided them with a financial incentive to restructure their operation into a more efficient one based on their 'inside' knowledge. The transfer of state property to financial intermediaries was another alternative to outright privatization. The advantages were that it was less time consuming and people with specialized skills would have been in charge. Post Keynesians view labor-managed firms favorably. Post Keynesians believed worker motivation would have increased to make enterprises efficient and profitable, at the same time mobilizing support for the transition process. Labor-managed firms required government financial assistance and an appropriate institutional structure so that they were not disadvantaged. Labor-managed firms could have become a transitional mechanism, allowing people gradually to adjust their behavior in a participatory environment. It was up to the reformers to exploit and further develop the existing cooperative property structure.

3.3 Institutions

Post Keynesians have been criticized by institutionalists on the grounds that their study of institutions is unsubstantial. Hodgson (1988, p. 241) argued that there exists a foundation for the extension of Post Keynesian analysis using the institutional paradigm: 'it was with institutionalism as a midwife that Keynesian macroeconomics was born' (Hodgson, 1993, p. 260). Actually, Post Keynesians are now realizing that the institutional framework can assist their understanding of economic behavior. A synergistic synthesis of a Post Keynesian-Institutional approach is attempted in this section with special reference to the transition economies.

Most of the institutional literature on transition perceived that the creation of guaranteed property rights was the only ultimate goal consistent with the neoclassical approach to transition. Consequently, the neoclassical transition model recommended economic policies independent of the present institutional structure because these were supposed to be present in all societies. This presumably reflected their basic assumption of perfect knowledge. In the certain or calculable probabilistic world of neoclassical economics, there is no need for forward contracts since there cannot be any deviation from the foreseeable agreed terms of the contract. However, equations do not embody institutions.

For example, monetary policy can never be independent of institutional structure in the financial sector (Arestis and Howells, 1992, p. 135).

For the Post Keynesians, economic policy cannot ignore institutions since the institutional framework of an economic system is a basic element of its economic dynamics. Economic processes, which are the subject of Post Keynesianism, are dynamic, while economic equilibria, the subject of neoclassicism, are static. Post Keynesians emphasized path-dependence, the presence of which results in past states influencing later conditions. Economic action, in times of uncertainty, is part of the economy in real time. The economy cannot be separated from history: 'institutions matter and history matters' (Smyth, 1998, p. 378). Thus, 'our actions are informed by history and limited by history' (Brockway, 1998, p. 164). Economic action takes place in historical time where past experiences – we are creatures of the past – together with the incremental evolution of institutions, influence present actions that determine the future. The future is different from the past: 'This means that the system is indeterminate because the future is indeterminate' (Peterson, 1996, p. 156). Economic behavior is highly influenced by institutions, since individuals are not only atomistic beings, but also most importantly social beings. That is because economic behavior is positioned in socially constructed institutional structures and not in an impersonal market process. Economic behavior takes place within a 'socio-economic context', with individual constraints 'which promote and prevent, reward and punish his or her actions' (Kregel, et al., 1992, p. 85). Political-economic reforms fail not because market liberalization proceeds quickly or slowly, but because supportive institutional reforms develop too slowly. The pace of institutional development determines the pace of reforms.

Culture was extremely important in the development of the institutional structure. Culture provided a language-based conceptual framework for encoding, interpreting, processing, and utilizing information, thus influencing the way informal constraints were specified. Conventions and norms were culture-specific. The future is uncertain and not calculable, so rational expectations in the neoclassical sense are impossible. Most economic activity is based on accepted conventions. For example, preferences were not exogenous in transition economies. Socially defined conventions about consumption substantially influenced consumer preferences. Because information was difficult to acquire, and limited, individuals depended on socially determined behavior and conventions. Thus the income available to the consumer in transition economies, combined with socially defined conventions about consumption patterns, determined consumer choice. The neoclassical transition models, however, ignored the specific elements of culture in the development of the institutional structure. In the neoclassical transition models there was no concern with the efficient design of institutions, the political and cultural consequences and how the existing institutions influenced transition to a market economy. Shock therapists ignored the importance of implanted social institutions and the role of the state in the market. In contrast, Post Keynesians stressed that 'actors, ideas, and politics are important to the shape of new institutions' (Fligstein, 1996, p. 1080). Institutions develop as a result of local characteristics and a specific cultural framework; that is, social experience and social norms. This was because pre-existing institutions influence the shape of what would have been developed. Hence the development of the institutional structure should be conceived as a path-dependent process. This meant readjusting existing institutions to the changing economic framework. Institutional change was path-dependent and culturally dependent, making 'the process of transition so difficult and uncertain' (Grossman, 1997, p. 254). Institutions could not have changed at the same pace or developed into a single institutional form and should not, therefore, have been treated as single variables.

Societies bolster a productive balance between self-interest and civic values through specific institutions. The historical development of markets was associated with pre-existing institutions that made possible the development of market societies in such a way as to maintain 'liberty, prosperity, and justice in their societies for many generations' (Davidson and Davidson, 1996, p. 15). Consequently, the aim of market institutions was to encourage self-interest and, at the same time, safeguard the society from any tarnish of civic values by individualism. Institutions control the diverse individual interests in an efficient manner. Failure by suitable institutional structures to restrain the pursuit of self-interest inhibits the development of a cohesive society. This, the Post Keynesians argued, was exactly what happened in transition economies. Corruption could not have been reduced in transition economies until the institutions of a market economy were fully established. When the state started to disintegrate, which resulted in an inability to foster a civilized institutional framework, the only path remaining was that of a criminal sociopath. In such circumstances, the Post Keynesians would have been in agreement with the new institutionalists that 'neither self-enforcement by parties nor trust can be completely successful ... Equally, however, the returns on opportunism, cheating and shirking rise' (North, 1990, p. 35) in transition economies. Consequently, a broad variety of institutions of non-market coordination were necessary for high-performance market orientation in transition economies.

If the members of the society loose their confidence in state institutions to enforce contracts, the monetary system breaks down and the society returns to barter. The experience of the transition economies reveals exactly this outcome, because it was impossible to attain macroeconomic stabilization prior to an appropriate institutional development. The shock therapy approach removed, in one shot, the old institutional structure, without replacing it, allowing the free market to set up the appropriate institutional structure. Relying on the market to produce efficient institutions and concluding that their survival and superiority was the result of efficiency, ignored path-dependence, and multiple equilibria. This was the reason for the substantial fall in output, which reinforced the Post Keynesian proposition that economic reforms should not have been initiated before the introduction of institutional reforms. The privatization of state enterprises should have taken place at a much later stage, once an efficient institutional structure had been established.

Contrary to the neoclassical transition models, the setting up of the institutional structure required government action: 'it cannot be left to chance or left until later' (Rider, 1994b, p. 8). Government institutions provide certainty in an uncertain market system. The institutional structure not only facilitates the smooth functioning of the market process, but also provides solutions to market failures. There had to be a regulatory framework that internalized any externalities. Particularly in terms of monopoly power, the aim of the institutional structure should have been to restrain market power and ensure that there was adequate competition. Consequently, 'the solution then is for countries in transition to 'get the institutions right' (not prices, as neoclassical theorists have maintained)' (Grossman, 1997, p. 251). Should the institutional structure have been developed as a result of free market transactions? Post Keynesians would have disagreed absolutely. Firstly, it would have been an extremely time-consuming process. In addition, the market was incapable of satisfying effective demand immediately, so it would have been unable to respond to the immediate demand for a complicated institutional structure. Accordingly, the institutional structure could not have been left entirely to market forces: its development was an active and deliberate process. The 'deficiencies [of the shock therapy model] are associated with the side-stepping of the institutional hysteresis associated with any market or government action' (Yavlinsky and Braguinsky, 1994, p. 90).

Institutions embody habits, routines, and customs employed by economic actors, including the government and financial institutions. Informal constraints, which were culturally embedded, would not have changed immediately in response to the changes in the formal rules. Informal constraints have great survival potential because, in spite of changes in formal rules, they resolve basic exchange problems among the participants, whether they are social, political, or economic. The inconsistency between formal market institutions and the informal ones 'will always lead to different interpretations and applications of such laws' (Grossman, 1997, p. 252), producing outcomes that could have had significant implications for the effectiveness of the reform program. The overall constraints would have to have been restructured to produce a new equilibrium, or the unresolved tension would have resulted in political instability. Simply changing formal institutions is not sufficient. However, informal institutions are hard to change and require a gradual process.

The analysis of alternative strategies for institutional development revealed contrasting results for the Post Keynesians and shock therapists. The shock therapy approach, while prescribing an immediate transition to the market economy, argued that it was only through a process of trial and error that the market could deliver efficient operative institutions, thus necessitating a gradual process of institutional development. Meanwhile, the Post Keynesians, while advocating a gradual transition process, recommended immediate state intervention to develop, implement and enforce market institutions to create the pre-conditions for a civilized market economy: effectively an institutional shock therapy. The most appropriate method depended on how social reality was viewed and what was considered acceptable, desirable and feasible. It depended on assumptions about economic behavior, the method of analysis and the goals associated with the transition process. Essentially, the choice depended on what was considered to be efficient: a market mechanism providing market-produced institutions, or state intervention providing state-produced market institutions.

3.4   Monetary Policy and the Financial System

In contrast to the neoclassical economists, who consider money to be neutral, the Post Keynesians view money as 'a dominant – if not the single most important – institution in systems of market capitalism' (Peterson, 1996, p. 157). Money is not just a medium of exchange and a measure of value but also a store of value which, in a monetary economy, individuals value more than income itself: it is a means of limiting losses in a profit-and-loss economy. The Post Keynesians view non-neutrality of money and endogenous money supply as crucial in inducing changes in the real sector. Non-neutrality of money exists under both flexible and sticky wages and prices. As a result, it is not possible to split the capitalist economy into separate real and monetary sectors. Monetary policy is extremely important, since it has implications for income distribution. Post Keynesians propose that monetary policy, money, and finance are integral in understanding the economy.

Post Keynesian monetary theory begins with money as a unit of account. Production for the market is always monetary production under uncertainty, and money can never be neutral in an economy that operates in historical time. Consequently, Post Keynesians require an active domestic and international monetary policy. In the Keynes-Kalecki-Kaldor tradition, investment is an autonomous factor. It cannot be represented as a stable, downward-sloping function of the interest rate. The autonomy of investment is possible because of the credit system from which firms can borrow. Investment determines how much credit firms seek from outside sources. Credit often comes from the banking system, which leads to the creation of money. Furthermore, a supplier of investment goods may grant credit, for example, to the purchaser. Thus, the level of credit taken on by the firm is determined by, rather than being the determinant of, the level of investment. Essentially, the stock of money, in contrast to the monetarist view, is endogenous. It is determined by the level of investment, which also implies that investment takes place independently of the level of current savings. However, banks and financial institutions may be short of liquidity as a result of monetary tightening initiated by the central bank, or may be unwilling to lend due to excessive risk, or firms may be constrained by a low level of corporate cash flow. The endogeneity of money, as a result of credit provided by financial institutions, is central to the Post Keynesian view of the economic world. Money responds to the needs of production through the credit provided by the banks. The central bank determines the rediscount rate and the banks provide loans to creditworthy customers at the rediscount rate, plus a risk-related mark-up. New loans create new deposits.

The development of a modern banking system in the transition economies was essential, the Post Keynesians argued, because it established the relations between debtors and creditors which were the foundation of capitalism (Kregel et al., 1992, p. 1). A financial system, which has the ability to create money as a result of market transactions, was essential in the operation of a market economy. However, the financial system is 'a necessary but not sufficient condition for lifting an economy out of an unemployment morass' (Davidson and Davidson, 1996, p. 150). Liquidity is essential for economic activity in a market economy where the future is uncertain and full of surprises: 'Liquidity is freedom' (Davidson, 1994, p. 225). However, any time individuals wanted to increase their liquidity this comes at a cost to consumption resulting in a reduction in output and employment. It is the responsibility of the government to increase government expenditure, effectively acting as a lender of last resort, when there is a deficiency of private spending, to ensure full employment in a civilized economy. The expansion of government expenditure results in an increase in the demand for money and the banking system responds by endogenously expanding the money supply. This endogenous money supply increase will take place *pari passu* with additional orders for purchases of goods and inputs, which is correlated with an income-generated finance process.

With respect to the financial structure, the neoclassical transition model examined the problem of transition in the context of a hard budget constraint. A soft budget constraint would have violated the concept of relative scarcity, a fundamental aspect of the market process. The recommended hard budget constraint was based on the assumption that savings determine investment and also that Say's Law applied. Experience, however, showed that the introduction of a hard budget constraint, especially for state-owned enterprises, did not establish a hard budget constraint. 'This is absolutely unthinkable under the monetarist paradigm but quite natural in other frameworks of economic analysis' (Yavlinsky and Braguinsky, 1994, p. 100). That is because neoclassical economics does not have a theory of money and so, therefore, is not applicable to the real world (Wray, 1996, p. 141).

The fact that demand for credit by enterprises is endogenously determined is an important feature distinguishing the Post Keynesian from the neoclassical approach. Banks respond to the demand for loans and not to the independent demand for deposits. For the individual firm, at the micro level and in the absence of borrowing, the level of savings determines the level of investment. Conversely, in the context of the whole economy, at the macro level, it is investment that determines savings. What holds for one enterprise does not hold for all enterprises. Hard budget constraints do not really exist because, given the cost of obtaining credit, firms have a soft budget constraint whether they operate in a market or a centrally administered system. Any move towards a market economy would certainly have failed if reformers ignored the existence of the soft budget constraint. Thus 'the problem of shortage can in no way be solved by reducing the role of planning and state control in the economy as suggested by Kornai' (Szego, 1991, p. 336). After the implementation of neoclassical stabilization policies in the transition economies, the soft-budget constraint persisted and so too did the output reduction due to uncertainty. Consequently, Post Keynesians argued, there was a need for government intervention in financial markets. The government's role was to increase confidence in the financial system by providing the appropriate incentives and regulation for the development of a healthy financial system.

The new economic conditions required the development of a two-tiered banking system comprising the central bank, which prints money and controls the stock of money, and the private banking sector, which accepts deposits and provides credit. For the Post Keynesians, the central bank should not have been independent, as the neoclassical transition model claimed, because this would have required the central bank to formulate monetary policy independently of civic values, which required full employment. 'The tendency toward independent central banking (both at national and international levels) can be seen as a rejection of the spirit of Keynes since it has become associated with the idea that the control of inflation must dominate other macroeconomic policy objectives' (Arestis and Bain, 1995, p. 161). An independent central bank model did not allow governments to use the money supply to fund budget deficits. Thus the only option available to transition economies was to reduce the budget deficit by reducing government expenditure in an environment of high pre-existing social transition costs. The theoretical and empirical suggestion of the link between the independence of the central bank and price stability is the result of very restrictive assumptions, based on very strong and narrow views of how the economy operates. Additionally, banking innovations have undermined monetary targeting.

The removal of bad debts from the balance sheet of the banks was essential, so that they could function effectively. The process of liability destruction involved the removal of all liabilities that were not based on economic assets, thus facilitating the restructuring of the financial system. Hence the Post Keynesians recommended government intervention to establish a healthy financial system, which facilitated restructuring. This required some banks to be state owned to counterbalance the market power of private commercial banks.

3.5   Fiscal Policy

The transition economies have suffered from chronic fiscal problems. Private enterprises have excelled at avoiding tax under the current inadequate institutional structure. Depression has accompanied privatization, inhibiting any increase in tax revenue. Therefore, Post Keynesians argued that transition economies, to achieve a successful transformation, had to take into account the revenue factors when considering such policy areas as privatization and international trade. Aggregate demand is the key policy instrument in influencing the economic activity in a market economy. Post Keynesians argue that the level of aggregate demand, determined by individual actions, is insufficient to create full employment at the going real wage. It is the responsibility of the government to adjust aggregate demand to the level of full employment since, in a decentralized market; there are no automatic mechanisms to ensure an appropriate level of aggregate demand. Thus budget deficits during recessions, as in the transition case, were essential to maintain full employment. However, these budget deficits should have been the result of productive government expenditure on private-public infrastructure development in order to stimulate employment and, thus, promote a civilized society. The deficits should not have been due to reductions in taxes, such as the Reagan supply-side deficits. Increasing investment is much more effective than increasing consumption; that is because investment directly influences aggregate supply and consumption indirectly. Davidson (1994, p. 79; 1996, p. 503) characterizes government fiscal policy as a 'balancing wheel'. This recommendation was in contrast to the neoclassical-dominated international institutions' proposal, which imposed the shock therapy approach. The International Monetary Fund (IMF) and World Bank's conditional loans were based on reducing government expenditure and achieving a balanced budget (Martinez-Vazquez, Rioja, Skogstad and Valen, 2001, p. 503).

For the Post Keynesians, the development of a tax system should be based not only on revenue considerations but also on the social and cultural background of the society. There is a definite link between tax compliance and civic values. In a civilized society, there is a conscious payment of taxes by members of the society and non-compliance is not considered an alternative: 'Taxes are the price of civilization' (Tobin, 1994, p. 338). Non-compliance is the result of the diminishing role of civic values in a society. In these circumstances, the decision whether to pay taxes or not comes under scrutiny as a result of the 'rational' computation associated with the benefits and costs of deceiving. In addition, enforcement mechanisms for non-compliance will be ineffective as long as there is an imbalance between self-interest and civic values. Simplicity of the tax system encourages compliance. The development of a civilized society in the transition economies would have encouraged tax-paying norms consistent with civic values, whereby individuals would have had to pay their taxes as part of their moral duty. 'In a civilized society where civic values and self-interest flourish, the citizens must be willing not only to die for their country but also to pay for it' (Davidson and Davidson, 1996, p. 217). This perception of tax-paying norms was in contrast to the neoclassical transition models, in which individuals were motivated not by moral duty but, rather, by self-interest and according to which it would have been impossible to increase tax compliance. Tax-paying norms, appropriate for a civilized market economy, required a radical transformation of behavior by individuals previously under a centrally administered structure. This was in line with the Post Keynesian goal of developing a society based on civic values.

3.6   International Trade and Foreign Aid

Post Keynesians recognized the positive benefits associated with international trade. Meanwhile, because open economies are more complex than closed economies, the market outcome would have been even less likely to be a socially desirable outcome. Active government intervention was essential from the start to restructure external trade and payments appropriate to a civilized market economy.

Contrary to the neoclassical view, Post Keynesians argued that an appropriate level of protection would have been essential for enterprises to survive on an uneven playing field. The experience of mature market economies revealed that there development and industrialization was strongly linked with protectionist measures. Consequently, globalization did not automatically result in trade liberalization; rather, there seemed to be powerful forces that supported the construction of trade barriers. In the Post Keynesian model the effect of protection on the prices of finished products is quite small and due mainly to tariffs on inputs, while the effect on production depends on demand. In the neoclassical model, the effect of protection on prices of finished goods is complete, while materials tariffs are never significant and production effects are entirely determined by supply. Thus tariffs produce a demand and not a supply reaction, and price changes are minor (Norman, 1996, pp. 523, 528). Consequently, based on the Post Keynesian model, transition economies should not have expected a substantial reduction in prices or inflation by the removal of tariffs.

Post Keynesians argued that a flexible exchange rate system encouraged only financial currency speculation and not production, discouraged forward contracts, and encouraged stagnation in the domestic and world economy. It prompted countries to solve the problems of unemployment and inflation by shifting them onto their trading partners, in an uncivilized way. Post Keynesians note that *The Financial Times* and the *Economist*, which supported the freely floating exchange rate and pressured the international community to adopt it, have changed their view. They have admitted it was a failure and that the advantages were grossly overestimated (Davidson, 1994, p. 264; Davidson and Davidson, 1996, p. 182).

Under a flexible exchange system expansionary monetary and fiscal policy result in exchange rate depreciation, a reduction in aggregate demand, inflation and capital flight, leading to both budget and trade deficits. 'Exchange-rate considerations limit individual countries from pursuing autonomous monetary policies: balance-of-payments considerations limit them from pursuing full-employment fiscal policies' (Palley, 1998b, pp. 345–6). That is because it is not possible to achieve full employment and balanced trade at the same time by maintaining purchasing power parity. Thus it 'is a barbaric conservative policy that can improve one's own job position only by exporting unemployment. The ultimate effect of these policies is to reduce the standard of living of both deficit and surplus nations' (Davidson and Davidson, 1996, p. 184). The resulting trade wars, for example during the 1930s, created instability and were to the detriment of the whole international community. In a world of imperfect competition and market power, domestic firms forced consumers to pay higher prices to make their products effectively cheaper overseas, cross-subsidizing export growth. The emphasis of the shock therapy approach on comparative advantage, as a means by which international trade would take place, ignored the role of economies of scale, which might have been more important than comparative advantage. In such circumstances, the substantial reduction in output initiated by the implementation of the shock therapy transition model had a negative impact on international trade because firms were unable to exploit economies of scale, which proved to be far more important than was assumed by neoclassical analysis.

The comparative advantage theory of international trade was developed in a specific historical period where natural resource endowments and capital-labor ratios determined economic location. Today, this has been replaced by an era of knowledge-intensive industries where comparative advantage is human made rather than created by Mother Nature and history. Natural resources have ceased to dominate economic activity. Long-run economic growth is the result not only of the country's resource endowments but also, most importantly, of its capacity to satisfy both domestic and foreign knowledge-intensive production processes. Differences in production opportunity costs are due to resource endowments, which reflect what each society believes to be civilized working conditions. The presence of high and persistent unemployment and of very large transaction costs contradicts the assumptions of comparative advantage. Hence that Post Keynesians argue comparative advantage is irrelevant. Industry policy should facilitate strategic economic advantage.

The financial assistance provided by the mature market economies has been disappointing. The transition economies had to depend on their own resources. In addition, due to the relative scarcity of foreign capital and international aid, transition economies competed only in providing concessions. This may have enabled them to acquire the necessary financial resources, Post Keynesians conceded, but it has had irreversible consequences for the future. It has created a heavy reliance on the voluntary movement of capital and handouts from international organizations, reducing national sovereignty and jeopardizing the development of a civilized society. The transition economies would have been able to stand on both feet only after an extensive debt cancellation program, together with substantial foreign aid, not only to assist the transition program, but also to maintain political support and the development of a civilized society. Foreign aid benefited the donor economy as well as the recipient transition economy because it helped to stimulate increased international trade and strengthened relationships in the international community. A prime example is the Marshall Plan's large military and economic aid programs after World War II. The European countries received financial aid to buy American products. This facilitated restructuring in both Europe and the United States. The development of a civilized society, as Post Keynesians argued, requires an international financial system that prohibits the movement of financial capital for speculative reasons. Indeed, Keynes argued that capital controls, both inward and outward, should be permanent. Thus, the Post Keynesians concluded that the transition economies, due to the freely floating exchange rate and the free international market, were contributing to the international debt problem, which threatened the viability of the international financial system.

The problems with international trade in the transition economies reflect the struggle associated with the current international financial system, in which there is no international lender of last resort willing to stabilize exchange rates. Keynes called for an international central bank under a fixed exchange-rate system, an international reserve bank being a lender of last resort. The international central bank would have had the power to create an international currency and its supply would have been determined by future growth needs and potential. 'Such an institution requires, at the very least, powers greater than those granted to the IMF at the Bretton Woods conference' (Arestis and Bain, 1995, p. 166). Keynes insisted on the creation of an International Clearing Union (ICU) based on a bancor unit of account. He helped to devise the Bretton Woods Agreement to encourage intervention, fix exchange rates, and control financial capital. In this scheme, creditor nations would have shared the burden of adjustment of the deficit nations and encouraged economic development in the international economy.

Thus, for the Post Keynesians, coordination of international trade was essential, especially for the republics of the ex-Soviet Union. Even though the break up of the Soviet Union and COMECON resulted in a variety of transition processes, which increased the complexity and the dimensions of the process, there still should have been coordination between the ex-COMECON countries. 'The economies of these states are still so greatly entangled that it is much less costly to gradually change the existing system of the division of labor than to abolish it at once' (Yavlinsky and Braguinsky, 1994, p. 103). For example, intra-trade between the ex-Soviet Union republics comprised 80 per cent of their total trade. Trade diversion would have been extremely costly and these products would not have been able to gain access in the international markets. Additionally, trade restrictions between transition economies would have reduced output, magnifying the social cost of transition. As a result, economic links between enterprises in the ex-COMECON countries were necessary, subject to the free movement of goods, labor, and capital.

Post Keynesians viewed the recommendation for establishment of a payments union by neoclassical gradualist economists as a positive element in the transition process. However, they were very critical of the temporary nature of the payments union in establishing only convertibility, after which it would have ceased to exist since no other goal justified its existence. A Post Keynesian approach would have favored a permanent mechanism for international trade between transition economies, which offered stability and the development of a civilized society. The Payments Union would have evolved, if it were established – and there is no reason not to establish it today – to an Eastern European Clearing Union similar to the International Clearing Union suggested by Keynes for the international financial system. Through the clearing union, a fixed exchange system would have eliminated the instability and negative outcomes caused by the flexible exchange rate system. There would have been no advantage in engaging in export-led growth and importing inflation. In this international system, fiscal and monetary policies would still remain the responsibility of the sovereign state. Through the clearing union 'as in all civilized games, all participants are winners who reap benefits' (Davidson and Davidson, 1996, p. 206).

The free trade initiated by the shock therapy approach was 'overshooting in the sense that it is causing deindustrialisation' (Yavlinsky and Braguinsky, 1994, p. 103). The challenge for transition economies was 'to savor the taste of trade without allowing trade to become an all-consuming force that threatens the development of social and economic life within a community' (McClintock, 1996, p. 225). The Post Keynesian model recommended an adaptive strategy that combined open but managed trade with government expenditure adjustment programs. 'A fixed exchange rate regime operating in tandem with intelligent internal demand and incomes management policies will create an environment where all nations simultaneously can be winners and economic growth increases globally without any nation necessarily running into a balance of payments constraint' (Davidson, 1994, p. 256). Economic policy coordination has, therefore, become a necessary condition for achieving sustained economic prosperity in the new globalize economic environment. A concurrent generalized expansion of income across countries, through a co-coordinated approach, might have helped to mitigate the problems of trade deficits and capital flight driven by international differences in inflation and interest rates. This would have enabled countries to stay on an expansionary course. In the absence of such coordination, the adverse policy incentives that promoted the macroeconomics of austerity and the lowering of the wage floor would have inevitably asserted themselves.

3.7   Social Policy

Transition economies failed to estimate the dangers associated with the inadequate provision of social services. Such policies were necessary for the reform process. Post Keynesians argue that social provisioning in the transition economies was necessary due to the high social cost involved. Supplementation of income and the provision of social services were society's responsibility, and the legal right of each disadvantaged individual. 'Conscience cannot allow us to ignore the poor, either at home or abroad – to be less than concerned, less than generous' (Galbraith, 1996, p. 276). Society recognizes those who need assistance by using civic values as the yardstick. People need financial support and essential social services as well as time to become familiar with the new economy; hence, it must be a gradual process. It was recognized by Post Keynesians that people were unable to use their potential resource capacity to provide a decent standard of living. Under the abnormal economic conditions of transition, 'income distribution is too important to be left solely to the capricious forces of the market' (Davidson and Davidson, 1996, p. 177).

Application of the neoclassical transition model resulted in large social costs, massively reduced production, and unemployment. Meanwhile, under the instructions of the IMF and World Bank, dominated by the free market ideology, the transition economies reduced social protection and public investment 'probably to levels below those needed to sustain reforms' (Wang, 1996, p. 22). The demise of the health care system resulted in the life expectancy of Russian men dropping to 57 years, similar to that in many Third World nations (Intriligator, 1998, p. 243; Gustafson, 1999, pp. 183–4). The increase in mortality and morbidity rates was a momentous embarrassment for the international organizations, such as the World Bank, which had been allocating resources to achieve appropriate health standards (Ellman, 1994, p. 2). Even Aslund (1995, p. 287), one of the architects of shock therapy, recognized this unacceptable result.

A civilized society, in the mould proposed by the Post Keynesians, required a social policy that addressed chronic unemployment. Unemployment causes psychological problems. Hence social policies were necessary to reduce anti-social behavior due to unemployment. The social policy of Post Keynesians is based on the right to work and to a basic income (Jackson, 1999, p. 639). Post Keynesians are in favor of the government assuming the role of employer of last resort, offering public service jobs to anybody who wants to work at a low fixed wage. This eliminates involuntary unemployment and achieves full employment. This wage becomes a constraint upon private sector wage increases that are not linked with productivity. This is a desirable way of achieving price stability, instead of creating the 'natural rate of unemployment'. Employers would have benefited from a pool of trained and work-oriented workers. The program would have been funded from the budget and, at the same time, there would have been a reduction in welfare payments. The employer of last resort program was politically feasible and did not require a substantial amount of financial resources (Mosler, 1997–8; Jackson, 1999, p. 639). In addition, basic income is defined as a cash benefit given to all members of the society irrespective of their personal and financial circumstances. It enables individuals to survive without having to work. It would allow individuals to express their work preferences, freely taking up jobs that they would prefer, thus increasing their productivity. 'In sum, neither the claim that social security distorts competitive labor markets, nor that it reduces net national saving stand up to close inspection. The empirical evidence is that households view social security wealth as compensation' (Palley, 1998a, p. 108).

4 The Post Keynesian Process of Transition

The Post Keynesians would have started the reform process by reforming the institutional structure. The institutional structure involved formal institutions, the regulation of the financial system incorporating a state controlled central bank and the tax system. By the end of Year 1, once the formal institutional structure has been developed, individuals would develop informal institutions lasting throughout the transition period. After the development of the formal institutional structure, the process of the restructuring of state enterprises, the privatization of small-medium enterprises and the establishment of the clearing union should have taken place in Year 2 in accordance with the newly established formal institutions under fixed prices, protection, and fixed exchange rate. Discretionary monetary and fiscal policies and industry-incomes policies, as part of the overall market planning, should have been initiated throughout the reform process in order to assist with the restructuring of enterprises and the achievement of full employment. To assist individuals with the transition costs the minimum income and other assistance programs, such as retraining, should have been established in line with the restructuring of enterprises. In this way, restructuring of state enterprises could have gone ahead without substantial resistance by workers. The right to work can only be initiated after the enterprises are restructured. The gradual price liberalization should have taken place only after enterprises are restructured in Year 6. Conditional foreign aid was essential throughout the reform program. The sequencing of the reforms is presented in Table 6.1.

5 The Cost of Transition

Using the cost criteria of the transition process identified in Chapter 3, it can be argued the implementation of the Post Keynesian model in transition economies resulted in high economic cost, however lower than shock therapy, since it involved the transformation of centrally administered socialism into a economic system dominated by private property and markets. The Post Keynesian approach had also the highest political cost, since people misunderstood the extensive government intervention with centrally administered socialism. With regard to the ideological cost the people in CEEFSU placed the Post Keynesian model at the medium level ideological cost since the approach was consistent with the desire to establish a capitalist economic system. With regard to the International Financial cost the international financial institutions and governments in mature market economies were not keen to provide funding to the transition economies, which implemented the Post Keynesian approach. Lastly, with regard to the Foreign Direct Investment Cost the Post Keynesian model has the highest cost, since multinationals were not enthusiastic to finance projects in transition economies if they had implemented the Post Keynesian model.

6 Conclusion

Keynes' fundamental argument, as Moore (1979, p. 134) reiterated, was that 'economics is essentially a moral and not a natural science. It employs introspection and value judgments'. The Post Keynesians propose that the market outcomes should be desirable from a societal point of view that, in turn, requires discretionary government policies. Consequently, institutional and non-economic factors become relevant in the model, not as imperfections but as important elements of the transition process. Limiting the growth of aggregate demand through restrictive fiscal and monetary policy does not reduce inflation. It reduces output and increases interest rates and unemployment. That is exactly what happened in transition economies. Thus 'laissez-faire is not optimal'.

The implementation of the shock therapy approach took place in an environment where 'most practical economists in Russia know very little about mainstream economics, but mainstream economists know very little about the Russian economy. As could easily be expected, one area of knowledge is really no substitute for the other' (Yavlinsky and Braguinsky, 1994, p. 103). If the historical experience of the successful post-war reconstruction of Western Europe approximated the economic conditions of transition economies – which is doubtful – the successful policies adopted then totally contradict those implemented in CEEFSU. During reconstruction, price ceilings and subsidies were maintained and economic planning was implemented. Monetary and fiscal reforms and policies were adopted and the European Payments Union was established, with the aim of restoring trade among countries. Exchange rates

Table 6.1
The Post Keynesian Process of Transition

		1	2	3	4	5	6	7	8	9	10
1. Price Liberalization	Price Deregulation							▓	▓	▓	▓
Stabilization	Market Planning, Industry Incomes Policy	▓	▓	▓	▓	▓	▓				
2. Privatization	Restructuring State Enterprises			▓	▓	▓	▓				
	Privatization of Small and Medium Enterprises				▓						
3. Institution	Formal Institutions	▓	▓								
	Informal Institutions			▓	▓	▓	▓	▓	▓	▓	▓
4. Monetary Policy and the	Financial Regulation			▓	▓	▓	▓	▓	▓	▓	
Financial System	Discretionary Monetary Policy	▓	▓	▓	▓	▓	▓	▓	▓	▓	▓
5. Fiscal Policy	Discretionary Fiscal Policy	▓	▓	▓	▓	▓	▓	▓	▓	▓	▓
	Tax Structure	▓	▓								
6. International Trade and	Clearing Union			▓	▓	▓	▓	▓	▓	▓	▓
Foreign Aid	Tariffs	▓	▓	▓	▓	▓	▓	▓	▓	▓	▓
	Conditional Foreign Aid	▓	▓	▓	▓	▓	▓	▓	▓	▓	▓
7. Social Policy	Minimum Income	▓	▓	▓	▓	▓	▓	▓	▓	▓	▓
	Right to Work							▓	▓	▓	▓
	Years	**1**	**2**	**3**	**4**	**5**	**6**	**7**	**8**	**9**	**10**

were controlled and capital flows restricted, and the USA provided financial and technical support under the Marshall Plan. Lastly, markets were influenced and guided by an active state, with the aim of supporting the initiatives of firms. The state was able to implement these policies only under a consensus process, which encouraged cooperation rather than conflict. The successful post-war reconstruction of Western Europe reveals that 'there is no single policy that can restore high-wage full employment. Instead, a successful program will have to be multidimensional and comprise structural reform, monetary policy, fiscal policy, international economic policy' (Palley, 1998b, pp. 349, 350). Therefore, Post Keynesians rejected any idea that there could have been a completely 'free market' economy in the transition economies.

In terms of today's global economic problems, including those of the transition economies, 'Keynes had the correct answers for his times and they are the right answers for today' (Cornwall and Cornwall, 1997, p. 540). Keynes would have argued that aggregate demand policies, together with policies to reduce inflation, were necessary for transition economies. The political leaders of the transition economies and the public were misled by the prevailing ideology of the free market in relation to the role of the government and budget deficits. Government discretionary policies were not the problem, but part of the solution. The policies implemented, based on orthodox economic analysis, failed to reduce unemployment and develop a civilized society, making it even more difficult to attain the Post Keynesian goal. A different program was required, consistent with the Post Keynesian propositions to initiate recovery. 'It is then not a question of whether the State should intervene in the economy but rather that it is an inherent part of the economy and the question relates to the form and purpose of state activity' (Arestis and Sawyer, 1993, p. 23). Thus a hand-off approach is totally inappropriate because it is socially undesirable.

The advice of shock therapy was wrong, arrogant and catastrophic (Minsky, 1996a, p. xii; Cox, 1998, p. 9; Ticktin, 1998, p. 73; Arnot, 1998, pp. 220, 222, 234; Lo, 1995, p. 80). Yavlinsky and Braguinsky (1994, p. 115) suggested 'in the old days, engineers who constructed a railway bridge in Russia had to stand under it when the first train crossed. One should either stake one's life in this transformation or do something else ... and ask all those advisors who care so little about the countries they try to help that they are unable even to theorize properly to stay at home'. 'Crony capitalism' was increasingly paralleled by 'crony research and advice', more than 30,000 Western 'consultants' had visited Moscow since the change of regime, many of them interested in assistance not to ordinary Russians but to themselves (White, 2000, p. 141). In such an environment the Post Keynesians propositions did not had a chance of consideration. They met 'strong political and institutional barriers – the same barriers that have blocked the use of Keynesian policies in recent years' (Jackson, 1999, p. 661). Given the research agenda of the IMF and World Bank for transition economies, 'no wonder economics has again become the dismal science' (Davidson, 1992, p. 462).

Chapter 7

The Pluralistic Market Socialist Model of Transition

1 Introduction

According to much of the literature and the dominant perception of the IMF, the World Bank and mature market economies, adoption of the capitalist market economy was the only possible way to avoid stagnation in CEEFSU. In reaction to the failures of Stalinism, capitalism – conceptualized today as a 'normal society' (Blackburn, 1991a, p. x) – came to be seen the only viable alternative for the people of CEEFSU, even though a capitalist class did not exist. However, this view was not necessarily accurate. The course of events might have taken another route, and it might have resulted in the adoption of a market socialist economic system. Capitalism was not necessarily the mode of production into which all societies were bound to evolve. Since the transition process did not automatically lead to a capitalist economic system, market socialism was worthy of serious consideration.

Market socialism in CEEFSU was not attractive because any form of socialism was considered to be a form of Stalinism. In the meantime, however, capitalism was linked with prosperity, the rule of law, democracy and the elimination of shortages, despite the experiences of mature market economies. In the transition economies there was a 'celebration of the market, the virtues of free enterprise and greed unlimited' (Miliband, 1991, p. 6), which did not promote the socialist goal. However, according to the market socialists, the collapse of centrally administered socialism should not have been interpreted as the exhaustion of all egalitarian prospects or a failure of untried forms of socialism, especially market socialism: 'That [the irrelevance of socialism] is far from the truth' (Roemer, 1999a, p. 64). Writing premature obituaries for socialism is very popular these days. But 'socialism is not Stalinism' (Galeano, 1991, p. 254) and the market socialist proposal avoided any elements associated with the Stalinist inefficiencies. The collapse of Stalinism caused a re-examination of fundamentals of socialist construction.

It was argued that the failure of centrally administered socialism could have been avoided if the most important principles of market socialism had been adopted by way of introducing markets and allowing the people to participate in the formation of the plans by establishing a democratic political process. This did not imply the inevitability of socialism but, rather, its historical possibility as a desirable goal to strive for: a radical egalitarian ideal worth pursuing. In fact, the collapse of Stalinism has assisted the cause of market socialism. It has cleared the way for consideration of potentially efficient and democratic forms of socialism by initiating a new purpose for public ownership. This is 'a moment of opportunity, not defeat' (Thompson, 1991, p. 107).

2   Primary Elements of the Pluralistic Market Socialist Model

2.1   Economic Analysis

Marxism is derived from the works of Karl Marx, and it forms the basis for the economic analysis used by market socialists. It has always been central to the construction of democratic and egalitarian alternatives to capitalism, as well as egalitarian reforms of capitalism itself. Market socialists highlighted the need to incorporate power and class into economic analysis and believed that these resulted from the private ownership of the means of production. Markets distribute income according to relative power. In neoclassical economic theory, 'class and sectoral conflict tend to be ruled out almost by assumption' (Nell, 1996, p. 154). Post Keynesians are in the same boat – like other 'vulgar' economists – as they have little to say about concepts such as economic power, class struggle, alienation, or exploitation. Mathematical formulas developed by neoclassical and Post Keynesian economists create the illusion that economics is a value-free science: figures are preferred to words despite the inability to fit the human factor into equations.

Marx was silent about the construction of socialism and what socialism specifically involved; the details did not matter. Marx declined to write recipes for the social cookbooks of socialism. So socialists believed that the economic institutions and processes of socialism would have emerged naturally and spontaneously; consequently, they did not require serious forethought. Marxian economics is a broad theory of the historical evolution of economic life. Thus concepts such as 'the state withers away' and 'the antithesis between physical and mental labor vanishes' did very little to assist socialists in developing a coherent socialist economic system. In the meantime, Marx cannot be blamed for what was subsequently applied as socialism. Such a claim would be 'just about as logical as placing the responsibility for the Spanish Inquisition at the feet of Jesus Christ' (Cox, 1998, p. 10).

Marx ruled out any role for the market in a socialist economy. In contrast, both Bukharin and Trotsky were in favor of the use of 'the market evil'. Contrary to Marx, market socialists argued that the market mechanism was the most efficient way of co-coordinating decentralized decision-making. They encouraged economic innovation in order to produce and distribute the goods that people need for self-realization. They believed markets could have been used to achieve socialist ends. According to Abalkin (1988, p. 42), 'the market is no capitalist invention'. The market socialists embraced market relations in every aspect of economic life and rejected Stalin's 'two-property thesis'. According to the two-property thesis, market relations were only legitimate if an exchange of property occurred between participants in the transaction. Between state-owned enterprises there was no exchange of property in any transaction. Thus market relations were not warranted and relations between state-owned enterprises had to be centrally administered (Stalin, 1972, pp. 1–29).

There was recognition in the transition economies that market failures existed, as in every market system, in the form of externalities and public goods, economies of scale, unjust distribution of income and advertising. These failures were attributed to market capitalism rather than to markets *per se*: the markets of a socialist economic system need not be anything like the markets of capitalism. Therefore, there was neither a simple-minded endorsement of markets, nor their straightforward dismissal. Market socialism combined the strengths of the market system with those of socialism to achieve both efficiency and equality. The issue was not whether there were to be markets but, rather, what kind of markets and with what kind of consequences. There was no such thing as a 'market': markets were institutionally dependent. Markets did not require capitalists or the concentration of economic power and wealth in the hands of a small class. Market socialists disagreed with Kornai (1995a, p. 54) that market socialism was an oxymoron and that the failure of the Yugoslav model was proof of the failure of the concept of market socialism. Market socialists attacked the 'anarchy' of both the market and of central planning. Hence, instead of trying to abolish market relations as an integral feature of socialism and of a Marxist view of socialist transition, socialism should attempt to improve them.

The theory of market socialism is still being developed. Today, Lange's contribution to the theory of market socialism is considered archaic because it ignored incentive issues. The market socialist model developed here is an amalgamation and a stylized version of the work of a number of socialist economists. In addition to the traditional sources of market socialism, I have incorporated the non-market socialists Devine (1988) and Albert and Hahnel (1991) in my analysis. Their model of negotiated coordination planning is incorporated into my market socialist model because of its valuable insights into the process of economic planning.

2.2   What is a Good Society?

The market socialist model is concerned with the optimal combination of public and private property, centralization and decentralization, of markets and planning and of individualism and the social good. Socialism does not, and will never be able to, abolish scarcity. What it offers is a different way of dealing with economic problems: conscious intervention by communal institutions, a 'visible hand', and greater social ownership through the reduction of private ownership of the means of production. The call for the abolition of exploitation is a call for an egalitarian distribution of resources, because exploitation is the result of the unequal distribution of the means of production and not of surplus labor. However, socialism is not only about redistributing income. It is also about designing institutions and relationships, which foster independence, self-respect, and dignity, which give people a greater degree of control over their lives and the capacity to exercise responsibility for their actions. Self-realization stands for the development and application of individual talents in a direction that gives meaning to a person's life.

Market socialism is quite different from capitalism, in either the neoclassical or the Post Keynesian forms, in that a market socialist society tries to achieve different goals and a different economic system. For the neoclassical economists, it was utopian to believe that a society could have been founded on a norm of egalitarianism. Greed is good – or at least a necessary evil: a motivating force that can be tamed by the right institutions. Nonetheless, for neoclassical economists, the dominance of planning questioned the ability of the market to function efficiently. Also, planning resulted in corruption. Meanwhile, Post Keynesian policies of intervention in markets could not have overcome the macroeconomic problems that were rooted in the market process. Economic and political power would have tended to undermine the successful implementation of Post Keynesian policies; therefore, there was no Keynesian solution for transition economies.

Socialism has a well-defined set of ends and values of freedom, democracy, social justice, community, efficiency, self-management, solidarity, preventing exploitation of the weak, reducing alienation, greater equality of opportunity, income, wealth, status, and power and the satisfaction of basic needs. Market socialists had traditionally criticized capitalism and Stalinism for violating the four central values of equality, democracy, autonomy, and community. This was because capitalist and Stalinist societies were inherently based on domination and exploitation, which heavily influenced human relations. Market socialists condemn both capitalist and Stalinist exploitation because they are characterized by unjust inequality of ownership and control of the means of production. The profit incentive system in capitalism and the nomenclature system in Stalinism compelled economic actors to treat any other considerations as, at best, secondary. Both economic systems increased inequality of income, wealth, and privileges, which affected economic growth and productivity by obstructing the evolution of productivity-enhancing governance structures. These outcomes were due to the highly concentrated private ownership of capital under capitalism and the highly concentrated levels of power under Stalinism. In contrast, in market socialism, human needs would be the driving force, not the market or power.

Marx highlighted the inherent tendency of markets to generate exploitation, inequality, and instability. Exploitation arises from inequalities in endowments of production, lack of competitive conditions and inescapable market uncertainties. Even if such sources of inequality were abolished, material incentives, such as rewards in the form of market wages for different skills, would have been essential. Inequalities would not have been unjust in the transition economies as long as they resulted from need or merit. Differences in skills resulted from varying educational opportunities, talents and abilities and the degree of material resources, all of which were attributable to factors for which people had no responsibility. Environmental conditions had to be equalized, from 'arbitrary factors of inherited wealth, social position and the "genetic lottery" of talents to determine the life chances of individuals' (Satz, 1996, p. 71). As a result, the disadvantaged would have to be compensated so that people could enter the market on the fairest possible terms. The overall interest of society cannot just be reduced to a sum of individual self-interests.

Market socialists aim to rectify market failures in a number of ways. Firstly, market socialists endeavor to ensure full employment by the public regulation and democratic planning of investment. Secondly, market socialists strive for a reduction in inequality of income by encouraging the growth of enterprise forms in which primary income is distributed more equally. Thirdly, market socialists intend to introduce a highly discretionary tax system to facilitate the redistribution of income. Market socialism provides conscious social direction by combining markets with planning in a way that makes the best use of both instruments. Otherwise the free market would have been self-destructive, fostering class differences and promoting a lack of freedom. The market is the only alternative to bureaucracy, and self-management is not in conflict with efficiency. Thus socialism is about equal entitlement to the means of production, with the question of how people choose to use their endowments in the production process left open.

A socialist view of freedom centers on the idea of effective choice. A person who is free has many options from which to choose, but these options must be real rather than hypothetical. The neoclassical economists accept only a negative view of freedom, which is characterized by an absence of intentional coercion. However, freedom has both a negative and a positive face. Positive freedom is having the ability and hence the appropriate resources to act effectively. This is interpreted in market socialism as embodying three forms of equality: an equal guaranteed basic livable income; equal access to capital resources; and a limit to market-generated inequalities. In market socialism, 'the free development of each becomes the condition for the free development of all' (Roemer, 1996b, p. 12).

Consequently, a market socialist economy would have combined public ownership of large, established corporations with a high degree of reliance on markets. Yunker (1997, p.ix) argued that such an economy, in its everyday operations, would have appeared almost identical to the market capitalist economy of today. There would, however, have been one critical difference: profits and interest generated by publicly-owned corporations would have been distributed to the general public as a social dividend or minimum income supplement to labor income, instead of being paid out in proportion to financial asset ownership.

2.3   Speed

Capitalism required a class of capitalists and a class of proletarians. These classes did not come into existence naturally and spontaneously. It was impossible for Russia, with a history of nearly 1,000 years of autocratic rule, to convert rapidly to capitalism since social norms, attitudes and the way of thinking restricted the development of capitalist institutions. The early hopes and expectations for a rapid transition 'were naïve at best' (Weisskopf, 1996, p. 286; Kagarlitsky, 1993, p. 88; Zwass, 1999, p. 236). The market socialists argued that the teleological theories of progress behind the neoclassical models of transition, and to some degree behind the Post Keynesian model, were inapplicable.

Given shock therapy's insistence on the need for speed, there was no time for a native capitalist class of small private entrepreneurs to mature over decades or centuries into large corporations. For the shock therapy approach to be able to set up the basis for 'normal' capitalist accumulation, capitalists had to be created as soon as possible. 'There was no feasible way his [Sachs's] privatization could be done legally, legitimately or morally' (Holmstrom and Smith, 2000, p. 9). This class had to be 'hot housed', virtually overnight. In the end, a combination of elements was essentially drafted to privatize the economy, using criminal methods: the underground Mafia, the nomenclatura and segments of the intelligentsia. Thus 'spontaneous privatization' was a deliberate strategy by the nomenclatura and criminal elements to transform itself into a capitalist class. Indeed, economic advisors – the highly paid missionaries and the Harvard Institute for International Development (HIID) – bear much of the responsibility for the creation of CEEFSU's criminal capitalists. Currently, there is an investigation into whether, and to what extent, the HIID broke US laws. It has been claimed that they channeled hundreds of millions of dollars from the US Agency for International Development into the hands of corrupt privatizers. Also, it is being ascertained to what extent Harvard academic advisors personally profited in the process (Holmstrom and Smith, 2000, p. 9).

For the market socialists, the introduction of market relations in CEEFSU has not delivered the desirable results. Burawoy and Krotov (1993), Burawoy (1996) and Reardon (1996) argued that the collapsed of centrally administered socialism and the implementation of shock therapy gave rise to merchant rather than industrial capitalism. In merchant capitalism exchange dominated production and trade was orchestrated by the state by distributing export quotas, licenses and money credit. This was because, in an environment of chronic shortages in transition economies, enterprises were motivated by the maximization of profits, not through production but through trade, buying cheap and selling dear. The new entrepreneurs, the previous managers, operate in an environment of monopolistic behavior, illegal transactions and against weak state competitors. The introduction of market relations could not have eliminated such behavior, as there was a blossoming of premodern forms of exploitation. Monopoly and barter increased because of the disintegration of the party state. The withering away of the party state led to the reconstruction of the economy and the emergence of a fragmented, anaemic and ineffective liberal democracy, incapable of introducing a market economy with hard budget constraints. Hence, the new entrepreneurs, rather than thinking long-term, tended to seek quick enrichment and, in fact, were highly ambivalent toward capitalism, since they were used to weak state competitors, behind-the-scenes transactions and monopolistic behavior.

Merchant capitalism did not evolve into industrial capitalism. Rather it inhibited the development of capitalism by conserving anti-capitalist forms of production upon which it survived. That is to say, merchant capitalism, as both Weber and Marx demonstrated, was a development away from bourgeois industrial capitalism. Corruption under the previous regime was a result of necessity, due to the shortcomings of the central administration of the allocation of resources. Today, however, due to the adoption of the shock therapy process of transition, corruption has become the predominant medium of accumulation. This unprecedented level of corruption resulted not only in a loss of tax revenue but also in the erosion of the evolutionary process of the development of the capitalist class. In addition, capitalist ideology based on the rule of law has been eroded. The voluntary relationships between economic actors in the market system have been replaced by a combination of greed and fear, making the development of a civilized capitalist system impossible. 'Today, as yesterday, the process of primitive accumulation is not a pretty one' (Holmstrom and Smith, 2000, p. 4). Consequently, 'there is no market road to a market economy: it requires a strong centralized state that dictates the transition to economic actors' (Burawoy, 1996, p. 275).

The transition to market socialism from central administration would, therefore, have been a slow and lengthy process. The transformation of social relations into entirely different settings that were not centrally administered and non-capitalist could only have taken place through a gradual process. Progress would have been evolutionary, incrementalist, a succession of small forward steps. The belief that it could have taken place in one shot and achieved desirable results was inconsistent both with social reality and with the goals associated with socialism. Moreover, 'any harmful effects which participation may pose for economic efficiency can be minimized by gradualism' (Howard and King, 1992, p. 379).

According to the market socialists, experience teaches us that transition was likely to be a lengthy process, interrupted by setbacks, fraught with tensions, conflicts, difficulties and errors. To a large extent, policies were implemented on a trial-and-error basis, making people aware of the need for radical solutions. The transformation required considerable learning capacity on the part of everybody. Policies should not have been formed as they were under the old administrative methods, on the basis of what is desirable and possible. Policies should have been based on compromise between interest groups. 'But if it is to be a socialist society of free men and women, there can be no other way' (Howe, 1994, p. 65). Contrary to popular myth, an attempt to make an immediate transition to a market capitalist economy did not offer a tried-and-true path to prosperity any more than would an attempt to build a democratic market socialist economy.

2.4   Political Structure

According to the market socialists, any reform that required greater initiative and more personal responsibility in the economic sphere, while maintaining rigid party control over political life, simply would not have worked. Democratic politics was considerably more important for the success of market socialist system than it was for the success of a capitalist system. Full and deepened democracy was an essential precondition of socialism. This was recognized by both Marx and Kautsky in their analysis of the Paris Commune.

Open criticism, free discussion, differences of opinion and the peaceful competition of interest groups were crucial to any progress, to any meaningful changes in the economic structure toward market socialism. 'The political method of democratic government is an essential principle, not an accidental accompaniment of a just society' (Durbin, 1976, p. 557). Those who assert a fundamental incompatibility between socialism and democracy normally rely on the association of socialism with the one-party political systems common to all Stalinist countries.

If the transition from capitalism to socialism was a democratic challenge, as Jacobs (1999, p. 539) argued, this was even truer for the transition economies. In a democratic capitalist society, people participate in the decision-making process; however, effective decision-making remains with the capitalists. Democratic affairs in capitalist societies were a matter for specialists, the politicians, and 'participation in the capitalist market generates a sense of passivity, isolation, and self-absorption inimical to effective democratic citizenship' (Simon, 1996, p. 51). In addition, majority voting did not lead to efficient economic outcomes. Thus there was no presumption that the capitalist democratic process would have resulted in efficiency-pursuing government. Reforms would only have taken place as long as the dominance of the capitalist class was not threatened. The only way that any effective policies in the interest of the majority could have been introduced was by eliminating the power of capital. This would have required the abolition of private property and its appropriation by the majority of the people: the working class. Popular control in both the state and the economy was the only alternative for CEEFSU: that is, socialist democracy.

In general, socialist revolutions were not born in conditions favorable to democracy. Market socialism could only have been peacefully and democratically introduced in transition economies by strictly legal and democratic processes. A market socialist party in CEEFSU would have had to convince the majority of people that it stood for humane government, as well as material improvement and a more rational use of resources than capitalism. 'There is no undemocratic road to socialism. If we were forced to conclude that there cannot be a democratic road to socialism, then we would also have to conclude that the entire socialist enterprise is illusory' (Howe, 1994, p. 65).

Multi-party politics were consistent with socialism, inasmuch as social classes existed in socialism and were heterogeneous. Doing away with political parties results in repression. Conflicts between groups existed, based upon their different economic interests. Under market socialism, there would have been several political parties competing for power, and some would have been 'bourgeois'. In the meantime, democracy is a risky process. Advocates of market socialism recognized the possibility that, if the system did not perform as well as hoped, citizens would have restored capitalism. Then, perhaps, some years later, the socialists might again have won the elections. Therefore, the language must change from 'countries are socialist ... [to] ... socialist parties in power' (Roemer, 1994a, p. 110). However, socialism might have been well embodied in the constitution, which might have limited the permissible degree of accumulation of private property in productive assets and constitutionally have protected non-private property. The justification for a 'supermajoritarian' requirement to reverse the socialist principles was that the social cost of change would have been substantial; changes in property relations should not have endangered long-term planning and investment (Roemer, 1996b, p. 33).

In market socialism, the sectoral and spatial distribution of investment would have been subject to both political as well as economic pluralism. The national five-year plan would have been based primarily on the plans of the enterprises, which themselves were derived from projected market demand. In addition to taking into account the interdependence associated with investment decisions, the planning process would have been a process of debate. Even the greatest precision in the economic calculus will never eliminate the necessity for making political decisions, in drawing up plans of development. 'No neutral decision rule is at hand because the contending claims are usually non-zero-sum' (Maier, 1991, p. 56). It follows that the optimization of economic decisions embodied not only the system and techniques of economic calculus but also a corresponding political mechanism within which conflicting interests could have been clarified and compromised upon. The democratic process itself could have helped to educate voters as to the real alternatives they faced and to engage their cooperation rather than their resistance to needed measures. All would have participated in decision-making so that the decisions taken, in the name of society, were as close as possible to real social preferences.

Plans would have been approved by an elected parliament and implemented within market relations mediated by the discretionary power of the state. For the regulation of, and application of, plans, political pluralism (effective participation of the people) and economic pluralism (market relations) were necessary. A market socialist economy involved a continuing role for the state, one that was much subtler, more indirect, and more benign than running an administrated socialist economy. In contrast to earlier central plans, reliance would have been primarily on market instruments. The plan was characterized by flexibility, to the point of naming it 'slack planning'. Additionally, democracy makes the state's task more difficult, since a variety of inconsistent objectives will be reflected in the preferences of individuals, groups of citizens and political parties' preferences. The trade unions would have had an important role as well. They would have been more active in participating in the social sections of the plans and even in setting forth their own alternative proposals. Thus market socialism was not a regime of technocrats but a form of economic management that left ample room for pluralism and democratic processes of decision-making.

The analysis of the political structure of market socialism contradicts the current dominant perception in CEEFSU that socialism is inherently authoritarian and oppressive, and that capitalism alone is capable of providing freedom and democratic rule. In reality, Russia has a 'decorative parliament' (Kagarlitsky, 1996b, pp. 306–7). The demands for democratic processes, not only in the political structure but also in the economic structure, could only have taken a socialist form. Livingstone (1993, p. 103) argued that 'everything I saw confirms that democracy will either be socialist or it will not exist'. Actually, market socialism would have significantly improved the quality of democracy in transition economies.

An analysis of the political structure of market socialism reveals a contradiction. While democracy was necessary, in order to facilitate the reforms in the transition economies, it also exaggerated the existing difficult economic situation by allowing the people to show dissatisfaction. In my view, this contradiction could have been avoided through ideological change. Revolutionary transformation in the economic and political environment was impossible without a revolution in the minds of the people, in their psychology and mentality.

2.5   Ideological Structure

Ideology always plays a profound role in any political-economic system, especially in the process of change, because each economic system is based on certain values. Non-material factors, such as ideas, theories, ideologies, knowledge, values, norms, attitudes and expectations, were important in transition economies because they could have both induced and hindered change. The ideology transmitted in CEEFSU was that of the triumph of capitalism. 'Proletarian internationalism has given way to liberal universalism' (Sakwa, 1998, p. 73), and 'the word imperialism is out of style and no longer to be found in the dominant political lexicon, even though imperialism is present and does pillage and kill' (Galeano, 1991, p. 254). The 'propensity to truck and barter' was presented as innate in human nature and essential for the speed of transition to global capitalism. The fall of Stalinism resulted in the 'retraditionalisation' of society and the 'delegitimisation of state action' (Sakwa, 1998, pp. 192–3). All this was in line with the worldwide acceptance of free-market ideology.

The market socialists argued that there is no real conflict between socialist equality and freedom, when both are properly conceived. However, for freedom to prevail, self-interest was paramount. In the transition economies, it was unrealistic to assume that people would not have behaved in a self-interested manner in their personal economic decisions: 'Attempts to eradicate it are futile' (Porket, 1998, p. 239). However, the individual pursuit of self-interest, when subjected to checks and balances and without the influence of a capitalist class, would have been economically and socially beneficial. Hopefully, once people had experienced equality and negotiated coordination under socialism, learning would have occurred, perceptions would have changed, and consciousness might have been transformed. In addition, when an egalitarian ethos had been established, people might have become less self-interested. Meanwhile, the influence of the capitalist class on educational policy would have been absent. A specific institutional and educational structure, which promoted cultures of cooperation, would have contributed significantly to overcoming the principal-agent problem, reduced free riding and also increased the likelihood of compromise. The ideological reform had the aim of encouraging the appropriate response. In the contemporary climate of opinion, it is too easy for proponents of socialism in CEEFSU to be casually dismissed as naïve idealists. However, people were brought up to expect full employment and universal welfare and, therefore, were unlikely to give their wholehearted support to the sort of capitalist model imposed.

2.6   Initial Conditions

Market socialists agreed with Marx, that the construction of socialism in each country would have had to take into account the specific idiosyncrasies and uniqueness of each nation's experience and could not have been applied like a 'cookbook recipe'. The same argument could have been used for the construction of market socialism in the transition economies. Transition economies could have been transformed only within the limits of their own traditions and possibilities. There was no single model. In the meantime, the imposition of the shock therapy model was based on an inadequate understanding of the institutions of the previously state-socialist countries, and it ran counter to the historical traditions, present-day realities, and actual possibilities of transition economies. Despite all their systemic similarities, the transition economies differed considerably from each other in many respects. The transition to market socialism was, by its nature, a path-dependent process. Path-dependency meant not only that transformation would have been affected by the initial state and, therefore, by the history of the system and country undergoing transformation, but also that steps taken earlier would have influenced the direction and speed of later policy choices. Shock therapy apologists sometimes repeat the excuse: 'you can't make an omelet without breaking a few eggs.' Cohen (1998, p. 249) argued that, if we were to learn anything from the past, 'there would be no omelet, only a mass of broken eggs in the form of crushed hopes and lives'.

3 Secondary Elements of the Pluralistic Market Socialist Model

3.1 Price Liberalization and Stabilization

The introduction of market relations in centrally administered socialism would have led to the establishment of a new form of accountability for the producer, in relation to the citizen as a consumer, via the market test. By lifting some restrictions on the market, it was expected that individual activity would have helped to satisfy consumer demand. Price movements through competition in the market would have adjusted socially undesirable differences in the profitability of different types of products. It was the responsibility of the transition government to intervene in order to dampen price fluctuations and the associated effects on incomes. The high level of market concentration that resulted from the introduction of full market relations was of critical concern. It was necessary to restrict unjustified monopoly power and to develop market competition among the enterprises. Competition in market socialism was treated as the antithesis of monopoly power, not as a potential generator of monopoly power. In contrast to Lange and Taylor's (1939) model of competitive market socialism, market socialists envisaged an economic system where discretionary power existed.

Without a price reform in the transition economies, it would have been impossible to secure any assessment of costs and the results of production, to ensure an equivalent exchange of goods and services, to stimulate scientific and technological progress and, finally, to encourage the economizing of resources. This meant, among other things, an end to subsidies, which undermined the incentive for producing efficiently and resulted in a wasteful attitude by consumers. Subsidies also imposed a considerable burden on the state budget. The typical firm would have to have been self-supporting. Higher prices, at which demand and supply balance, were in the interest of society because they eliminated possible corruption by the administrators of the shortage. However, the price formation process would have to have been transparent: a public process subject to public checks, not one controlled by enterprises. In mature market economies, most enterprises form their prices by adding a mark-up to the unit cost. However, the costs and the mark-ups are not known. In a socialist market, the barriers to information would have been dissolved. There was a need for government intervention because market forces could not have generated all the information needed for decision-making in the social interest. The producer would have worked in a climate of publicity, consultation, criticism, and measurement. In a socialist market, with the absence of the serious spillover effects of monopoly power and the social and political barriers to information disclosure, production for profit would have been socially desirable. While economic efficiency demanded that enterprises should not have been subsidized, clearly articulated social goals should have been supported by the society.

Differential remuneration in the transition to market socialism was necessary if labor services were to be used in the most advantageous way, in addition to eliciting the desired effort. The system of work remuneration under centrally administered socialism did not depend on efficiency considerations. Market socialists reject 'mindless egalitarianism' and seek to reward, materially and morally, those who work harder. It is efficient to develop the talents in which people have comparative advantages. The differences in the value of the marginal product of labor in various occupations should be equal to the differences in the marginal disutility involved, necessitating differentiation in income. Consequently, inequality will continue to exist. However, in an egalitarian socialist society, quite small differences of pay could have been quite highly valued (Blackburn, 1991b, p. 224). While wage levels would have been subject to the law of supply and demand, they would have been shaped by collective bargaining undertaken by free trade unions and bounded by social regulations such as incomes policies. This would have been supplemented with adequately designed and funded education and job-training programs.

The abolition of subsidies was expected to lead to the closing of a large number of enterprises, or at best to layoffs, as enterprises sought ways to function efficiently by meeting the market test. The question was whether or not market socialism allowed unemployment. Unemployment was rejected as being inconsistent with socialism. Market socialists argued that, in a plan-based economy geared to meeting the needs of society as fully as possible; there was no need for unemployment. Even if some fundamental technological improvements made entire trades no longer necessary, the plan should have been able to foresee this in advance and take the appropriate corrective action. Market socialism was capable of adjusting distribution through an incomes policy, so as to achieve full employment output without inflation.

While enterprises were to become accountable to citizens as consumers, the management of enterprises would also have been accountable to society via a national allocative plan. 'The genuine difference between socialism and capitalism is not negating either plan or market but in the particular interests which the plan and market serve' (Socialism: Theory and Practice Round Table, 1989, p. 20). In a market economy, markets could not allocate investment efficiently, due to positive and negative externalities. During the transition, it was essential to involve the state in investment planning. The responsibility of the state was to internalize the externalities associated with investment, to produce public goods and to compensate for incomplete markets.

In the market, decisions about whether to invest were complicated, especially during transition. Capital accumulation relied on complex judgments about the likely demand and cost conditions for many years into the future. Decisions had to be based on a balance of expertise, technical knowledge, and guesswork. However, the market, especially during transition, fails to provide sufficient information to the investor about the future. A set of futures markets, necessary for agents to make suitable contingency plans in times of uncertainty, does not exist in reality. That is because it was natural for people to be rather cautious, and also due to the uncertainties in investment being so great during transition: there was a systematic tendency to under-invest in a market system. Moreover, there was a bias towards projects with fewer uncertainties and risks. Playing it safe was of course a characteristic of the banking system, whose role was to fund investment projects. Yet it is often the riskiest projects that drive the motor of economic development. In short, 'while markets may be excellent for fine-tuning responses to changing demand and technology, they may not be good at stimulating large, non-marginal changes in the structure of the economy' (Estrin and Winter, 1990, p. 112). The market socialist state must, therefore, counteract these tendencies by intervening to provide firms with information about the economic environment: prices and market trends. This can be achieved through an indicative plan to foster both the general rate of accumulation and investment in relatively risky projects, and plan to innovate for the future. The central authority was qualified to forecast the rate of technological progress and guarantee that most investment projects would have reflected the interests of the society and not shortsighted individual self-interest.

The dominant perception CEEFSU was that planning must always mean administrative allocation of resources, as it did under Stalinism. However, to attempt to include the whole economy in an all-embracing disaggregated central plan was impossible, self-defeating, inefficient, and also undesirable on social and political grounds. Planning is an economic activity of coordination for different sectors of an economy. Plans are definite, overall, governing guidelines, constructed regularly at certain periods for the development of a large number of mutually varied, dependent economic activities. The outcome of centrally planning investment would have been less wasteful, since it would have eliminated duplication, more efficient, and desirable from society's point of view. Pachter (1976, p. 795), Stiglitz (1993, p. 24) and Devine (1988, pp. 5,

15) argued that only a market socialist system could have made its investment decisions in full view of all economic, political, social and human factors. Planning was an unavoidable component of modern economic management in any society, especially in a socialist society, in order to realize particular outcomes such as greater social justice. Effective planning required the use of markets. In this regard, the market socialist model bears a close resemblance to the Sik (1967) model, which is based on the interventionist Keynesian tradition of market planning. The market process and economic planning were distinct, yet mutually supporting assignments.

The nature of government intervention in market socialism was qualitative and not quantitative. The desired investment levels and pattern of society would have been implemented not through a command system but by manipulating the interest rates at which different industrial sectors borrowed funds from state banks. Central planning was expected to give way to a variety of forms of market planning. Therefore, only under strong state regulation through planning could the transition to the market have taken place in transition economies.

The plan had to determine priorities. It should reflect the priorities of society as a whole and those of the separate social groups whose interests were recognized as being especially important. Prioritizing was a complex process and had to be based on social compromise within an open and pluralistic-democratic system. Social and investment priorities were inevitably political decisions for instrumental and desirable reasons. Indicative planning was a decentralized and democratic process of consultation and discussion, concerned exclusively with plan construction and elaboration. The process provided a forum in which information could have been pooled. Also, diverse interest groups could have confronted one another about spillover effects, giving voters an equal voice in determining the plan's objectives. In itself, the plan did not contain an implementation procedure. As every actor 'bargains' through successive 'iterations', the process of negotiated coordination, rather than price taking, would have occurred. 'Such a procedure contains rather more teeth than might at first sight appear' (Estrin and Winter, 1990, p. 116), because one of the major actors in a market socialist economy was the state. However, the use of the political process to decide investment planning 'opens up the Pandora's box of rent seeking, the wasteful use of resources by interest groups who aim to influence the outcome of the process' (Roemer, 1994a, p. 106). Yet, under socialism, the tension between sectional and social interest would have been explicit, with the possibility of partial reconciliation and also some transformation of the perceptions and levels of social awareness of those involved.

3.2 Privatization

In conditions of general uncertainty, it was impossible to carry out privatization without weakening economic links and undermining managerial confidence and efficiency. This resulted in destabilizing production, destroying productive forces, increasing unemployment and generally deepening the crisis. Privatization simply resulted in enriching the managers, without any benefit to the workers or to production. The collapse of central administration passed power from the central authority to the managers, who appropriated – 'stole' – the enterprise's assets through spontaneous privatization, transforming themselves into a new bourgeoisie. In Russia, due to the sluggish institutional structure, the former Russian nomenclatura, often in collaboration with Mafia-like groups, allegedly composed of former KGB officers, was more successful than its Central European counterparts in turning public property into private wealth. Eyal, Szelenyi and Townsley (1997, p. 62) characterized post-Stalinist Central Europe as 'capitalism without capitalists', while the emerging Russian structure was 'capitalists without capitalism'. Those running Russia are 'the same old crooks (quite literally) who ran it before', the 'self-professed Communists turned-anti-Communists', but nowadays they have money to spend and invest abroad (Ticktin, 1998, p. 90; Cohen, 1998, p. 244). Trotsky had argued that it was self-evident that members of the 'bureaucracy' would, in the end, have preferred to own property, rather than to administer state enterprises.

The myth behind the development of the widespread ownership of private property through the free distribution of vouchers – 'peoples' privatization' (Braguinsky, 1998, p. 231) – had not materialized, nor had the dream of 'people's capitalism'. For the transition towards capitalism to succeed, it was essential to gain the support of the managers. Support was gained by allowing management to keep its privileged position and, at the same time, to substantially increase their fortunes despite the 'free distribution of shares'. Control still rested with management, who disregarded the owners of vouchers. They considered vouchers to be inconvenient, as they did not help raise capital but required a dividend payment. In many cases in Russia, managers encouraged workers to buy more shares in the enterprise so as to strengthen their own control, which resulted in the concentration of large amounts of capital in the hands of the few. Finally, the bureaucracy 'got what it wanted: a title to property and the right for the first time to be defined as a 'class' in its own right' (Ticktin, 1998, p. 90). In such an environment 'it is not the state which is privatizing the soviet enterprise, but the soviet enterprise which is privatizing the state' (Clarke, 1992, p. 5). In reality, privatization was a misnomer; it was, in fact, 'decentralization' (Eyal, Szelenyi and Townsley, 1997, p. 71; Cohen and Rogers, 1996, p. 102).

At the end, 'not only despite, but because of marketization' (Parish and Michelson, 1996, p. 1045) through the free distribution of vouchers, a dominant class of private owners emerged. Market socialists were not at all surprised by the outcome. The voucher privatization of state enterprises in transition economies was reminiscent of Roemer's coupon economy. Roemer (1996a, p. 386) and Bardhan (1993, p. 149) demonstrated that, if vouchers representing shares in the nation's firms were equally distributed to all citizens and held as traditional private property, with the right to sell, such vouchers would have rapidly become concentrated in the hands of a few. It was individually optimal for the weak and disadvantaged to sell the vouchers. Under Roemer's version of market socialism, the poor and the middle class would have been only able to exchange, not liquidate, their vouchers and, therefore, would have remained the dominant voucher-holders.

For the market socialists, the initial distribution of ownership was a major concern, because it would have determined the distribution of power and influenced equity and efficiency. Because markets did not approximate perfect competition and were dominated by domestic and international monopolies, the initial distribution of power increased inequalities. In addition privatization, through the distribution of free vouchers, did not change the competitive environment. Thus monopoly power was not reduced and success in business was linked inextricably to the personal relations enjoyed. As a result, the entry of new firms was obstructed and innovation stifled.

The transition economies lacked private capitalists with the necessary financial capital to purchase enterprises, making foreign ownership the only alternative. It was not by coincidence that foreign capital came to the rescue of transition economies. This was an act of purposeful action by the mature market economies, ensuring that foreign ownership was the only permissible medium of privatization. A process, like shock therapy, implicitly had the goal of initiating the destruction of any institutional barrier inhibiting the penetration, influence, and power of foreign capital. The market socialists argued that the International Monetary Fund and the World Bank were responsible for creating the depression in transition economies through the collapse of domestic markets and COMECON, the development of the hard budget constraint, and the provision of foreign aid conditional on satisfying specific 'shock therapy' targets. In such an environment, the only interested buyers come from abroad at a price 'for next to nothing' (Gowan, 1995, p. 45). There was 'a brutal struggle to steal everything they could get their hands on' (Holmstrom and Smith, 2000, p. 7). Equally important was the pressure exerted on governments from transition economies to sell state assets and public utilities to multinational companies (the only possible buyers) to reduce fiscal deficits, lower inflation and discipline the labor market by inducing high unemployment. Effectively, multinationals practiced 'cherry-picking' in the name of global integration and national disintegration. Packages of incentives and legal regulations were often negotiated on a case-by-case basis, making the process appear arbitrary and even corrupt. As Bucknall (1997, p. 8) stated, 'it must be great fun remaking nations, a chance few ever get, and it must be even better when it is personally profitable'. Nevertheless, 'this does not so much suggest a new era on the globe as something rather old fashioned which, in the days of communism, used to be called imperialism' (Gowan, 1995, p. 60).

Practically every dictionary defines socialism as public ownership of land and capital. In the case of CEEFSU, the first task should have been to maintain state property. However, market socialists would have introduced fundamental changes in property relations. Forms of ownership, it was argued, were determined by, among other things, the varying degree of concentration of the productive forces. Diverse forms of technology gave rise to diverse forms of socialization: technology was not neutral. Thus to impose a common form of ownership was inconsistent with social reality. It could hardly have been correct to describe the progress of socialism as a mechanical increase in the share of state-owned assets at the expense of other forms of ownership. The simplistic view that state property was clearly superior to all other forms of ownership could not be sustained. Markets and planning could have been used in conjunction with a number of different kinds of ownership institutions, both private and collective.

The market socialists argued that state ownership *per se* did not guarantee efficiency. If the structure of state ownership conflicted with the changing economic realities, state ownership would have been a negative rather than a positive element in economic development. State property was no longer seen as sufficient or even necessary for socialism. Within the market socialist economic system, and based on state property, a variety of property forms could have existed. Thus all forms of property – individual, cooperative, and state – were important and were consistent with socialism.

This argument did not dismiss the role of state property in the socialist economy. State-owned enterprises would have been large enterprises characterized by monopoly power. State ownership would have ensured that the behavior of large enterprises was in line with the social good. State enterprises would have been both instructed and motivated to maximize the long-term rate of profit and thereby also efficiency. Managers of state-owned firms would have been induced to pursue profits, not only by making their salaries and bonuses subject to achieved profits but also by threatening job security. Decision-making in state firms would have been based not on the conventional hierarchical structure of firms, but rather on a democratic process in which all workers participated.

Market socialists argued that co-operatives were consistent with socialist principles. Enterprises in market socialism would normally have taken the form of workers' co-operatives, with capital supplied externally. Under this structure, ownership and control would have been exercised by all members of the co-operative, in the form of group property. All members of the co-operative would have been equal, with no distinction between employers and employees and no exploitation of labor. While a hierarchy is necessary for the coordination of production processes even in co-operatives, authoritarian hierarchies were not a natural result. There was a positive relationship between participation in decision-making and productivity, as well as between profit sharing and productivity. In firms that allowed the workers to make the decisions, the workers could have drawn from their shop-floor experience to make the correct decisions and responded rapidly. Where work yielded utility, and since co-operatives eliminated the exploitation of labor by capital, co-operatives could have performed better than hierarchical firms. In a democratically self-managed enterprise, workers, as a group, had a strong interest in assuring good job performance by monitoring the labor process of individual workers. Empirically, the claim that hierarchical firms necessarily outperform labor-managed firms was yet to be proven.

The co-operative form of ownership would have filled the gap left by the state sector. It would have counter-balanced state monopolies and stimulated changes in the state sector. Unsuccessful state enterprises might have become co-operatives. In the case of the media, where independence and freedom of information were crucial, ownership should have been in the form of a co-operative, making executives responsible only to their employees. Strangely enough, Roemer (1996a, p. 388; 1994d, p. 301) was against worker-ownership as a co-operative structure. Roemer has repeatedly argued that increasing employee control over the workplace is not a necessary element of the socialist vision. In this vein, an egalitarian distribution of profits was far more important than democratic control over the workplace. I believe that socialism required dramatically increased democratic control, in the form of workers' ownership of medium-sized enterprises. Moreover, the trend in modern technology was towards teamwork, custom-made products and small establishments, which also foster self-management.

The new perception of property relations under market socialism went further than the co-operative form. Private property should have been legalized, thereby recognizing that it had a role in a socialist system. Market socialists would have encouraged privately owned firms; however, they would have been restricted to small-scale enterprises, with large-scale privately owned capitalist firms being abolished. 'Capitalist firms that are sufficiently small do not pose a serious threat to the well-being of others' (Winter, 1990, p. 157). Capital should have been socialized and rented to firms. Private property was considered complementary to state and group ownership. Individuals should have been permitted to operate their own enterprise subject to certain regulations administered by local government. The regulations would have covered areas such as the level of activity permitted and the obligation to pay tax on profits and a 'capital use tax', since the means of the production was owned by society. It should also have been possible for a private entrepreneur to employ a few people. While this would have made him/her an exploiter, he/she would have had to work within, as well as manage, the enterprise. This would have been subject to conditions such as the number of people employed, or the value of capital assets, which would have varied across sectors. Private property was considered the most effective structure for the development of labor-intensive activities, especially in the service sector, and this was one of the major weaknesses of centrally administered socialism. Perhaps the most important reason for legalizing individual property was the need to liquidate the black market and associated activities. By bringing the shadow economy into the open, its activities could have been taxed and regulated.

Once privately owned enterprises reached a predetermined size and gained regional market power, the sole ownership rights of the private owners should have been abolished, appropriate compensation paid and the firms transformed into co-operatives. This was analogous to the capitalist entrepreneur, who sells out to the corporation when he/she is prepared to expand the business beyond its small size. But there is one important difference: a capitalist entrepreneur sells out voluntarily to the other self-interested firm wanting to purchase the investment. Under market socialism it would have been compulsory, with compensation determined by the state. Did the proper compensation for the original entrepreneur result in illegitimate enrichment? No, as long as the social-ist market and the price mechanism was functioning correctly. From a societal point of view, there would have been no unearned income arising simply from the capitalization of small ownership of capital and land.

Once co-operatives reached a predetermined size and gained economy-wide monopoly power, the co-operatives' rights should have been relinquished, after appropriate compensation, and their assets transferred to state ownership through legislation. Market socialists view the property structure of the enterprise as directly linked with monopoly power and the principal-agent problem. While small private ownership of the enterprise would not have given rise to power, as the firm grows its power increases, requiring a change in ownership. As the power of the firm increases with its size, ownership would also have been altered from private, to co-operative, to state. In this way, no individual or group of people would have gained substantial power in the economy. They would have been unable to accumulate substantial wealth, and incapable of influencing economic policy by virtue of their economic control of significant sectors of the means of production. In this market environment, state-owned firms must compete with one another and with cooperative and private enterprises. Thus it would have been wrong to conclude from the experience of firms in a command economy that state-owned firms would have behaved in a similar manner under a market socialist economy.

The ownership structure, discussed in the previous paragraphs contradicts the one proposed by Yunker. For Yunker (1997, pp. 15, 157, 178), entrepreneurial enterprises would have remained in private ownership so long as they remained genuinely entrepreneurial. An 'entrepreneurial enterprise' is defined as any busi-ness enterprise still being personally managed by its founder or owner (Yunker, 1988, pp. 75–6). Thus, any individual who achieved a substantial fortune under capitalism by genuine entrepreneurship – as opposed to ordinary financial speculation in which there is no managerial effort involved – would have been equally capable of achieving this fortune under market socialism. Upon volun-tary departure from personal management of an entrepreneurial enterprise, the owner would have realized the capitalized value of his/her personal ownership interest by selling the enterprise to an existing publicly owned enterprise. Thus Bill Gates, who personally manages Microsoft, would still have been able to retain his ownership rights under Yunker's market socialist model, even though Microsoft exercised substantial global monopoly power. This would be unacceptable for the property structure that I propose for market socialism.

A political democratic process would have determined the distribution of profits, in the form of a non-transferable and non-convertible 'social dividend'. Oscar Lange proposed the 'social dividend' system in the late 1930s. Initially he based it on work performance, but later made it independent of effort. Roemer (1994c, p. 292), however, opposed a proposal based on work performance. Under social ownership, citizens would have been given their per capita share of the total coupon/voucher value of the productive property in the economy, upon reaching the age of maturity. Whereas Roemer uses the term 'coupons', I refer to 'vouchers' in keeping with the voucher privatization in CEEFSU. Citizens would have been entitled to trade these stocks at prices quoted on a competitive stock market, but they could not have cashed in their portfolio. These trades would have been carried out with a 'coupon currency', as the only acceptable legal tender on the stock market. In turn, firms could have traded coupons received from issuing stock at the State Treasury for investment. The net revenues of the publicly owned business enterprise sector would not have been added to general government tax revenue. Rather, the net revenues would have been distributed directly to the public in the form of a social dividend proportionate to individual labor income. At death, the citizen's vouchers would have been sold and the coupon revenues returned to the Treasury. The Treasury, in turn, would have issued coupon endowments to citizens reaching the age of maturity. Various financial institutions, not shareholders, would have monitored firms. This would have ensured that dividends were paid in a more egalitarian way than they would have been in a capitalist society. Under market socialism, corporate profits would have been distributed to all citizens, whereas under capitalism these funds would have financed the consumption of capitalists.

One of the major criticisms of the coupon/voucher capital market system is that it could generate a 'lottery culture' that would reduce the capacity of citizens' political participation (Simon, 1996, p. 52). To avoid this, Roemer (1992, p. 270) suggested the establishment of mutual funds. A share in a firm would have entitled the owner of a mutual fund to a share of the firm's profits, and a share in a mutual fund would have entitled the holder to a share of the mutual fund's profits. It could be asked: 'why not forget about coupons/vouchers and directly use government revenue drawn from taxes on income, profit and capital?' Such revenue would be designed to provide income to the government for public expenditures and to maintain a guaranteed basic-livable income for all citizens. I would favor a market socialist model that instead universalized participation in conventional capital markets, universalized basic-livable income. A guaranteed basic-livable income would eliminate the need for a coupon/voucher market and the associated socially undesirable speculative behavior. It would eliminate the need for a Department of Social Security and would increase individual security and thus productivity. In contrast to Yunker (1988, p. 74; 1997, p. 179; 1994, p. 10; 1986, p. 683), the guaranteed basic-livable income would be provided without a work performance condition or means test.

For industrial democracy and self-management to be meaningful, the members of each enterprise would need to have a substantial degree of control over their work environment. This would be reflected in areas such as decisions about the products to be made and the methods of production. Small co-operatives might want to decide most issues by general meetings. Larger ones would probably adopt a more formal system of management, with top executives chosen by, and answerable to, the membership, but given a large degree of discretion in their day-to-day decision-making. Such an arrangement would avoid the problem that 'if everyone wanted to speak in general meetings, there would be no time available for anything else!' (Nove, 1994a, p. 211). However, it would be a mistake to regard time spent in decision-making as inherently unproductive. Workers' self-management at the enterprise level be a democratic process of decision-making and would foster and reinforce democracy at the political level. Workers would still need unions to protect them from overzealous managers, even if they had the power to remove management. Under market socialism, the national government would have had no authority to hire and dismiss managers of corporations. Managers would have been accountable to the rank-and-file employees through elections.

3.3   Institutions

Marx emphasized the importance of supporting institutions for accumulation and the fact that institutional choice did not take place in a vacuum. Moreover, given human behavior, and to ensure socialist outcomes from a market mechanism, the environment had to be altered so that the market outcomes were consistent with the social interests of efficiency, equity, self-management and solidarity. The transition to a socialist market would surely have required the development of new institutions, though possibly no more than those required for the transition to capitalism.

Under market socialism there would indeed have been markets, but there would also have been a wide range of other social, political and legal institutions that constrained them. Institutional norms would have fostered participation in self-management and the establishment of information disclosure laws and the implementation of periodic 'social audits' to monitor infringements of ecological and egalitarian standards. In this context, collusive behavior and cartels would have been illegal. Such institutions could only have been the result of targeted societal and state action. Market exchange also requires an informal system of institutions; similar to those that have evolved painstakingly over time, and in a variety of ways, in various market economies. The development of informal relationships in transition economies needed positive encouragement, the importance of which was often underestimated. Roemer (1996b, p. 35) stated that 'I remain agnostic on the question of the birth of the so-called socialist person, and prefer to put my faith in the design of institutions that will engender good result with ordinary people'.

In CEEFSU, institutions of private property did not exist. There was no independent judiciary and no bourgeois state to enforce private property rights. Yet, without these guarantees, most capitalists remain reluctant to put money into productive investments. Hence there has been little productive investment and little development, and the economy continues to sink even after privatization. The result was widespread corruption – the term Mafia lost its exclusive Italian connotation (Holmstrom and Smith, 2000, p. 1) – in which the new bourgeois was developed in a process of 'kleptocracy' (Eyal, Szelenyi and Townsley, 1997, p. 62). What shock therapy economists did not recognize was that the institutions of Western capitalism, including the legal, political and economics infrastructure were not easily to replicate. As a result, trust in such institutions was seriously undermined and slowly disappeared.

3.4   Monetary Policy and the Financial System

Under market socialism, capitalist shares and stock exchanges would have been removed and the production sector would have been financed entirely through a competitive credit market: that is, by a variety of socially-owned financial institutions, state and regional banks, pension funds and philanthropic trusts. However, those financial institutions with monopoly power would have been state-owned. For Roemer (1994a, pp. 76–7), firms in a coupon/voucher economy would have been organized around a small number of main banks. These banks would have been primarily responsible for organizing loan consortia to finance the operations of the firms within their groups and monitoring these firms. By monitoring the firms and ensuring sound management and profitability, the firms would have been able to pay back their loans. Having profitable firms, as clients would have given the banks a good reputation, making it easier for them to raise money to finance the operations within their respective groups. The role of banks would have been similar to that of those in the German and Japanese economies.

Roemer (1996b, p. 31; 1994a, pp. 76–7, 84; 1992, p. 272) and Miller (1994, p. 259) were in favor of banks operating independently of the state and not using political criteria when making decisions about firms. The banks' independence from political control would have been enforced by a series of legal and economic measures. I am against this proposal, since the independence of the state banks contradicts the proposition of the accountability of financial institutions to society through the planning process. Roemer (1996b, p. 31; 1994a, p. 78) and Bardhan (1993, p. 149) noted that there were arguments favoring the monitoring system over a take-over process, since investors were more likely to have inaccurate information about firms and their management. Investors are myopic: stock prices fall when firms take actions that are optimal in the long run but risk short-run profits. In a bank-centric monitoring system, dividends and institutional owners of firms would not have fired management if it pursued a long-run investment policy that resulted in low short run coupon/voucher prices (Roemer, 1994a, p. 81). In these new banks, money managers would have been rewarded for nurturing new enterprises to achieve an efficient long-run performance. The only serious restriction would have been that capital speculation by individuals over high-risk productive assets would no longer have been possible.

The coupon/voucher mechanism had to be supported by sophisticated financial institutions and regulation to prevent speculation, swindling and cheating. Actually, Bardhan (1993, p. 154) and Bardhan and Roemer (1992, p. 115) argued that the bank-centric monitoring system might have been less difficult to introduce in some developing countries, similar to the transition economies, where there was a pre-existing set of public investment banks and financial institutions. However, the same argument could have been used not only for a Romer-Bardhan-Yunker bank-centric monitoring system but also for the democratic-plan-centric monitoring system of state banks that I propose.

The instruments that the government could have used to influence the pattern of investment are discounts and surcharges on the market interest rate. The central bank would have manipulated the money supply – Post Keynesians would have denied this was possible – and would have been empowered to lend money to firms, with a specific interest rate discount or surcharge for each consumer-good sector. Lange proposed that to regulate investment interest rates should be used by the socialist government As it was assumed that the market was able to reach the Walrasian equilibrium, it could also have been assumed that the market would have been able to reach the Lange equilibrium: 'One assumption is as robust as the other' (Roemer, 1994a, p. 103).

It was anticipated that the bankruptcy rate among publicly owned firms under market socialism would have been approximately the same as it was among privately owned businesses under market capitalism. The imposition of a hard budget constraint and the possibility of bankruptcy would have provided the same incentive toward efficiency as it does presently. However, an anti-cyclical monetary and fiscal policy would have safeguarded against business depressions, in which bankruptcies become widespread, owing to general market failure rather than to individual firm inefficiencies.

In addition to the criticisms of the social dividend structure, the lottery culture and the disincentive for political participation already mentioned, Barkan and Belkin (1991, p. 570) argued that the bank-centric monitoring system would have reintroduced a form of ownership with bank-and-firm clusters, creating a quasi-privatized system. In response to this, Roemer (1992, p. 270) altered the model by introducing mutual funds. Each mutual fund would initially have held the same portfolio as all the large firms in the country. The coupons/vouchers distributed to adult citizens would have entitled each to a per capita share of the income of each mutual fund. However, a mutual fund structure has its own problems. These financial intermediaries would have been able to extract rents because potential borrowers would have had nowhere to go. They might have engaged in openly predatory activity, forcing firms to accept the bank's direction and control. Financial markets were not balanced through the interest rate mechanism. On the contrary, financial intermediaries always ration credit by withholding credit from borrowers who are not considered credit-worthy. Since lenders tend to share the same criteria, such 'strategic non-lending' has been a major mechanism through which class power has been exercised. For example, Yang (1993, p. 8) argued that, while collective ownership was a feasible option in a market system, it must be less efficient than private ownership since it was not prevalent. This argument does not take into account the difficulty that worker co-operatives have faced in borrowing capital, which has been a major obstacle to their development under capitalism. Effectively, the proposal of independent profit-maximizing state banks monitoring firms in the economy replicated the widely emphasized Marxist literature on the domination of the economy by 'financial capital'.

A complex socialist economy would have required new types of financial intermediaries, which would have been owned by the state if they had market power, to promote greater workplace democracy and to negotiate coordination through planning. As already stated, the market socialist model proposed for the transition economies, in contrast to that of Roemer and Yunker, did not require a social dividend but, rather, a guaranteed livable income, and not a bank-centric-monitoring system but, rather, a democratic-plan-centric monitoring system for firms.

3.5   Fiscal Policy

A market-based economy, even if it were socialist, would have been characterized by instability in investment and thus in employment, by hopefully to a lesser degree than in capitalism. Consequently, a discretionary fiscal policy would have been required in times of recession to increase investment and employment. There would have been no reason in the socialist society for resources to be unemployed. Planning, discretionary fiscal and monetary policies and an indirect mechanism involving tax and credit incentives would have ensured full employment. The funds required for government expenditure and investment would have been raised by turnover taxes on individual income and the profits of industrial enterprises. Privately owned businesses would have been subject to a 'capital use tax', since capital stock is social. This tax rate would have been based on the average rate of return on capital in the economy, which is equal to the rentals on natural resource use plus the return on assets employed minus the value of investments (Yunker, 1997, pp. 178, 208; Devine, 1988, p. 205). Progressive tax on income and wealth and appropriate transfer payments would have reduced inequalities. In contrast to Yunker and Roemer Transfer payments would have taken the form of a guaranteed livable income and not the form of a social dividend.

Market socialists have been very critical of the unfairness and inequity of capitalism, which is magnified by the fact that inheritance is clearly an important factor in determining the distribution of wealth. The resulting inequalities persist from generation to generation. In most capitalist economies, the majority of the rich are rich because they started from a privileged position. 'To have any appreciable chance of becoming a wealthy capitalist, you must be lucky enough to receive a substantial inheritance, or (if you do not receive an inheritance) you must be prodigiously, extraordinarily and unbelievably lucky in capital markets' (Yunker, 1997, p. 96). This highlighted the crucial importance of breaking the inequality cycle by drastically hindering the capacity of the wealthiest section of the population to pass on their accumulating fortunes through the generations. Under market socialism, the changing character of ownership and inheritance taxes would ensure equality of opportunity and the elimination of the unequal generational wealth distribution. Roemer (1996b, p. 20; 1994a, p. 120) argued that even if people have justly earned their estates, under conditions of equal opportunity, it did not follow that they have the right to exacerbate differential opportunity in the next generation by distributing their estates to favored individuals. The requirement of equality of opportunity for the next generation is also a goal for market socialists.

3.6   International Trade and Foreign Aid

Free participation in international trade was, without doubt, an extremely important factor in the economic success of transition economies. 'In most industrial sectors today nationalization implies the need for internationalization' (Murray, 1987, p. 92). This view was consistent with Marx's assertion that 'the emancipation of the workers is not a local, nor a national, but an international problem' (Barratt-Brown, 1995, p. 338; Yunker, 1997, p. 32). Actually, 'market socialism in one country' was not realistic (Roemer, 1994b, p. 291; 1991b, p. 573) because 'no firm is an island into itself' (Murray, 1987, p. 92). The relative isolation of the Soviet Union from the international transfer of technological knowledge had devastating consequences on its efficiency and contributed to its ultimate collapse.

Experience revealed that free trade did not benefit everyone equally. The concept of comparative advantage had its origins not so much in economics as in politics, and was created within the context of colonialism, war, nationalist rivalries, and military power. Prices and wages undoubtedly reflect the exchange of equivalents that, in turn, are the products of specific historical processes.

Instead of mutual free trade, each government acts on its own to reduce its country's imports, either directly by import controls or indirectly by the general deflation of the purchasing power of the country. This simply means that other governments follow suit and the whole level of world trade is set far below what is optimum. To expand such mutually beneficial trade would have required that governments planned international trade. Nove (1994b, p. 369) was concerned about the stability of the international trade system 'that the East Europeans are now so keen to join'. Naturally, a customs union of several market socialist countries in CEEFSU would have been both possible and desirable: a common socialist market with close cooperation and perhaps a common currency. The socialist customs union would have provided the means to avoid the destructive elements of free international trade with the capitalist countries and, at the same time, might have become a vehicle for the development of market socialism. A supranational planning body would have ensured that prevailing regulations and interventions in member socialist countries encouraged social equality and ecological responsibility for entire global production. These regulations would have incorporated standards for conditions of production such as health and safety, rights to overtime, redundancy and maternity pay, sickness benefits and rights, and facilities for workers. The fundamental basis of the socialist customs union would have been 'the precondition for the free development of each would be the free development of all' (Blackburn, 1991b, p. 233). In this way, the international market for equity and debt capital would have continued without essential change, but within a framework of the socialized ownership of investment resources. While the proposal for a socialist customs union was quite similar to the Post Keynesian recommendation for a permanent international clearing union, there were some important differences. The socialist customs union would have been based on an international socialist market, guided by a supranational planning body based on the principles of consultation, debate, democracy, and self-government between member countries.

Roemer (1994b, p. 291; 1991b, p. 573) favored participation of foreign capital in the socialist economy. The mandate of market socialism was to equalize incomes in the national economy, and domestic income could have increased through the participation of foreign capital. The socialist control of investment would, however, have required some regulation of foreign investment. Meanwhile, socialist transition countries would have been able to use their members' resources without damaging the socialist cause and falling into the trap of providing concessions to international capital by eliminating restrictions. Legal safeguards would have been needed to prevent international capital from 'flying'. A system of internationally negotiated controls on capital flight would have been necessary, whereby countries would have been required to return capital that was moved abroad in violation of a nation's laws. Such returned funds would have been confiscated if the owner were convicted of illegal capital exports. In this way, an internationally sanctioned system would have provided a powerful deterrent. Early drafts for the establishment of the IMF, written by the Roosevelt administration, contained provisions for precisely these measures to assure the return of illegal flight capital that was transferred abroad. However, they never materialized (Block, 1994, p. 379).

The international organizations and mature market economies were certainly not sending massive amounts of aid eastwards to facilitate the transition. There was no second Marshall Plan. However, this did not preclude massive political intervention from outside to ensure that the transition economies adopted the 'right' course of economic action. According to market socialists, the development policies pursued and funded by the IMF and the World Bank were inimical both to the interests of the people and to the natural environment in CEEFSU. Meanwhile, neither international organizations nor mature market economies wished to see the transition economies descend into complete chaos. Hence the strategy was to provide limited and conditional support for market reforms to allow for the international exploitation of parts of the transition economies, integrate the transition economies into the world financial system, and permit a very narrow sector of their domestic population to enrich themselves. This, of course, would not have led to the rebirth of the transition economies. Nor would it have improved the lives of the ordinary people. However, it would have kept the elite of the transition economies quiet internationally and prevented disturbances in Russia spilling over into the wider world. If the mature market economies could have gained access to cheap resources, then so much the better for them.

If the mature market economies really wished to improve the chances of a democratic consolidation in transition economies they should have forgiven old debts, offered generous new aid, and dismantled their own trading restrictions. Instead, the conditional nature of IMF and World Bank funding assured investors that transition governments would not bend to popular pressures to abandon the shock therapy policies. IMF and World Bank financial and technical assistance programmes to CEEFSU stipulated that recipients could neither place restrictions on foreign neither direct investment nor encourage development banking. For example, the terms of a World Bank loan agreement constrained the ability of the Polish Development Bank to issue direct, subsidized industrial loans. Moreover, these international organizations barred transition economies from pursuing gradualist reforms or state intervention still less contemplating the possibility of market socialism. The dependence of the IMF and World Bank on the US capital market for their funds has effectively transformed these institutions into agents of United States foreign policy.

3.7   Social Policy

Social protection was embedded in centrally administered socialism and was expressed as a cumulative series of rights. Today in CEEFSU poverty is endemic, together with humiliation and economic collapse. Transition govern-ments have been pressed by the IMF and the World Bank to cut public spending and, in particular, to eliminate the large public subsidies for housing and food. Privatization exposed the population to the risks of the market without any in-stitutionalized safeguards and ensured the loss of guaranteed shelter and cheap food, which constituted a denial of the collectivist ethic of the previous system. The IMF insisted on spending cuts in education, medicine, culture, and even assistance to people disabled by the Chernobyl nuclear disaster. This was in contrast to the controversial *World Development Report on Poverty*, produced by the World Bank when Joseph Stiglitz was chief economist, which argued that effective safety nets should have been created before free-market reforms were introduced. The market socialists argued that the transition process required an adequate social policy. Its creation should have been an integral part of the transition design, since as it was required to cushion the most vulnerable groups of the population, as well as to ensure political support.

The goal associated with market socialism was greater equality at the be-ginning, so that people entered the market on an equal footing, to achieve the equalization of positive freedoms in production. Indeed, raising the income of the poor would have been the most important single step to improving their opportunities for self-realization and greater welfare. To achieve this, house-holds would have required access to a guaranteed basic-livable income without being forced to sell labor power to enterprises even though they were socially owned. The survival of the members of the society, at a basic but decent stan-dard, should have been independently guaranteed 'No questions asked, no strings attached' to a sufficient income (Van Parijs, 1991, p. 130). Under these circumstances, individuals would have been able to exercise genuine choice about selling their labor power to enterprises, rather than being compelled to sell by necessity. A transfer system based on the guaranteed basic-livable income is not targeted at those who have shown to be 'inadequate'. It involves less administrative control over its beneficiaries and is far less likely to stig-matize, humiliate or shame them or undermine their self-respect. Van Parijs (1991, pp. 130; 1997, p. 327) dismissed the argument that the introduction of a guaranteed basic-livable income was unfair and resulted in exploitation: those who choose to live off their basic income do not unfairly free ride and exploit those citizens who do make the required contribution.

A guarantee basic-livable income for all citizens has been linked with the classic market socialist concept of the social dividend as outlined by Oscar Lange, recently refined by Roemer and Yunker, as it is presented in this chapter. It was that part of the national income which was not distributed as wages or interest but which belonged to the people as owners of the means of production. For Roemer (1994c, p. 292), the social dividend would have been a form of guaranteed income. However, the social dividend, as proposed by Roemer, would have fluctuated in line with market conditions and not necessarily have provided an adequate income. For Yunker, it would have fluctuated, in addition to market conditions, on the basis of labor effort: the social dividend would be a fixed percentage of labor income. In fact, under Roemer's calculations the actual profit dividend each person would have received would not have been enormous (Roemer, 1996b, p. 18; Wright, 1996b, p. 131). On Yunker's proposal, people unable to work would not have received a social dividend. I prefer the provision of a guaranteed basic-livable income instead of the social dividend concepts suggested by Roemer and Yunker. Profits of state enterprises would become a part of government revenue, which would have funded the guaranteed basic-livable income, not the social dividend. An unconditional basic income would have been a grant paid to every citizen, irrespective of his or her occupational situation and marital status, and without regard to his or her work performance or availability for work. There would have been a framework of objective minimum standards, which would have been determined with the help of scientists and approved after public debate, facilitating social solidarity and the promotion of social justice. The implementation of the guaranteed basic-livable income would have freed the resources of the Department of Social Security, given that the taxation office would have administered the system. The Department of Social Security would be transformed and have concentrated on the provision of services. The highly progressive tax system would have ensured that those who did not require the guaranteed basic-livable income returned the gain through normal taxation. In transition economies, the funding of the guaranteed minimum income would not have been affected by fiscal constraints. The elimination of the privileges of the bureaucracy and the gradual removal of subsidies and the soft budget constraint would have provided adequate funding.

In line with this thinking, health, education and welfare services should have been distributed according to need. Under conditions of full employment, the right-to-work for all citizens would have been firmly established, without giving up the guaranteed basic-livable income. Having these elements of social and taxation policies in place, and with no private ownership in the means of production, there would have been no private fortunes and no legal means of making money by speculation. Inequality would have been reduced substantially.

4   The process of reform

According to the market socialist approach to the transition, the first priority was the establishment of the institutional structure to assist the development of the socialist market that would have facilitated the development of informal institutions. At the same time, the establishment of financial regulation, the tax structure, guaranteed basic-livable income, and the founding of the socialist customs union should have been initiated. The privatization of small firms and the transfer of medium firms to labor management could have followed in Year

1. The restructuring of large state enterprises could have been initiated in Year 2 lasting to the end of Year 3. Discretionary fiscal and monetary policy together with incomes and industry policies would be maintained throughout the transition process. After the restructuring of state enterprises was completed in Year 4, together with the gradual liberalization of prices, tariffs with the capitalist countries would have been permanent, while tariffs with the members of the socialist customs union would have been eliminated. Unconditional foreign aid would have facilitated the process. The right to work could only be implemented after the restructuring of state enterprises was complete in Year 4. The market socialist process of transition is demonstrated in Table 7.1.

5 The Cost of Transition

Using the cost criteria of the transition process identified in Chapter 3, the pluralistic market socialist model of transition would had one of the lowest economic costs, but higher than neoclassical gradualist and the Chinese models, since it involved the maintenance of state ownership for large enterprises and a number of elements of centrally administered socialism. The pluralistic market socialist approach had the highest political cost (together with the Post Keynesian model), since people were not willing to experiment with market socialism. With regard to the ideological cost the people in CEEFSU placed the pluralistic market socialist model at the high end of ideological cost (but lower than the Chinese model) since the approach was inconsistent with the desire to establish a capitalist economic system. With regard to the International Financial cost the international financial institutions and governments in mature market economies were not enthusiastic to provide funding to the transition economies, which implemented the pluralistic market socialist approach. Lastly, with regard to the Foreign Direct Investment Cost the pluralistic market socialist model has the highest cost (together with the Post Keynesian model), since multinationals were not enthusiastic to finance projects in transition economies if they had implemented the pluralistic market socialist.

6 Conclusion

In what way can the market socialist model proposed for the transition economies be called socialist? What was distinctive about a transition process that tried to establish a 'socialist' system? Ideologically, the model borrowed concepts and analysis from the liberal view, particularly the interventionist variant. It may even be argued that the transition process would have been contradictory. It tried to achieve a consistent socialist system through 'capitalist' means such as markets, prices, profits, market planning, 'bourgeois democracy' and self-interest. Strangely enough, the norms and institutions of capitalism appeared to be essential to socialism.

Table 7.1
The Market Socialist Process of Transition

Years		1	2	3	4	5	6	7	8	9	10
1. Price Liberalization	Price Deregulation										
Stabilization	Market Planning Industry-Incomes Policy										
2. Privatization	Restructuring Large State Enterprises										
	Privatization of Small Enterprises										
	Medium Enterprises: Co-operatives										
3. Institution	Formal Institutions										
	Informal Institutions										
4. Monetary Policy and the Financial System	Financial Regulation										
	Discretionary Monetary Policy										
5. Fiscal Policy	Discretionary AD Policy										
	Tax Structure										
6. International Trade and Aid	Socialist Customs Union										
	Tariffs										
	Unconditional Foreign Aid										
7. Social Policy	**Guaranteed Basic-Livable Income**										
	Right to Work										
	Years	1	2	3	4	5	6	7	8	9	10

Supporters of market socialism accept that capitalism has been able to sustain a high level of economic growth. Centrally administered socialism was not able to match those levels. For socialism to have a chance in the transition economies, the economy would have had to adopt mechanisms that were not peculiarly 'capitalist'. According to Radzikhovsky (1990, p. 12), 'an economy cannot be ideological correct or incorrect, it can only be efficient and inefficient'. If market socialism did not discriminate against 'capitalist' mechanisms, what was left to distinguish a capitalist from a socialist economic system? Socialism stands, by definition, for humane rule and the subordination of economics to humanity. However, was market socialism simply 'capitalism with a human face'?

Socialism, as envisaged by supporters of the model, was able to provide economic growth and, equally importantly, provide higher forms of accountability than capitalism. This was what was so special about socialism. It was no longer central administration replacing the market, or state property replacing private property, or even a single party system replacing 'bourgeois democracy'. These were not characteristics of socialism but, rather, of Stalinism, which did not have any relevance to socialism. For market socialists, socialism was described as a system superior to capitalism because it was able to eliminate some forms of power and, where power still existed, to control it more effectively than under capitalism. Although capitalism had achieved both high efficiency and accountability, socialism could have gone even further. The fact that non-pluralistic socialism failed to achieve these goals was an argument against Stalinism, not against socialism.

Although the market socialist model aimed to reproduce the accountability of capitalism, it also envisaged new forms of accountability. In particular, it incorporated national allocative planning and workers' election of management, which had been inhibited under capitalism due to the power of domestic and international capital. One of the problems with a high concentration of private ownership in capitalist societies was its consequent influence on the political process. In the market socialist model, this was less likely to happen. Also less likely would be for the media to be influenced by particular interests. This is in contrast to what is currently happening in Russia. Therefore, it was argued that with the elimination of some and the effective control of the remaining centers of power, market socialism can achieve equality of opportunity for self-realization, welfare, political influence, and social status.

Hence the market socialist reforms would have provided the basis for the development of a socialist ideology, which did not bear much resemblance to socialism as previously practiced. Like all ideologies, it advocated the establishment of a superior form of society. It borrowed methods and analysis from competing ideologies, particularly classical liberal and liberal interventionist concepts. The outcome would have been different from all liberal as well as non-pluralistic forms. The model proposed a pluralistic society where the forms of ownership would have facilitated a level of accountability beyond the grasp of a capitalist society. Such ideology is termed 'socialist interventionist', while the economic system is market socialism. While it bears a close resemblance to the liberal interventionist model, it attempted to transcend the levels of individualism and accountability achieved so far in capitalist societies. As Rider (1998, p. 166–7) stated, market socialism is a 'model that uses mainstream tools to accomplish non-mainstream goals'.

While market socialists were very critical of the Stalinist system, they did not develop a coherent guide for the development of socialism in transition economies. The starting-point of the writings of market socialists was capitalism, but in reality in CEEFSU the starting-point was centrally administered socialism. Market socialists had to answer the call for the development of a socialist market in CEEFSU. The transition economies faced a momentous task of institution building. No matter what kind of market system was desired, the costs of designing market socialism would have been no greater than the costs of building a capitalist system. Miller (1994, p. 262) argued that the market element of market socialism had to be in place before the socialist element. However, this was in contradiction to the transition process initiated in CEEFSU. In contrast, it could have been argued that the evolution of centrally administered socialism in CEEFSU towards market socialism would have been the easiest and least destabilizing path. Market socialism had an advantage over other models of transition. One of the most important goals – that the majority of property should be socially owned – was realized. What remained was the development of market relations in accordance with these socialist goals. In the transition to a market economy, the transition economies had to take advantage of any elements in the old system that were potentially conducive to successful operation within a new decentralized competitive market socialist system. In particular, the skills and the education of workers and their detailed knowledge about production processes might have been best harnessed by a system in which management remained more accountable to insiders than to external financiers.

The transition to market socialism required the development of a practical, workable form of socialism 'to replace the misguided and half-baked proposals of the past' (Yunker, 1997, p. 195; Brighouse, 1996, p. 187). However, market socialism still remains a hypothetical possibility, not only for transition economies but also for anywhere in the world, because it has not yet been implemented anywhere. Economic analysis did not necessarily support the conclusion that market socialism *would* have worked better than capitalism, but rather, that it *might* have worked better than capitalism. Consequently, the relative performance of market socialism was an empirical rather than a theoretical question. In response to this criticism, Yunker (1997, pp. 143, 151) and Stauber (1977, p. 244) claimed that market socialism would have operated 'almost exactly' like contemporary capitalism. However, only an actual experiment with market socialism would have provided truly definitive evidence on its economic performance. However, this did not appear possible due to the cry from CEEFSU of 'no more socialist experiments on us', even though experiments could not have been avoided in any kind of transition to a market economy. It was Stalin who had called on people to make sacrifices for the sake of socialism. The word 'socialism' was discredited, and brought bad memories to the people in CEEFSU. In transition economies there was a political fatigue; there had been enough societal experiments and there was no taste for new ones. People in the transition economies wanted a system that had proven its workability, independently of whether capitalism was good, bad or indifferent.

The question then arises: to what extent was the proposed strategy of market socialism politically feasible? The dominant ideology imposed upon transition economies was unfavorable to egalitarian alternatives such as market socialism. The kind of market socialism advocated here could only have been politically possible if a substantial sector of state-owned firms had been maintained and political parties calling for a more egalitarian denationalization had possessed influence. 'If privatization can be stopped, Eastern Europe presents mouth-watering possibilities for experimentation with market socialism' (Shleifer and Vishny, 1994, p. 165). In fact, there was strong evidence that, due to privatization, popular cynicism and the lack of credible advocates of an alternative approach, the idea that market socialism as a viable option for transition economies 'was effectively dead' (Weisskopf, 1996, p. 282; Rider, 1998, p. 179).

Whether market socialism would have been an alternative to capitalism for the transition economies, or anywhere else in the world remains an open question. However, there was no need for market socialism to defend itself against the charge of being utopian. 'Utopia is a prerequisite of social upheavals, just as unrealistic efforts are the precondition of realistic ones' (Kolakowski, 1976, p. 687).

Chapter 8

The Non-Pluralistic Model of Market Socialism: The Chinese Approach

1 Introduction

Nearly a quarter of century ago, China's Communist leadership, under Deng Xiaoping, initiated a marketization process in its centrally administered socialist economic system, which was modeled on Stalinist principles. The start of these reforms is usually identified with the Communist Party Plenum in December 1978. Thus the period of reform has been at least double that in CEEFSU. China's reforms differed markedly from those implemented in the transition economies of CEEFSU. There were a few reasons for this. Firstly, China was exhausted from 20 years of dealing with Mao's messianic vision. Secondly, the Chinese leadership was not willing to adopt shock therapy and there was no desire to replicate the experience of Western Europe. Thirdly, China faced no economic crisis, only dissatisfaction with the pace of economic growth.

It has been widely accepted that the Chinese reforms have been successful. In sum, the economic growth rate is among the highest on record and fairly stable, it has been achieved without sacrificing external equilibrium, and inflation has been kept under control. Consequently, the experiences and outcomes of the various transition economies, which implemented different strategies, are puzzling. Why is it that shock therapy, which dismantled an inefficient economic structure in one shot, resulted in a large decline in economic growth, while in China, which initially preserved the inefficient planning system, a substantial increase in output resulted? Strangely enough, an argument used for the adoption of shock therapy by Sachs and Woo (1994, p. 105) was the supposed failure of the two-track Chinese approach. This suggests that there were serious problems with the methodology underlying the transition orthodoxy of shock therapy and that the Chinese experience offered a strong counter-example to the sweeping claim that the gradual reforms would fail. The Chinese experience with reform has been an embarrassment to orthodox economics.

However, whether China's reforms and successes could have been replicated other transition economies was hotly debated. McKinnon (1993b), McMillan and Naughton (1992) and Blackburn (1991d) argued that China's success demonstrated the superiority of an evolutionary, experimental and bottom-up reform over the comprehensive and top-down shock therapy approach. Not surprisingly, a number of Russians expressed interest in experimenting with the Chinese model. Actually, the neoclassical gradualist approach analyzed in Chapter 5 was highly influenced by the Chinese process of transition. Woo (1994), Sachs and Woo (1994), Qian and Xu (1993), Lin, Cai and Li (1996, p. 201), Gordon, (1992, p. 54), Li (1999, p. 133), Johnson (1994, p. 67) and Hughes (1994, p. 135) argued that the success of the Chinese reforms was due to neither gradualism nor to experimentation but, rather, to China's unique initial conditions. It was argued that the model did not have any implications for other transition economies that faced different initial conditions. Thus 'the recommendation that Russia should take the same path as China amounts to telling apples to be pears' (Aslund, 1993, p. 99). Nevertheless, the economic problems in pre-reform China were common to all centrally administered economies and so the Chinese model of transition could have held some interest to CEEFSU, if the transition process had resulted in the establishment of a market capitalist system. As already explained, the transition economies were not interested in adopting a market socialist model, even if it was Chinese-style. Actually, this appears to be true. The dynamic process of reform in China revealed the unfolding of market capitalism, not market socialism. It is in this context that an investigation of the applicability of the Chinese process of reform as an alternative model of transition, in the tradition of political economy, can take place.

2 Primary Elements of the Non-Pluralistic Model of Market Socialism

2.1 Economic Analysis

Mao, like Marx, ruled out any role for the market in a socialist economy. In contrast, Deng Xiaoping agreed with the pluralist market socialists about the integral role of markets in a socialist economic system. Deng Xiaoping, the architect of economic reform, proclaimed that it did not matter whether the cat was red or white as long it caught mice (Zwass, 1999, p. 224). Mao's response to Deng's statement was: 'if it is all the same to them whether it is a white cat or a red cat, they will not mind if it is imperialism or Marxism-Leninism' (Weil, 1996, p. 269). Deng also proclaimed the slogan 'enrich yourselves' and that it was all right for a few to get rich first and pull the others along with them later. Market-oriented reforms, specifically the extension of markets and a significant reduction in the role of central planning, have been crucial elements in explaining China's economic success. Naturally, 'markets do not require private ownership to function' (Bowles and Xiao-Yuan, 1994, p. 60).

2.2   What is a Good Society?

When the Chinese leaders initiated the reforms in the late 1970s, they did not question the feasibility or desirability of the 'socialist' economic system, recognizing that a free market economy was inappropriate for China. China's leaders did not imagine that they could quickly, in one shot, create the wealth of mature market economies. There was consensus that a desirable balance between planning and markets could only be found through experimentation and the system's evolution, not through sweeping and radical propositions. China had already experienced a succession of disasters by attempting policy 'leaps' such as 'The Great Leap Forward'. Consequently, China's reforms were not conceived as part of a grand plan or a blueprint. There were never-ending changes in the official definitions of China's economic system, which were, in part, a reflection of the lack of clear objectives in the reform process. Initially it was coined as, 'the planned economy leads, the market economy supports'. This was followed by 'a planned commodity economy', then 'a socialist market economy with Chinese characteristics'. Presently, it is defined as 'a socialist market economic system'.

The reforms have consisted of small step-by-step changes. The ultimate goal was not announced, nor was any timetable for the transition mentioned. Some of the changes were initiated spontaneously, at ground level, and only after they were successful were they ratified by government and implemented as official policy. The reforms proceeded by trial and error, with frequent mid-course corrections and reversals of policy. The goal was modest: avoiding disaster and achieving some improvements through cautious changes; attempting to 'perfect' the existing public ownership-based planned economy via bettering efficiency and incentives and correcting for structural imbalances. Therefore, China did not concern itself with what it should have done but, rather, with what it could have done: trying whatever measures would propel economic growth and transform a command economy into a market economy.

There is wide disagreement among economists whether China is a market socialist economic system. On the one hand, the combination of the partial reliance on the market and active local state and social ownership leads some economists to characterize China's economy as a decentralized, developmental market-socialist system. Most importantly, the doctrine of the dictatorship of the proletariat by the Communist Party upholds the socialist character of the society. The economic structure in China resembles Lenin's New Economic Policy.

On the other hand, Weil (1996, pp. 21, 39) argued that the concept of 'socialism' in China has become 'muddied' and 'blurred', in view of the fact that two parts of the system, the state and the liberalized sectors, were so closely combined. The socialist character of the economic system in China could be confused by the fact that 'the public' owns a major portion of the economy through state ownership, which is indicative of 'socialism'. However, as already mentioned in Chapter 7, state ownership, as such, cannot be accepted as a sufficient condition for a socialist system. In addition, the continuing direct investment by the government in expanding enterprises, the use of the state for regional and sectoral redistribution and the degree of macroeconomic control could also be indicative of socialism. However, these elements were suggestive of the macroeconomic guidance of the emerging market rather than socialism. Effectively, the Chinese reform policies are quasi-capitalist policies. This Chinese definition of socialism does not have any resemblance to the propositions of the pluralistic market socialists presented in Chapter 7. Hence, the long-term commitment to the socialist market concept in China appears doubtful: 'It does not matter if a regime calls itself red or white, as long as it exploits the working classes for profit' (Weil, 1996, p. 26). Therefore, despite the continued claim by the government that its system is socialist, it could be argued that in China, even though there is a high degree of public ownership, workers and peasants are still exploited for the benefit of the political and economic elite.

Although the government did not intend to transform the socialist economic system into a capitalist economy, the economic reforms, during the last decade, effectively opened the door to decentralization, commercialization, privatization, as well as democratization and effectively making the 'Chinese-style' transition process relevant as an alternative model of transition for CEEFSU. For this reason, the lessons of China's experience with respect to the viability of market socialism are arguably of more academic than practical importance.

2.3   Speed

The Chinese transition process has been metaphorically represented as 'crossing the river by feeling the stones underfoot' (Johnson, 1994, p. 60; Zhou, 1992, p. 200; Kornai, 1995a, p. 37; Yu, 1993, p. 3) and to 'go a step and look for the next' (Weiying and Yi, 1995, p. 6). The Chinese process of reform is often cited as the leading example of a feasible and successful gradualist and evolutionary transformation to marketization, with the possible exception of the 'mini bangs' or 'controlled explosions' necessary to get the process started.

The Chinese approach to reform was characterized as piecemeal, partial, incremental, bottom-up, experimental, adaptive through learning and marked by frequent shifts of direction and ad hoc responses to unanticipated outcomes. Notwithstanding, 'economic reform Chinese style is not an accident. There is a political logic for it' (Cao, Qian and Weingast, 1999, p. 125). The choice of gradualism had to do with China's turbulent modern history of long periods of instability, which made the leadership acutely aware of avoiding over-hasty system changes. In this context, a gradual approach to economic reform was inevitable, in contrast to Mao Zedong's policies of 'big bangs' in the form of 'The Great Leap Forward' and the 'Cultural Revolution'.

A salient feature of China's reform was that it proceeded on an ad hoc and trial-and-error basis. Piecemeal reform measures were introduced, on an experimental basis, in a single region or sector and, if successful, were then extended to enterprises in other regions or sectors of the country. Therefore, the reform started with experimentation: from minor reform to moderate reform, and from moderate reform to major reform. Consequently, China's reforms were massively time-consuming. During transition, due to the absence of social policies, great emphasis was placed in avoiding 'chaos' and large-scale unemployment. Wherever possible, the aim was to minimize the social and economic costs of change and displacement; thus, there was a strong case for incrementalism and extensive state action.

Chinese economic reforms were evolutionary, with a 'stop-go cycle' and 'an easy-to-hard sequence'. An evolutionary process means that many small and half-hearted reform measurers accumulate into a radical one over time. The easy-to-hard sequence involved firstly agriculture and foreign trade and, only later, industry. Reform in rural areas preceded that in urban areas. Actually, Jin and Haynes (1997, p. 83) argued that the best way to characterize the Chinese transition process was not as a gradual approach, but rather as a dualist leading-sector approach. At the end, the process generated a self-perpetuating dynamic, which was successful in raising productivity in all sectors. Consequently, the easy-to-hard sequence may not necessarily be different from the optimal sequence, since the easiest reform might be the precondition for the hardest. The Chinese reformers interpret optimization as the minimization of social cost. By splitting and spreading the transition costs over a long period and by changing policy direction after a small policy error during experimentation, the process was optimal, both politically and economically.

However, the apparent 'success' of the gradual Chinese process of transition can be rationalized by shock therapy supporters as a result of the 'special' initial conditions that existed in China prior to the reform process. These special initial conditions were associated with a number of positive outcomes. They included the development of the private sector, the high savings rate, the structural characteristics of the economy, the Chinese diaspora, the deliberate mass campaigns against the bureaucracy, and, finally, the fact that China was not so centrally planned as the Soviet Union and Eastern Europe. Of these reasons, the first two, the positive measures for the development of the private sector and the high savings rate, could only have been part of the general economic theory of transition, which were consistent with a shock therapy approach. The remaining reasons were specific to the Chinese economic state of affairs prior to the reform, making the model inapplicable to CEEFSU.

Hence a successful transition outside China, for the shock therapy supporters, could only have taken place via the shock therapy approach and gradualism could only have failed. Meanwhile, the Chinese experience demonstrated that a gradualist approach could only have been realized, as the shock therapy supporters argued, where special initial circumstances existed. There is a contradiction here. The shock therapy process was supposedly based on simple truths and applicable to any transition economy, independent of the initial conditions. By arguing that the success of the gradualist Chinese approach was due to the specific characteristics of the economy, the universality of the shock therapy approach was undermined. The experience of China weakened the arguments for the shock therapy approach. This anomaly was explained by Parker, Tritt and Woo (1997, p. 15), who argued that in Hungary, Poland and Russia the transition process involved structural adjustment since they were already industrialized urban societies, while in China and Vietnam it involved 'normal economic development' since they were overwhelmingly subsistence peasant agricultural economies. Nevertheless, this argument reinforces the position that initial conditions play an important role in determining the speed of the reform process, which the shock therapy champions ignored. This argument undermines the generality of the shock therapy approach. China's experience raised the possibility that a gradual process of 'growing out of plan' was a feasible alternative to creative destruction (Rawski, 1992, p. 16; Weitzman and Xu, 1994, p. 142; Gelb, Jefferson and Singh, 1993, p. 19; Jefferson and Rawski, 1994, p. 66; Nolan, 1995, pp. 7, 110).

2.4   Political Structure

The reform movement in China, as in CEEFSU, combined demands for both political and economic reform. Reform implied 'opening up' the party's monopoly to political pluralism and freeing the economy from state controls, so that market forces could be rejuvenated. Nevertheless, the emphasis placed on the political relatively to the economic reforms varied across countries, as did the decision whether they should have been attempted at the same time or with one preceding the other. Gorbachev chose to implement political reform first, with Eastern Europe following suit. Chinese reformers followed Mao who, in the development of the economy, supported 'putting politics in command' (Weil, 1996, pp. 218–9). There was a belief in China that only with the presence of the Communist Party could there be economic growth while still ensuring the construction of a socialist society. Deng consistently maintained that the only feasible political setting in which to reform the command economy successfully was under strong, unified party leadership. Consequently, the Chinese non-pluralistic regime was not prepared to allow the degree of political liberalization required to establish a pluralistic form of market socialism, as described in Chapter 7.

The key to the disintegration of the Soviet nation-state lay with the decision taken by Gorbachev to pursue *glasnost* and *perestroika*. In the end, in CEEFSU, there were radical political changes; however, economic reform progressed haltingly. Under these conditions, support for a more radical program of 'shock therapy' quickly gained ground, strongly affected by the rapid growth in the influence of Western ideas. Actually, the revolutionary overthrow of the Communist Party was the central building block for the transition orthodoxy, as it was intrinsically desirable and functionally useful to economic progress. In the sharpest contrast, there was a near-consensus among the Chinese leadership that political democratization was not part of the political agenda.

The Chinese reforms seem to suggest that economic reform should have preceded political reform. It appears that in countries like China, which has a large population and was very unevenly developed, democratization should have been the result of economic reform, by first ensuring the development of the productive forces and increases in income. Initially, people are likely to highly value improvements in their living standard more than democratic rights. Moreover, their rankings of the relative importance of these goals can alter sharply as their income level and security changes.

The reform processes in China have maintained political stability and, on the whole, state control of the macro economy. This stands in contrast to the political instability, which has hindered CEEFSU's transition. Democracy in Russia and Eastern Europe was too myopic and paid too much attention to meeting short-term political goals. Thus it was necessary for China to have a non-pluralistic political system, which positively influenced investment with the aim of stimulating economic growth. 'The limits of reform are thus set by political actors' (Nee and Matthews, 1996, p. 405). China's non-pluralism was vastly better at governing China than Gorbachev or Yeltsin at governing the USSR and Russia. The criterion by which to evaluate a political reform should be whether or not it contributes to social stability and economic development.

Under circumstances where the economic system has not been fundamentally changed, the destabilizing of the political structure would only make it impossible for the economic reform to proceed. Marketization of a centrally administered economy is an evolutionary process with interactions between self-interested agents; however, economic policy must be implemented independently from the interests of the economic elite. If the leaders were occupied with competition for power and endless debates, the economic reform program, 'even if it were completely correct, would end up as a mere scrap of paper' (Li, 1994, p. 311). The absence of powerful interest groups, whose demands interfere with attempts at consensus, could be considered an advantage for the Chinese reform process. China's non-pluralistic leaders did not need to be troubled about a loss of political legitimacy, but instead focused on political stability. Hence, while a weak and unstable government was likely to retard the progress of economic transformation, a strong and stable government was likely to accelerate it. 'Good government' did not necessarily imply democratic government. Thus the relative stability enforced by non-pluralism in China deserved part of the credit for China's economic success.

Because of its Pareto-improving property, the dual-track approach minimized political opposition to reform ex ante. Enforcement of the plan track was crucial for preserving the pre-existing rents. The power for sufficient state enforcement was required to carry out a reform that created no losers, only winners, by introducing two set of laws in two different regions. In such a process, the strong state was able to use its power to prevent a rapid growth of asset inequality and protect the weaker members of society, who might otherwise have suffered more during the transition process. Maintaining political stability in China has been an important factor in encouraging foreign investment, which was required to finance growth.

The introduction of market forces has brought about fundamental changes not only in the economy but also in the character of the state itself. Market reforms alter relations of dependence in the government hierarchy, greatly affecting the party's ability to monitor, sanction, and reward. This has reduced its capacity to govern, as both its legitimacy and its monitoring and enforcement capacity declined. Ultimately, however, the non-pluralistic political structure produces collusion between political-bureaucratic and economic elites, and holds economic progress hostage to the interests of those elites. Actually, the enrichment of state officials was absolutely vital to the success of reform, which has been tolerated in China precisely because of its non-pluralistic character.

As long as China's rulers insist on complete political control, they will always choose loyalty over competence, and this facilitated by an anachronistic cadre selection process. There is widespread popular disillusionment with the Communist Party over corruption and lost ideals, even among its own rank and file, which demonstrates the erosion of the party's credibility and its monopoly on power. China today has developed a social structure quite different from that, which existed before the reform era. But this has emerged gradually, without sharp breaks with the past, as the power-holders of old were transformed into a new type of elite. Party cadres understand that they would be better off in a capitalist than in a state socialist society.

Nevertheless, China, politically, may eventually have to be reformed. It would be naïve to assume that the commercialization of economic relationships and the invigoration of the private sector would not have affected the country's political relations. People increasingly desired democracy partly, as a result of their better economic position and partly due to the influence of foreign investment. A more professionally run economy would eventually have to undermine China's non-pluralistic political environment. 'Thus, wittingly or not, Deng has in effect abandoned not only Marxism but also Leninism' (Segal, 1994, p. 45). Decentralization has reached a point where its advantages with respect to reform are close to being outweighed by the hurdles it puts in the way of policy-making and consensus building. The political rules and their constitutional underpinnings need to be reappraised in light of changed economic circumstances. Without a new political contract that brings clarity to the rules of the center and provinces, no amount of tinkering with monetary and fiscal instruments would enhance effectiveness. The Chinese leaders seem to forget that within the current model there is still an unresolved tension between the dynamic economic change and the continuing political centralization. China will no doubt discover that an open market economy is basically incompatible with a closed, repressive polity (Marangos 1997; Marangos 1999). Thus it is not Gorbachev who should have learned from China, but China should learn from what happened to the former USSR. While central administration 'does not necessarily have to end with an explosion' it can be brought to a conclusion 'by a confused and peacefully orchestrated process' (McNeill, 1998, pp. 68, 69).

The first major clash resulting from the growing resistance to the effects of marketization and especially the rampant corruption was the uprising of 1989 in Tiananmen Square, led by students and intellectuals and joined by many workers as it proceeded. The challenge to the Communist Party's authority was repressed brutally and the continued dominance of the Communist Party was signaled by the crackdown as non-negotiable. The response of the government in the aftermath of Tiananmen seems to have been to accelerate the economic reforms, in order to present the Chinese masses with a *fait accompli*, to 'complete' marketization, while Deng Xiaoping was still alive to guide the process. Chaohua, Dan and Minqi (1999, p. 64), Minqi (1996, p. 1) and Wood (1994, p. 40) argued that the failure of the 1989 democratic movement actually paved the way for capitalist development in China. 'Democracy was repressed, but capitalism was saved' (Minqi, 1996, p. 4).

The future reform challenges in China will almost surely be political. Non-pluralistic China faces the profound task of defining relations between a weakening central government and strengthening regional governments, to bring the requisite central power under democratic control and to build a democratic system of check and balances. What is interesting to note is that Chinese society itself is swiftly changing, no matter what the government does. No political authority can halt this process. The critical question is how the change will happen. Nevertheless, the fact remains that 'it is doubtful that a pluralistic regime could have produced a significantly better overall record of growth' (Putterman, 1995, p. 1064; Nolan, 1995, p. 308).

2.5   Ideological Structure

It was very important for the reformers to find a way of making all these reforms ideologically acceptable to the public, due to the fact that it takes time for people to get accustomed to a market economy (Weiying and Yi, 1995, p. 10). Despite the current domination of marketization, most ordinary people had not yet totally lost their trust in the old system. The claim that the system is, and must remain, socialist was not simply a matter of official rhetoric. Many Chinese rejected the idea that the country should become fully capitalist, which was widely viewed as a prescription for disastrous social chaos. In spite of this, the success helped gradually to change the attitudes not just of ordinary people but also the more conservative and fearful leaders.

The proposed changes were presented as acceptable departures within the tradition of Marxism-Leninism-Maoism. There was a shift from revolutionary to pragmatic ideology. This was reflected in the slogan: China should adopt 'pick-ism'; that is, it should adopt useful components from different models (Smyth, 1998, p. 236). In this way, reformers were seeking to make the reform highly acceptable by articulating their theoretical underpinnings. There was no denying that the culture of the leadership and the people was socialist. Consequently, the reforms had to be shaped within socialist principles so that they would be accepted. Mao's vision of a more egalitarian and sustainable form of development, which takes into account the need to avoid polarization, remained a legacy to the people of China.

Indeed, this ideology shares many common elements with Lenin's ideology as it was manifested in the words and deeds of his leadership in the early 1920s. The eulogy of the New Economic Policy has been widely used in China for justifying views on marketization. Presently, it serves to justify the concept of a non-coercive, mixed economy dependent on individual and co-operative forms of incentives. The leadership has consistently spoken of the economy as one in which public ownership; planning and 'socialist' values are central to socio-economic life. China did not achieve a high level of capitalist development – even though the country enjoyed a strong capitalist tradition – before its socialist revolution, so it must employ institutions usually associated with capitalism to prepare it for a higher stage of socialism. This was essentially the reasoning Lenin used in the early 1920s to justify the New Economic Policy in the Soviet Union. Actually, nowadays, the attitude of intellectuals, bureaucrats and local governments towards the reforms is no longer one of unconditional support but is instead guided by the dictates of self-interest. The intellectual mainstream in China is undoubtedly pro-capitalist and is studying Western theories of how markets work.

2.6   Initial Conditions

Mao's effort to follow the teachings and practices of Marx, Lenin and Stalin was influenced by both China's salient national characteristics and its international environment. That is why Stalinism in China was not the Stalinism of the Soviet Union and Eastern Europe. The official definition of the goal of China's economic reforms was 'a socialist market economy with Chinese characteristics'. The Chinese were groping towards a solution to the transition problem by taking into account the initial conditions of the economy. The effectiveness of any policy prescription for transition depended on the opportunities and circumstances of the economy. Therefore, the specific design and sequence of reforms in China was 'induced' – path-dependent – rather than 'imposed', as in CEEFSU.

3 Secondary Elements of the Non-Pluralistic Model of Market Socialism

3.1   Price Liberalization–Stabilization

By 1984 the Chinese government had become convinced of the necessity of a price reform. China was forced to move away from administrative means of controlling prices towards market instruments, as the administrative measures were inefficient in an increasingly liberalized financial setting. However, its approach to price liberalization was to give social stability a high priority, and the maintenance of social cohesion was a key criterion by which price reform was to be implemented. It was decided to reform the structure of relative prices only gradually, and to do so in a controlled and planned fashion, recognizing that price controls were necessary.

The mechanism chosen and implemented in May 1984 was the two-track system. Under this system, there were centrally specified input and output quotas, within which sales and purchases were centrally directed at low prices, which were controlled. Above these quotas, and for production sectors for which did not have quotas, firms producing outputs and inputs were allowed to set prices for their products according to market conditions. This formally established the double-track price system: the co-existence of centrally determined prices and market-determined prices.

The establishment of the dual price system preserved planned allocation while incrementally drawing output into the market system and softening the risk of economic reform. By 'changing a big earthquake into several tremors', price reform was implemented (Chen, Jefferson and Singh, 1992, pp. 208–9). The incremental aspect of the dual-track system also allowed for the tandem implementation of price and enterprise reforms. The emergence of a market economy did not mean the immediate collapse of all components of the existing system. The granting of partial micro-autonomy represented a small crack in the traditional economic system.

However, partial autonomy also implied that entrepreneurs gained partial control over the allocation of the newly created stream of resources. The unexpected result of the micro-management reform was the rapid creation of new enterprises in the market track by autonomous entrepreneurs, driven by profit motivation, allocating the new stream of resources to the previously suppressed sectors. It improved incentives in the state enterprises and collective farms so that a closer link between personal rewards and individual efforts was established without privatization. Meanwhile, since the planned allocation mechanism and distorted macroeconomic environment was preserved, the state still had control over the old stream of resources and guaranteed that those resources were allocated to the priority sectors.

Consequently, the aim of the dual-track price system was to reduce the marginal price distortion in the state enterprises' production decisions while leaving the state a measure of control over material allocation. Nonetheless, if the growth rate of the new sector is higher than that of the old sector, then the old sector will continually decline as a proportion of the economy, without explicit reform actions being taken against the old sector. 'China is growing out of plan' (McMillan and Naughton, 1992, p. 133). The expansion of the suppressed sectors would not have resulted in a decline in the priority sectors because a new stream of resources supported the expansion of the suppressed sectors. Because the Chinese reform preserved the centralized organisation of production but allowed the emergence of product markets, it led to a general expansion of output in state industry as well. Thus, instead of abandoning planning, China introduced markets at the margin, parallel to planning, establishing an example of outstanding good planning.

Lau, Qian and Roland (2000, p. 121) demonstrated that a 'dual-track' mechanism, as used in China, can serve to implement an efficient Pareto-improving economic reform. The introduction of the market track provided the opportunity for economic agents who participated in it to be better off, whereas the maintenance of the plan track provided implicit transfers to compensate potential losers from the market liberalization by protecting the status quo rents. Thus the dual-track approach is Pareto-improving and efficient.

Chinese economic reforms, not only price reform, had been progressing through a dual-track system. The dual-track system was also used in most of the other reform areas. The dual structure of ownership, while keeping state ownership relatively unchanged, meant that non-state sectors were encouraged to grow. The dual governance of the market and the plan included a dual-track pricing system, a dual exchange rate system, and dual geographical divisions, with the establishment of special economic zones. The dual fiscal division of responsibilities and incentives was represented by a system of revenue-sharing contracts between different levels of government.

The dual price system is, of course, not ideal. There was a paradox associated with the dual-track price reform process. The intention of the dual-track system was to reduce administrative intervention in the economy; however, in order to maintain orderly operation of the dual-track system more government intervention capable of enforcing the quotas was required. Thus the double-track system perpetuated government control and price distortions. This provided strong incentives to engage in various sorts of malpractice, including failure to meet quota obligations, disguised price increases for quota sales and the diversion of quota allocations to the market. Most importantly, the dual-track approach initiated a buy-out process of the vested interests, on the one hand, and institutionalized state opportunism and corruption, on the other. Hence China's economic reforms were hijacked by state opportunism and corruption, which promoted the interests of the ruling elite at a cost to society. While the dual-track pricing system is a temporary expedient to smooth the reform process, McMillan and Naughton (1992, p. 137) and Fan (1994, p. 154) argued that it was about time for its abolishment.

Inflation, as experience demonstrated, was an inevitable phenomenon when a country transforms from a centrally planned to a market economy. However, China's other big advantage, in 1978, was that that it began the reform with no overt inflation and not much repressed inflationary pressure. During the reform period, the government was not prepared to sacrifice growth to pursue zero inflation. However, it was equally concerned not to allow the rate of inflation to rise to a level sufficient to threaten social stability and to divert investment into speculation away from investment in physical assets. Thus the aim was to keep macroeconomic stability, with low and tolerable inflation. The result was a pattern of fluctuating growth, with the government prepared to intervene sharply to lower inflation, primarily through direct controls on government expenditure, once the rate crossed a critical threshold. The state's ability to control the inflation rate depended both on the effectiveness of the state's apparatus in raising revenue, and its capacity to resist interest group pressure for inflationary increases in state expenditure (Nolan, 1995, p. 226). The partial reform in the large-scale state enterprise sector and the banking system account for the inflation and the stop-go nature of Chinese growth in the period 1988 to 1993, while inflation reached low double digits only during 1985, 1988 and 1989 (Xiao, 1991a, p. 1; Perkins, 1994, p. 43). Consequently, although inflation has been curtailed, its underlying structural causes remain fundamentally unaltered.

The labor market has not been freed up to any significant degree. That is because price liberalization was certain to create demands for compensating increases in money wages. An incomes policy was essential: without incomes policy there was a great danger of a spiral of cost-push inflation developing. Moreover, habits of trade unions and government responses could quickly have become ingrained, so that it would have been hard to break out of the wage-money-price spiral once the process was in motion. The breakdown of the incomes policy was one of the main causes of high inflation in the late 1980s (He, 1994, p. 212).

Unlike the Soviet Union and Central and Eastern European labor markets, which were characterized by labor shortage, China has an enormous oversupply of labor (Lau, 1997, p. 52). Keeping unemployment within the state sector provided much more favorable political and social conditions for the non-state sector to expand and for the whole economic reform to go smoothly. It is worth noting that the necessity for enterprises to retain, or even increase, their surplus labor under central direction provided them with a legitimate excuse for a soft budget constraint.

Once the Third Plenum of the Eleventh Party Congress initiated reform in late 1978, the responsiveness, capabilities, and flexibility of lower levels of government were critical for success. The close and intimate knowledge of the local economy, command over the machinery of political mobilization, and the organizational resources to implement policies proved to be instrumental for economic growth. Reform was to be based on local experimentation and orchestrated by local political machines, which minimized political risks for the central government and the danger of poorly conceived actions being widely applied. A decentralized 'bottom-up' approach to reform was adopted. Dependence on vertical connections with government officials was replaced by greater reliance on social networks linking actors within and across communities. For that reason, the maintenance of a strong, relatively unified Communist Party was critical to combining cautious and controlled decentralization with some form of overall control. A strong central government was able to keep order, maintain movement in the chosen direction and hold the several regions together. Decentralization in China has involved the devolution of administrative and fiscal power from the state to provincial and local governments and to state-owned enterprises.

As a result decentralization, alongside the gradual growth of a market economy, produced a desire to promote the local economy, comparable to that of the nation-state. Consequently, it appears that the central government was no longer as powerful as it was in the past. Thus the basic question over China's future revolves around the degree to which the central authority will give way to the increasingly dynamic periphery.

3.2   Privatization

In CEEFSU, privatization emerged as a radical strategy to counteract the problems that haunted centrally administered economies, such as bureaucracy, lack of enthusiasm and initiative, and inefficiency. Meanwhile, the Chinese reformers argued, and disaggregated data actually showed, that ownership was entirely irrelevant to the day-to-day operations of the enterprise. The Chinese experience of transition demonstrated that state ownership had remained a critical actor in the transition process. China rejected the privatization approach followed by CEEFSU. While the Russians rapidly and criminally privatized state enterprises right at the start of reform process, the Chinese have, so far, maintained state ownership, management and planning for the bulk of the industrial economy. China's experience of industrial reform suggested that economists tended to overstate the importance of early privatization programs during the transition process.

China's success demonstrated the continued economic relevance of social ownership: markets do not require private ownership to function. It was argued that privatization of the state sector is always necessary but immediate privatization was not. Privatization would have been more feasible and smoother after a large non-state sector emerged. Much of China's gains have been due to 'pseudo-privatization' of rural land and of rural industry to 'owners' who were not always private, such as township and village enterprises, and did not enjoy all the attributes of ownership; however, they have faced incentives similar to private owners. Overall, China has pursued a pragmatic approach with regard to ownership, not an ideological one.

The Chinese reformers chose to deal first with their biggest economic problem, agriculture, partly because it was the easiest political route to take. It was much easier to assign autonomy to the individual plots that farmers were working on. Furthermore, Chinese agriculture was easier to reform than Russian agriculture because of the big difference in labor intensity. China started with agricultural reform by breaking up the large collective farms into smaller, more efficient, units and introducing the household responsibility system. Under the household responsibility system peasant households were the basic units of farm production. The village collective, on the other hand, takes charge of managing land contracts, maintaining irrigation systems and providing peasants with equitable access to farm inputs, technology, information, credit and the services of farm machinery, product processing, marketing, primary education and health care. This new form of village collective organisation overcomes the main drawbacks of the commune system, while preserving the principal merits of economic organisation characterized by public ownership of the means of production. Initially, household contracts for the use of the land lasted for 15 years, then were extended to thirty years, and now have, for all practical purposes, been made indefinite. Hence it virtually amounts to individual ownership. Up to now, Chinese reformers have not contemplated the formal privatization of land.

The most significant change in the structure of the Chinese economy has been the rise in the industrial output produced by the collective sector, the township and village enterprises (TVEs). This sector consists largely of enterprises under the administrative control and ownership of local governments at the township and village levels. Township and village enterprises operate under close supervision from the township or village industrial departments, which contribute start-up funds, appoint managers and are intimately involved in major strategic decisions. The growth of TVEs benefited from the success of China's agricultural reforms, which greatly expanded the supply of rural savings, freed millions of workers to seek non-farm employment and boosted rural demand for consumer goods. The non-state sector in China, dominated by TVEs, has been the main engine of industrial growth in the reform period. TVEs were able to satisfy numerous niches in the developing market economy. China's experience demonstrates that the fastest economic improvements in industry can result from creating an environment where new industries can emerge and that privatization proved to be an unimportant part of the explanation for the accelerated growth.

The crucial point is that the TVEs represent localized collective ownership, compared to the centralized state ownership embodied by the state-owned enterprises. This difference renders TVEs and state-owned enterprises fundamentally different in nature. Even though both are publicly owned in the legal sense and are subject to government regulations, there is a lot of autonomy associated with TVEs. In addition, TVEs have closer relations with the community where they are located than do their state-owned counterparts. TVEs have been characterized by better governance, greater autonomy, clear-cut incentives, less regulations and social obligations, greater competition, and hard budget constraints. Employment is not guaranteed; TVEs do go bankrupt and workers do lose their jobs. In short, TVEs operate in a highly competitive environment and managers, local workers and local officials appear to behave as shareholders with consistent objectives.

There is widespread disagreement regarding the effective property structure of the TVEs. That is because TVEs have vaguely defined ownership structures. On the one hand, there is the argument that TVEs are some kind of 'quasi-private' disguised private enterprises. Private firms have registered as collectives to overcome political discrimination: 'wearing a red cap'. On the other hand, there is the argument that a typical TVE is not a private firm, but a genuine collective firm. Independently of the ownership structure of TVEs, Smith (1993, p. 90) and Woo (1997, p. 322) argued that almost certainly these collectively owned industries will undergo a metamorphosis from collective enterprises to capitalist enterprises, or be privatized outright.

The high efficiency and rapid growth of the TVE sector has exerted a deep influence on the state sector in two major respects. Firstly, competition has forced state enterprises to work very hard to avoid making losses. Secondly, instead of being replaced by massive privatization, as in CEEFSU, the relative role of state enterprises has been gradually reduced as they are out-competed and outgrown by the TVEs, since the state enterprises are less efficient. Consequently, in this process of transition there seems to be no need to privatize state-owned enterprises, which may result in the loss of political control. In the 1980s, in an effort to ameliorate the urban employment problem, the state removed many of the restrictions on the urban service sector and, as a result, restaurants, small traders and many personal services prospered.

Regulations on 'Transforming the Management Mechanisms of State-owned Industrial Enterprises', under the slogan 'separation of ownership and control', formalized the autonomy of state-owned enterprises and their responsibilities and the financial consequences of their independent business decisions. State firms were allowed to 'reject' or 'refuse' official instructions, including mandatory plan directives that fell outside narrowly defined boundaries. Overzealous officials who encroached upon enterprise autonomy would 'bear responsibility for a criminal act'. Enterprises could 'select employees according to their merits' and 'dismiss and fire workers and staff' (Jefferson and Rawski, 1994, p. 62). Profit is now the main objective in Chinese industry. As a result, China's approach to large state enterprises was first to corporatize them, without privatization.

There is disagreement with regard to the effectiveness of the attempts to reform the state sector. Naughton (1994, p. 483), Jefferson and Rawski (1994, p.ii), Rawski (1992, p. 1) and Singh and Gelb (1994, p. 252) argued that, due to the reforms introduced, state-owned enterprises had a moderately rapid total factor productivity growth record, which induced efficiency-enhancing responses. Conversely, Sachs and Woo (1994, p. 118), Smith (1993, p. 63), Cao, Fan and Woo (1997, p. 37) and Huang and Duncan (1996a, p. 14) argued that the state sector in China has continued to perform poorly. It makes heavy losses, lags in total factor productivity growth, depends on state subsidies, and apparently is suffused with economic corruption. The inability to make their own decisions in accordance with market conditions resulted in low competitive capacity and weak vitality for growth. The central government continued to prop up much of state-owned industry through low-cost bank loans and other subsidies, perpetuating the syndrome of the soft budget constraint. 'In short, the state enterprises were like puppets' (Lin, Cai and Li, 1996, p. 207). A contradiction regarding the reform has appeared due to increasing managerial authority: the state finds that its own continued ownership and control hinders their independent progress. Huang and Duncan (1996a, p. 16) and Xiao, (1991b, p. 11) argued that privatization and providing a uniformly competitive environment is the solution. Yet to relinquish the last vestiges of government possession is to abandon all pretence of a socialist system.

Nevertheless, actual privatization is taking place in China through spontaneous privatization and 'state asset stripping' by local cadres who are often transformed into entrepreneurs. This was the means by which hard-line opponents of reform were given some stake in the new system in order for reform to progress smoothly. Meanwhile, the government is quite successful in privatizing small and less important businesses, effectively permitting the growth of a sizeable private and semi-private capitalist economy outside the state sector. If present trends continue, Weil (1996, p. 36) and Smith (1993, p. 86) argued that the 'collective sector' would gradually merge with the private capitalist sector. It does not thereby follow that a large state sector would be a permanent part of China's market economy.

In 1995, China began a reform in privatizing and restructuring the state-owned enterprises under the slogan 'grasping the large and letting go the small' (Cao, Qian and Weingast, 1999, pp. 104, 105; Lau, 1999, p. 58). It was announced that 1,000 of the largest state-owned enterprises were to remain under state control and that the 13,000 large and medium-sized state-owned enterprises, as well as most of the 350,000 smaller companies, were to be denationalized (Zwass, 1999, pp. 229, 230; Lau, 1999, p. 58). The sale of state enterprises occurs by auctioning or corporate transformation, where most shares are sold to private individuals, or a share-based cooperative system (SBC), where shares are sold mostly to employees. The all-familiar picture has emerged in China, where firms were either bought by foreigners or the share distribution favored managers who have acquired shares from workers who often immediately re-sell their share allocation. The SBC, with its supposedly 'co-operative' features, was obviously a useful formula to disguise de facto privatization.

The privatization process has been initiated by local governments and tolerated, sometimes even encouraged, by the central government. It has become in the local government's interest to privatize or restructure state enterprises due to the hard budget constraints of local governments and the increased competition from the non-state sector that has made it increasingly costly to maintain these inefficient enterprises. It has also been a strategic move, as in all elements of the reform process, to assign the responsibility of privatization to the local governments. Local governments can pursue the reform at a speed suitable to local conditions. The central government does not force local governments to reform all at once or all at one speed. Thus, if the local government found that workers were not being absorbed as fast as predicted, it could slow down the pace of privatization or lay-offs. This, in part, accounts for the unevenness of privatization across localities.

3.3   Institutions

The Chinese experience demonstrated that the development of institutional arrangements required specific knowledge of the historic time, region, culture and government, since institutions are public goods. While the development of market institutions is tremendously important, they take time to actually materialize. Due to the fact that China's reform effort was experimental, based on improving performance rather than establishing a Western-style market system, it is not surprising that institutional change has also been gradual, uneven, and unfinished. Maintaining, instead of destroying, existing institutions avoided the time-consuming process for individuals to reconstruct their knowledge about the workings of the economy. In fact, the dual-track approach used minimal additional information, compared with other possible liberalization schemes. The dual-track approach utilized the existing information contained in the original plan and enforced the plan through existing institutions. No new information or institutions were required.

To a Western-trained economist, the centrality to any transformation process of establishing well-defined private property seemed so self-evident as to hardly merit discussion. Actually, one of the major problems with the CEEFSU transitions concerned the inability to establish well-defined private property rights. In China, the process of institutional development avoided any collapse in output. Actually, the unusual institutional arrangements in China challenge many popular notions about economic reform. In contrast to property rights theory, the Chinese 'ownership maze' demonstrated that while ownership claims are tacitly recognized, property rights in the formal sense are vague, ill defined and fuzzy. In the Chinese economy, transparent, legally protected individual property rights were the exception not the rule. Public ownership characterized by confused property rights was the norm. Most importantly, China's reforms have been successful in stimulating economic growth in spite of their failure to clarify property rights.

In China, institutional development was viewed as a product of simply re-moving controls. Consequently, the emphasis placed on informal institutions, rather than formal contracts, seemed to be a response to deficiencies in the explicit institutional structure. Therefore, once the integrity of the traditional economic system was cracked by the introduction of enterprise autonomy, institutional changes occurred in a way that was self-propelling. China's path-dependent institutional reforms have followed a path that can be explained by induced rather than designed institutional innovation. Basically, the absence of a well-defined legal framework encouraged implicit inter-firm arrangements. In addition, the absence of well-developed capital markets contributed to the growth of informal rural credit co-operatives. It is clear that informal arrange-ments are preferable to none at all.

The experience of other transition economies suggested that there had to be a significant period of conversion to market tradition before a strong set of formal institutions could evolve. That it would have taken time for a market tradition to be developed is pertinent. Thus introducing formal institutions might not be possible, at least in the shorter term. In a period of transition, such implicit and uncodified property rights and informal institutions had several advantages, de-pending on the degree of market imperfection and the pattern of market demand. Indeed, the need for an explicit legal framework was reduced, because implicit contracts were self-enforcing. The TVE enters into informal contracts based on its reputation, which is considered a core asset common to all TVEs. It is the effects of reputation and custom that underpin the functioning of informal institutions. Although obscure, property rights may lead to shortsightedness in investment decisions. Ownership incentives and risk sharing have, so far, outweighed this shortsightedness in investment decisions.

The property rights of TVEs can only be exercised collectively through the representatives of the community. There is no residual claimant in the traditional sense. In fact, 60 per cent or more of the after-tax profits of TVEs cannot legally be distributed directly to the residents, but must be reserved for the TVEs. Most of this reserve fund is re-invested, with the remainder used as a collective welfare fund, since it is intended for social purposes. A transformation strategy centered on custom and vaguely defined cooperatives, even with a hard budget constraint, would seem the farthest thing imaginable from the conventional wisdom of property rights theory. However, due to this bizarre institutional structure, the dynamism of the economy came mainly from the swift entry of new, small, non-state enterprises. Implicitly, the Chinese reformers followed Hayek (1944), who argued that efficient institutional arrangements could only emerge through a spontaneous process, as the unintended consequence of in-teractions between self-interested actors. Consequently, informal institutions might be more efficient than formal institutions.

Nevertheless, so far two questions have not been addressed: under what circumstances might informal institutions be more efficient than formal institutions? Why are vaguely defined cooperative TVEs as efficient as private firms? It seems fair to say that standard property rights theory aspires to be universal or culture-free. The theory assumes, explicitly or implicitly, that all people are indiscriminately non-cooperative, regardless of their cultural background. Weitzman and Xu (1994, pp. 136–7, 139) argued that conventional property rights theory might be inadequate because it missed a critical dimension: co-operative culture, the capability or desire to be cooperative. Meanwhile, governance arrangements have a high correlation with historical background and the social, cultural and commercial environment. Corporate governance operates at both the formal and informal regulatory levels, where customs, business culture, ethics, historical background, and social and commercial environments have an important role.

Let the outcome to a repeated non-cooperative prisoner's dilemma game be quantified by the parameter λ (lamda), which has a value between zero and one. A high value of λ, close to one, means a non-cooperative solution that resembles the outcome of cooperative collusion. A low value of λ, close to zero, means a non-cooperative solution that differs from the outcome of cooperative collusion. The parameter λ represents the ability of a group of people to resolve prisoner's dilemma and free-riding problems internally, without the imposition of explicit rules of behavior. With a value one of λ, people in a group would be able to solve the free rider problems internally. With an λ equal to zero people in a group would not be able to solve the free rider problems. With a λ between zero, and one, people in the group would be able to cooperate effectively, the more so the larger to value of λ.

A lot of anecdotal evidence could be cited to justify the general proposition that East Asia is a high-lamda society relative to Europe, which by comparison is more of a low-lamda society (Weitzman and Xu, 1994, p. 139). Well-defined property rights may not be so crucial in a high-lamda society; an implicit contract may be more efficient than an explicit contract. High-lamda individuals prefer implicit to explicit contracts because there is a saving of time and energy in negotiating, formulating and enforcing the contract and there might be an incentive effect for the implicit contract.

Li (1996, p. 3) explained the usage of informal institutions in China by the fact that the market environment can be characterized as a grey market. A grey market is one in which transactions may be blocked due to government regulations. However, a government bureaucrat can work around the obstacles and make the transaction possible. Thus, the grey market gets it name due to the uncertainty regarding whether the transaction will be 'white' or 'black', i.e. legal or illegal. Facing a grey market, the entrepreneur has an incentive to include the government as an ambiguous owner. Ambiguous property rights arise when the owner's rights are not guaranteed beforehand. Instead, owners have to fight for actual control ex post. Strangely enough, the otherwise private firm is optimally chosen to have an ambiguous owner and property rights. The benefit of ambiguous property rights is that, when the transaction is black, the firm can get help from bureaucrats. In other words, the arrangement of ambiguous property rights is a response to the greyness of the market, which is a form of market imperfection. Hence, by choosing to register the firm as a collective, entrepreneurs intentionally invite the local government to share the rights of control. Once the local government is involved in the operation of the firm, it is difficult to pre-assign control rights and the division of control becomes blurred: control rights are ambiguous.

It has been widely recognized that the reform process in China has resulted in an unacceptable level of corruption and rampant, unregulated and often illicit speculation. Such official corruption reduces the effectiveness of the dual-track system and undermines political support for the reform. Corruption was due to the fact that the maintenance of political stability was an obsession for the reforming government. Political stability required continued commitment to the old political institutions. The maintenance of political stability enabled the state to remain comparatively effective in maintaining reasonably predictable rules. However, corruption effectively diminishes the relative power and advantages of the administrative elite.

It has been suggested that the solution to these unprecedented levels of corruption is the institutionalization of private property rights, which are secure and transferable. In addition, the informal institutional arrangements in the economic system have become internally inconsistent. Informal institutions entail costs, which become more manifest as the non-state sector grows in size and informal avenues are no longer sufficient, requiring the excessive use of direct administrative means. Subsequently, in this context, the reform of property rights in China is more important than immediate privatization. Increasingly, economic actors can coordinate their interests though market institutions and social networks, bypassing the local party organisation to some extent. The question is whether a communist government, accustomed to political monopoly and unfettered control over economic resources, can create a legal and regulatory framework within which enterprises can further broaden their autonomy and establish institutional guarantees of private property. This would effectively 'get rid of the communists and install a bourgeois state' (Smith, 1993, p. 97).

3.4   Monetary Policy and the Financial System

The aim of the reforms in the financial sector was to establish and improve the two-tier banking system, where the central bank would focus on supervision and setting monetary targets. However, Chinese reforms have been criticized by orthodox economists because they did not establish an independent central bank and a consciously independent monetary policy. That is because, in a government-controlled planned economy, China's leadership was alleged to have been printing currency, fuelling a dangerously inflated bubble economy instead of responding to increases in money demand. However, as mentioned in Chapter 7, an independent central bank is inconsistent with socialist principles.

The Chinese reformers have also initiated reform in the financial system. Compared to the single-bank system before 1979, there is now a financial system under a central bank, including four big 'specialized' commercial banks and several other small universal banks, a far-reaching network of urban and rural credit cooperatives, and hundreds of finance and investment companies. The big four commercial banks in China, established in 1994, are known as the 'specialized banks' as each of them specializes in one of the following sectors: industry and commerce, agriculture, construction, foreign trade and international capital flows. The specialized banks finance important projects that may not meet commercial loan standards. The aim of the gradual reform of the financial sector was to avoid the experience of transition economies that permitted unrestricted wildcat banking, which resulted in inflationary explosions. In China, there was no monetary overhang, which contrasted strongly with CEEFSU.

However, to the orthodox economists' dismay, the independence of China's banking establishment was compromised effectively not only by the central government but also by the local governments. Considering that banks operated under the close supervision of local governments, they were careful to listen to local governments' priorities: acting in the interests of the region was more important than profits. Local governments did not like to see local banks remit excess reserves to the central government or to see banks lend excess reserves to banks in other localities, even to branches of the same bank. 'The rule of the game has been to keep deposits with the local boundary' (Chen, Jefferson and Singh, 1992, p. 217).

A prominent feature of China's financial system was the considerable appetite of enterprises for investment resources, motivated by low, often negative, real interest rates. Turning funding over to banks, however, did not necessarily harden the budget constraint. Due to the existence of distortions in both product and factor markets and the fact that the managers followed government instructions, this provided the state enterprises with legitimate excuses for demanding government subsidies, tax concessions and preferential credits, and made the enforcement of the Enterprise Bankruptcy Law exceedingly difficult. Consequently, the budget constraint was soft. Effectively, only a handful of enterprises were actually made bankrupt. The difficulties came mainly from the lack of a social security system. It was politically dangerous to displace employees of bankrupted firms onto the job market without unemployment support. Some loss-making industries, such as energy, transportation, and infrastructure sectors were considered too important to fail.

The Chinese introduced a bankruptcy law to move away from the guaranteed bailout and, in 1986 the first bankruptcy was announced with great fanfare in Shenyang (Perkins, 1988, p. 616). Since 1992, the central and local governments have shown a willingness to use the bankruptcy law and, more commonly, to merge or restructure loss-making enterprises. 'The blank check is becoming a thing of the past' (Yusuf, 1994, p. 83). The hard budget constraint at the local governmental level, in effect, had been translated into a hard budget constraint also for the local enterprise. Therefore, the TVE sector was characterized by a hard budget constraint and market competition. The experience of the TVE sector has demonstrated that hard budget constraints can be imposed upon socially owned enterprises through market competition, and that it is possible to motivate public entrepreneurs and workers through appropriate compensation schemes without privatization.

Nowadays, stock markets have become 'neutral' economic forms utilized by socialism. The official opening of the Shanghai Securities Exchange and the Shenzhen Stock Exchange in 1990 and 1991 marked the rebirth of the Chinese stock market. However, the stock market cannot be relied on as a device to solve the problems of capital shortage and X-inefficiency in state-owned enterprises. Western experience shows that fast economic growth can be achieved without a developed stock market. Although the stock market can provide the advantage of sharing risk and facilitating capital mobility, at the same time the government uses discriminatory tax incentives to encourage firms to become listed in order to promote the development of the stock market. The share market could only have been developed naturally when the demand for its services arose. Therefore, the right approach to the development of a stock market in China was 'demand following' rather than 'supply-leading' (He, 1994, p. 214). Thus, in the case of China, reforming the present banking system and making it more competitive was far more urgent than setting up stock exchanges.

In this context, there is disagreement between economists about the effectiveness of the monetary and financial reforms. Yusuf (1994, p. 88) argued that China's monetary management was surprisingly effective, while Hornik (1994, p. 31) argued that the Chinese macro economy lacked monetary and fiscal discipline. The disagreement stems from the debate about whether the ultimate goal is market socialism or market capitalism. Barratt-Brown (1995, p. 243) and Weil (1996, p. 76) argued that, by 1994, China was moving towards a fully-fledged capital market and private banking system with openings for foreign capital. A Foreign Exchange Market and foreign banks were already operating in China. Even more remarkable, the issuing of shares in former state properties, not only to Chinese residents but also to foreigners, was under consideration. What would be left of socialism in China? What direct power would the government have over the economy when, as was proposed, the Central Bank was made independent? How was this different from a capitalist economy with a government employing the indirect measures at its disposal to influence the decisions of capital-owners, national and foreign, within the overall pressures of the going rate of profit?

3.5   Fiscal Policy

While budgetary deficits are frequently associated with inflationary pressures and external imbalances, this did not appear to be the case in China during the process of fiscal decentralization. Chinese reformers argued that the purpose of fiscal policy should not have been to maintain a mechanical balance between revenues and expenditures, but rather to promote economic growth. Actually, the primary problem of the Chinese economy today is inadequate aggregate demand and under-utilization of capacity. The present capacity utilization rate is only around 50 per cent (Chaohua, Dan and Minqi, 1999, pp. 85, 89). Under these conditions, an increase in the deficit would help to reduce unemployment, rather than unleash inflation. However, due to the unprecedented level of corruption, public funds were frequently channeled into speculative activities, in which losses accrued to the state and gains were privately pocketed. As direct subsidies have declined, enterprises have become more dependent on financing from banks and financial markets. The very power of credit flows meant that their control has become intensely political. As decentralization proceeded, the management of credit was determined by political bargaining. Only a fear of the political damage which rampant inflation may have caused enabled the central government to impose some restraint on monetary increases. Effectively, budgetary policy was an exercise in political economy. Without progress in the political sphere, technical solutions would not have worked.

China differs from other countries in that the central government collects very few of its own taxes. Apart form customs duties and selected excises, the central government relies on local government for the collection of tax revenues, most of which originate with state industry. Some portion of tax revenues collected locally was remitted to the center, as specified by a system of financial responsibility contracts. Under this scheme, local governments remit a fixed target of revenue to the center. In view of the fact that actual collection of taxes was primarily a local, rather than a central, responsibility, it comes as no surprise to learn that the central government has found itself obliged to bear the brunt of the revenue squeeze. This squeeze resulted from the falling state enterprises' profits, the universal efforts to avoid paying taxes, and the soft budget constraint.

By giving lower-level governments a bigger stake in the prosperity of the local economy, fiscal decentralization has been crucial in cementing their support for increasingly more difficult reforms. As a consequence, the share of revenue going to the central government has dropped. In 1981, the central government's share of revenue was 57 per cent; by 1993 this had dropped to below 39 per cent. Thus the national state bodies of 'socialist' China were greatly under-funded. At the same time, the Chinese budget deficit soared from 2.6 billion Yuan or $US 442 million in 1981, to 23.8 billion Yuan or $US4.1 billion in 1992: a tenfold increase. If government debt was included, the figure rises to 90.5 billion Yuan or $US16 billion. This is equal to some 3.8 per cent of GNP. This massive loss of revenue has fuelled the almost desperate drive to cut government responsibility for social security, health, and education, and to force all state institutions to be self-financed. Furthermore, it has also meant that the government increasingly lacked funds for the investment programs for the reforms themselves, thus exaggerating dependency on foreign funding. Perhaps, most significantly in the long run, under-funding of the central government has undermined the ability of the state to use the very macroeconomic financial methods on which it depended to control the market and, thus, to maintain its claim to 'socialist goals'.

The VAT, introduced in 1986, was first applied to fourteen selected commodities. The VAT was designed to replace the product tax as the major indirect tax on the production of goods. However, the complicated tax structure created new problems and the newly introduced tax system itself was abandoned. It was replaced by the Contract Responsibility System, which was characterized by extensive bargaining between the center and enterprises and was also seriously distorted and insufficient. The tax liabilities of enterprises should have eliminated distortions and not been subjected to discretion by the creation of an explicit taxation system as a substitute for the former implicit revenue system.

In order to avoid these problems, new economic regulations, issued in November 1993, included a shift from government dependence on a share of profits to a more tax-based system and an increasingly even distribution of the tax revenues between the center and the localities. In 1994 China introduced a major tax reform, initiating clear distinctions between national and local taxes and establishing a national tax bureau and local tax bureaux, each responsible for their own tax collections. It was determined that value added tax would become the major indirect tax to be collected by the central government and shared with local government at a fixed ratio of 75:25 (Cao, Qian and Weingast, 1999, p. 116). However, regionalism has already become so far advanced, and the ties between local government officials and enterprises so close, that there was great resistance to changing the tax system. The decline of national authority may simply not be reversible by the belated top-down attempt to reassert control from the center.

3.6   International Trade and Foreign Aid

In 1979, trade liberalization policies were introduced to facilitate exports and, for the first time, to allow for foreign investment. In essence, these efforts involved the break-up of the monopoly of foreign trade held by the central government, transferring this authority to local governments. Special economic zones were set up to free foreign investors and domestic exporters from red tape. Real devaluation, natural comparative advantage and the entrepreneurial energies of a receptive expatriate community also contributed to China's trade performance. Nevertheless, it is doubtful that trade would have grown in the way that it did if restrictive national regulations had not been substantially mitigated by local authorities taking advantage of the possibilities offered by extensive decentralization.

Extensive state action, through protection, was needed to construct a competitive industrial sector, so that China could shift from a traditional anti-comparative advantage and heavy industry oriented development to a strategy that relied on comparative advantage. In this process, one of the key functions of planning was to identify sectors that were likely to become internationally competitive and to take measures to assist them.

China went to great lengths to attract foreign capital and foreign technology. Both rapid economic growth and higher incomes increasingly depended on the input of ever-larger amounts of capital from abroad, and expatriate investors were a potentially important source of linkage with the world economy. In contrast to China, transition economies had relied too much, and to some extent even passively, on foreign aid and foreign advice in carrying out economic reform. In the Chinese case, foreign advice was accepted only selectively. 'China's reform programme was largely shaped despite, not because, of foreign advice' (Nolan, 1995, p. 23).

Powerful pressures from the international system and the desire to join the WTO have greatly influenced China's internal transition. The desire to join the WTO also prompted China to reduce import duties and to eliminate many import quotas in favor of tariffs. The foreign exchange reform established a managed floating system and unified the dual exchange rate system on January 1 1994 (Lin, Cai and Li, 1996, p. 218; Perkins, 1994, p. 33; McKinnon, 1993a, p. 78).

However, 'opening to the world' can only be accomplished by increasing conformity to capitalist norms, which raises fundamental issues for Chinese domestic society and its re-subordination to outside powers. The Chinese themselves are caught between their desire to hold on to an historic independence, which is seen as inseparable from the protection of national sovereignty, and their need for foreign investment and trade. In the first place, whether largely foreign-funded capitalist development, intentionally introduced by the government, can be controlled, or whether the most powerful figures in the current leadership even want to control it, is a fundamental issue today. From this perspective, the only question is whether there will be conversion to a totally private form of capitalism. No doubt a complete reversion to a capitalist system is the goal of many within the burgeoning privatized sector, while some elements within the government, especially those most closely tied into foreign ventures and joint enterprises, must share these ultimate aims. In reality, local governments competing to attract overseas capital typically bend to investors' demands. Moreover, many local cadres cultivate good relations with foreign owners in their own personal interest. Even though they know perfectly well what the working and living conditions in foreign owned factories are, they would never intervene to do anything about them. In addition, illegal outflow of private funds, amounting to US $20 billion annually, even before the Asian financial crisis of 1997–8, has induced further illegal capital flight (Lau, 1999, p. 70). In this way, the internal 'socialist' market and the external 'capitalist' market have been employed to stimulate and accelerate economic growth, and have become inextricably linked, to the point that they are not distinguishable.

3.7 Social Policy

In China, employment in an enterprise provides a full set of social benefits. A job within an enterprise almost always comes with employer-provided housing with minimal maintenance costs, free health care, maternity payments, worker's compensation and other forms of insurance, a pension, and other resources such as schools and recreational facilities. This set of social services, funded by the enterprise, has been metaphorically named the 'iron rice bowl' (Minqi, 1996, pp. 1, 2; Weil, 1996, p. 33). The amount, and even the nature of social benefits, are unspecified and vary among enterprises. Consistent with the dominance of informal institutions, the social benefits are not determined by explicit agreements but, instead, are a 'consensual' sharing of enterprise resources. Consequently, the productivity of China's state enterprises might be underestimated, since the social benefits produced in the enterprises are not included as an output. As well, the argument that the collective-private sector is efficient while state enterprises are inefficient might be due to the fact that state enterprises offer much higher social benefits than the collective enterprises. Thus, while the expenditure of the central government in China on welfare is minuscule, in CEEFSU the welfare provision was funded by direct budgetary expenditures.

The 'iron rice bowl' is a form of socialism that organizes society in its entirety, including its class relations and the degree of egalitarianism. These socialist elements have remained, up until now, surprisingly, resistant to a direct attack by the liberalization process. The current enterprise-based social security system imposes uneven burdens on enterprises and impedes labor mobility The absence of a national, non-enterprise based social security system also makes it difficult for the government to allow inefficient enterprises to go bankrupt. Consequently, there is pressure to change the structure of social provision. This is due to the fact there has been a sharp increase in the cost of funding social services because of the growth of China's population and the deterioration of the financial position of state enterprises. In general, though, the net result of the reform process was an improvement in the most basic indicators of welfare: death rates, life expectancy, official infant mortality and the number of people living in absolute poverty (Nolan and Sender, 1994, p. 335; Gelb, Jefferson and Singh, 1993, p. 8; Johnson, 1994, p. 62). However, there is disturbing evidence that unreported mortality rates for newborn females rose because of the severity of the One Child Campaign (Nolan and Sender, 1994, p. 336).

Equitable distribution of the benefits of economic progress is essential in a socialist country. Some of the socialist features of the pre-reform system remain in place: public ownership, universal access to basic education, food security and community help for those who are impoverished through no fault of their own. In a decentralized market system, even with social ownership of the means of production, it was inevitable that rewards were more closely tied to productivity. In addition, income inequality can be expected to increase, and this has materialized in China. Bowles and Xiao-Yuan (1994, p. 69) argued that this has been allowed to progress to the point where the economic viability of the socially owned sector in the poorer regions has been threatened. They also assert that this clearly cannot be solved without a more active and redistributive role for the central government, which is inconsistent with current Chinese policy.

4 The Process of Reform

Based on the aforementioned analysis a process of transition towards a market economy can be established as the Chinese non-pluralistic model of transition summarized in Table 8.1. The initiation of the transition process (Year 0 on the Table) would take place with the establishment of a dual-track price system, which would be maintained throughout the transition process (Years 0 to 10 on the Table) and the removal of restrictions on new entry, which promotes the establishment of non-state enterprises. The promotion of non-state enterprises is only required for 3 Years from 0 to 3, after which the market process would be adequate in stimulating new enterprises. Concurrently, the development of informal institutions would unfold, with the formation of the TVEs and private enterprises being subject to hard budget constraints. The hard budget constraint for non-state enterprises would be maintained throughout the transition process, while soft budget constraints would exist for state-owned enterprises. After the promotion of non-state enterprises in Year 4, the privatization of small state enterprises is followed for the next 2 Years (Year 3 to 5) together with the restructuring of large state enterprises, lasting until the end of the transition process in Year 10. Tax reform was then initiated after the privatization of small state enterprises in Year 5. Throughout the reform process, central planning, incomes policy, soft budget constraints for large state enterprises, discretionary monetary and fiscal policies, tariffs and the 'iron rice bowl' funded by enterprises were maintained.

5 The Cost of Transition

Using the cost criteria of the transition process identified in Chapter 3, the Chinese model of transition has the lowest economic costs, together with the neoclassical gradualist model, since it involved the maintenance of centrally administered directives. The Chinese approach had the medium of the range of political cost together with the shock therapy, since both models had initially large political support. With regard to the ideological cost the people in CEEFSU placed the Chinese market socialist model at the highest level of ideological cost since the approach was inconsistent with the desire to establish a democratic capitalist economic system. With regard to the International Financial cost the international financial institutions and governments in mature market economies were not willing to provide funding to the transition economies, which implemented the Chinese market socialist approach. Lastly, with regard to the Foreign Direct Investment Cost the Chinese model of transition has the lowest cost (together with the neoclassical gradualist model), since multinationals were enthusiastic to finance projects in the special economic zones consistent with the free market approach.

6 Conclusion

China has been successful in stimulating economic growth, achieving an economic development process that has taken several decades in industrial countries. The policies chosen were the result of complex historical factors, leading to fundamentally different approaches and outcomes than those attained in CEEFSU. However, many problems continue to exist in the transition to a market economy in China. Areas of poverty remain as a result of significant regional disparities along with crime, corruption, bribery and extortion. Administrative interference, price manipulation, inefficient state-owned enterprises, and attempts to monopolise production and trade at the local level, all underscore the need for checks and balances for an effective market economy. The majority of the literature, of course, recommends the initiation of reforms aimed at establishing a full market capitalist system, since 'China's rapid growth momentum cannot be sustained without deeper reforms' (Gelb, Jefferson and Singh, 1993, p. 20).

China's market-oriented reform appears to have become irreversible. China today stands on the brink, facing fundamental choices as to the direction the country should take. Actually, the name of the system may have had little effect on its actual practices. The balancing act of the Chinese leadership between the revolutionary socialism implemented by Mao, emphasizing public ownership and welfare, mass-based collectivism and egalitarianism, and the market reforms of Deng Xiaoping, with their increasingly capitalistic characteristics, privatized forms of property and class polarization, have now reached a level of contradiction that must be resolved. Indeed, our analysis of China's reforms reveals that the dynamic process of change tilts towards market capitalism.

While the Chinese model has produced rapid economic growth, the system has come to look increasingly like capitalism with Chinese characteristics,

Table 8.1
The Chinese Process of Transition

	Years	1	2	3	4	5	6	7	8	9	10
1. Price Liberalization Stabilization	Dual-Track Price System	■	■	■	■	■	■	■	■	■	■
	Central Planning-Incomes Policy	■	■	■	■	■	■	■	■	■	■
2. Privatization	Restructuring State Enterprises				■	■	■	■	■	■	■
	Promotion of Non-state Enterprises	■	■	■	■	■	■	■	■	■	■
	Privatization of Small Enterprises				■	■					
3. Institutions	Formal Institutions										
	Informal Institutions	■									
4. Monetary Policy and the Financial System	Hard Budget Constraint for Non-SOEs	■	■	■	■	■	■	■	■	■	■
	Soft Budget Constraint for large SOEs	■	■	■	■	■	■	■	■	■	■
	Discretionary Monetary Policy	■	■	■	■	■	■	■	■	■	■
5. Fiscal Policy	Discretionary Fiscal Policy	■	■	■	■	■	■	■	■	■	■
	Tax Reform							■			
6. International Trade and Aid	Tariffs	■	■	■	■	■	■	■	■	■	■
	Foreign Aid										
7. Social Policy	Enterprise Funded Iron Rice Bowl	■	■	■	■	■	■	■	■	■	■
	Years	1	2	3	4	5	6	7	8	9	10

instead of socialism with Chinese features. Ironically, despite its retention of socialist language and even Communist rule, building capitalism around the edges of a still-functioning state socialist system has proved to be a more viable path to capitalism than the processes adopted in CEEFSU. Consequently, since the Chinese transition to a market economy would most likely evolve into a market capitalist system, the process becomes relevant as an alternative strategy for CEEFSU. The transition economies were not interested in a market socialist model of transition, but our analysis of the Chinese reforms does not lead logically to the easy conclusion that Russia and Eastern Europe should have followed the Chinese path. China was not Eastern Europe and Eastern Europe was not China.

Independently of the applicability of the Chinese economic reforms to CEEFSU, the maintenance of non-pluralism as a strategy incorporated in the transition process renders the Chinese model undesirable for CEEFSU. To a certain extent, the whole sequencing debate was irrelevant. Most states have little choice of direction. 'Political outcomes are far from a matter of choice by governments' (Nolan, 1995, p. 156). Gorbachev attempted to begin the Soviet Union reforms with economic change, only to be stifled by entrenched bureaucratic and industrial interests. Without glasnost, without political reform, there would have been little chance for economic change. Gorbachev's own visit to China during the Tiananmen demonstration must have strongly reinforced his feeling that the Chinese reforms were not be a feasible route for the Soviet Union. Who would like to recommend to CEEFSU trading democracy for growth? Stalinism was externally imposed on Eastern Europe, and it was very difficult to imagine a Communist Party government retaining legitimacy through the transition process. Moreover, the transformation in the Soviet Union was taking place against the backdrop of revolution in Central and Eastern Europe in 1989. This was itself a direct consequence of perestroika and glasnost. The unleashing of perestroika and glasnost in the Soviet Union had produced a similar impact on social consciousness in Central and Eastern Europe. The mass demands for democracy and independence from an artificial unification of historically independent states were unleashed with perestroika and glasnost in the Soviet Union, and with them the propensity for the respective countries to split into separate political units. When Gorbachev made it clear that the Soviet Union would not intervene, as it had done in 1968, one by one the Communist-led governments started to collapse. Hence the success of the Chinese economic reforms was fundamentally based on a non-pluralistic political structure, which effectively made the process inapplicable to CEEFSU. Therefore, it was not the 'special initial conditions' of China that made the model inappropriate but, rather, the switch to a democratic political structure in transition economies. The governments of transition economies neither had the mandate, nor wanted to reimpose tight state direction of the economy and politics.

Part III

Conclusions

Chapter 9

Was There an Optimal Model
of Transition?

1 Introduction

In the preceding chapters, alternative models of transition were developed, based on a political economy approach. It was stressed that comparisons between models were inappropriate before demonstrating the goals and method of analysis, which are associated with assumptions regarding economic behavior, institutions, ideology, and initial conditions. An attempt would be made to identify whether, from the models developed, an optimal model of transition existed. Without doubt, the issue of determining an optimal model is complex. It is too much to expect very precise and conclusive results that are applicable everywhere. But to assert that economists should not at least attempt to recommend a solution to the transition problem is intellectually myopic, not to say disingenuous. 'Of course, social science does not equip us to give a definite answer' (Lipton and Sachs, 1992, p. 249). Consequently, my ambition is modest: to provide some insights to this important problem. The following conclusions are meant to be applicable with some general tendency.

An evaluation of each model of transition was presented at the conclusion of each chapter corresponding to the model under examination. It was asserted that the shock therapy model was short-lived. Support for the governments implementing the shock therapy process was very high initially but started to deteriorate when the social cost increased. The result was that governments, which implemented shock therapy lost power after only one term in office. The new governments reversed the course of reform and proceeded with a gradual transition approach. The neoclassical model of transition was riddled with an apparent contradiction. A competitive capitalist economic system, the ultimate goal of neoclassical economists, required a government with no discretionary power. However, the neoclassical gradualist model of transition required re-regulation and re-nationalization during the transition process. The neoclassical gradualist supporters failed to reveal how, from an economic system with the presence of government discretionary power during the transition period, the economic system would be transformed into a competitive capitalist economic system.

Transition governments, the mature market economies and international financial institutions disregarded the Post Keynesian propositions of transition. The Post Keynesian recommendation for extensive government intervention, not only during the transition period, but also as a permanent feature of the economic system, was associated with centrally administered socialism. The Post Keynesian propositions for transition economies faced a set of unwelcome political and institutional barriers; the same ones that blocked the use of Post Keynesian policies in mature market economies.

The market socialist model was not attractive because any form of socialism was considered a form of Stalinism. The word 'socialism' was discredited and brought bad memories to the people in CEEFSU. In transition economies there was political fatigue. There had been enough societal experiments and there was no taste for new ones. People in transition economies wanted a system that had proved its workability. Thus the transition economies were not interested in adopting a market socialist model, even if it was Chinese-style. The maintenance of non-pluralism as a strategy incorporated in the Chinese transition process rendered the Chinese model undesirable for CEEFSU. The governments of transition economies neither had the mandate, nor wanted to reimpose tight state direction of the economy and politics.

Tentatively, we can state that the market socialist models in either form, pluralistic or non-pluralistic, did not have any chance of being implemented due to the fact the both the people and governments in CEEFSU desired the establishment of a market capitalist system. In addition, the non-pluralistic nature of the Chinese model was intolerable. The Post Keynesian model had the same fate, since the maintenance and dominance of government intervention was considered undesirable. Effectively, the only alternative was the neoclassical model of transition in either shock therapy or gradualist form. The experience of transition economies reveals the dominance of the neoclassical gradualist model of transition. As demonstrated, no transition economies implemented the Post Keynesian or market socialist models. Those governments that implemented the shock therapy model lost power and were not able to maintain the necessary shock therapy reforms, and the newly appointed governments implemented the neoclassical gradualist model. In addition, the governments that initially implemented the neoclassical gradualist model were able to maintain internal and external support for their reforms. Nowadays, all transition economies are implementing the gradualist variant of the neoclassical model. Competition between models resulted in the 'survival of the fittest'. Thus, the neoclassical gradualist model can be interpreted as the optimum model of transition under the internal and external constraints faced by transition economies. It can be argued that, in hindsight, the neoclassical gradualist model maximized social welfare under the given internal and external constraints. A more formal process deriving the optimum model of transition is attempted below.

2 A Formalist Approach in Deriving the Optimal Model of Transition

For each political economy model of transition developed in the preceding chapters a set of primary and secondary elements were presented together with the process of transition and an indication of the cost of transition. By assuming that each element of the cost of transition has equal weight, each transition model can be ranked from highest to the lowest cost on the basis of each element of the cost of transition.

2.1 Economic Cost

The shock therapy process of transition involved the highest reduction in output and employment, followed by the Post Keynesian model, then the Market Socialist model. The neoclassical gradualist model, together with the Chinese model, has the least economic cost. The neoclassical gradualist approach used as prototype the Chinese model of transition and maintained centrally administered directives.

2.2 Political Cost

The Post Keynesian model and the Pluralistic Market Socialist model did not have any or very small political support, while the shock therapy and the Chinese models had initially political support but as time passed the political support was substantially reduced. The Neoclassical gradualist model appears to be the model with stable political support.

2.3 Ideological Cost

Given that people in CEEFSU were willing to tolerate and accept a combination of radical and gradual changes initially in the reform process towards the establishment of a capitalist system, the model with the highest ideological cost would be the Chinese model, followed by the pluralistic market socialist model, then the Post Keynesian. The people in CEEFSU place both the neoclassical gradualist and the shock therapy models at the lowest ideological cost, since both approaches were consistent with the willingness of change towards a capitalist economic system. However, the neoclassical gradualist approach involved a less radical change in behavior.

2.4   International Cost

International Financial Aid Cost. International financial institutions and mature market economies were willing to substantially fund the transition economies that implemented shock therapy, and to a lesser extent the neoclassical gradualist model. They were not willing to finance transition economies that implemented any of the remaining models.

2.5   *Foreign Direct Investment Cost.* International financial capital would not be willing to invest in transition economies, which implemented the Post Keynesian, or the pluralistic market socialist model. While financial capital financed projects in the transition economies that implemented the shock therapy approach, the instability caused by the radical reforms was a deterrent, and the dominant form of privatization was through free distribution of vouchers. The neoclassical gradualist model offered stability in the reforms, as did the Chinese model, with the establishment of special economic zones, which were consistent with a free market approach. Privatization took place by auctions in the neoclassical gradualist approach.

The ranking can be interpreted as a cost index for each element of the cost of transition. Tentatively, the following table can be created:

We can rewrite the table based on the ranking of each model of each element of the transition cost. In the case of an equal ranking the average is taken as an indicator of ranking.

Table 9.1
Ranking of Alternative Models of Transition on the
Basis of Elements of Cost of Transition

	Economic Cost	Political Cost	Ideological Cost	International Financial Aid Cost	Foreign Direct Investment Cost
One (Highest)	Shock Therapy	Post Keynesian	Chinese Model	Post Keynesian	Post Keynesian
Two	Post Keynesian	Market Socialism	Market Socialism	Market Socialism	Market Socialism
Three	Market Socialism	Chinese Model	Post Keynesian	Chinese Model	Shock Therapy
Four	Neoclassical Gradualist	Shock Therapy	Shock Therapy	Neoclassical Gradualist	Neoclassical Gradualist
Five (Lowest)	Chinese Model	Neoclassical Gradualist	Neoclassical Gradualist	Shock Therapy	Chinese Model

Table 9.2
Cost Indices of Alternative Models of Transition

Transition Model	Shock Therapy	Neoclassical Gradualist	Post Keynesian	Market Socialism	Chinese Model
Economic Cost	1	4.5	2	3	4.5
Political Cost	3.5	5	1.5	1.5	3.5
Ideological Cost	4	5	3	2	1
International Financial Aid Cost	5	4	2	2	2
Foreign Direct Investment Cost	3	4.5	1.5	1.5	4.5

The best estimate of the 'true' ranking of the five alternative models of transition is provided by the order of the various sums of ranks Rj, when the Kendall Coefficient of Concordance W is significant. If one accepts the cost criteria by which I have ranked the alternative models of transition, and assuming equal weights, then the best estimate of the 'true' ranking of the alternative models according to the cost criteria is provided by the order of sums of ranks (Siegel, 1956, p. 238).

Kendall's Coefficient of Concordance

$$W = \frac{s}{\frac{1}{12}k^2(N^3 - N)}$$

$$s = \sum \left(Rj - \frac{\sum Rj}{N} \right)^2$$

k = number of sets of rankings (= 5 cost criteria)
N = the number of elements ranked (= 5 models of transition)
Rj = sum of ranks

$$\sum Rj = 75, \quad \frac{\sum Rj}{N} = \frac{75}{5} = 15,$$

$$s = (16.5-15)^2 + (23-15)^2 + (10-15)^2 + (10-15)^2 + (15.5-15)^2 = 116.5$$

$$\frac{1}{12}5^2(5^3 - 5) = 250$$

$$W = \frac{111.6}{250} = 0.466$$

W expressed the degree of agreement amongst the 5 cost criteria in ranking the 5 models of transition. W = 0.466 is significant at 0.05 because s = 116.5 > 112.3 the value of significance (Table R in Siegel, 1956, p. 238). Consequently, we can use the order of the sum of ranks as the best true ranking of the five models of transition based on five cost criteria of transition. Thus:

Ranking of the Alternative Models of Transition
based on the Cost of Transition =
= Economic Cost + Political Cost + Ideological Cost +
+ International Financial Aid Cost + Foreign Direct Investment Cost.

The order of sum of ranks reveals the following order:
The optimality criterion tilts towards the neoclassical gradualist model. The reduction in output was smaller than under shock therapy; political support for the reform was maintained after the election results; foreign aid was provided, albeit less than in the shock therapy model; and foreign direct investment was substantial due to auctioning of the state enterprises, in contrast to the free distribution of shares by the shock therapy model. Thus it appears that the neo-

Table 9.3
Ranking of Alternative Models of Transition on the
Basis of Total Cost of Transition

Model	Total Cost of Transition From Highest To Lowest
Post Keynesian Market Socialism	10
Chinese Model	15.5
Shock Therapy	16.5
Neoclassical Gradualist	23

classical gradualist model of transition reduces the cost of transition, satisfying the optimality criterion. The neoclassical gradualist model can be interpreted as the optimum model of transition under the aforementioned internal and external constraints. An acceptance of the 'efficient market hypothesis' would conclude that competition between alternative transition models would only result in the 'survival of the fittest'. It can be argued that the neoclassical gradualist model maximized social welfare under the given internal and external constraints.

Thus the lowest cost of transition is associated with the neoclassical gradualist model of transition. Of course, the aforementioned analysis has its weaknesses. The weights assigned to each cost are the same, which is not necessarily correct, and there is interdependence between the elements of cost. With regard to the benefits of transition, the pre-existing factors or the initial conditions are ignored. In defense of the calculating process of identifying the optimum model of transition, the process has been able to provide an explanation, using a purely formalistic analysis, of the eventual dominance of the neoclassical gradualist model of transition. Further research may be able to provide a more robust outcome, identifying the net benefits of transition by using fewer assumptions. However, an attempt would be made, in the following, to determine the impact of the initial conditions and of the institutional structure on the cost of transition.

3 The Influence of the Initial Conditions on the Cost of Transition

If initial conditions mattered, what would be the impact of initial conditions on the cost of transition? As analyzed, the shock therapy approach did not show any concern about the initial conditions. The neoclassical economists showed some concern about the initial conditions during transition but these differences would be ironed out as the transition economies draw near to the establishment of a free market. Post Keynesians considered the initial conditions important and it was the role of the government when implementing discretionary policies during and after the completion of the transition process to incorporate them into their policies. For the market socialists, both pluralistic and non-pluralistic, initial conditions were extremely important in shaping the development of socialism.

The influence of the initial conditions in determining the process and cost of transition is directly linked with the perception that each model had with respect to whether what elements, if any, of the existing structure of the centrally administered socialism should remain. Each model of transition had to determine whether any aspects of the initial conditions of centrally administered socialism were consistent with, and desirable in, a market economy, as perceived in the definition of a good society of each model. It is obvious that the more elements are maintained from centrally administered socialism in the market economic system, the less the reforms that are required, thus the less the cost of transition. The shock therapy approach did not show any concern for the initial conditions since it advocated the destruction of all the elements of centrally administered socialism, so as to instigate 'creative destruction': from the ashes of the destruction of centrally administered socialism the free market would naturally be created. The neoclassical gradualists economists showed some concern for the initial conditions since during the transition process elements of the centrally administered economy would be maintained and gradually eliminated. Consequently, the role of the initial conditions and as such elements of centrally administered socialism in influencing the process of transition, for the neoclassical gradualist economists, would be only important in the beginning of the transition. As the transition process gradually gained momentum the elements of central administration would disappear and as such the initial conditions would become unimportant.

The Post Keynesians perceived that the initial conditions influence the transition process due to the fact that a number of elements of the centrally administered economic system should be maintained. For example, discretionary fiscal and monetary policies, incomes and industrial policies, fixed exchange system and the coordination of international trade through a customs union. However, with the completion of the transition process, based on the definition of a good society from a Post Keynesian perspective, the economy would be dominated by private property and markets. Consequently the transition process required a substantial amount of reforms and the destruction of a number of the elements of centrally administered socialism, thus increasing the transition cost. Of course, the increase in the transition cost would be to a lesser extent than the neoclassical gradualist and a lot less than the shock therapy.

The pluralistic market socialist approach considered the initial conditions extremely important since the model maintained most elements of centrally administered socialism. However, the model required the transformation of medium enterprises to cooperatives and small enterprises into private property increasing the cost of transition but to a lesser extent than the aforementioned models. The Chinese model maintained all the elements of centrally administered socialism and allowed the development of markets by eliminating restrictions and 'grow out of plan'. As a result, the Chinese process of transition by putting emphasis on the maintenance of the elements of centrally administered socialism and per se on the initial conditions would have the lowest transition cost, if only the initial conditions mattered.

4   The Influence of the Institutional Structure on the Cost of Transition

If the institutional structure were important, how would institutions impact on the cost of transition? As analyzed, the shock therapy and the neoclassical gradualist approaches to institutional development appear to be quite similar. In both cases, market institutions can only result from market forces, however, the proposal of the neoclassical gradualist economists allowed institutions to develop concurrently with market relations. For shock therapy supporters, the first goal was the development of market relations, on the assumption that the institutions would have followed in due time. Meanwhile, the Post Keynesians, while advocating a gradual transition process, recommended immediate state intervention to develop, implement and enforce market institutions to create the pre-conditions for a civilized market economy. Similarly, the pluralistic market socialists while advocating a gradual transition process, recommended immediate societal and state action in developing the socialist institutions. In contrast, to the aforementioned institutional approaches, the Chinese approach to institutional development placed emphasis on informal institutions, encouraged implicit inter-firm arrangements in the absence of a well-defined legal framework.

The emphasis on private property rights has been at the fundamental issue of the dominant neoclassical strategy in both developing and transitional economies. Actually, one of the major problems with the CEEFSU transitions concerned the inability to establish well-defined private property rights and the protection of private property that has resulted in the rise in crime and corruption to intolerable levels. The New Institutionalist literature is relevant here. New Institutionalism applied to the transition process, which has mainly influenced the neoclassical gradualist transition model and to some extent shock therapy, emphasizes that the central issue of transition had to be the establishment of well-defined private property and the protection of private property. Individual rights to use, sell, and exchange property were paramount. Individuals must be free to enter contracts and these contracts have to be enforced. Private property rights need to established and enforced through the expansion of autonomous court system. It appears that the necessity of establishing private property rights to be self-evident as to hardly merit thoughtful discussion, as the New Institutionalists argued. However, this is not necessary true.

For the shock therapy supporters the establishment of private property rights could only take place after the establishment of market relations while for the neoclassical gradualists it would take place concurrently with the development of market relations. Once government imposed controls and distortions have been removed and private property rights installed, an economy dominated by the private sector would be the natural outcome; the market was a natural phenomenon that had been suppressed by the state. Once state properly designs and enforces contract rights then transaction costs can be reduced and markets can naturally proliferate. The World Bank and IMF recognize that the regulatory environment is also important to enhance private investment. However, any regulation of private investment activity should be made transparent and non-discretionary.

For the pluralistic market socialists the establishment of private property rights was not a major concern since the majority of property would be socially owned. Local government may well easily regulate small enterprises, the only form of enterprises that could be privately owned. For the Chinese reformers private property rights was not an issue at all.

In synergistic synthesis of a Post Keynesian- (old) Institutional approach, the Post Keynesians are influenced by Veblenian-type constructs, which see institutions as mental constructs or habits of thought common to the generality of individuals. Markets are also seen not as exchange mechanisms, but as social institutions. While there is widespread recognition that government must play an important role in building these institutions, surely markets as institutions must evolve not only through state policy but also through their own internal dynamics. Economic actors are most effective in combining learning and monitoring for themselves and for others; local knowledge, local culture and local networks influence the development of new organizational forms.

To (old) Institutionalists, property rights are much more than legally recognized entities. It involves a particular mode of thinking that is historically specific. To (old) Institutionalists the concept of property inherent in the functioning of capitalism is very different than the ideas of what constitutes legitimate property under socialist regimes in CEEFSU. For capitalist type exchanges to operate and become widely acceptable both the polity and the society must reconceptualize the legitimacy of markets. The expansion of market activity and the encouragement of investment and accumulation require stability in the concepts that represent property rights. Once a particular mode of thinking becomes habitual, markets will operate with greater fluidity. Both the society and the polity will then be committed to an acceptable form of property rights, which will ensure their reproduction.

Consequently, the concept of markets needs to regress from the neoclassical notions of self-interested individuals to the concept that perceives markets as broad institutional structures and arrangements that support and govern the process of exchange. This involves a more dynamic concept of market development and transition, which focuses on new institutional arrangements, which reduce the transformation risks and transaction, costs, associated with market development in transition economies. Policies should be based on dynamic, structural and institutional embeddedness aimed at overcoming the failures and incapacities of neoclassical models of transition. Individuals are complex dynamic social beings connected to the ever changing broader domain of institutional and structural development.

As soon as we see markets as social constructs, the question of the social and economic purpose of market arises. Market failures are the result of not achieving a specific set of goals. Therefore the process of transition involves the design of market institutions with specific purpose in mind. In this context, the experience of South East Asia is relevant here, in which market structures and institutions aimed at promoting rapid industrialization surface partly through state design and partly though the evolution of private institutions.

Hence, the synergistic synthesis of a Post Keynesian-(old) Institutional approach emphasizes the institutionalization of property rights not the legalization of property rights and as such developing an effective institutional process of private property rights substantially reducing the cost of transition comparing with the neoclassical models of transition. The market socialists were not so concern with this issue.

5 Conclusion

A political economy approach as adopted in this book results in alternative models of transition. For each model developed a set of primary and secondary elements were provided, together with a process of transition and an estimation of the cost of transition. The perspective adopted was that the transition process required a change in society in all of its dimensions; as such the transition process was not only an economic experiment, it also involved transformation of societies and of social and political structures. This approach to the transition process is quite different from the approaches and critiques adopted in the economic literature. As for example, Stiglitz (1994, 2002) has concentrated on an economic policy and philosophy that viewed the relationship between government and markets as complementary, both working in partnership, and recognized that while markets were at the center of the economy, there was an important, if limited, role for government to play. Stiglitz's critique of the transition process adopted by transition economies and sponsored by the IMF and World Bank is based on the line of reasoning that there is no a priori basis for arguing that the government should not intervene in the market, and there seems to be strong arguments for government intervention, even though there is a possibility of 'government failure'. As for another example, McKinnon (1992b) has concentrated in providing an optimum order of economic liberalization, if privatization was postponed, as an alternative interim method of hardening budget constraints. Both of these approaches and generally in the economic literature the transition process has not been analyzed in a holistic approach; that can only be possible from a political economy perspective.

We do not have any method to tell us what would exactly have happened if alternative models were pursued. We cannot run a controlled experiment, to try an alternative strategy by going back in time. Economists cannot predict the future in detail. They can only examine the past, observe the present, and have a cautious view about the future. The same applies for the transition process. The key question still remains: When will the transition process be complete? We still need to be patient and wait for the outcome of the reforms.

Appendix

1 Poland

Type of Transition:	Shock therapy.
Reforms Begin:	1 January 1990.
Gradual Shift:	19 September 1993.
Financial Assistance:	18 April 1991 to 17 April 1994: 1224.0 million SDRs.
	8 March 1993 to 7 March 1994: 476.0 million SDRs.

24 August 1989: Sejm (Lower House) elects as Prime Minister Tadeysz Mazowiescki, a leading member of the Solidarity trade union, mandating him to form a Solidarity-led coalition government embracing all four main parties in parliament.

12 September 1989: Prime Minister Mazowiescki formed a coalition government dominated by members of Solidarity. The junior partners were the Polish United Workers Party, the United Peasants Party and the Democratic Party. The new government aimed to abolish the command economy as soon as possible.

12 October 1989: The government published a plan to establish as quickly as possible a market economy and envisaged the full introduction of market mechanisms and institutions by the start of 1991.

December 1989: Economic and budget reform and an austerity package approved by the Solidarity-led government was presented to the Sejm by the Finance Minister Leszek Balcerowicz on the 17 December and was passed by the Sejm on 29 December. Balcerowicz described the package as one involving deep surgical cuts, which would begin on 1 January 1990. The aim was to balance the budget and to reduce inflation substantially by April 1990, cut wages by 25 per cent in real terms, remove price controls and cut government subsidies. By cutting state support, an increase in unemployment was expected and the government budgeted for an increase of 400,000 registered unemployed. The main objective of the package was to lay the basis for creating a market economy by expanding the private sector, liberalizing the foreign exchange rules and creating internal convertibility of the currency.

January 1990: Price increases were introduced on 2 January 1990, in line with the Solidarity-led government's IMF-backed austerity program. Coal prices rose six fold, electricity, gas and petrol fourfold and public transport fares doubled. Real incomes fell by 36 per cent, since the government introduced a wage freeze and the currency devalued by 31.5 per cent. Prime Minister Mazowiecki faced a damaging strike on 16 January in the Silesian coalmines, which were Poland's main foreign currency earner. However, he repeated that austerity measures were essential to economic reform and recovery.

25 November 1990: First-round presidential election results: Walesa 39.96 per cent, Tyminski 23.10 per cent and Mazowieski 18.08 per cent. Three other candidates gained 18.86 per cent.

9 December 1990: The second round of presidential elections resulted in a victory of Walesa with 74.3 per cent of the vote.

27 October 1991: Multiparty elections for the 460-seat Semj as well for the 100-seat Senate. In a turnout of only 43.2 per cent no party gained more than 13 per cent of the vote, producing a severely fragmented legislature.

5 December 1991: In the Sejm Walesa nominated Jan Olszewski as Prime Minister to form a center-left coalition, consisting of Olszewski's Center Alliance, the Christian National Union, the Peasant Party and some independents.

February 1992: The new government's socioeconomic policy was unveiled at a joint press conference by Prime Minister Jan Olszewski. Its key elements were a relaxation of the previous tight monetary controls in an effort to halt a recession. The government's state of the nation report on 10 February, had acknowledged both achievements of 1989–91 and the then critical state of the economy.

5 March 1992: The government's program to relax monetary controls, invest in state enterprises and increase imports, with the aim of taking the economy out of recession, was rejected by the Sejm by 171 votes to 138. The former communists of the Democratic Left Alliance and the right wing Confederation of an Independent Poland opposed the program on the grounds that it was too rigorous, while the Democratic Union and the Liberal Democratic Congress opposed it because it was not tough enough.

23 March 1992: Although Olszewski had originally favored a relaxation of the previous government's tight monetary controls; he now called on the Sejm to recognize the importance of retaining the confidence of the IMF.

26 May 1992: In a letter to the speaker of the Sejm Walesa announced that he had lost confidence in the government and proposed the formation of a new government.

5 June 1992: The Sejm passed a motion of no confidence in the government of Prime Minister Olzewshi by 273 to 119 with 33 abstentions. The nomination for Prime Minister of W. Pawlak was approved by 261 to 149 with 7 abstentions.

2 July 1992: Pawlak resigned as Prime Minister after failing to form a government. Hanna Suchocka was proposed as Prime Minister. Following Walesa's agreement the Sejm approved Suchocka by 233 votes to 61 with 113 abstentions.

October 1992: Suchocka government's priorities were to cut the growing budget deficit, speed up privatization and depoliticise pay bargaining. The new economic plan was formulated in consultation with the IMF.

February 1993: The budget was approved.

15 April 1993: Peasant Alliance withdrew from seven-party center-right coalition.

28 May 1993: The Suchocka government failed by one vote to survive a vote of no confidence in the Sejm. The origins of the vote of no confidence lay in an industrial dispute over a pay claim by Solidarity on behalf of teachers, nurses and public sector workers.

30 May 1993: President Walesa dissolved Parliament and called a general election, under a new rule whereby a party had to cross a threshold 5 percent of the votes in order to be allotted parliamentary seats and an alliance had to obtain at least 8 per cent of the votes.

19 September 1993: The general election results showed that a coalition was needed in order for a government to be formed. The election saw a decisive shift towards those left-center parties with roots in the old system, promising a somewhat slower pace of market reform. The Alliance of the Democratic Left (ADL) – which included the Social Democracy of the Polish Republic, the Polish Socialist Party and the OPZZ trade union – and the Polish Peasant Party, both with roots in the former regime, emerged as victors, with 20.4 per cent and 15.4 per cent of the vote and 171 and 132 seats respectively.

26 October 1993: Pawlak was sworn in as Prime Minister after a coalition government was formed between the Alliance of the Democratic Left (ADL) and the Polish Peasant Party. The government program stressed that it would continue market reforms but would seek to distribute the cost of reforms equally and provide support to those who suffered.

2 February 1995: Walesa took the first formal steps to dissolve parliament, taking the contested budget to the Constitutional Court.

6 February 1995: Walesa calls for Pawlak's resignation, citing incompetence and lack of progress with economic reforms. The shock therapy approach to transition was significantly altered after the 1993 elections, due largely to the fact that a great number of citizens were suffering. After Pawlak's forced resignation, President Walesa nominated Jozef Olesky as the new Prime Minister.

November 1995: New elections saw the emergence of a new Prime Minister and cabinet, with the weakened SLD-PSL coalition remaining in government.

November 1995: The leading candidates in the Presidential Poll were Walesa, Kwasniewksi (the chairman of the former Democratic Left Alliance) and Pawlak (the Prime Minister until February 1995, representing the Polish Peasant Party). Aleksander Kwasniewski defeated Walesa in the second round of the Presidential elections, winning 51.7 per cent of the vote to Walesa's 48.3 per cent. Kwasnieswki was committed to economic reform and to Poland's accession to the European Union and to NATO.

22 December 1995: Lech Walesa's term in office as President ended.

September 1997: These elections finally saw the ousting of the Alliance of the Democratic Left and its coalition from government. Solidarity regained power in the form of the Freedom Union (UW), the remnant of Solidarity's original parliamentary party, in coalition with Electoral Action Solidarity (AWS). The coalition was expected to continue the policies of restructuring, deregulation, privatization, trade liberalization and EU accession. The 37-party AWS, however, was hard to hold together. It resisted the pace of economic change sought by the UW and pursued a more conservative social agenda. The new Solidarity-led government elected Jerzy Byzek as the new Prime Minister. Another notable appointment was Freedom Union (UW) leader Leszek Balcerowicz, who became the Deputy Prime Minister and had overall responsibility for economic policy. Whilst serving as Finance Minister in 1989–91, Balcerowicz had been the author of Poland's shock therapy free market reforms in 1990.

Conclusion: The Mazowiescki government, and to lesser extent the Suchocka government, with the support of the President Walesa, implemented the shock therapy approach. The growing dissatisfaction with the impact of the reforms on the public, which was not alleviated by foreign financial assistance, resulted in the both the Mazowiescki and Suchocka governments facing and losing an early election, placing in power a coalition government that favored of a gradual approach. Walesa also lost the presidential elections, a victim of the implementation of the shock therapy approach in a democratic environment without substantial foreign financial support.

2   Czechoslovakia: Until 31ˢᵗ December 1992

Transition Type: Shock Therapy.
Reforms Began: 1 January 1991.
After the break-up of Czechoslovakia into two separate republics, the Czech Republic continued with shock therapy and Slovakia pursued a gradual approach to economic reforms.

2.1   Czech Republic

Transition Type: Shock therapy.
Reforms: 1 January 1993.
Gradual shift: 1 January 1996 (slowing down some economic reforms, mainly privatization, health and railways).
Financial Assistance: 1 January 1993: 589.6 millions of SDRs.

1 January 1993: The Czech Republic continued with its radical reforms, maintaining Vaclav Havel as President, and Vaclav Klaus as Prime Minister.

31 May-1 June 1996: Prime Minister Vaclav Klaus suffered an unexpected setback in the general election, losing his parliamentary majority.

27 June 1996: Klaus signed a coalition agreement to form a minority government, which would control 99 of the 200 seats. Klaus conceded that there would be greater decentralization and a slower pace of health and welfare reform.

May 1997: The government suffered a currency crisis, Klaus fought for his political survival. President Havel accused the government of 'losing its direction', further heightening tensions.

30 November 1997: Prime Minister Vaclac Klaus resigned following the withdrawal from the Civil Democratic Party-led government of two junior coalition partners – the Christian Democratic Union-Czech People's Party, and the Civil Democratic Alliance. This further weakened the coalition's power.

Conclusion: The implementation of shock therapy by the Klaus government without any substantial foreign assistance resulted in the loss of its majority in the parliament after one term in office. While Klaus was able to remain in power, the minority government had to substantially distort the shock therapy program so as to remain in power. However, ultimately Klaus was forced to resign, putting an end to the shock therapy process.

2.2   Slovakia

Transition Type:	Gradual
Reforms begin:	1 January 1993
Financial Assistance:	1 January 1993: 257.4 million SDRs
	22 July 1940 to 22 March 1996: 180.3 million SDRs

30 September 1994: The Movement for a Democratic Slovakia, led by Vladimir Meciar, was voted in after winning a high percentage of votes. Meciar's platform stressed a slower transition and improved economic conditions. Meciar also spoke against the then current voucher privatization program, alleging that control of state assets would go to 'anonymous persons' and that foreign capital might 'buy out the country'. Instead he favored existing management and workers and giving Slovaks the right to refuse privatization.

March 1998: President Michal Kovac resigned after serving out his second five-year-term in office. The post of President remained vacant as the parliament had failed to muster the three-fifths majority needed to elect one.

September 1998: These elections finally ousted from power the controversial Prime Minister Vladimir Meciar and his party, Movement for a Democratic Slovakia. Meciar had dominated Slovak politics since 1989, and was heavily criticized by the international community for 'backsliding' on economic and democratic reforms. Opposition parties won a majority of seats in the Slovak National Council; however, in the absence of a president, parliament chairman Ivan Gasparovic called upon Mikulas Dzurinda, leader of the Slovak Democratic Coalition, to form a new government. After weeks of negotiations, opposition parties agreed to form a four-party coalition under Dzurinda's leadership, pursuing a gradual reform process.

3 Bulgaria

Type of transition:	Shock therapy, but with slow implementation
Reforms began:	1 February 1991
Gradual shift:	18 December 1994
Financial Assistance:	17 April 1992–16 April 1993: 155.0 million SDRs
	11 April 1994–11 April 1995: 116.0 million SDRs

1 February 1991: The coalition government of L. Berov led the reform program, which continued throughout 1992. This government was committed to an adjustment program designed to stabilize the economy and to transform it into a market economy. Shock therapy was implemented slowly due to the fact that the Berov government was in power with a fragile coalition. No political party had a majority in Parliament and the successive coalition governments had only a fragile parliamentary basis. In fact, throughout 1993 and 1994 the Berov Government suffered no less than 6 votes of no confidence.

2 September 1994: The Berov government resigned and called for an early election.

18 December 1994: The election results showed that the coalition remained in power; however, its power, which was already quite fragile, was weakened further by the better than expected results of the Bulgarian Socialist Party. A gradual approach was adopted.

Conclusion: The democratic process in Bulgaria did not facilitate the implementation of the shock therapy approach. It has been stressed that the shock therapy process required a strong government to be able to implement the necessary reforms. This did not materialize in Bulgaria. The inadequate amount of foreign financial assistance was not able to secure immediate reforms.

4 Russia

Type of transition: Shock therapy under the Gaidar government
Reforms begin: 2 February 1992
Gradual shift: 2 December 1993
Financial Assistance: 5 August 1992 to 4 January 1993: 719.0 million SDRs
                          30 June 1993: 1078.3 million SDRs

February 1992: With the support of the Russian President Boris Yeltsin the Gaidar reforms were implemented throughout 1992 and 1993. New reform attempts began in October 1993 after Yeltsin stormed the parliament.

12 December 1993: The change in Russia's approach to transition came with the general elections of 1993. Eight of the thirteen participating parties or coalitions passed the 5 per cent threshold; however, overall the election produced no decisive result, although Zhirinovsky's Liberal Democratic Party of Russia did surprisingly well. The initial panic subsequently turned into a generally held opinion that the LDP's success was largely a protest vote against the dire economic circumstances of a large section of the population due to the shock therapy. This shows that, if the elections had been held on a proportional system, the LDPR would have been the single largest group in the Duma.

20 December 1993: Prime Minister Chernomyrdin spoke out against shock therapy, personally criticizing Gaidar and blaming him for the LDPR success which he interpreted a vote of protest against the reforms: 'We should face the truth and admit that many people voted against the hardships and mistakes of the current reforms…naturally any 'shock' methods must be precluded in the future…the election defeat is a personal evaluation of Gaidar's work, not as a representative of the whole government but as the person responsible for the Economics Ministry' (Jeffries, 1996, p. 127).

January 1994: An embattled Yelsin was forced to sacrifice the radical reformers in government. Two leading radical reformers, Yegor Gaidar and Boris Fedorov, resigned. A new cabinet featured several centrists in key positions despite the reported objections of Yeltsin, strengthened the authority of the centrist Prime Minister Viktor Chernomyrdin. A Presidential decree reduced the number of Deputy Prime Ministers from nine to five, and specified that the new Government was to consist of twenty-three ministries including three new ones. Few reformers were retained in the Cabinet. Exceptions included the radical Deputy Prime Minister responsible for privatization, Anatoly Chubais, and the moderates Sergei Shakhrai and Aleksandr Shokhin, who lost their status as Deputy Prime Ministers but remained as ministers. In contrast, key centrists remained in place, such as First Deputy Prime Minister Oleg Soskovets. Gaidar, the First Deputy Prime Minister and Minister of the Economy, widely credited as the architect of economic reform, resigned on 16 January 1994. Gaidar claimed his decision was due to 'unceasing pressure from conservative political circles...I cannot work without having the necessary levers at my command' (Jeffries, 1996, p. 129). In a letter of resignation to Yeltsin, he argued that he regarded some recent government policies were 'dangerous' and singled out two for criticism: the planned economic union with Byelarus and the decision to construct a new building to house the Federal Assembly at an estimated cost of $US 500 million. Boris Fedorov, Minister of Finance and Deputy Prime Minister, resigned formally on 26 January 1994. Fedorov said that his resignation had been forced by the government's new conservative course, which he described on 26 January 1994 as, ' an economic coup' by 'red industrialists' with 'a lifeless and incompetent ideology of state planning'. Among those at whom Fedorov's remarks were directed were Chernomyrdin himself, a career industrialist before he entered politics; the Russian Central Bank chair, Viktor Gerashenko, and the Deputy Prime Minister responsible for Agriculture, Aleksandr Zaveryvkha. On 26 January Fedorov predicted that the new government would be confronted by hyperinflation and a concomitant fall in living standards, leading to a 'social explosion' of protest against impoverishment. Despite the resignations, Yeltsin reaffirmed his commitment to defend reforms and to ensure stability and the continuation of the democratic course.

20 January 1994: Chernomyrdin declared that the period of market romanticism had ended. A government spokesman stressed that the mechanical transfer of Western economic methods to Russian soil had done more harm than good. The Chernomyrdin government would take account of the special characteristics of Russia, the Russian people and Russian traditions in economic policy making. Despite these remarks, and the resignations of Gaidar and Fedorov,

Chernomyrdin insisted that the government would continue efforts to lay the foundations for a market economy.

Conclusion: The shock therapy approach in Russia was short-lived. The Gaidar-inspired government lost the public's and Yelsin's support under the social impact of the reforms. The foreign financial assistance provided was not adequate to encourage public support for the Gaidar program. The disappointing election result forced Gaidar and his fellow reformists in the government to resign, which ended of the shock therapy process.

5 Albania

Type Of Transition: Initially gradual then shock therapy.
Reforms Began: June 1991-July 1992 gradual.
                        July 1992- 29 June 1997 shock therapy.
Gradual Shift: 29 June 1997.
Financial Assistance: 26 Aug 1992 to 25 Aug 1993: 20 million SDRs.
                        14 July 1993 to 13 July 1996: 42.4 20 million SDRs.

June 1991: The Socialist national stability coalition took office, with Prime Minister Fatos Nano and opted for a gradualist approach to market reforms. However, conflicts and delays in the reform process led to increasing dissent among the coalition parties, culminating in a government crisis in December 1991 and a decision to hold general elections in March 1992.

March 1992: The Berisha government was voted in, and initiated ambitious economic reforms to halt economic deterioration and put the country on the path to a market economy.

July-August 1992: The new government, headed by A. Meksi, proceeded with a shock therapy approach.

Early 1994: The Berisha regime was showing worrying signs of authoritarianism. On the arrest of former Prime Minister Fatos Nano, public political rallies were banned, except those of the Democratic Party. Indoor meetings organized by opposition parties were routinely disrupted and banned.

6 November 1994: Berisha held a referendum on a new constitution after failing to achieve a 2/3 majority in parliament. The referendum was unsuccessful, with only 40 per cent voting 'yes'. After the failure of the referendum nine out of nineteen cabinet ministers were replaced.

End of December 1994: Both coalition partners of the Democratic party, the Republican Party (one representative) and the Social Democratic Party (seven representatives), announced the end of their cooperation on the grounds that the government was incapable of fighting corruption and inefficiency.

May 1996: The May elections saw a landslide victory for the Berisha regime. However, it was widely reported that this was due to irregularities in the conduct of the election. The Berisha regime collapsed when pyramid deposit-taking schemes collapsed and rioting broke out.

11 February 1997: The Republican Party withdrew from the PDS-led coalition, demanding that the government resign.

March 1997: One third of the country was in the hands of rebels demanding that Berisha resign. Berisha ordered the government of A. Meksi to resign and declared a national sate of emergency.

29 June 1997: General elections were held, with the Socialist Party of Albania (SPA) taking office and ousting Berisha's government. The SPA had made progress in restoring central control. However, rising crime and the losses incurred by the failed pyramid schemes, was making the SPA's job difficult. The SPA's main focus was to maintain strict economic discipline if the IMF and World Bank were to assist the country.

Conclusion: Due to the inadequate financial support the shock therapy approach was maintained by authoritarian methods. However, authoritarianism cannot survive for long. With the violent overthrow of Berisha and the shock therapy approach, which was directly linked with authoritarianism, the reform process was discredited and gradualism was the natural course of the new government.

6 Estonia

Type of Transition:	Shock therapy.
Reforms Began:	September 1992.
Gradual Shift:	5 March 1995.
Financial Assistance:	16 September 1992–
	15 September 1993: 27.9 Million of SDR.
	27 October 1993- 26 March 1995: 23.2 million SDRs.
	12 April 1995: 13.9 million SDRs.

20 September 1992: Multiparty elections were held more than a year after the nation formally declared independence, on 21 August 1991. In the interim period, the country had three legislative bodies competing with each other, while two successive governments handled daily matters. The long-awaited elections produced a fragmented Parliament with almost 30 parties and coalitions, from which a coalition government emerged with a slim and fragile majority. The elections produced a five-party coalition (the Fatherland Coalition) of conservatives and Christian Democrats led by Prime Minister Mart Laar. Parliament elected Lennart Meri as president. This government proceeded with a shock therapy approach to transition.

June 1994: Controversy over the leadership of Prime Minister Mart Laar and his self-confessed 'dictatorial' style divided the ruling Fatherland group. The Ministers of Justice and Defense, Kaido Kama and Indrek Kannik, had resigned in May. At a special party congress on 11 June 1994, Kama and Ulo Nugis, speaker of the Riigikogu (legislature) both unsuccessfully challenged Laar, who had pledged to resign as Prime Minister if defeated, for the post of chair of the Fatherland group. The Estonian Liberal Democratic Party (ELDP) withdrew from the Fatherland group after its proposal for a secret vote of confidence for Laar was defeated in the Riigikogu. Tiit Kabin, chair of the seven-party ELDP faction in the Riigikogu, claimed objections to the way the government was run.

September 1994: A motion of no confidence in Prime Minister Mart Laar was easily carried in the legislature on 26 September 1994. The motion was backed by 60 of the legislature's 101 deputies. Laar, a reformist and member of the right-wing Fatherland group, remained in office pending the appointment of a successor by President Lennart Meri. The vote of censure followed the 2 September 1994 revelation by the Bank of Estonia President Siim Kallas, that Laar had secretly ordered the sale of 2000 million Russian roubles to the breakaway republic of Chechnya back in October 1992, thus breaking an agreement with the IMF to return the roubles to the Russian Central Bank. In response to this revelation, Fatherland's coalition partners the Rural Centrist Party and the Social Democratic party demanded Laar's resignation.

5 March 1995: Sixteen parties/coalitions contested the election and nine failed to reach the 5 per cent threshold. There was a decisive swing to center-left parties.

16 April 1995: The new government took office and Prime Minister Tiit Vahi promised to continue with the policies of the previous government, but had made commitments to help farmers (with low-interest loans and tax concessions) and old-age pensioners.

Conclusion: An electorate, which had seen its standard of living decline to an unacceptable level, ousted the Mart Laar government, which had pursued a shock therapy model of transition under limited foreign financial assistance. An alliance of impoverished peasants and unskilled workers, the prime victims of the free market and liberal foreign trade regime, defeated the Mart Laar government.

7 Latvia

Transition Type: Shock therapy.
Reforms Started: 5 June 1993.
Gradual Shift: 25 July 1997.
Financial Assistance: October 1993-March 1995: 23.25 million SDRs.
                      December 1993: 45.73 million of SDRs, of which 22.87
                      were on a 15-month standby, provided after achiev-
                      ing specific targets.
                      24 May 1996: 30 million of SDRs.

21 August 1991: Latvia declared independence. The ruling party was the Latvian Popular Front.

5 June 1993: Parliamentary elections saw right wing parties dominate the new assembly. A new party called Latvian Way won the majority of votes. The new President was Guntis Ulmanis of the Latvian Peasants Union, and the Prime Minister was Valdis Birkavs. Agreement on agricultural policy formed the basis of the coalition, with the aim that by 1996 at least 75 per cent of state enterprises be privatized. Enterprises without a future were to be closed down.

14 July 1994: Prime Minister Valdis Birkav's government resigned following the resignation of three cabinet ministers and the withdrawal of the Latvian Peasant Party from the coalition, due to at the coalition's failure to introduce protectionist measures for domestic production.

March 1995: Its new government was formed: a coalition of Latvia's Way, Political Union of Economists and Independents. Prime Minister Maris Gailis of Latvia's Way. The coalition had the aim to continue the reforms.

Elections of September 30-October 1 1995: Results produced a fragmented parliament. The largest party was the Saimnieks, which had a center-left platform. The main losers in this election were Latvia's Way and other mainstream parties, who lost to populist parties such as Saimnieks. This result was attributed to voters' deep dissatisfaction with the dislocation caused by economic and social reforms. During this time Latvia suffered a major banking crisis. The largest commercial bank in the Baltics, Baltija Bank, collapsed, after a few other banks had gone bankrupt or lost their licenses. This bank in particular had been offering extremely high interest rates to attract money to finance ventures with questionable prospects. The bank failed to complete its 1994 audit, and customers started to withdraw deposits. The government stepped in and took over the management of the bank. An administrator was appointed to determine the fate of the bank, including possible liquidation. The confidence crisis also affected the foreign exchange market; where there were large capital outflows and calls for a devaluation of the Lat. Monetary policy was tightened.

November 1995: President Ulmanis asked Maris Grinblats, the Prime Ministerial candidate of the right-wing National Bloc, to form a government. Grinblats failed to secure support from parties on the left. On 29 November, President Ulmanis asked the Prime Ministerial candidate of the National Reconciliation Bloc, Ziedonis Cevers, to form a Government. Cevers also failed. On the third attempt to form a working government, the Saiema approved by 70 votes to 24 the formation of a coalition under Andris Skele, who was chosen as a compromise candidate. Skele's government comprised of his Saimnieks party, Latvia's Way, the Union for Fatherland and Freedom, the Latvian National Conservative Party, Latvia's Unity Party, Latvia's Farmer's Union, the Christian Democratic Union, and Latvia's Green Party. Skele's government priorities were to balance the budget and to encourage foreign investment. Skele was a champion of rapid privatization of land.

May 1996: Skele dismissed Deputy Prime Minister and Agriculture Minister Alberts Kauls, prompting the withdrawal of the Unity Party from the coalition government. Kauls, a supporter of strong state regulation of the agricultural sector, appeared at odds with Skele. Kauls criticized the administration's agricultural policy and had told a farmer's meeting in Skrunda that the government was destroying agriculture. In justifying the dismissal of Kauls, Skele stated that he was not prepared to have any member of the government advocating collectivization or administrative restriction. This was confirmed when Kauls's five fellow Unity Party legislators withdrew their support from the coalition. Speaking soon after his dismissal, Kauls predicted that the government would fall in less than two months.

18 June 1996: Ulmanis was re-elected as President.

21 October 1996: Deputy Prime Minister Cevers resigned due to personal differences with Prime Minister Andris Skele. Personal differences had been apparent for some time, with Cevers criticizing the 'authoritarian style' of Skele's leadership. Relations were also inflamed by Skele's 'draconian' budget plan, which sought to eliminate the country's budget deficit. This plan had led to protests both inside and outside the legislature, and, although Cevers supported the principle of a deficit-eliminating budget, he and his Saimnieks party had called for specific changes to the draft, particularly in relation to its planned taxation of pensions.

January 1997: Prime Minister Skele resigned on 20 January 1997, and was renominated by President Ulmanis on 29 January following consultation with the 100-member Saiema. Skele had resigned after widespread criticism over his choice of businessman Vasilijs Melniks as Finance Minister to replace Aivars Kreituss. Ulmanis had urged the Saiema to reject the appointment of Melniks, who had been the subject of a corruption investigation, but was cleared of any wrongdoing. Following Skele's resignation, Melniks also resigned. The resignation of Skele was unexpected. At the end, he formed an eight-party coalition spanning the political spectrum, which he managed to hold together despite internal dissension. Skele was seen as a key figure in the acceleration of economic reforms and aimed to make Latvia more attractive to investors. Skele was renominated for the post of Prime Minister after negotiations demonstrated that he continued to command a majority in the Saiema. It was reported also that the President believed him to be the best choice for continued implementation of economic reforms.

13 February 1997: After elections the Saiema approved a new Latvian government under Prime Minister Andris Skele by seventy votes to seventeen with one abstention. The new Cabinet involved ministers from five of the parties.

25 July 1997: Prime Minister Andris Skele announced the resignation of his government following the collapse of the ruling five-party coalition. The government, which had been formed in February, faced serious corruption allegations in the months that followed. On 28 July 1997, President Guntis Ulmanis invited the outgoing Minister of Economy, Guntars Krasts, to form a new Government.

August 1997: Of the 100 members Saiema, 73 voted in support of Krasts's new five-party center-left coalition. The government emphasized the importance of continued reform and a balanced budget. However, the budget deficit was increasingly growing at an increasing rate and the privatization of large-scale industries have been very slow, due to governmental disputes.

September 1997: The credential and applications committee of the Saiema found that thirty-four of the total forty-eight deputies investigated had contravened anti-corruption legislation.

October 1997: The IMF approved credit to support the government's 1997–1999 economic program.

Conclusion: Latvia is another nation, which pursued a shock therapy approach to economic reforms. The continuation of rapid reforms under Skele's authoritarian rule, however, is an exception to the rule that shock therapy governments lost power after one term and retreated to a more gradualist approach to reform. Why was it that in the other transition economies the governments that implemented shock therapy nations lost power and the reform direction changed from shock therapy to gradualism, whilst in Latvia a rapid approach continued? This can be explained by the authoritarian rule of the Sleke government, in addition to financial help received from the IMF. Evidently, one must compare the amount of IMF assistance given to Latvia and to other shock therapy nations of similar size and level of industrialization. Latvia received 153.9 million SDRs in total while Estonia received 65 million SDRs and Albania 62.4 million SDRs. Latvia received more financial assistance than Estonia and Albania combined, yet it is a nation of similar population, size and industrialization to Estonia. The large amount of foreign aid to Latvia was justified by the IMF in terms of the country's: 'remarkable degree of stability' (Economic Commission for Europe, 1993, p. 233) implying that both the Birkavs and Skele governments were implementing a reform process consistent with the guidelines of the IMF. Thus Latvia could afford to sustain the burden of the reforms directly as a result of its foreign assistance under authoritarian rule. This example highlights how crucial foreign aid was in helping these nations implement the shock therapy process, facilitated as well by an authoritarian political process. In Latvia foreign assistance was able to maintain the authoritarian rule for some time in contrast with what took place in Albania. However, the return in power of the Skele government was short-lived; it lasted only 5 months before collapsing under serious corruption allegations. This also highlights the problem associated with the provision of ample foreign aid: it encourages corruption. Thus, it is fair to say that, as of August 1997, when Skele's government resigned and Krasts forms a government, a slowing down of economic reforms took place. The social costs of sustaining the reforms made it very difficult to balance the budget and to privatize state enterprises, thus allowing the government to create a budget deficit.

Bibliography

Abalkin, L. (1988), 'Economic Reforms and Lessons of the Past', *Social Sciences*, Vol.19, No.4, pp. 38–45.

Abell, P. (1990), 'An Equitarian Market Socialism', in J. Le Grand and S. Estrin (eds), *Market Socialism*, Oxford University Press, Oxford, pp. 78–99.

Abel, I. and Bonin, J.P. (1993), 'State Desertion and Convertibility: The Case of Hungary', in I.P. Szekely and D.M.G. Newberry (eds), *Hungary: An Economy In Transition*, Cambridge University Press, Cambridge, pp. 329–341.

Aganbegyan, A. (1988), *'The Challenge: Economics of Perestroika'*, Hutchinson, London.

Albert, M. and Hahnel, R. (1991), *'The Political Economy of Participatory Economics'*, Princeton University Press, Princeton.

Alchian, A. and Demsetz, H. (1972), 'Production, Information Costs and Economic Organization', *American Economic Review*, Vol.62, No.5, December, pp. 777–95.

Aleksashenko, S. (1992), 'The Economic Union of Republics: Federation, Confederation, Community', in A. Aslund (ed.), *The Post-Soviet Economy: Soviet and Western Perspectives*, St. Martin's Press, New York, pp. 115–131.

Alexeev, M. (1991), 'If Market Clearing Prices Are So Good Then Why Doesn't (Almost) Anybody Want Them?', *Journal of Comparative Economics*, Vol.15, No.2, pp. 380–390.

Alonso, J.A. and Garcimartin, C. (1998–9), 'A New Approach to Balance-of-Payments Constraint: Some Empirical Evidence', *Journal of Post Keynesian Economics*, Vol.21, No.2, pp. 259–82.

Amariglio, J. and Ruccio, D.F. (1994), 'Postmodernism, Marxism, and the Critique of Modern Economic Thought', *Rethinking Marxism*, Vol.7, No.3, pp. 7–35.

Amsden, A.H. (1996), 'Late Industrialization: Can More Countries Make It?', in C.J. Whalen (ed.) *Political Economy for the 21st Century*, M.E. Sharpe, Armonk, New York, pp. 245–261.

Anderson, J.H., Lee, Y. and Murrell, P. (2000), 'Competition and Privatization Amidst Weak Institutions: Evidence from Mongolia', *Economic Inquiry*, Vol.38, No.4, October, pp. 527–549.

Andorka, R. (1994), 'Causes of the Collapse of the Communist System: Present Situation and Future Prospects in Hungary', in J.H. Moore (ed.), *Legacies of the Collapse of Marxism*, George Mason University Press, Virginia, pp. 19–34.

Anonymous. (1990), 'No Halfway House', *The Economist*, Vol.314, No.7647, 24 March, pp. 17–9.

Applebaum, E. (1979), 'The Labor Market', in A.S. Eichner, (ed.), *A Guide to Post-Keynesian Economics*, Macmillan, New York, pp. 100–119.

Arestis, P. and Bain, K. (1995), 'The Independence of Central Banks: A Non-conventional Perspective', *Journal of Economic Issues*, Vol.29, No.1, pp. 161–74.

Arestis, P. Dunn, S. and Sawyer, M. (1999), 'Post Keynesian Economics and Its Critics', *Journal of Post Keynesian Economics*, Vol.21, No.4, pp. 527–49.

Arestis, P. and Howells, P. (1992), 'Institutional Developments and the Effectiveness of Monetary Policy', *Journal of Economic Issues*, Vol.26, No.1, pp. 135–57.

Arestis, P. and Sawyer, M. (1993), 'Political Economy: An Editorial Manifesto', *International Papers in Political Economy*, Vol.1, No.1, pp. 1–38.

Argyrous, G. (1996), 'Economic Evolution and Cumulative Causation', in G. Argyrous and F. Stilwell (eds), *Economics as a Social Science. Readings in Political Economy*, Pluto Press, Annandale, NSW, pp. 112–9.

Argyrous, G. and Stilwell, F. (eds), (1996a), *Economics as a Social Science. Readings in Political Economy*, Pluto Press, Annandale.

Argyrous, G. and Stilwell, F. (1996b), 'Introduction', in G. Argyrous and F. Stilwell (eds), *Economics as a Social Science. Readings in Political Economy*, Annandale, Pluto Press, pp. x–xi.

Argyrous, G. and Stilwell, F. (1996c), 'Why Do Economists Disagree?', in G. Argyrous and F. Stilwell (eds), *Economics as a Social Science. Readings in Political Economy*, Annandale, Pluto Press, pp. 49–51.

Arneson, R.J. (1993), 'Market Socialism and Egalitarian Ethics', in P.K. Bardhan, and J.E. Roemer (eds), *Market Socialism: The Current Debate*, Oxford University press, Oxford, pp. 281–297.

Arneson, R.J. (1996), 'What Do Socialists Want?', in E.O. Wright (ed.), *Equal Shares. Making Socialism Work. The Real Utopias Project, Volume II*, Verso, London, pp. 209–230.

Arnot, B. (1998), 'From Collapse to Disintegration: the Russian Economic Transition', in M. Cox (ed.), *Rethinking the Soviet Collapse. Sovietology, The Death of Communism and the New Russia*, BookEns Ltd., London, pp. 219–240.

Arrighi, G. (1991), 'Marxist Century, American Century', in R. Blackburn (ed.), *After the Fall. The Failure of Communism and the Future of Socialism*, Verso, London, pp. 126–165.

Ash, T.G. (1996), 'Introduction', *Social Research*, Vol. 63, Summer, pp. 287–9.

Asimakopulos, A. (1979), 'Tax Incidence' in A.S. Eichner (ed.), *A Guide to Post–Keynesian Economics*, Macmillan, New York, pp. 61–70.

Aslund, A. (1989), 'Soviet and Chinese Reforms–Why They Must Be Different', *The World Today*, Vol. 45, November, pp. 188–191.

Aslund, A. (1992a), '*Post–Communist Economic Revolutions. How Big a Bang?*', The Center for Strategic and International Studies, Washington.

Aslund, A. (ed.), (1992b), '*The Post–Soviet Economy. Soviet and Western Perspectives*', St. Martin's Press, New York.

Aslund, A. (1992c), 'Introduction', in A. Aslund (ed.), *The Post–Soviet Economy. Soviet and Western Perspectives*, St. Martin's Press, New York, pp. 1–5.

Aslund, A. (1993), 'Comment on 'Gradual versus Rapid Liberalization in Socialist Economies' by McKinnon', *Proceedings of the World Bank Annual Conference on Development Economies*, World Bank, Washington, pp. 95–99.

Aslund, A. (1994a), 'Lessons of the First Years of Systematic Change in Eastern Europe', *Journal of Comparative Economics*, Vol.19, No.1, August, pp. 22–38.

Aslund, A. (1994b), 'The Case for Radical Reform', *Journal of Democracy*, Vol.5, No.4, October, pp. 63–74.

Aslund, A. (1994c), 'The Role of the State in the Transition to Capitalism', in J.H. Moore (ed.), *Collapse of Marxism*, George Mason University Press, Virginia, pp. 181–198.

Aslund, A. (1995), *'How Russia Became a Market Economy'*, The Brookings Institution, Washington.

Aslund, A. (1997a), *'Russia's Economic Transformation in the 1990s'*, Pinter, London.

Aslund, A. (1997b), 'Introduction', in A. Aslund (ed.), *Russia's Economic Transformation in the 1990s*, Pinter, London, pp. 1–10.

Aslund, A. (1997c), 'A Critique of Soviet Reform Plans', in A. Aslund (ed.), *The Post–Soviet Economy. Soviet and Western Perspectives*, St. Martin's Press, New York, pp. 167–180, reprinted in A, Aslund (ed.), *Russia's Economic Transformation in the 1990s*, Pinter, London, pp. 11–24.

Aslund, A. (1997d), 'Epilogue', in A. Aslund (ed.) *Russia's Economic Transformation In the 1990s*, Pinter, London, pp. 182–190.

Aslund, A. (1997e), 'Observations on the Development of Small Private Enterprise in Russia', *Post–Soviet Geography and Economics*, Vol.38, No.4, pp. 191–205.

Aslund, A., Boone, P.P. and Johnson, S. (1996), 'How to Stabilize: Lessons From Post–Communist Countries', *Brooking Papers on Economic Activity*, No.1, pp. 217–291.

Atesoglu. (1998), 'Inflation and Real Income', *Journal of Post Keynesian Economics*, Vol.20, No.3, pp. 487–92.

Auerbach, P., Desai, M. and Shamsavari, A. (1988), 'The Transition From Actually Existing Capitalism', *New Left Review*, No.170, July/August, pp. 61–79.

Aven, P.P. (1997), 'Problems in Foreign Trade Regulation in the Russian Economic Reform', in A. Aslund (ed.), *Economic Transformation in Russia*, St. Martin's Press, New York, pp. 80–93, reprinted in A. Aslund, *Russia's Economic Transformation in the 1990s*, Pinter, London, pp. 56–67.

Balcerowicz, L. (1993), 'Common Fallacies In The Debate On The Economic Transition In Central and Eastern Europe', *European Bank For Reconstruction And Development*, Working Paper No. 11, October.

Balcerowicz, L. (1994), 'Understanding Postcommunist Transitions', *Journal of Democracy*, Vol.5, No.4, October, pp. 75–89.

Balcerowicz, L., Blaszczyk, B. and Dabrowski, M. (1997), 'The Polish Way to the Market Economy 1989–1995', in W.T. Woo, S. Parker and J.D. Sachs (eds), *Economies in Transition. Comparing Asia and Europe*, MIT Press, Cambridge, Mass., pp. 131–160.

Bardhan, P.K. (1993), 'On Tackling the Soft Budget Constraint in Market Socialism', in P.K. Bardhan and J.E. Roemer (eds), *Market Socialism: The Current Debate*, Oxford University Press, Oxford, pp. 145–155.

Bardhan, P.K. (2000), 'The Nature of Institutional Impediments to Economic Development', in M. Olson and S. Kahkonen (eds), *A Not-So-Dismal Science: A Broader View of Economics and Societies*, Oxford University Press, Oxford, pp. 245–267.

Bardhan, P. and Roemer, J.E. (1992), 'Market Socialism: A Case for Rejuvenation', *Journal of Economic Perspectives*, Vol.6, No.3, pp. 101–116.

Bardhan, P.K. and Roemer, J.E. (1993), 'Introduction', in P.K. Bardhan and J.E. Roemer (eds), *Market Socialism: The Current Debate*, Oxford University Press, Oxford, pp. 3–17.

Bardhan, P.K. and Roemer, J.E. (1994), 'On the Workability of Market Socialism', *Journal of Economic Perspectives*, Vol.8, No.2, Spring, pp. 177–81.

Barkan, J. and Belkin, D. (1991), 'Comment', *Dissent*, Vol.38, No.4, Fall, pp. 569–572.

Barratt–Brown, M. (1995), *Models in Political Economy*, Second Edition, Penguin Books, Melbourne.

Begg, D. (1993), 'Discussion of Part Seven', in I.P. Szekely and D.M.G. Newbery (eds), *Hungary: An Economy in Transition*, Cambridge University Press, Cambridge, pp. 341–344.

Belkin, D. (1994a), 'Why Market Socialism? From the Critique of Political Economy to Positive Political Economy', in F. Roosevelt and D. Belkin (eds), *Why Market Socialism?*, M.E. Sharpe, Armonk, New York, pp. 3–47.

Belkin, D. (1994b), 'The Turning Point: A Review of Brus and Laski, From Marx to the Market', in F. Roosevelt and D. Belkin (eds), *Why Market Socialism?*, M.E. Sharpe, Armonk, New York, pp. 155–164.

Berg, A. (1994), 'Does Macroeconomic Reform Cause Structural Adjustment? Lessons from Poland', *Journal of Comparative Economics*, Vol.18, No.1, February, pp. 376–409.

Bergson, A. (1991), 'The USSR Before the Fall: How Poor and Why', *Journal of Economic Perspectives*, Vol.5, No. 4, Fall, pp. 29–44.

Bergson, A. (1992), 'Communist Economic Efficiency Revisited', *American Economic Review Papers and Proceedings*, Vol.82, No.2, May, pp. 27–30.

Berle, A.A. Jr. (1954), *The 20th Century Capitalist Revolution*, Harcourt, Brace and Company, New York.

Berliner, J.S. (1988), 'The Economics of Overtaking and Surpassing' in J.S. Berliner (ed.) *Soviet Industry From Stalin To Gorbachev: Essays On Management and Innovation*, Studies in Soviet History and Society, Series Ithaca, Cornell University Press, New York pp. 159–87.

Berliner, J.S. (1993), 'Innovation, the Soviet Union, and Market Socialism', in P.K. Bardhan and J.E. Roemer (eds), *Market Socialism: The Current Debate*, Oxford University Press, Oxford, pp. 190–203.

Bigler, R.M. (1996), 'Back in Europe and Adjusting to the New Realities of the 1990s in Hungary', *East European Quarterly*, Vol.30, Summer, pp. 205–34.

Bim, A. (1992), 'The Role of the State in Transitional Postcommunist Economies', in A. Aslund (ed.), *The Post–Soviet Economy. Soviet and Western Perspectives*, St. Martin's Press, New York, pp. 181–195.

Binns, P., Cliff, T. and Harman, C. (1987), *Russia: From Workers State to State Capitalism*. London: Bookmarks.

Blackburn, R. (1991a), 'Preface', in R. Blackburn (ed.), *After the Fall. The Failure of Communism and the Future of Socialism*, Verso, London, pp. ix–xv.

Blackburn, R. (1991b), 'Fin de Siecle: Socialism After the Crash', in R. Blackburn (ed.), *After the Fall. The Failure of Communism and the Future of Socialism*, Verso, London, pp. 173–249.

Blackburn, R. (1991c), 'Fin de Siecle: Socialism after the Crash', *New Left Review*, No.185, January/February, pp. 5–67.

Blackburn, R. (1991d), 'Russia Should Be Looking East, Not West', *New Left Review*, No.198, September–October, pp. 137–140.

Blair, R. (1994), 'Comment', in F. Roosevelt and D. Belkin (eds), *Why Market Socialism?*, M.E. Sharpe, Armonk, New York, pp. 241–242.

Blanchard, O. (1996), 'Theoretical Aspects of Transition', *American Economic Review Papers and Proceedings*, Vol.86, No.2, May, pp. 117–22.

Blanchard, O., Boycko, M., Dabrowski, R., Dornbusch, R., Layard, R. and Shleifer, A. (eds), (1993), *Post-Communist Reform: Pain and Progress*, The MIT Press, Cambridge, Mass.

Blanchard, O. and Dabrowski, M. (1993), 'The Progress of Restructuring in Poland', in O. Blanchard, M. Boycko, R. Dabrowski, R. Dornbusch, R. Layard, and A. Shleifer (eds), *Post-Communist Reform. Pain and Progress*, The MIT Press, Cambridge, Mass., pp. 109–149.

Blanchard, O., Dornbusch, R., Krugman, P.P., Layard, R. and Summers, R. (eds), (1992), *Reform in Eastern Europe*, MIT Press, Cambridge, Mass.

Blanchard, O. and Layard, R. (1993), 'Overview', in O. Blanchard, M. Boycko, R. Dabrowski, R. Dornbusch, R. Layard, and A. Shleifer, (eds), *Post-Communist Reform: Pain and Progress*, The MIT Press, Cambridge, pp. 1–14.

Blankenagel, A. (2000), 'Legal Reforms in Russia: Visible Steps, Obvious Gaps, and an Invisible Hand?', *Journal of Institutional and Theoretical Economics*, Vol.156, No.1, pp. 99– 119.

Blecker, R.A. (1998), 'International Competitiveness, Relative Wages, and the Balance–of–Payments Constraint', *Journal of Post Keynesian Economics*, Vol.20, No.4, pp. 495–526.

Block, F. (1994), 'Remaking Our Economy: New Strategies for Structural Reform', in F. Roosevelt and D. Belkin (eds), *Why Market Socialism?*, M.E. Sharpe, Armonk, New York, pp. 371–381.

Block, F. (1996), 'Finance and Market Socialism', in E.O. Wright (ed.), *Equal Shares. Making Socialism Work. The Real Utopias Project, Volume II*, Verso, London, pp. 159–169.

Blommenstein, H. and Marrese, M. (ed.), (1991), *Transformation of Planned Economies: Property Rights and Macroeconomic Stability*, OECD, Paris.

Boettke, P.J. (1999), 'The Russian Crisis: Perils and Prospects for Post–Soviet Transition', *American Journal of Economics and Sociology*, Vol.58, No.3, July, pp. 371–384.

Bofinger, P. (1991), 'Options for the Payments and Exchange Rate System in Eastern Europe', *European Economy*, No.2, Special Issue, pp. 243–62.

Bogomolov, O. (1990a), 'The Changing Image of Socialism', *Social Sciences*, No.3, pp. 84–94.

Bogomolov, O. (1990b), 'Socialism's Changing Image', *Moscow News*, No.28, p. 3.

Boone, P.P. and Fedorov, B. (1997), 'The Ups and Downs of Russian Economic Reforms', in W.T. Woo, S. Parker and J.D. Sachs (ed.), *Economies in Transition. Comparing Asia and Europe*, MIT Press, Cambridge, Mass., pp. 161–188.

Bowles, S. and Gintis, H. (1990), 'Rethinking Marxism and Liberalism from a Radical Democratic Perspective', *Rethinking Marxism*, Vol.3, No.3–4, Fall–Winter, pp. 37–43.

Bowles, S. and Gintis, H. (1993), 'The Revenge of Homo Economicus: Contested Exchange and the Revival of Political Economy', *Journal of Economic Perspectives*, Vol.7, No.1, pp. 83–102.

Bowles, S. and Gintis, H. (1996), 'Efficient Redistribution: New Rules for Markets, States, and Communities', *Politics and Society*, Vol.24, No.4, December, pp. 307–342.

Bowles, S. and Gintis, H. (2000), 'Walrasian Economics in Retrospect', *Quarterly Journal of Economics*, Vol.115, No.4, November, pp. 1411–1439.

Bowles, P. and Xiao–Yuan, D. (1994), 'Current Success and Future Challenges in China's Economic Reforms', *New Left Review*, No.208, November/December, pp. 49–76.

Boycko, M. (1991), 'Price Decontrol: The Microeconomic Case for the 'Big Bang' Approach', *Oxford Review of Economic Policy*, Vol.7, No. 4, pp. 35–45.

Boycko, M., Shleifer, A. and Vishny, R. (1993), 'Privatising Russia', *Brookings Papers on Economic Activity*, No.1, pp. 139–92.

Bracher, K.D. (1989), *The Age of Ideologies*, Weidenfeld and Nicolson, London.

Brada, J.C. (1996), 'Privatization is Transition – Or is it?', *Journal of Economic Perspectives*, Vol.10, No.2, Spring, pp. 67–86.

Braguinsky, S. (1998), 'Democracy and Economic Reform: Theory and Some Evidence from the Russian Case', *Contemporary Economic Policy*, Vol.16, No.2, April, pp. 227–40.

Bratkowski, A.S. (1993), 'The Shock of Transformation or the Transformation of the Shock? The Big Bang in Poland and Official Statistics', *Communist Economies and Economic Transformation*, Vol.5, No.1, pp. 5–28.

Breth, R. and Ward, I. (1982). *Socialism: The Options*. Melbourne: Hargreen Publishing Co.

Brighouse, H. (1996), 'Transitional and Utopian Market Socialism', in E.O. Wright (ed.), *Equal Shares. Making Socialism Work. The Real Utopias Project, Volume II*, Verso, London, pp. 187–208.

Brockway, G.P. (1998), 'Path Dependency and Animal Spirits', *Journal of Post Keynesian Economics*, Vol.21, No.1, pp. 163–5.

Brooks, K., Guasch, L.J., Braverman, A. and Csaki, C. (1991), 'Agriculture and the Transition to the Market', *Journal of Economic Perspectives*, Vol.5, No.4, Fall, pp. 149–161.

Brown, S. (1992), 'Federalism and Marketisation in the Soviet Union' in A. Aslund (ed.), *The Post–Soviet Economy. Soviet and Western Perspectives*, St. Martin's Press, New York, pp. 132–164.

Brown, A. (1996), 'The Russian Transition in Comparative and Russian Perspective', *Social Research*, Vol.63, No.2, Summer, pp. 403–15.

Brus, W. (1976), 'Political Economy and Socialism', in E.L. Wheelwright and F.J.B. Stilwell (eds), *Readings in Political Economy: Volume 2*, Australian and New Zealand Book Company Pty. Ltd, NSW, pp. 251–253.

Brus, W. (1985), 'Socialism – Feasible and Viable?', *New Left Review*, No.153, September/October, pp. 43–62.

Brus, W. (1993), 'Marketisation and Democratisation: The Sino–Soviet Divergence', *Cambridge Journal of Economics*, Vol.17, No. 4, December, pp. 423–441.

Brus, W. and Laski, K. (1989), *From Marx to the Market: Socialism in Search of an Economic System*, Oxford University Press, Oxford.

Bucknall, K.B. (1997), '*Why China has Done Better that Russia since 1989*', Working Papers in Economics, Griffith University, Department of Economics, No.14, April.

Buchanan, J.M. (1986), *Liberty, Market and the State*, Wheatsheaf, Brighton.

Burawoy, M. (1996), 'Why Coupon Socialism Never Stood a Chance in Russia: The Political Conditions of Economic Transition', in E.O. Wright (ed.), *Equal Shares. Making Socialism Work. The Real Utopias Project, Volume II*, Verso, London, pp. 265–276.

Burawoy, M. and Krotov, P. (1992), 'The Soviet Transition To Capitalism: Worker Control and Economic Bargaining In The Wood Industry', *American Sociological Review*, Vol.57, February, pp. 16–38.

Burawoy, M. and Krotov, P. (1993), 'The Economic Basis of Russia's Political Crisis', *New Left Review*, No.198, pp. 49–69.

Byrd, W.A. and Lin, Q. (eds), (1990), *China's Rural Industry: Structure, Development and Reform*, Oxford University Press, Oxford.

Calvo, G.A. and Frenkel, J.A. (1991), 'Credit Markets, Credibility and Economic Transformation', *Journal of Economic Perspectives*, Vol.5, No.4, Fall, pp. 139–148.

Campbell, R.W. (1991), *The Socialist Economies in Transition*, Indiana University Press, Bloomington.

Cao, Y.Z., Fan, G. and Woo, W.T. (1997), 'Chinese Economic Reforms: Past Successes and Future Challenges' in W.T. Woo, S. Parker and J.D. Sachs (ed.), *Economies in Transition. Comparing Asia and Europe*, MIT Press, Cambridge, Mass., pp. 19–40.

Cao, Y., Qian, Y. and Weingast, R. (1999), 'From Federalism, Chinese Style to Privatization, Chinese Style', *Economics of Transition*, Vol.7, No.1, pp. 103–31.

Caporaso, A. and Levine, D.P. (1993), *Theories of Political Economy*, Cambridge University Press, Cambridge.

Carrington, S. (1992), 'The Remonetisation of the Commonwealth of Independent States', *American Economic Review Papers and Proceedings*, Vol.82, No.2, May, pp. 22–26.

Cataphores, G. (1994), 'The Imperious Austrian: Schumpeter as Bourgeois Marxist', *New Left Review*, No.205, May/June, pp. 3–30.

Chaohua, W., Dan, W. and Minqi, L. (1999), 'A Dialogue on the Future of China', *New Left Review*, No.235, May/June, pp. 60–106

Chen, K., Jefferson, G.H. and Singh, I. (1992), 'Lessons from China's Economic Reform', *Journal of Comparative Economics*, Vol.16, No.2, June, pp. 201–25.

Chipman, L. (1981), *Liberty, Justice and the Market*, Center for Independent Studies, Sydney.

Chomsky, N. (1991), *Deterring Democracy*, Verso, London.

Chubais, A. and Vishnevskaya, M. (1997), 'Main Issues of Privatization in Russia', in A. Aslund and R. Layard (eds), *Changing the Economic System in Russia*, St. Martin's Press, New York, pp. 89–98, reprinted in A. Aslund, *Russia's Economic Transformation in the 1990s*, Pinter, London, pp. 68–78.

Clague, C. (1992), 'Introduction: The Journey to a Market Economy', in C. Clague and G. Rausser (ed.), *The Emergence of Market Economies in Eastern Europe*, Blackwell, Cambridge, pp. 1–22.

Clague, C. and Rausser, G. (ed.), (1992), *The Emergence of Market Economies in Eastern Europe*, Blackwell, Cambridge.

Clarke, S. (1992), 'Privatization and the Development of Capitalism in Russia', *New Left Review*, No.196, November/December, pp. 3–28.

Clower, R. (1999), 'Post–Keynes Monetary and Financial Theory', *Journal of Post Keynesian Economics*, Vol.21, No.3, pp. 399–414.

Coase, R.H. (1992), 'The Institutional Structure of Production', *American Economic Review*, Vol.82, No.4, June, pp. 713–719.

Cohen, G.A. (1989), 'Are Freedom and Equality Compatible?', in J. Elster and K.O. Moene (eds), *Alternatives to Capitalism*, Cambridge University Press, Cambridge, pp. 113–126.

Cohen, G.A. (1994), 'Back to Socialist Basics', *New Left Review*, No.207, September/ October, pp. 3–16.

Cohen, S.F. (1998), 'Russia: Tragedy or Transition', in M. Cox (ed.), *Rethinking the Soviet Collapse. Sovietology, The Death of Communism and the New Russia*, BookEns Ltd., London, pp. 241–250.

Cohen, J. and Rogers, J. (1993), 'Associative Democracy', in P.K. Bardhan and J.E. Roemer (eds), *Market Socialism: The Current Debate*, Oxford University Press, Oxford, pp. 236–252.

Cohen, J. and Rogers, J. (1996), 'My Utopia or Yours?', in E.O. Wright (ed.), *Equal Shares. Making Socialism Work. The Real Utopias Project, Volume II*, Verso, London, pp. 93–109.

Coleman, J.S. (1993), 'The New Social Structure and the New Social Science', in C. Lemert (ed.), *Social Theory: The Multicultural and Classic Readings*, Westview Press Inc., Colorado, pp. 563–566.

Comiso, E. (1992), 'The Political Conditions of Economic Reform in Socialism' in J. Kovacs and M. Tardos (eds), *Reform and Transformation in Eastern Europe. Soviet Type Economies on the Threshold of Change*, Routledge, London, pp. 225–45.

Cooter, R. (1992), 'Organization as Property: Economic Analysis of Property Law Applied to Privatization', in C. Clague and G. Rausser (ed.), *The Emergence of Market Economies in Eastern Europe*, Blackwell, Cambridge, pp. 77–98.

Cornwall, J. (1979), 'Macrodynamics', in A.S. Eichner (ed.), *A Guide to Post–Keynesian Economics*, Macmillan, New York, pp. 19–33.

Cornwall, J. and Cornwall, W. (1997), 'The Unemployment Problem and the Legacy of Keynes', *Journal of Post Keynesian Economics*, Vol.19, No.4, pp. 525–41.

Cox, E. (1993), 'The Economics of Mutual Support: A Feminist Approach', in S. Rees, G. Rodley and F. Stilwell (eds), *Beyond the Market: Alternatives to Economic Rationalism*, Pluto Press Australia Ltd, NSW, pp. 270–276.

Cox, M. (1998), 'Introduction', in M. Cox (ed.), *Rethinking the Soviet Collapse. Sovietology, The Death of Communism and the New Russia*, BookEns Ltd., London, pp. 1–12.

Crotty, J.R. (1980), 'Post–Keynesian Economic Theory: An Overview and Evaluation' *American Economic Review, Papers and Proceedings*, Vol.70, No.2, May, pp. 20–5.

Csaba, L. (1995), *The Capitalist Revolution in Eastern Europe: A Contribution to the Economic Theory of Systemic Change*, Edward Elgar Publishing Limited, Hants.

Dabrowski, M. (1997), 'The First–Year of Russian Transformation', in A. Aslund and R. Layard (eds), (1993), *Changing the Economic System in Russia*, St. Martin's Press, New York, pp. 1–18, reprinted in A. Aslund, *Russia's Economic Transformation in the 1990s*, Pinter, London, pp. 41–55.

Dahl, R. (1994), 'Social Reality and 'Free Markets': A Letter to Friends in Eastern Europe', in F. Roosevelt and D. Belkin (eds), *Why Market Socialism?*, M.E. Sharpe, Armonk, New York, pp. 339–348.

Daly, M. (1993), 'No Economy is an Island', in S. Rees, G. Rodley and F. Stilwell (eds), *Beyond the Market: Alternatives to Economic Rationalism*, Pluto Press Australia Ltd, NSW, pp. 72–90.

Davidson, G. and Davidson, P. (1996), *Economics For A Civilized Society*, Second (Revised) Edition, Macmillan, London.

Davidson, P. (1992), 'Would Keynes Be A New Keynesian?', *Eastern Economic Journal*, Vol.18, No.4, pp. 449–63.

Davidson, P. (1994), *Post Keynesian Macroeconomic Theory*, Edward Elgar, Hants.

Davidson, P. (1996), 'Reality and Economic Theory', *Journal of Post Keynesian Economics*, Vol.18, No.4, pp. 479–508.

Davies, R.W. (1969), 'Planning a Mature Economy in the U.S.S.R.', in J.S. Prybyla (ed.), *Comparative Economic Systems*, Appleton–Century–Crofts, New York, pp. 259–272.

Davis, A. (1993), 'Economic Health', in S. Rees, G. Rodley and F. Stilwell (eds), *Beyond the Market: Alternatives to Economic Rationalism*, Pluto Press Australia Ltd, NSW, pp. 119–135.

De Carvalho, F.J.C. (1995–6), 'The Independence of the Central Bank: A Critical Assessment of the Arguments', *Journal of Post Keynesian Economics*, Vol.18, No.2, pp. 159–75.

De Menil, G. (1997), 'Trade Policies in Transition Economies: A Comparison of European and Asian Experiences', in W.T. Woo, S. Parker and J.D. Sachs (eds), *Economies in Transition. Comparing Asia and Europe*, MIT Press, Cambridge, Mass., pp. 257–298.

Dequech, D. (1999), 'Expectations and Confidence Under Uncertainty', *Journal of Post Keynesian Economics*, Vol.21, No.3, pp. 415–30.

Desai, P. (1989), *Perestroika in Perspective*, Torinis and Co., London.

Devine, P. (1988), *Democracy and Economic Planning: The Political Economy of a Self–Governing Society*, Westview Press, Colorado.

Dewatripont, M. and Maskin, E. (1993), 'Centralization of Credit and Long–term Investment', in P.K. Bardhan and J.E. Roemer (eds), *Market Socialism: The Current Debate*, Oxford University press, Oxford, pp. 169–174.

Dewatripont, M. and Roland, G. (1992a), 'The Virtues of Gradualism and Legitimacy in the Transition to a Market Economy', *The Economic Journal*, Vol.102, No.411, March, pp. 291–300.

Dewatripont, M. and Roland, G. (1992b), 'Economic Reform and Dynamic Political Constraints', *Review of Economic Studies*, Vol.59, No.201, pp. 703–730.

Dietrich, M. (1986), 'Organisational Requirements of a Socialist Economy: Theoretical and Practical Suggestions', *Cambridge Journal of Economics*, Vol.10, No.4, pp. 319–332.

Dietz, R. (1992), 'The Reform of Soviet Socialism as a Search for Systemic Rationality: A Systems Theoretical View', in M.J. Kovacs and M. Tardos (eds), *Reform and Transformation in Eastern Europe. Soviet Type Economies on the Threshold of Change*, Routledge, London, pp. 19–39.

Dillard, D. (1987), 'Money as an Institution of Capitalism', *Journal of Economic Issues*, Vol.21, No.4, pp. 1623–47.

Dittus, P.P. (1994), 'Bank Reform and Behavior in Central Europe', *Journal of Comparative Economics*, Vol.19, No.3, December, pp. 335–361.

Dobb, M. (1973), *Theories of Value and Distribution since Adam Smith*, Cambridge University Press, Cambridge.

Dornbusch, R., (1993), 'Payments Arrangements among the Republics' in O. Blanchard, M. Boycko, R. Dabrowski, R. Dornbusch, Layard, and A. Shleifer, *Post-Communist Reform: Pain and Progress*, The MIT Press, Cambridge, Mass., pp. 81–108.

Doucouliagos, C. (1995), *'The Efficiency Of The Labor–Managed Firm: Theoretical And Empirical Considerations'*, PhD Thesis Department of Economics, Faculty of Business and Economics, Monash University.

Dow, S.C. (2002), *Economic Methodology: An Inquiry*, Oxford University Press, Oxford.

Dreze, J.H. (1993), 'Self–Management and Economic Theory: Efficiency, Funding, and Employment', in P.K. Bardhan and J.E. Roemer (eds), *Market Socialism: The Current Debate*, Oxford University press, Oxford, pp. 253–265.

Driver, C. (1996), 'Stagnation as a Problem of Transition: Arguments and Proposals', *Cambridge Journal of Economics*, Vol.20, No.5, pp. 553–564.

Dugger, W.M. (1996), 'Redefining Economics: From Market Allocation to Social Provisioning', in C.J. Whalen (ed.), *Political Economy for the 21st Century*, M.E. Sharpe, Armonk, New York, pp. 31–43.

Dunn, S.P. (1999), 'The Future of Post Keynesian Economics?', *Journal of Economic and Social Policy*, Vol.4, No.1, pp. 1–16.

Durbin, E. (1976), 'A Social View of Democracy', in I. Howe (ed.), *Essential Works of Socialism*, Yale University Press, London, pp. 557–563.

Dyker, D.A. (1987), *The Soviet Union under Gorbachev*, Croom Helm, London.

Easterly, W. and Fischer, S. (1994), 'What We Can Learn from the Soviet Collapse', *Finance and Development*, Vol.31, No.4, December, pp. 2–5.

Economic Commission for Europe, (1992), *Economic Survey Of Europe in 1991–1992*, New York.

Economic Commission for Europe, (1993) *Economic Survey Of Europe in 1992–1993*, New York.

Economic Commission for Europe, (1994) *Economic Survey Of Europe in 1993–1994*, New York.

Economist, (1994), 'Inequality', 5 November, pp. 19–23, reprinted in G. Argyrous and F. Stilwell (eds), (1996a), *Economics as a Social Science. Readings in Political Economy*, Pluto Press, Annandale, pp. 13–16.

Economist Intelligence Unit Limited, (1996), *EIU Country Report–Poland First Quarter 1996*, London.

Economist Intelligence Unit, (1998), *World Outlook 1998–Forecasts of Political and Economic Trends in over 180 Countries*, London.

Edwards, S. (1992), 'Stabilization and Liberalization for Economies in Transition: Latin American Lessons for Eastern Europe', in C. Clague and G. Rausser (eds), *The Emergence of Market Economies in Eastern Europe*, Blackwell, Cambridge, pp. 129–160.

Eichengreen, B. (1993) 'A Payments Mechanism for the Former Soviet Union: Is the EPU a Relevant Precedent?', *Economic Policy*, No.17, October, pp. 309–53.

Eichner, A.S. (ed.), (1979a), *A Guide to Post–Keynesian Economics*, Macmillan, New York.

Eichner, A.S. (1979b), 'Introduction', in A.S. Eichner (ed.), *A Guide to Post–Keynesian Economics*, Macmillan, New York, pp. 3–18.

Eichner, A.S. (1979c), 'A Look Ahead', in A.S. Eichner (ed.), *A Guide to Post–Keynesian Economics*, Macmillan, New York, pp. 165–84.

Eisner, R. (1998), 'Save Social Security from its Saviors', *Journal of Post Keynesian Economics*, Vol.21, No.1, pp. 77–92.

Elliot, J.E. (1996 [1984]), 'The Institutionalist School of Political Economy' in D.K. Whynes (ed.), *What is Political Economy?*, Basil Blackwell, pp.

59–89, reprinted in G. Argyrous and F. Stilwell (eds), *Economics as a Social Science. Readings in Political Economy*, Pluto Press, Annandale, NSW, pp. 108–111.

Ellman, M. (1994), 'Transformation, Depression and Economics: Some Lessons', *Journal of Comparative Economics*, Vol.19, No.1, August, pp. 1–21.

Elson, D. (1988), 'Market Socialism or Socialization of the Market?', *New Left Review*, No.172, November/December, pp. 3–44.

Elson, D. (1991), 'The Economics of a Socialized Market', in R. Blackburn (ed.), *After the Fall. The Failure of Communism and the Future of Socialism*, Verso, London, pp. 310–314.

Elster, J. and Moene, K.O. (1989), 'Introduction', in J. Elster and K.O. Moene (eds), *Alternatives to Capitalism*, Cambridge University Press, Cambridge, pp. 1–35.

Elster, J., Offe, C. and Preuss, K. (1997), *Institutional Design in Post–Communist Societies: Rebuilding the Ship at Sea*, Cambridge University Press, Cambridge.

Engels, F. (1977), 'Engels to J. Bloch' in K. Marx and F. Engels, *Selected Letters*. Foreign Language Press, Peking, pp. 75–8.

Enzensberger, H.M. (1991), 'Ways of Walking: A Postscript to Utopia', in R. Blackburn (ed.), *After the Fall. The Failure of Communism and the Future of Socialism*, Verso, London, pp. 18–24.

Erber, E. (1994), 'Virtues and Vices of the Market: Balanced Correctives to a Current Craze', in F. Roosevelt and D. Belkin (eds), *Why Market Socialism?*, M.E. Sharpe, Armonk, New York, pp. 349–362.

Ericson, R.E. (1991), 'The Classical Soviet–Type Economy: Nature of the System and Implications for Reform', *Journal of Economic Perspectives*, Vol.5, No.4, Fall, pp. 11–27.

Estrin, S. (1990), 'Workers Co–operatives: Their Merits and their Limitations', in J. Le Grand and S. Estrin (eds), *Market Socialism*, Oxford University Press, Oxford, pp. 165–192.

Estrin, S. and Le Grand, J. (1990), 'Market Socialism', in J. Le Grand, and S. Estrin (eds), *Market Socialism*, Oxford University Press, Oxford, pp. 1–24.

Estrin, S. and Miller, D. (1994), 'Reply', in F. Roosevelt and D. Belkin (eds), *Why Market Socialism?*, M.E. Sharpe, Armonk, New York, pp. 243–246.

Estrin, S. and Winter, D. (1990), 'Planning in a Market Socialist Economy', in J. Le Grand and S. Estrin (eds), *Market Socialism*, Oxford University Press, Oxford, pp. 100–138.

Esty, D.C. (1997), 'Environmental Protection During the Transition to a Market Economy', in W.T. Woo, S. Parker and J.D. Sachs (eds), *Economies in Transition. Comparing Asia and Europe*, MIT Press, Cambridge, Mass., pp. 357–385.

Eswaran, M. and Kotwal, A. (1989), 'Why are Capitalists the Bosses?', *The Economic Journal*, Vol.99, No.394, March, pp. 162–76.

Eyal, G., Szelenyi, I. and Townsley, E. (1997), 'The Theory of Post–Communist Managerialism', *New Left Review*, No.222, March/April, pp. 60–92.

Fan, Q. (1994) 'State–owned Enterprise Reform in China: Incentives and Environment', in Q. Fan and P. Nolan (eds), *China's Economic Reforms*, St. Martin's Press, Hampshire, pp. 137–156.

Fazzari, S.M., Ferri, P. and Greenberg, E. (1998), 'Aggregate Demand and Firm Behavior: A New Perspective on Keynesian Microfoundations', *Journal of Post Keynesian Economics*, Vol.20, No.4, pp. 527–58.

Fedorov, B.G. (1992), 'Monetary, Financial and Foreign Exchange Policy', in A. Aslund (ed.), *The Post–Soviet Economy. Soviet and Western Perspectives*, St. Martin's Press, New York, pp. 102–111.

Fedorov, B.G. (1997), 'Macro–economic Policy and Stabilization in Russia', in A. Aslund (ed.), (1995), *Russian Economic Reform at Risk*, Pinter, London, pp. 9–18, reprinted in A. Aslund (ed.) *Russia's Economic Transformation in the 1990s*, Pinter, London, pp. 109–126.

Feltenstein, A. (1994), 'The Uncertainty of Economic Success When Economic Regimes are Uncertain: A Study of Transition Periods' *Journal of Comparative Economics*, Vol.19, No.2, October, pp. 217–236.

Femminis, G. and Ruggerone, L. (1999), 'On the Role of Sector Size in Determining the Transition Path', *The Manchester School*, Vol.67, No.4, September, pp. 588–602.

Fischer, S. (1992), 'Privatization in East European Transformation', in C. Clague and G. Rausser (eds), *The Emergence of Market Economies in Eastern Europe*, Blackwell, Cambridge, pp. 227–244.

Fischer, S. (1993), 'A Payments Mechanism for the Former Soviet Union: Is the EPU a Relevant Precedent?: Discussion', *Economic Policy*, Vol. 17, October, pp. 347–350.

Fischer, S. (1994), 'Discussion, Structural Factors In The Economic Reforms Of China, Eastern Europe And The Former Soviet Union', *Economic Policy*, Vol.19, pp. 131–5.

Fischer, S. (1996), 'Comment and Discussion on: How to Stabilize; Lessons from Post–communist Countries', *Brooking Papers on Economic Activity*, No.1, pp. 292–313.

Fischer, S. and Frenkel, J. (1992), 'Macroeconomic Issues of Soviet Reform', *American Economic Review Papers and Proceedings*, Vol.82, No.2, May, pp. 37–42.

Fischer, S. and Gelb, A. (1991), 'The Process of Socialist Economic Transformation', *Journal of Economic Perspectives*, Vol.5, No.4, Fall, pp. 91–105.

Fischer, S. and Sahay, R. (2000), 'Taking Stock', *Finance and Development*, Vol.37, No.3, pp. 2–6.

Fischer, S., Sahay, R. and Vegh, C.A. (1996), 'Stabilization and Growth in Transition Economies: The Early Experience', *Journal of Economic Perspectives*, Vol.10, No.2, Spring, pp. 45–66.

Fish, M.S. (1994), 'Russia's Fourth Transition', *Journal of Democracy*, Vol.5, No.3 July, pp. 3–42.

Fleurbaey, M. (1993), 'Economic Democracy and Equality: A Proposal', in P.K. Bardhan and J.E. Roemer (eds), *Market Socialism: The Current Debate*, Oxford University press, Oxford, pp. 266–278.

Fligstein, N. (1996), 'The Economic Sociology of the Transition from Socialism', *American Journal of Sociology*, Vol.101, No.4, January, pp. 1074–81.

Folbre, N. (1996), 'Roemer's Market Socialism: a Feminist Critique', in E.O. Wright (ed.), *Equal Shares. Making Socialism Work. The Real Utopias Project, Volume II*, Verso, London, pp. 57–70.

Frank, R. (1985), *Choosing the Right Pond: Human Behavior and the Quest for Status*, Oxford University Press, New York.

Friedman, M. (1962), *Capitalism and Freedom*, University of Chicago Press, Chicago.

Friedman, M. (1980), *Free to Choose*, Macmillan, Melbourne.

Friedman, M. and Friedman, R. (1996, [1980]), 'The Power of the Market', in M. Friedman and R. Friedman, (1980), *Free to Choose*, Secker & Warburg, London, reprinted in G. Argyrous and F. Stilwell (eds), *Economics as a Social Science. Readings in Political Economy*, Pluto Press, Annandale, NSW, pp. 77–81.

Frydman, R., Rapaczynski, A. and Turkewitz, J. (1997), 'Transition to a Private Property Regime in the Czech Republic and Hungary', in W.T. Woo, S. Parker and J.D. Sachs (eds), *Economies in Transition. Comparing Asia and Europe*, MIT Press, Cambridge, Mass., pp. 41–102.

Furubotn, E. (1976), 'The Long Run Analysis of the Labor–Managed Firm: An Alternative Interpretation', *American Economic Review*, Vol.66, No.1, March, pp. 104–23.

Furubotn, E.G. (2000), 'Legal Reforms in Russia: Visible Steps, Obvious Gaps, and an Invisible Hand?', *Journal of Institutional and Theoretical Economics*, Vol.156, No.1, pp. 120–124.

Gaidar, Y. (1997), 'The IMF and Russia', *Papers and Proceedings: The American Economic Review*, Vol.87, No.2, May, pp. 13–16.

Galbraith, J.K. (1993), 'Change and the Planning System', in C. Lemert (ed.), *Social Theory: The Multicultural and Classic Readings*, Westview Press Inc., Colorado, pp. 411–414.

Galbraith, J.K. (1996), 'The Good Society: The Economic Dimension' in G. Argyrous and F. Stilwell (eds), *Economics as a Social Science. Readings in Political Economy*, Pluto Press, Annandale, pp. 272–6.

Galbraith, J.K. (1998), 'John Maynard Keynes: From Retrospect to Prospect', *Journal of Post Keynesian Economics*, Vol.21, No.1, pp. 11–13.

Galeano, E. (1991), 'A Child Lost in the Storm', in R. Blackburn (ed.), *After the Fall. The Failure of Communism and the Future of Socialism*, Verso, London, pp. 250–254.

Gardner, S.H. (1998), *Comparative Economic Systems*, Second Edition, The Dryden Press, Orlando.

Gelb, A., Jefferson, G. and Singh, I. (1993), *'Can Communist Economies Transform Incrementally? The Experience of China'*, Transition and Macro Adjustment Division, Policy Research Department, World Bank, Washington, DC.

Geld, A. and Gray, C. (1991), *The Transformation of Economies in Central and Eastern Europe. Issues, Progress and Prospects*, The World Bank, Washington.

Gerschenkron, A. (1962), *Economic Backwardness in a Historical Perspective*, Cambridge, Harvard University Press, Massachusetts.

Gerschenkron, A. (1968), *Continuity in History and Other Essays*, Cambridge, Harvard University Press, Massachusetts.

Giersh, H. (1989), *The Ethics of Economic Freedom*, Centre for Independent Studies, St. Lornards, NSW.

Gill, G. (1988), *The Rules of the Communist Party of the Soviet Union*, Macmillan Press, London.

Glasman, M. (1994), 'The Great Transformation: Polanyi, Poland and the Terrors of Planned Spontaneity', *New Left Review*, No 205, May/June, pp. 59–86.

Gordon, M.J. (1992), 'China's Path to Market Socialism', *Challenge*, Vol.35, No.1, January/February, pp. 53–6.

Gordon, D.M., Weisskopf, T.E. and Bowles, S. (1996), 'Social Structures Of Accumulation', in G. Argyrous and F. Stilwell (eds), *Economics as a Social Science. Readings in Political Economy*, Pluto Press, Annandale, NSW, pp. 256–259.

Gorz, A. (1991), 'The New Agenda', in R. Blackburn (ed.), *After the Fall. The Failure of Communism and the Future of Socialism*, Verso, London, pp. 287–297.

Gowan, P. (1995), 'Neo–Liberal Theory and Practice for Eastern Europe', *New Left Review*, No.213, September/October, pp. 3–60.

Grabel, I. (2000), 'The Political Economy of 'Policy Credibility': The New–Classical Macroeconomics and The Remaking of Emerging Economies', *Cambridge Journal of Economics*, Vol.24, No.1, January, pp. 1–19.

Graham, C. (1997), 'Strategies for Addressing the Social Costs of Market Reforms: Lessons for Transition Economies in East Asia and Eastern Europe', in W.T. Woo, S. Parker and J.D. Sachs (ed.), *Economies in Transition. Comparing Asia and Europe*, MIT Press, Cambridge, Mass., pp. 325–356.

Gramsci, A. (1971), *Selections from the Prison Notebooks*, International Publishers, New York.

Granville, B. (1997), 'Farewell Rouble Zone', in A. Aslund (ed.), (1995), *Russian Economic Reform at Risk*, Pinter, London, pp. 65–88, reprinted in A. Aslund (ed.) *Russia's Economic Transformation in the 1990s*, Pinter, London, pp. 101–118.

Gregory, P.R. and Stuart, R.C. (1999), *Comparative Economic Systems*, Sixth Edition, Houghton Mifflin Company, Boston.

Grigoriev, L. (1992), 'Ulterior Property Rights and Privatization' in A. Aslund (ed.), *The Post–Soviet Economy. Soviet and Western Perspectives*, St. Martin's Press, New York, pp. 196–208.

Grilli, V. 'A Payments Mechanism for the Former Soviet Union: Is the EPU a Relevant Precedent ?: Discussion', *Economic Policy*, Vol. 17, October, pp. 346–347.

Grosfeld, I. (1990), 'Reform Economics and Western Theory: Unexploited Opportunities', *Economics of Planning*, Vol.23, No.1, March, pp. 1–19.

Grossman, P.Z. (1997), 'On the New Institutionalist Story about the Former Socialist Economies', *Journal of Economic Issues*, Vol.31, No.1, March, pp. 251–4.

Gustafson, T. (1999), *Capitalism Russian–Style*, Cambridge University Press, Cambridge.

Habermas, J. (1991), 'What Does Socialism Mean Today? The Revolutions of Recuperation and the Need for New Thinking', in R. Blackburn (ed.), *After the Fall. The Failure of Communism and the Future of Socialism*, Verso, London, pp. 25–46.

Halliday, F. (1991), 'The Ends of Cold War', in R. Blackburn (ed.), *After the Fall. The Failure of Communism and the Future of Socialism*, Verso, London, pp. 78–99.

Hammer, L.C. and Akram–Lodhi, A.H. (1998), 'In 'the house of spirits': Toward a Post Keynesian Theory of the Household?', *Journal of Post Keynesian Economics*, Vol.20, No.3, pp. 415–33.

Hansson, A. (1992), 'The Emergence and Stabilization of Extreme Inflationary Pressures in the Soviet Union', in A. Aslund (ed.), *The Post–Soviet Economy. Soviet and Western Perspectives*, St. Martin's Press, New York, pp. 67–84.

Hare, P.G. (1991), 'Hungary: In Transition to a Market Economy', *Journal of Economic Perspectives*, Vol.5, No.4, Fall, pp. 195–201.

Harrington, M. (1994), 'Markets and Plans: Is the Market Necessarily Capitalist?', in F. Roosevelt and D. Belkin (eds), *Why Market Socialism?*, M.E. Sharpe, Armonk, New York, pp. 83–108.

Hayek, F.A. (1948), *Individualism and Economic Order*, University of Chicago, Chicago.

Hayek, F.A. (1986, [1944]), *The Road to Serfdom*, Ark Edition, London.

Hayek, F.A. (1979), *Social Justice, Socialism and Democracy: Three Australian Lectures*, Centre of Independent Studies, Sydney.

He, D. (1994), 'The Stock Market and Industrial Performance: Lessons form the West for Stock Market Development in China', in Q. Fan and P. Nolan (eds), *China's Economic Reforms*, St. Martin's Press, Hampshire, pp. 191–217.

Heilbroner, R. (1994), 'Foreward', in F. Roosevelt and D. Belkin (eds), *Why Market Socialism?*, M.E. Sharpe, Armonk, New York, pp. xv–xvi.

Heilbroner, R. (1996a), 'Economics, Political and Otherwise', in G. Argyrous and F. Stilwell (eds), *Economics as a Social Science. Readings in Political Economy*, Pluto Press, Annandale, NSW, pp. viii–ix.

Heilbroner, R. (1996b), 'The Ideology of Capital', in G. Argyrous and F. Stilwell (eds), *Economics as a Social Science. Readings in Political Economy*, Pluto Press, Annandale, NSW, pp. 32–35.

Heilbroner, R. (1996c), 'Economics in the Twenty–first Century', in C.J. Whalen (ed.) *Political Economy for the 21st Century*, M.E. Sharpe, Armonk, New York, pp. 265–274.

Heilbroner R. and Barkan, J. (1994), 'From Sweden to Socialism? An Exchange' in F. Roosevelt and D. Belkin (eds), *Why Market Socialism?*, M.E. Sharpe, Armonk, New York, pp. 175–80.

Helpman, E. and Krugman, P. (1985), *Market Structure and Foreign Trade. Increasing Returns, Imperfect Information, and the International Economy*, The MIT Press, Cambridge, Mass.

Herr, H. and Westphall, A. (1991), 'Economic Coherence and the Transformation of Planned Economies Into Monetary Economies', *Journal of Post Keynesian Economics*, Vol.13, No.3, Spring, pp. 307–327.

Hirshleifer, J. (1996, [1977]), 'The Expanding Domain of Economics', in J. Hirshleirfer, (1977), *The Passions and the Interests; Political Arguments for Capitalism Before its Triumph*, Cambridge University Press, Cambridge, reprinted in G. Argyrous, and F. Stilwell (eds), (1996a), *Economics as a Social Science. Readings in Political Economy*, Pluto Press, Annandale, NSW, pp. 90–93.

Hobsbawn, E. (1991), 'Out of the Ashes', in R. Blackburn (ed.), *After the Fall. The Failure of Communism and the Future of Socialism*, Verso, London, pp. 315–325.

Hodgson, G.M. (1988), *Economics and Institutions*, Polity Press, Oxford.

Hodgson, G.M. (1993), *Economics and Evolution: Bringing Live Back to Economics*, Polity Press, Cambridge.

Holmstrom, N. and Smith, R. (2000), 'The Necessity of Gangster Capitalism: Primitive Accumulation in Russia and China', *Monthly Review*, Vol.51, No.9, February, pp. 1–15.

Horne, J. (1995), 'The Economics of Transition and the Transition of Economics', *The Economic Record*, Vol. 71, No.215, December, pp. 379– 392.

Hornik, R. (1994), 'Bursting China's Bubble', *Foreign Affairs*, Vol.73, No.3, May/June, pp. 28–42.

Horvat, B. (1992), 'Nationalization, Privatization or Socialization: The Emergence of the Social Corporation', in F. Targetti (ed.), *Privatization in Europe. West and East Experiences*, Dartmouth.

Horvat, B. (1994), 'Comment', in F. Roosevelt and D. Belkin (eds), *Why Market Socialism?*, M.E. Sharpe, Armonk, New York, pp. 319–321.

Howard, M.C. and King, J.E. (1992), *A History Of Marxian Economics, Volume II, 1929–1990*, Macmillan, London.

Howard, M.C. and King, J.E. (1993), 'Is Socialism Economically Feasible? An Analysis in terms of Historical Materialism', Discussion Paper No.1, Department of Economics, School of Economics and Commerce, LaTrobe University, January.

Howard, M.C. and King, J.E. (1994), 'Is Socialism Economically Feasible? An Analysis in Terms of historical Materialism', *Review of Political Economy*, Vol.6, No.2, pp. 133–152.

Howard, M.C. and King, J.E. (1999), '*The Stalinists' Counter–Revolutions*', Paper Presented at the Howard Sherman Festschrift Conference in February, at the University of California, Riverside.

Howe, I. (1994), 'Thinking About Socialism: Achievements, Failures, and Possibilities', in F. Roosevelt and D. Belkin (eds), *Why Market Socialism?*, M.E. Sharpe, Armonk, New York, pp. 51–82.

Howe, I. and Coser, L. (1976), 'Images of Socialism', in I. Howe (ed.), *Essential Works of Socialism*, Yale University Press, London, pp. 835–850.

Howell, J. (1994), 'Striking a New Balance: New Social Organizations in Post–Mao China', *Capital & Class*, No.54, Autumn, pp. 89–111.

Howells, P.G.A. (1997), 'The Demand for Endogenous Money: A Rejoinder', *Journal of Post Keynesian Economics*, Vol.19, No.3, pp. 429–35.

Howells, P. and Hussein, K.A. (1999), 'The Demand for Bank Loans and the 'State of Trade'', *Journal of Post Keynesian Economics*, Vol.21, No.3, pp. 441–454.

Huang, G. (1994), 'Problems of Monetary Control in China: Targets, Behavior and Mechanism', in Q. Fan and P. Nolan (eds), *China's Economic Reforms*, St. Martin's Press, Hampshire, pp. 46–73.

Huang, Y. and Duncan, R. (1996a), '*State Enterprise Reforms in China: A Critical review of the Policy Measures and their Impacts*', Paper Presented at the Workshop at the Deakin University Melbourne, 4 October.

Huang, Y. and Duncan, R. (1996b), '*Which Chinese Enterprises Make Losses?*', Paper Presented at the Workshop at the Deakin University Melbourne, 4 October.

Hudson, J. (1999), 'A Generalized Theory of Output Determination', *Journal of Post Keynesian Economics*, Vol.21, No.4, pp. 663–78.

Hughes, G. (1994), 'Discussion Structural Factors in the Economic Reforms Of China, Eastern Europe And The Former Soviet Union', *Economic Policy*, Vol.19, pp. 135–139.

Hussain, A. (1993), 'Discussion of Part Five', in I.P. Szekely and D.M.G. Newbery (eds), *Hungary: An Economy In Transition*, Cambridge University Press, Cambridge, pp. 270–274.

Hussain, A. (1994), 'Private Sector Development in Economies in Transition', *Journal of Comparative Economics*, Vol.19, No.2, October, pp. 260–271.

Ickes, B.W. (1996), 'How to Stabilize: Lessons from Post–communist Countries: Comment', *Brookings Papers on Economic Activity*, No.1, pp. 298–305.

Illarionov, A., Layard, R. and Orszag, P.P. (1997), 'The Conditions of Life', in A. Aslund (ed.), (1994), *Economic Transformation in Russia*, St. Martins Press, New York, pp. 127–56, reprinted in A. Aslund (ed.) *Russia's Economic Transformation in the 1990s*, Pinter, London, pp. 137–158.

Inglehart, R. (1977), *The Silent Revolution*, Princeton, Princeton University Press, New Jersey.

International Monetary Fund, (1992), *Albania: From Isolation Toward Reform – Occasional Paper*, Washington DC, September.

International Monetary Fund, (1994), *Economic Reviews – Albania*, Washington DC, July.

Intriligator, M.D. (1998), 'Democracy In Reforming Collapsed Communist Economies: Blessing Or Curse?', *Contemporary Economic Policy*, Vol.16, No.2, April, pp. 241–246.

Jackson, W.A. (1999), 'Basic Income and the Right to Work: A Keynesian Approach', *Journal of Post Keynesian Economics*, Vol.21, No.4, pp. 639–62.

Jacobs, L.A. (1999), 'Market Socialism and Non–Utopian Marxist Theory', *Philosophy of the Social Sciences*, Vol.29, No.4, December, pp. 527–539.

Jameson, F. (1991), 'Conversations on the New World Order', in R. Blackburn (ed.), *After the Fall. The Failure of Communism and the Future of Socialism*, Verso, London, pp. 255–268.

Jarai, Z. (1993), '10 Per Cent Already Sold: Privatization In Hungary', in I.P. Szekely and D.M.G. Newbery (eds), *Hungary: An Economy In Transition*, Cambridge University Press, Cambridge, pp. 77–83.

Jefferson, G.H. (1993), 'Are China's Rural Enterprises Outperforming State–Owned Enterprises?', Transition and Macro Adjustment Division, Policy Research Department, World Bank, Washington, DC.

Jefferson G.H. and Rawski, T.G. (1994), 'Enterprise Reforms in Chinese Industry, *Journal of Economic Perspectives*, Vol.8, No.2, Spring, pp. 47–70.

Jeffries, I. (1996), *A Guide To The Economies In Transition*, Routledge, London.

Jensen, M. and Meckling, W. (1979), 'Rights and Production Functions: An Application to Labor–Managed Firms and Codetermination', *Journal of Business*, Vol.52, No.4, October, pp. 469–506.

Jianguo, W.T., Ling, M. and Smyth, R. (2001), 'Corporate Governance and Ownership Reform in China's State–Owned Enterprises', *Asian Profile*, Vo.29, No.2, April, pp. 93–107.

Jin, D. and Haynes, K.E. (1997), 'Economic Transition at the Edge of Order and Chaos: China's Dualistic and Leading Sectoral Approach', *Journal of Economic Issues*, Vol.31, No.1, March, pp. 79–101.

Johnson, J. (1994), 'Should Russia Adopt The Chinese Model of Reform?', *Communist and Post–Communist Studies'*, Vol.27, No.1, pp. 59–75

Kagarlitsky, B. (1993), 'Russia on the Brink of New Battles', *New Left Review*, No.192, pp. 87–97.

Kagarlitsky, B. (1996a), 'The Agony of Neo–Liberalism or the End of Civilization', *Monthly Review Press*, June, pp. 36–39.

Kagarlitsky, B. (1996b), 'Russia Chooses – and Loses', *Current History*, Vol.95, No.603, October, pp. 305–310.

Kagarlitsky, B. (1999), 'Rumblings in Russia', *The Progressive*, July, pp. 24–26.

Kalecki, M. (1996, [1943]), 'Political aspects of Full Employment', in J. Osiatynski *Collected Works of Michal Kalecki, Vol. 1*, Clarendon Oxford, reprinted in G. Argyrous and F. Stilwell (eds), (1996), *Economics as a Social Science. Readings in Political Economy*, Pluto Press, Annandale, NSW, pp. 146–149.

Kee, F.S. (1996), 'Pricing and the Business Enterprise', in C.J. Whalen (ed.), *Political Economy for the 21ˢᵗ Century*, M.E. Sharpe, Armonk, New York, pp. 87–102.

Keesing's Record of World Events, (1997), Vol, 43, No. 2, Cambridge.

Keesing's Record of World Events, (1997), Vol, 43, No. 5, Cambridge.

Keesing's Record of World Events, (1997), Vol, 43, No. 6, Cambridge.

Keesing's Record of World Events (1997), Vol 43, No. 11, Cambridge.

Kemp, D. (1988), *Foundation for Australian Political Analysis: Politics and Authority*, Oxford University Press, Melbourne.

Kenyon, P. (1979), 'Pricing', in A.S. Eichner (ed.), *A Guide to Post–Keynesian Economics*, Macmillan, New York, pp. 34–45.

Keynes, J.M. (1920), *The Economic Consequences of the Peace*, Macmillan, London.

Keynes, J.M. (1967, [1936]), *The General Theory of Employment, Interest and Money*, Macmillan, London.

Kim, I. (1994), 'The Political Economy of Investment Control in Post–1978 China', in Q. Fan and P. Nolan (eds), *China's Economic Reforms*, St. Martin's Press, Hampshire, pp. 74–103.

Kingston–Mann, E. (1999), 'How Do We Understand Russia's Crisis?', *Challenge*, Vol.42, No.1, January/February, pp. 34–42.

Klaus, V. (1995), 'Privatization Experience: The Czech Case', *Policy*, Vol.11, No.1, Autumn, pp. 45–47.

Kirkby, E. (1993), 'Broadening the Scope of Public Policy', in S. Rees, G. Rodley and F. Stilwell (eds), *Beyond the Market: Alternatives to Economic Rationalism*, Pluto Press Australia Ltd, NSW, pp. 105–109.

Kirzner, I.M. (1998), *How Markets Work. Disequilibrium, Entrepreneurship and Discovery*, Occasional Paper No.64, The Centre for Independent Studies, St. Leonards, NSW.

Kolakowski, L. (1976), 'The Concept of the Left', in I. Howe (ed.), *Essential Works of Socialism*, Yale University Press Ltd., London, pp. 682–698.

Kolodko, G.W. (1993), 'Stabilization, Recession, and Growth in a Post–socialist Economy', *MOCT–MOST: Economic Journal on Eastern Europe and the Former Soviet Union*, No.1, January, pp. 3–38.

Kolodko, G.W. (1998), 'The Russian Economy in Crisis', *The Harriman Review*, Special Issue, December, pp. 24–27.

Kolodko, G.W. (1999a), 'Incomes Policy, Equity Issues, and Poverty Reduction in Transition Economies', *Finance and Development*, September, pp. 32–34.

Kolodko, G.W. (1999b), 'Transition to a Market Economy and Sustained Growth. Implications for the Post–Washington Consensus', *Communist and Post–Communist Studies*, Vol.32, No.3, pp. 233–261.

Kolodko, G.W. (2000), 'Transition to a Market and Entrepreneurship: The Systemic Factors and Policy Options', *Communist and Post–Communist Studies*, Vol.33, No.3, pp. 271–293.

Koltay, J. (1993), 'Tax Reform in Hungary', in I.P. Szekely and D.M.G. Newbery (eds), *Hungary: An Economy In Transition*, Cambridge University Press, Cambridge, pp. 249–270.

Kornai, J. (1983), 'Equilibrium as a Category of Economics', *Acta Oeconomica*, Vol.30, No.2, pp. 145–159.

Kornai, J. (1986), 'The Hungarian reform Process: Visions, Hopes, and Reality', *Journal of Economic Literature*, Vol.24, No.4, December, pp. 1687–1737.

Kornai, J. (1988), 'Individual Freedom and Reform of the Socialist Economy', *European Economic Review*, Vol.32, No. 2/3, March, pp. 233–267.

Kornai, J. (1990), *The Road to a Free Economy*, W.W. Norton, New York.

Kornai, J. (1992a), *The Socialist System. The Political Economy of Communism*, Clarendon Press, Oxford.

Kornai, J. (1992b), 'The Postsocialist Transition and the State: Reflections in the Light of Hungarian Fiscal Problems', *The American Economic Review*, Vol.82, No.2, May, pp. 1–21.

Kornai, J. (1992c), 'The Principles of Privatization in Eastern Europe', *De Economist*, Vol.140, No.2, pp. 153–176.

Kornai, J. (1993a), 'Transformational Recession A General Phenomenon Examined through the Example of Hungary's Development', *In Economic Appliquee*, Vol.46, No.2, pp. 181–227.

Kornai, J. (1993b), 'The Evolution of Financial Discipline under the Postsocialist System', *Kyklos*, Vol.46, No.3, pp. 315–336.

Kornai, J. (1993c), 'Market Socialism Revisited', in P.K. Bardhan and J.E. Roemer (eds), *Market Socialism: The Current Debate*, Oxford University Press, Oxford, pp. 42–68.

Kornai, J. (1994), 'Transformational Recession: The Main Causes', *Journal of Comparative Economics*, Vol. 19, No. 1, August, pp. 39–63.

Kornai, J. (1995a), 'Transformational Recession: The Hungarian Example', *Academia Economic Papers*, Vol. 23, No. 1, March, pp. 1–55.

Kornai, J. (1995b), 'Lasting Growth as the Top Priority: Macroeconomic Tensions and Government Economic Policy in Hungary', *Acta Oeconomica*, Vol.47, No.1–2, pp. 1–38.

Kornai, J. (1995c), 'The Dilemmas of Hungarian Economic Policy', *Acta Oeconomica*, Vol.47, No.3–4, pp. 227–248.

Kornai, J. (1995d), 'Hardening of the Budget Constraint Under the Postsocialist System', *Japan the World of Economy*, Vol.8, No.2, pp. 135–151.

Kornai, J. (1995e), *Highway and Byways: Studies on Reform and Post–Communist Transition*, MIT Press, Massachusetts.

Kornai, J. (1996), 'Growth and Macroeconomic Disequilibria in Hungary', *Academia Economic Papers*, Vol.24, No.1, March, pp. 1–44.

Kornai, J. (1997a), *Struggle and Hope: Essays on Stabilization and Reform in a Post–socialist Economy*, Edward Elgar Publishing Limited, Cheltnam.

Kornai, J. (1997b), 'The Transition from Socialism: The Reform of the Welfare State and Public Opinion', *American Economic Association Papers and Proceedings*, Vol.87, No.2, May, pp. 339–343.

Kornai, J. (1997c), 'Editorial: Reforming the Welfare State in Postsocialist Societies', *World Development*, Vol.25, No.8, pp. 1183–1186.

Kornai, J. (1997d), 'The Reform of the Welfare State and Public Opinion', *The American Economic Review, Papers and Proceedings*, Vol.87, No.2, May, pp. 339–343.

Kornai, J. (1998), 'The Place of the Soft Budget Constraint Syndrome in Economic Theory', *Journal of Comparative Economics*, Vol.26, No.1, pp. 11–17.

Kornai, J. (1999), 'What the Change of System Does and Does Not Mean', *Economic Systems*, Vol.23, No.2, June, pp. 160–166.

Kornai, J. (2000), 'What the Change of System From Socialism to Capitalism Does and Does Not Mean', *Journal of Economic Perspectives*, Vol.14, No.1, Winter, pp. 27–42.

Kornai, J. and Daniel, Z. (1986), 'The Chinese Economic Reform–As Seen By Hungarian Economists', *Acta Oeconomica*, Vol.36, No.3–4, pp. 289–305.

Kosmarskii, V. (1992), 'Public Attitudes to the Transition' in A. Aslund (ed.), (1992b), *The Post–Soviet Economy. Soviet and Western Perspectives*, St. Martin's Press, New York, pp. 25–38.

Kotz, D.M. (1999), 'Socialism and Capitalism: Lessons from the Demise of State Socialism in the Soviet Union and China', Paper presented at the Festschrift in honor of Howard Sherman at the University of California at Riverside, February 12–14.

Kovacs, J. and Tardos, M. (eds), (1992), Reform and Transformation in Eastern Europe. Soviet–Type Economies on the Threshold of Change, Routledge, London.

Kowalik, T. (1994), 'Oskar Lange's Market Socialism: The Story of and Intellectual–Political Career', in F. Roosevelt and D. Belkin (eds), Why Market Socialism?, M.E. Sharpe, Armonk, New York, pp. 137–154.

Kregel, J. A. (1979), 'Income Distribution' in Eichner, A.S. (ed.), A Guide to Post–Keynesian Economics, Macmillan, New York, pp. 46–60.

Kregel, J.A. (1980), 'Markets and Institutions as Features of a Capitalistic Production System', Journal of Post Keynesian Economics, Vol.3, No.1, Fall, pp. 32–48.

Kregel, J., Matzner, E. and Grabher, G. (1992), The Market Shock, AGENDA Group, Vienna.

Krueger, A. (1992), 'Institutions for the New Private Sector' in C. Clague and G. Rausser (eds), The Emergence of Market Economies in Eastern Europe, Blackwell, Cambridge, pp. 219–23.

Krugman, P. (1991), Geography and Trade, Leuven University Press, Leuven.

Krugman, P. (1994), 'The Myth of Asia's Miracle', Foreign Affairs, Vol.73, No.6, November/ December, pp. 62–78.

Kung, J.K. (1995), 'Equal Entitlement versus Tenure Security under A Regime of Collective Property Rights: Peasants' Preference for Institutions In Post–Reform Chinese Agriculture', Journal of Comparative Economics, Vol.21, No.1, August, pp. 82–111.

Kuznetsov, E. (1992), 'Post–socialist Transition from a Neo–Schumpeterian Perspective. The Case of the Former Soviet Union', Communist Economies and Economic Transformation, Vol.4, No. 4, pp. 469–499.

LaClau, E. and Mouffe, C. (1993), 'Radical Democracy: Alternative for a New Left', in C. Lemert (ed.), Social Theory: The Multicultural and Classic Readings, Westview Press Inc., Colorado, pp. 541–544.

Lah, M. and Susjan, A. (1999), 'Rationality of Transitional Consumers: A Post Keynesian View', Journal of Post Keynesian Economics, Vol.21, No.4, p p. 589–602.

Laki, M. (1993), 'Chances for the Acceleration of Transition: The Case of Hungarian Privatization', East European Politics and Societies, Vol.7, No.3, Fall, pp. 440–451.

Lane, R.E. (1978), 'Autonomy, Felicity, Futility: The Effects of the Marked Economy on Political Personality', The Journal of Politics, Vol.40, No.1, pp. 2–24.

Lane, R.E. (1979), The Dialectics of Freedom in A Market Society, The Edmund James Lecture, Department of Political Science, University of Illinois at Urbana–Champaign. Delivered April 16.

Lane, R.E. (1991), *The Market Experience*, Cambridge Press, New York.

Lange, O. (1976), 'Marxian Economics and Modern Economic Theory', in I. Howe (ed.), *Essential Works of Socialism*, Yale University Press Ltd., London, pp. 717–735.

Lange, O. and Taylor, F.R. (1939), *On The Economic Theory Of Socialism*, University of Minnesota Press, Minneapolis.

Lange, O. and Taylor, F.R. (1976), 'On the Policy of the Transition to Socialism', in E.L. Wheelwright and F.J.B. Stilwell (eds), *Readings in Political Economy: Volume 2*, Australian and New Zealand Book Company Pty. Ltd, NSW, pp. 231–235.

Laquer, W. (1989), *The Road to Freedom: Russia and Glasnost*. Hyman, London.

Lau, R.W.K. (1997), 'China: Labor Reform and the Challenge Facing the Working Class', *Capital & Class*, No.61, Spring, pp. 45–80.

Lau, R.W.K. (1999), 'The 15th Congress of the Chinese Communist Party: Milestone in China's Privatization', *Capital & Class*, No.68, Summer, pp. 51–87.

Lau, L.J., Qian, Y. and Roland, G. (2000), 'Reform Without Losers: An Interpretation of China's Dual–Track Approach to Transition', *Journal of Political Economy*, Vol.108, No.1, February, pp. 120–43.

Lavigne, M. (1995), *The Economics of Transition – From Socialist Economy To Market Economy*, Macmillan Press Ltd, Basingstone.

Layard, R. (1993), 'Stabilization versus Reform? Russia's First Year', in O. Blanchard, M. Boycko, R. Dabrowski, R. Dornbusch, R. Layard, and A. Shleifer, *Post-Communist Reform: Pain and Progress*, The MIT Press, Cambridge, Mass., pp. 15–36.

Layard, R. and Richter, A. (1997), 'Labor Market Adjustment; The Russian Way', in A. Aslund (ed.), (1995), *Russian Economic Reform at Risk*, Pinter, London, pp. 119–47, reprinted in A. Aslund (ed.), *Russia's Economic Transformation in the 1990s*, Pinter, London, pp. 159–181.

Lee, F.S. (1990), 'Marginalist Controversy and Post Keynesian Price Theory', *Journal of Post Keynesian Economics*, Vol.13, No.2, pp. 252–64.

Lee, F.S. (1996), 'Pricing and the Business Enterprise', in C.J. Whalen (ed.), *Political Economy in the 21st Century*, M.E. Sharpe, Armonk, New York, pp. 87–102.

Le Grand, J. (1990), 'Markets, Welfare and Equality', in J. Le Grand and S. Estrin (eds), *Market Socialism*, Oxford University Press, Oxford, pp. 193–211.

Leijonhufvud, A. (1993), 'The Nature of the Depression in the Former Soviet Union', *New Left Review*, No.199, pp. 120–126.

Leijonhufvud, A. and Ruhl, C. (1997), 'Russian Dilemmas', *American Economic Review Papers and Proceedings*, Vol.87, No.2, May, pp. 344–348.

Levine, A. (1996), 'Saving Socialism and/or Abandoning It', in E.O. Wright (ed.), *Equal Shares. Making Socialism Work. The Real Utopias Project, Volume II*, Verso, London, pp. 231–249.

Li, J. (1994), 'The Characteristics of Chinese and Russian Economics Reforms', *Journal of Comparative Economics*, Vol.18, No.3, June, pp. 309–313.

Li, D. (1996), 'A Theory of Ambiguous Property Rights in Transition Economies: The Case of the Chinese Non–State Sector', *Journal of Comparative
Economics*, Vol.23, No.1, pp. 1–19.

Li, W. (1999), 'A Tale of Two Reforms', *RAND Journal of Economics*, Vol.30,
No.1, Spring, pp. 120–136.

Lin, J.Y. (1989), 'An Economic Theory of Institutional Change: Induced And
Imposed Change', *Cato Journal*, Vol.9, No.1, Spring/Summer, pp. 1–33.

Lin, J.Y., Cai, F. and Li, Z. (1996), 'The Lessons of China's Transition to a
Market Economy', *Cato Journal*, Vol.16, No.2, pp. 201–231.

Lindblom, C.E. (1977), *Politics and Markets: The World's Political Economic
Systems*, Basic Books, New York.

Lipton, D. and Sachs, J. (1990), 'Creating a Market Economy in Eastern Europe: The Case of Poland', *Brookings Papers on Economic Activity*, No.1,
pp. 75–147.

Lipton, D. and Sachs, J. (1992), 'Prospects for Russia's Economics Reforms',
Brookings Papers on Economic Activity, No.2, pp. 213–83.

Litwack, J.M. (1991), 'Legality and Market Reform in Soviet–Type Economies',
Journal of Economic Perspectives, Vol.5, No.4, Fall, pp. 77–89.

Liu, M. (1994), 'Commune, Responsibility System and China's Agriculture',
in Q. Fan and P. Nolan (eds), *China's Economic Reforms*, St. Martin's Press,
Hampshire, pp. 104–136.

Livingstone, K. (1993), 'Can Democracy Survive in Russia?', *New Left Review*,
No.192, pp. 98–104.

Lo, D. (1995), 'Economic Theory And Transformation Of The Soviet–Type
System: The Challenge Of The Late Industrialization Perspective', in M.Y.
Chang and P. Nolan (eds), *The Transformation of the Communist Economies.
Against the Mainstream*, MacMillan, London, pp. 78–110.

Macesich, G. (1991), *Reform and Market Democracy*, Praeger Pub., New
York.

Maddock, R. (1994/5), 'Trade and Trade Blocks', *Arena Journal*, No.4, pp.
31–39.

Magdoff, H. (1976), 'The Market as an Instrument of Existing Institutions', in E.L.
Wheelwright and F.J.B. Stilwell (eds), *Readings in Political Economy: Volume
1*, Australian and New Zealand Book Company Pty. Ltd, NSW, pp. 62–65.

Makowski, L. and Ostroy, J.M. (1993), 'General Equilibrium and Market Socialism: Clarifying the Logic of Competitive markets', in P.K. Bardhan and
J.E. Roemer (eds), *Market Socialism: the Current Debate*, Oxford University
press, Oxford, pp. 69–88.

Maier, C.S. (1991), 'The Collapse of Communism: Approaches for a Future
History', *History Workshop Journal*, No.31, pp. 34–59.

Mandel, E. (1977), *From Class Society to Communism. An Introduction to
Marxism*, Ink Links, London.

Mandel, E. (1989), *Beyond Perestroika*, Verso, London.

Mandel, E. (1992), *Power and Money*, Verso, London.

Marangos, J. (1992), *The Search for a Consistent and Viable Economic System
in the Soviet Union*, Minor thesis submitted to the Department of Economics,
Monash University, Melbourne.

Marangos, J. (1997), 'Market and Political Freedom' in D. Kartarelis (ed.), *Business & Economics for the 21st Century– Volume I*, Business and Economic Society International, Worcester, pp. 162–7.

Marangos, J. (1998), 'The Rise and the Fall of the Stalinist Economic System: A Social Science Perspective', *Journal of Development Planning Literature'*, Vol. 13, No 3, July–September, pp. 233–253.

Marangos, J. (1999), 'The Rise and the Fall of the Stalinist Economic System: A Social Science Perspective' in S.B. Dahiya (ed.), *The Current State of Economic Science*, Spellbound Publications, Rohtak, pp. 2685–2705.

Marangos, J. (2000–1), 'A Post Keynesian View of Transition to Market Capitalism: Developing a Civilized Society', *Journal of Post Keynesian Economics*, Vol.23, No.2, pp. 299–309.

Marangos, J. (1997). *'Models of Transitions for Russia and Eastern Europe'*, Paper presented at the 33rd Annual Meeting of the Midwest Business Association, Chicago, 12–14 March.

Marris, R. (1992), 'Privatization, Markets and Managers' in F. Targetti (ed.) *Privatization in Europe. West and East Experiences*, Dartmouth, Aldershot, pp. 33–42.

Martinez–Vazquez, J., Rioja, F., Skogstad, S. and Valen, N. (2001), 'IMF Conditionality and Objections. The Russian Case', *American Journal of Economics and Sociology*, Vol.60, No.2, April, pp. 501–17.

Marx, K. (1966), *A Critique of the Gotha Programme*, International Publishers, New York.

Marx, K. (1975), *Early Writings*, Introduced by Colletti, L. Trans. Livingstone, R. and Benton, G., Vintage Books, New York.

Marx, K. (1976, [1859]), 'Preface' and 'Introduction' to *A Contribution to the Critique of Political Economy*, Foreign Language Press, Peking.

Marx, K. and Engels, F. (1988, [1872]), *Manifesto of the Communist Party*, Foreign Language Press, Beijing.

Mau, V. (1992), Prospects for Russia's Economic Reforms: Comments and Discussion', *Brookings Papers on Economic Activity*, No.2, pp. 266–73.

McClintock, B. (1996), 'International Trade and the Governance of Global Markets', in C.J. Whalen (ed.) *Political Economy for the 21st Century*, M.E. Sharpe, Armonk, New York, pp. 225–244.

McKinnon, R.I. (1991), 'Financial Control in the Transition from Classical Socialism to a Market Economy', *Journal of Economic Perspectives*, Vol.5, No.4, Fall, pp. 107–122.

McKinnon, R.I. (1992a), 'Spontaneous Order on the Road Back from Socialism: An Asian Perspective', *American Economic Association Papers and proceedings*, Vol.82, No.2, May, pp. 31–36.

McKinnon R.I. (1992b), 'Taxation, Money, and credit, in a Liberalizing Socialist Economy', *Economics of Planning*, Vol.25, No.1, pp. 98–112.

McKinnon, R.I. (1993a), 'Gradual versus Rapid Liberalization in Socialist Economies. The Problem of Macroeconomic Control', *Proceedings of the World Bank Annual Conference on Development Economies*, World Bank, Washington, pp. 63–94.

McKinnon, R.I. (1993b), *The Order of Economic Liberalization: Financial Control in the Transition to a Market Economy*, The John Hopkins University Press, Maryland.

McKinnon, R.I. (1995a), 'Financial Growth and Macroeconomic Stability in the People's Republic of China, 1978–1992: Implications for Russia and Eastern Europe', in P.B. Rana and N. Hamid (eds), *From Centrally Planned To Market Economies: The Asian Approach*, Oxford University Press, Oxford, pp. 73–106.

McKinnon, R.I. (1995b), 'Gradual Rapid Liberalization in Socialist Foreign Trade', in P.B. Rana and N. Hamid (eds), *From Centrally Planned To Market Economies: The Asian Approach*, Oxford University Press, Oxford, pp. 107–117.

McKinnon, R.I. (1995c), 'Taxation, Money, and Credit in the Transition from Central Planning', in P.B. Rana and N. Hamid, (eds), *From Centrally Planned To Market Economies: The Asian Approach*, Oxford University Press, Oxford, pp. 35–72.

McLellan, D. (1969), 'Marx's View of Unalienated Society', *Review of Politics*, Vol.31, No.4, October, pp. 459–65.

McMillan, J. and Naughton, B. (1992), 'How to Reform a Planned Economy: Lessons from China', *Oxford Review of Economic Policy*, Vol.8, No.1, pp. 130–143.

McNeill, T. (1998), 'Soviet Studies and the Collapse of the USSR: In Defense of Realism', in M. Cox (ed.), *Rethinking the Soviet Collapse. Sovietology, the Death of Communism and the New Russia*, BookEns Ltd., London, pp. 51–72.

Meade, J. (1972), 'The Theory of Labor–Managed Firms and of Profit–Sharing' *Economic Journal*, Vol.82, No.325S (special issue), pp. 402–28.

Mellor, R. (1999), 'Changing Cities in Post–Soviet Russia', *New Left Review: Specters of Nihilism*, No.236, July–August, pp. 53–76.

Meurs, M. (1996), 'Market Socialism as a Culture of Cooperation', in E.O. Wright (ed.), *Equal Shares. Making Socialism Work. The Real Utopias Project, Volume II*, Verso, London, pp. 110–121.

Mihalyi, P. (1993), 'Hungary: A Unique Approach to Privatization – Past, Present and Future', in I.P. Szekely and D.M.G. Newbery (eds), *Hungary: An Economy In Transition*, Cambridge University Press, Cambridge, pp. 84–117.

Milenkovitch, D.D. (1992), 'An Organisational Theory of Socialist Economy' in J. Kovacs and M. Tardos (eds), *Reform and Transformation in Eastern Europe. Soviet Type Economies on the Threshold of Change*, Routledge, London, pp. 40–61.

Miliband, R. (1991), 'Reflections on the Crisis of Communist Regimes', in R. Blackburn (ed.), *After the Fall. The Failure of Communism and the Future of Socialism*, Verso, London, pp. 6–17.

Miller, D. (1990), 'Why Markets?', in J. Le Grand and S. Estrin (eds), *Market Socialism*, Oxford University Press, Oxford, pp. 25–49.

Miller, D. (1993), 'Equality and Market Socialism', in P.K. Bardhan and J.E. Roemer (eds), *Market Socialism: The Current Debate*, Oxford University press, Oxford, pp. 298–314.

Miller, D. (1994), 'A Vision of Market Socialism: How it Might Work–And Its Problems', in F. Roosevelt and D. Belkin (eds), *Why Market Socialism?*, M.E. Sharpe, Armonk, New York, pp. 247–262.

Miller, D. and Estrin, S. (1994), 'A Case for Market Socialism: What Does it Mean? Why Should We Favour It?', in F. Roosevelt and D. Belkin (eds), *Why Market Socialism?*, M.E. Sharpe, Armonk, New York, pp. 225–241.

Milne, F. (1993), 'Overcoming the Illusion of Monetary Scarcity', in S. Rees, G. Rodley, and F. Stilwell (eds), *Beyond the Market: Alternatives to Economic Rationalism*, Pluto Press Australia Ltd, NSW, pp. 203–221.

Minogue, K.R. (1983), 'Freedom as a Skill', in A.P.P. Griffiths (ed.), *Of Liberty*, Cambridge University Press, Cambridge, pp. 197–215.

Minsky, H.P. (1996a), 'Forward', in C.J. Whalen (ed.) *Political Economy for the 21st Century*, M.E. Sharpe, Armonk, New York, pp. xi–xiii.

Minsky, H.P. (1996b), 'Uncertainty and the Institutional Structure of Capitalist Economies', *Journal of Economic Issues*, Vol.30, No.2, pp. 357–68.

Minsky, H.P. and Whalen, C.J. (1996–7), 'Economic Insecurity and the Institutional Prerequisites for Successful Capitalism', *Journal of Post Keynesian Economics*, Vol.19, No.2, pp. 155–70.

Minqi, L. (1996), 'China: Six Years After Tiananmen', *Monthly Review*, Vol.47, No.8, January, pp. 1–13.

Mizsei, K. (1993), 'Regional Cooperation in East–Central Europe', in I.P. Szekely and D.M.G. Newbery (eds), *Hungary: An Economy In Transition*, Cambridge University Press, Cambridge, pp. 44–50.

Moene, K.O. and Wallerstein, M. (1993), 'What's Wrong with Social Democracy', in P.K. Bardhan and J.E. Roemer (eds), *Market Socialism: The Current Debate*, Oxford University Press, Oxford, pp. 219–235.

Molyneux, M. (1991), 'The 'Woman Question' in the Age of Perestroika', in R. Blackburn (ed.), *After the Fall. The Failure of Communism and the Future of Socialism Fall*, Verso, London, pp. 47–77.

Moore, B.J. (1979), 'Monetary Factors' in A.S. Eichner (ed.), *A Guide to Post–Keynesian Economics*, Macmillan, London, pp. 120–138.

Moore, B.J. (1997) 'Reconciliation of the Supply and Demand for Endogenous Money', *Journal of Post Keynesian Economics*, Vol.19, No.3, pp. 423–8.

Moore, M. (1994), 'How Difficult is it to Construct Market Relations? A Commentary on Platteau', *The Journal of Development Studies*, Vol.30, No.3, April, pp. 818–830.

Mosler, W. (1997–8), 'Full Employment and Price Stability', *Journal of Post Keynesian Economics*, Vol.20, No.2, pp. 167–82.

Moulin, H. and Roemer, J.E. (1989), 'Public Ownership of the External World and Private Ownership of Self', *Journal of Political Economy*, Vol.97, No.2, pp. 347–367.

Murray, R. (1987), 'Ownership, Control and the Market', *New Left Review*, No.164, July/August, pp. 87–112.

Murrell, P. (1991a), 'Can Neoclassical Economics Underpin the Reform of Centrally Planned Economies?', *Journal of Economic Perspectives*, Vol.5, No.4, Fall, pp. 59–76.

Murrell, P. (1991b), 'Symposium on Economic Transition in the Soviet Union and Eastern Europe', *Journal of Economic Perspectives*, Vol.5, No.4, Fall, pp. 3–9.

Murrell, P. (1992a), 'Evolution in Economics and in the Economic Reform of the Centrally Planned Economies', in C. Clague and G. Rausser (eds), *The Emergence of Market Economies in Eastern Europe*, Blackwell, Cambridge, pp. 35–54.

Murrell, P. (1992b), 'Evolutionary and Radical Approaches to Economic Reform', *Economics of Planning*, Vol.25, No.1, pp. 79–95.

Murrell, P. (1994a), 'Conservative Political Philosophy and the Strategy of Economic Transition', in J.H. Moore (ed.), *Legacies of the Collapse of Marxism*, George Mason University Press, Virginia, pp. 165–179.

Murrell, P. (1994b), 'The Institutions and Governance of Economic Development and Reform', *The World Bank Research Observer*, Washington, DC,, pp. 201–205.

Murrell, P. (1995), 'The Transition According to Cambridge, Mass', *Journal of Economic Literature*, Vol.33, No.1, March, pp. 164–178.

Murrell, P. (1996), 'How Far Has the Transition Progressed?', *Journal of Economic Perspectives*, Vol.10, No.2, Spring, pp. 25–44.

Murrell, P. and Olson, M. (1991), 'The Devolution of Centrally Planned Economies', *Journal of Comparative Economics*, Vol.15, No.2, pp. 239–265.

Murrell, P. and Wang, Y. (1993), 'When Privatization Should Be Delayed: The Effect of Communist Legacies on Organizational and Institutional Reforms', *Journal of Comparative Economics*, Vol. 17, No.2, pp. 385–406.

Myrdal, G. (1960), *Beyond the Welfare state: Economic Planning in the Welfare State and its Economic Implications*, Duckworth, London.

Naughton, B. (1994), 'What is Distinctive about China's Economic Transition? State Enterprise Reform and Overall System Transformation', *Journal of Comparative Economics*, Vol.18, No.3, June, pp. 470–490.

Nee, V. (1992), 'Organisational Dynamics of Market Transition: Hybrid Forms, Property Rights and Mixed Economy in China', *Administrative Science Quarterly*, Vol.37, No.1, March, pp. 1–27.

Nee, V. (1996), 'The Emergence of a Market Society: Creating Mechanisms of Stratification in China', *American Journal of Sociology*, Vol.101, No. 4, January, pp. 908–49.

Nee, V. and Matthews, R. (1996), 'Market Transition and Societal Transformation in Reforming State Socialism', *Annual Review of Sociology*, Vol.22, pp. 401–35.

Nell, E.J. (1996), 'The Revival of Political Economy', in G. Argryous and F. Stilwell (eds), *Economics as a Social Science, Readings in Political Economy*, Pluto Press Australia, N.S.W., pp. 150–153.

Nelson, J.M. (1994), 'Linkages Between Politics and Economics', *Journal of Democracy*, Vol.5, No. 4, October, pp. 49–62.

Nelson, R.R. (1995), 'Recent Evolutionary Theorizing About Economic Change', *Journal of Economic Literature*, Vol.33, No.1, March, pp. 48–90.

Niggle, C. J. (1991), 'The Endogenous Money Supply Theory: An Institutionalist Appraisal', *Journal of Economic Issues*, Vol. 25, No.1, March, pp. 137–151.

Nineteenth All–Union Conference of the CPSU, (1988), *Documents and Materials*, Novosti Press, Moscow.

Nolan, P. (1993), 'China's Post–Mao Political Economy: A Puzzle', *Contributions to Political Economy*, Vol.12, No.1, pp. 71–87.

Nolan, P. (1994), 'Introduction: The Chinese Puzzle', in Q. Fan and P. Nolan (eds), *China's Economic Reforms*, St. Martin's Press, Hampshire, pp. 1–20.

Nolan, P. (1995), *China's Rise, Russia's Fall*, St. Martin's Press, New York.

Nolan, P. and Sender, J. (1994), 'Death Rates, Life Expectancy and China's Economic Reforms: A Critique to A. K. Sen', in Q. Fan and P. Nolan (eds), *China's Economic Reforms*, St. Martin's Press, Hampshire, pp. 301–341.

Noonan, J. (2000), 'Socialism, Individuality, and the Public/Private Distinction', *Rethinking Marxism*, Vol.12, No.3, Fall, pp. 23–37.

Norgaard, O., Hindsgauf, D., Johannsen, L. and Willumsen, H. (1996), *The Baltic States After Independence*, Edward Elgar, Cheltenham.

Norman, N.R. (1996), 'A General Post Keynesian Theory of Protection', *Journal of Post Keynesian Economics*, Vol.18, No.4, pp. 509–31.

North, D.C. (1990), *Institutions, Institutional Change and Economic Performance*, Cambridge University Press, Cambridge.

North, D.C. (1997), *WIDER Annual Lectures 1: The Contribution of the New Institutional Economics to an Understanding of the Transition Problem*, United Nations University, Helsinki.

Nove, A. (1983), *The Economics of Feasible Socialism*, Allen and Unwin, London.

Nove, A. (1986), *Marxism and Really Existing Socialism*, Harwood Academic Publishers, New York.

Nove, A. (1987a), 'Trotsky, Markets, and East European Reforms', *Comparative Economic Studies*, Vol.29, No.3, pp. 30–39.

Nove, A. (1987b), 'Markets and Socialism', *New Left Review*, No.161, January/February, pp. 98–104.

Nove, A. (1989a), *Stalinism and After: The Road to Gorbachev*, Unwin Hyman, London.

Nove, A. (1989b), 'The Role of Central Planning under Capitalism and Market Socialism', in J. Elster and K.O. Moene (eds), *Alternatives to Capitalism*, Cambridge University Press, Cambridge, pp. 98–109.

Nove, A. (1994a), 'Feasible Socialism? Some Social–Political Assumptions', in F. Roosevelt and D. Belkin (eds), *Why Market Socialism?*, M.E. Sharpe, Armonk, New York, pp. 183–224.

Nove, A. (1994b), 'Market Socialism and Free Economy: A Discussion of Alternatives', in F. Roosevelt and D. Belkin (eds), *Why Market Socialism?*, M.E. Sharpe, Armonk, New York, pp. 363–370.

Nuti, D.M. (1991), 'Stabilization and Sequencing in the Reform of Socialist Economies', in S. Commander (ed.), *Managing Inflation in Socialist Economies in Transition*, The World Bank, Washington, DC,, pp. 155–173.

Oberschall, A. (1996), 'The Great Transition: China, Hungary, and Sociology Exit Socialism into the Market', *American Journal of Sociology*, Vol.101, No.4, January, pp. 1028–41.

Oblath, G. (1993), 'Hungary's Foreign Debt: Controversies and Macroeconomic Problems', in I.P. Szekely and D.M.G. Newbery (eds), *Hungary: An Economy In Transition*, Cambridge University Press, Cambridge, pp. 193–223.

Ofer, G. (1987), 'Soviet Economic Growth: 1928–1985', *Journal of Economic Literature*, Vol.25, No.4, December, pp. 1767–1833.

O'Hara, P.A. (1999), 'How Can Economics be an Institutional–Evolutionary Science?', *Journal of Economic and Social Policy*, Vol.4, No.1, pp. 127–43.

Oi, J. (1992), 'Fiscal Reform and the Economic Foundations of Local State Corporation in China', *World Politics*, Vol.45, No.1, October, pp. 99–126.

Olson, M., Jr. (1992), 'Preface', in C. Clague and G. Rausser (eds), *The Emergence of Market Economies in Eastern Europe*, Blackwell, Cambridge, pp. vii–x.

Olson, M., Jr. (1995), 'Why the Transition from Communism is so Difficult', *Eastern Economic Journal*, Vol.21, No.4, fall, pp. 437–461.

Olson, M., Jr. (2000), 'Dictatorship, Democracy, and Development', in M. Olson and S. Kahkonen (eds), *A Not–So–Dismal Science: A Broader View of Economics and Societies*, Oxford University Press, Oxford, pp. 119–137.

Olson, M., and Kahkonen, S. (2000), 'Introduction: The Broader View', in M. Olsen and S. Kahkonen (eds), *A Not–So–Dismal Science: A Broader View of Economies and Societies*, Oxford University Press, Oxford, pp. 1–3.

Oxenstierna, S. (1992), 'Trends in Employment and Unemployment', in A. Aslund (ed.), *The Post–Soviet Economy. Soviet and Western Perspectives*, St. Martin's Press, New York, pp. 39–63.

Pachter, H.M. (1976), 'Three Economic Models: Capitalism, The Welfare State, and Socialism', in I. Howe (ed.), *Essential Works of Socialism*, Yale University Press, London, pp. 787–808.

Palley, T.I. (1998a), 'The Economics of Social Security: An Old Keynesian Perspective', *Journal of Post Keynesian Economics*, Vol.21, No.1, pp. 93–110.

Palley, T.I. (1998b), 'Restoring Prosperity: Why the U.S. Model is not the Answer for the United States of Europe', *Journal of Post Keynesian Economics*, Vol.20, No.3, pp. 337–53.

Parish, W.L. and Michelson, E. (1996), 'Politics and Markets: Dual Transformations', *American Journal of Sociology*, Vol.101, No.4, January, pp. 1042–59.

Parker, S., Tritt, G. and Woo, W.T. (1997), 'Some Lessons Learned for the Comparison of Transitions in Asia and Eastern Europe', in W.T. Woo, S. Parker and J.D. Sachs (eds), *Economies in Transition. Comparing Asia and Europe*, MIT Press, Cambridge, Mass., pp. 3–19.

Pejovich, S. (1976), 'The Labor–Managed Firm and Bank Credit' in J. Thornton (ed.), *Economic Analysis of the Soviet–Type System*, Cambridge University Press, Cambridge pp. 242–54.

Pejovich, S. (1987), 'The Case of Self–Management in Yugoslavia' in S. Pejovich (ed.), *Socialism: Institutional, Philosophical and Economic Issues*, Kluwer Academic, Dordrecht, pp. 239–50.

Perkins, D. (1988), 'Reforming China's Economic System', *Journal of Economic Literature*, Vol.26, No.2, June, pp. 601–45.

Perkins, D. (1994), 'Completing China's Move to the Market', *Journal of Economic Perspectives*, Vol.8, No.2, Spring, pp. 23–46.

Peters, M. (1993), 'Welfare and Future of Community', in S. Rees, G. Rodley and F. Stilwell (eds), *Beyond the Market: Alternatives to Economic Rationalism*, Pluto Press Australia Ltd, NSW, pp. 171–188.

Peterson, W.C. (1996), 'Macroeconomics and the Theory of the Monetary Economy', in C.J. Whalen (ed.) *Political Economy for the 21st Century*, M.E. Sharpe, Armonk, New York, pp. 151–170.

Petrenko, F. (1989), 'Socialism and Pluralism', *Socialism: Theory and Practice*, November, Vol.45, No 11, pp. 18–24.

Plant, R. (1990), 'Socialism, Markets and End States', in J. Le Grand and S. Estrin (eds), *Market Socialism*, Oxford University Press, Oxford, pp. 50–77.

Poirot, C. (1996), 'Macroeconomic Policy in a Transitional Environment: Romania, 1989–1994', *Journal of Economic Issues*, Vol.30, No.4, December, pp. 1057–1075.

Poirot, C.S., Jr. (1997), 'The Return to Barbarism', *Journal of Economic Issues*, Vol.31 No.1, March, pp. 233–44.

Polanyi, K. (1975 [1944]), *The Great Transformation*, Octagon Books, New York.

Popov, G. (1989), 'Give Efficiency A Change', *Soviet Weekly*, July 8th, p. 15.

Popov, V. (2000), 'Shock Therapy Versus Gradualism: The End of the Debate. (Explaining The Magnitude of Transformational Recession)', *Comparative Economic Studies*, Vol. XLII, No.1, pp. 1–57.

Porket, J.L. (1998), *Modern Economic Systems and their Transformation*, St, Martin's Press Inc., New York.

Putterman, L. (1993), 'Incentive Problems Favoring Noncentralized Investment Fund Ownership', in P.K. Bardhan and J.E. Roemer (eds), *Market Socialism: The Current Debate*, Oxford University Press, Oxford, pp. 156–168.

Putterman, L. (1995), 'The Role Of Ownership And Property Rights In China's Economic Transition', *China Quarterly*, No.144, December, pp. 1047–64.

Putterman, L. (1996), 'Coupons, Agency and Social Betterment', in E.O. Wright (ed.), *Equal Shares. Making Socialism Work. The Real Utopias Project, Volume II*, Verso, London, pp. 139–158.

Qian, Y. and Xu, C. (1993), 'Commitment, Financial Constraints, and Innovation: Market Socialism Reconsidered', in P.K. Bardhan and J.E. Roemer (eds), *Market Socialism: The Current Debate*, Oxford University press, Oxford, pp. 175–189.

Qinglian, H. (2000), 'China's Listing Social Structure', *New Left Review*, Second Series, No.5, September–October, pp. 69–99.

Radice, H. (1993), '*Global Integration, National Disintegration? Foreign Capital In The Reconstitution Of Capitalism In Central And Eastern Europe*', Paper Presented at the Workshop, 'Legacies, Linkages and Localities: on the Social Embeddedness of Transformation in Central and Eastern Europe', WZB, Berlin, September 24–25.

Radzikhovsky, L. (1990), 'An Economy of Sacred Cows', *Moscow News*, No.23, p. 12.

Rana, P.B. (1995), 'Introduction: The Asian Approach to Reforming Transitional Economies', in P.B. Rana and N. Hamid (eds), *From Centrally Planned To Market Economies: The Asian Approach*, Oxford University Press, New York, pp. 1–33.

Rapaczynski, A. (1996), 'The Roles of the State and the Market in Establishing Property Rights', *Journal of Economic Perspectives*, Vol.10, No.2, Spring, pp. 87–103.

Raskall, P. (1993), 'Widening Income Disparities in Australia', in S. Rees, G. Rodley, and F. Stilwell (eds), *Beyond the Market: Alternatives to Economic Rationalism*, Pluto Press, Australia Ltd, NSW, pp. 38–52.

Rausser, G. (1992), 'Lessons for Emerging Market Economies in Easter Europe', in C. Clague and G. Rausser (eds), *The Emergence of Market Economies in Eastern Europe*, Blackwell, Cambridge, pp. 331–2.

Rausser, G. and Simon, L. (1992), 'The Political Economy of Transition in Eastern Europe: Packaging Enterprises for Privatization', in C. Clague and G. Rausser (eds), *The Emergence of Market Economies in Eastern Europe*, Blackwell, Cambridge, pp. 271–8.

Rawski, T. (1992), '*Progress without Privatization: The Reform of China's State Industries*', Transition and Macro Adjustment Division, Policy Research Department, World Bank, Washington, DC.

Reardon, J. (1996), 'An Assessment of the Transition to a Market in the Baltic States', *Journal of Economic Issues*, Vol.30, No.1, January, pp. 629–38.

Rees, S. (1993), 'Practices and Policies for Social Justice', in S. Rees, G. Rodley, and F. Stilwell (eds), *Beyond the Market: Alternatives to Economic Rationalism*, Pluto Press Australia Ltd, NSW, pp. 291–304.

Rees, S. and Rodley, G. (1993), 'A Proposal for the Provision Full Employment', in S. Rees, G. Rodley, and F. Stilwell (eds), *Beyond the Market: Alternatives to Economic Rationalism*, Pluto Press Australia Ltd, NSW, pp. 222–236.

Rees, S., Rodley, G. and Stilwell, F. (1993), 'Introduction', in S. Rees, G. Rodley, and F. Stilwell (eds), *Beyond the Market: Alternatives to Economic Rationalism*, Pluto Press Australia Ltd, NSW, pp. 7–12.

Resnick, S. and Wolff, R. (1994), 'Between State and Private Capitalism: What Was Soviet 'Socialism'?', *Rethinking Marxism*, Vol.7, No.1, pp. 9–30.

Resnick, S. and Wolff, R. (2002), 'Class Theory and History: Capitalism and Communism in the USSR', Routledge, New York.

Reuter, A.F.P., 'Clashes Flare in South as Lithuanians Reject Unity', *The Age*, 15 January, 1990, p. 7

Rider, C. (1994a), 'Privatization in the Transition Economies: A Critique', *Journal of Post Keynesian Economics*, Vol.16, No.4, Summer, pp. 589–603.

Rider, C. (1994b), '*Policy Implications of the Transition of the Post–Communist Societies*, Presented at the Eighth Annual Malvern Political Economy Conference, Great Malvern Worcs, August.

Rider, C. (1998), 'Oskar Lange's Dissent From Market Capitalism and State Socialism', in R. Holt and S. Pressman (eds), *Economics and Its Discontents: Twentieth Century Dissenting Economists*, Edward Elgar Publishing, Aldershot, pp. 165–182.

Ridley, A. (1993), 'Conclusion', in I.P. Szekely and D.M.G. Newbery (eds), *Hungary: An Economy In Transition*, Cambridge University Press, Cambridge, pp. 347–352.

Robinson, J. (1974), 'What had become of the Keynesian Revolution?', *Challenge*, Vol.16, No.6, pp. 6–11.

Robinson, J. (1979), 'Foreword', in A.S. Eichner(ed.), *A Guide to Post–Keynesian Economics*, Macmillan, New York, pp. xi–xxi.

Robinson, J. and Eatwell, J. (1976), 'Socialist Economies', in E.L. Wheelwright and F.J.B. Stilwell (eds), *Readings in Political Economy: Volume 2*, Australian and New Zealand Book Company Pty. Ltd, NSW, pp. 236–242, reprinted from J. Robinson and J. Eatwell, (1973), *An Introduction to Modern Economics*, McGraw–Hill, London.

Rodley, G. (1993), 'Achieving Change Beyond the Market: A Systems Approach', in S. Rees, G. Rodley, and F. Stilwell (eds), *Beyond the Market: Alternatives to Economic Rationalism*, Pluto Press Australia Ltd, NSW, pp. 277–290.

Roe, A. (1991), 'Managing Inflation in Socialist Economies', in S. Commander (ed.), *Managing Inflation in Socialist Economies in Transition*, the World Bank, Washington, DC, pp. 1–27.

Roemer, J.E. (1989), 'Public Ownership and Private Property Externalities', in J. Elster and K.O. Moene (eds), *Alternatives to Capitalism*, Cambridge University Press, New York, pp. 159–179.

Roemer, J.E. (1991a), 'Market Socialism: A Blueprint', *Dissent*, Vol.38, No.4, Fall, pp. 562–569.

Roemer, J.E. (1991b), 'Replies', *Dissent*, Vol.38, No.4, Fall, pp. 572–575.

Roemer, J. (1992), 'Can There Be Socialism after Communism', *Politics and Society*, Vol.20, No.3, September, pp. 261–276.

Roemer, J.E. (1994a), *A Future for Socialism*, Harvard University Press, Massachusetts.

Roemer, J.E. (1994b), 'Market Socialism, A Blueprint: How Such An Economy Might Work', in F. Roosevelt and D. Belkin (eds), *Why Market Socialism?*, M.E. Sharpe, Armonk, New York, pp. 269–281.

Roemer, J.E. (1994c), 'The Strategic Role of Party Ideology when Voters are Uncertain about how the Economy Works', *American Political Science Review*, Vol.88, No.2, June, pp. 327–335.

Roemer, J.E. (1994d), *Egalitarian Perspectives: Essays in Philosophical Economics*, Cambridge University Press, Cambridge.

Roemer, J.E. (1996a), 'Efficient Redistribution: Comment', *Politics and Society*, Vol.24, No.4, December, pp. 383–389.

Roemer, J.E. (1996b), 'A Future for Socialism', in E.O. Wright (ed.), *Equal Shares. Making Socialism Work. The Real Utopias Project, Volume II*, Verso, London, pp. 7–39

Roemer, J.E. (1999a), 'Egalitarian Strategies', *Dissent*, Vol.46, No.3, Summer, pp. 64–74.

Roemer, J.E. (1999b), 'The Democratic Political Economy of Progressive Income Taxation', *Econometrica*, Vol.67, No.1, January, pp. 1–19.

Roemer, J.E. and Silvestre, J. (1993), 'Investment Policy and Market Social-ism', in P.K. Bardhan and J.E. Roemer (eds), *Market Socialism: The Current Debate*, Oxford University press, Oxford, pp. 108–119.

Roland, G. (1994a), 'On the Speed and Sequencing of Privatization and Restructuring', *The Economic Journal*, Vol.104, No.426, September, pp. 1158–1168.

Roland, G. (1994b), 'The Role of Political Constraints in Transition Strategies, *Economics of Transition*, Vol.2, No.1, pp. 27–41.

Roland, G. and Sekkat, K. (1993), 'Market Socialism and the Managerial Labor Market', in P.K. Bardhan and J.E. Roemer (eds), *Market Socialism: The Current Debate*, Oxford University press, Oxford, pp. 204–215.

Rondinelli, D.A. and Yurkiewicz, J. (1996), 'Privatization and Economic Restructuring in Poland: An Assessment of Transition Policies', *American Journal of Economics and Sociology*, Vol.55, No.2, April, pp. 145–60.

Roosevelt, F. (1994a), 'Marx and the Market Socialism', in F. Roosevelt and D. Belkin (eds), *Why Market Socialism?*, M.E. Sharpe, Armonk, New York, pp. 123–136.

Roosevelt, F. (1994b), 'Comment: Questions about Market Socialism', in F. Roosevelt and D. Belkin (eds), *Why Market Socialism?*, M.E. Sharpe, Armonk, New York, pp. 263–268.

Roosevelt, F. and D. Belkin, (1994), 'Preface', in F. Roosevelt and D. Belkin (eds), *Why Market Socialism?*, M.E. Sharpe, Armonk, New York, pp. xvii – xix.

Rosati, D.K. (1994), 'Output Decline During Transition from Plan to Market: A Reconsideration', *Economics of Transition*, Vol.2, No.4, pp. 419–441.

Rosenthal, E. (2000), 'Old–Line Communists at Odds with Party in China', *New York Times*, reprinted in *New Left Review*, Second Series, No.5, Sep-tember–October, pp. 82–3.

Rosewarne, S. (1993), 'Selling the Environment: A Critique of Market Ecology', in S. Rees, G. Rodley, and F. Stilwell (eds), *Beyond the Market: Alternatives to Economic Rationalism*, Pluto Press Australia Ltd, NSW, pp. 53–71.

Rostowski, J. (1993), 'Comment on 'Gradual versus Rapid Liberalization in Socialist Economies' by McKinnon', *Proceedings of the World Bank Annual Conference on Development Economies*, Washington DC, pp. 101–107.

Rowthorn, R.E. (1993), 'Discussion of Part Seven', in I.P. Szekely and D.M.G. Newbery (eds), *Hungary: An Economy in Transition*, Cambridge University Press, Cambridge, pp. 344–346.

Runciman, W.G. (1995), 'The Triumph of Capitalism as a Topic in the Theory of Social Selection', *New Left Review*, No.210, March/April, pp. 33–47.

Sachs, J. (1990), 'What is to be done?', *The Economist*, January 13, pp. 19–24.

Sachs, J. (1991a), 'Crossing the Valley of Tears in East European Reform', *Challenge*, Vol. 34, No 5, September/October, pp. 26–32.

Sachs, J. (1991b), 'Sachs on Poland', *The Economist*, January 19, p. 67.

Sachs, J. (1992a), 'Privatization in Russian: Some Lessons from Eastern Eu-rope', *American Economic Review Papers and Proceedings*, Vol.82, No.2, May, pp. 43–48.

Sachs, J. (1992b), 'The Grand Bargain', in A. Aslund (ed.), *The Post–Soviet Economy. Soviet and Western Perspectives*, St. Martin's Press, New York, pp. 207–216.

Sachs, J. (1993a), *Poland's Jump to the Market Economy*, The MIT Press, Cambridge, Massachusetts.

Sachs, J. (1993b), 'Privatising Russia: Comments and Discussion', *Brookings Papers on Economic Activity*, No.1, pp. 184–5

Sachs, J. (1994), 'Toward Glasnost in the IMF', *Challenge*, Vol.37, No.3, May–June, pp. 4–11.

Sachs, J. (1995a), 'Why Corruption Rules Russia', *The New York Times*, November 29, pp. 22.

Sachs, J. (1995b), 'Consolidating Capitalism', *Foreign Policy*, Vol.98, Spring, pp. 50–64.

Sachs, J. (1996a), 'The Transition in the Mid Decade', *American Economic Review Papers and Proceedings*, Vol.86, No.2, May, pp. 128–33.

Sachs, J. (1996b), 'Economic Transition and the Exchange–Rate Regime', *American Economic Review Papers and Proceedings*, Vol.86, No.2, May, pp. 147–52.

Sachs, J. (1997a), 'An Overview of Stabilization Issues Facing Economies in Transition', in W.T. Woo, S. Parker and J.D. Sachs (eds), *Economies in Transition. Comparing Asia and Europe*, MIT Press, Cambridge, Mass., pp. 243–256.

Sachs, J. (1997b), 'Why Russia has Failed to Stabilize', in A. Aslund (ed.), *Russian Economic Reform at Risk*, Pinter, London, pp. 53–63, 1995, reprinted in A. Aslund (ed.) *Russia's Economic Transformation in the 1990s*, Pinter, London, pp. 127–136.

Sachs, J. and Lipton, D. (1990), 'Poland's Economic Reform', *Foreign Affairs*, Vol.69, No.3, Summer, pp. 47–66.

Sachs, J. and Lipton, D. (1997), 'Remaining Steps to a Market–Based Monetary System in Russia', in A. Aslund and D. Layard (eds), (1993), *Changing the Economic System in Russia*, St. Martins Press, New York, pp. 127–62, reprinted in A. Aslund (ed.), Russia's *Economic Transformation in the 1990s*, Pinter, London, pp. 79–100.

Sachs, J. and Woo, W.T. (1994), 'Experiences in the Transition to a Market Economy', *Journal of Comparative Economics*, Vol.18, No.3, June, pp. 271–275.

Sakwa, R., (1989), *Soviet Politics*. Rouledge, London.

Sakwa, R. (1998), 'Russian Political Evolution: a Structural Approach', in M. Cox (ed.), *Rethinking the Soviet Collapse. Sovietology, The Death of Communism and the New Russia*, BookEns Ltd., London, pp. 181–201.

Samonis, V. and Hunyadi, C. (1993), *Big Bang and Acceleration: Models for the Postcommunist Economic Transformation*, Nova Science Publishers Inc., New York.

Sarkozy, T. (1993), 'A Legal Framework for the Hungarian Transition, 1989–91', in I.P. Szekely and D.M.G. Newbery (eds), *Hungary: An Economy In Transition*, Cambridge University Press, Cambridge, pp. 239–248.

Satz, D. (1996), 'Status Inequalities and Models of Market Socialism', in E.O. Wright (ed.), *Equal Shares. Making Socialism Work. The Real Utopias Project, Volume II*, Verso, London, pp. 71–89.

Schlack, R.F. (1996), 'Economics of Transition: Hypotheses Toward a Reasonable Economics', *Journal of Economic Issues*, Vol.30, No.2, June, pp. 617–27.

Segal, G. (1994), 'China's Changing Shape', *Foreign Affairs*, Vol.73, No.3, May/June, pp. 43–58.

Segal, L. (1991), 'Whose Left? Socialism, Feminism and the Future', in R. Blackburn (ed.), *After the Fall. The Failure of Communism and the Future of Socialism*, Verso, London, pp. 274–286.

Selowsky, M. and Martin, R. (1997), 'Policy Performance and Output Growth in the Transition Economies', *American Economic Review Papers and Proceedings*, Vol.87, No.2, May, pp. 349–353.

Sensat, J. (1996), 'Socialism as an Attitude', in E.O. Wright (ed.), *Equal Shares. Making Socialism Work. The Real Utopias Project, Volume II*, Verso, London, pp. 250–262.

Sestanovich, S. (1992), 'Foreword', in A. Aslund (ed.), *Post–Communist Economic Revolutions. How Big a Bang?*, The Centre for Strategic and International Studies, Washington, pp. vii–ix.

Setterfield, M. (1998), 'Path Dependency and Animal Spirits: A Reply', *Journal of Post Keynesian Economics*, Vol.21, No.1, pp. 167–170.

Shackle, G.L.S. (1973), 'Keynes and Today's Establishment in Economic Theory: A View', *Journal of Economic Literature*, Vol.11, No.2, pp. 516–19.

Shanin, T. (ed.), (1983), *Late Marx and the Russian Road*, Routledge & Kegan Paul, London.

Shapiro, N. (1977), 'The Revolutionary Character of Post–Keynesian Economics', *Journal of Economic Issues*, Vol.21, No.3, pp. 541–60.

Share, M.B. (1995), 'Transition to Capitalism?', *Journal of Third World Studies*, Vol.12, Fall, pp. 572–80.

Shiller, R..J., Boycko, M. and Korobov, V. (1992), 'Hunting for Homo Sovieticus: Situational versus Attitudinal Factors in Economic Behavior', *Brookings Papers on Economic Activity*, No.1, pp. 127–81.

Shkredov, V. (1989), 'Socialism and Ownership', *Socialism: Theory and Practice Supplement*, No.1, pp. 8–16.

Shleifer, A. and Boycko, M. (1993), 'The Politics of Russian Privatization', in O. Blanchard, M. Boycko, R. Dabrowski, R. Dornbusch, R. Layard and A. Shleifer, *Post-Communist Reform: Pain and Progress*, The MIT Press, Cambridge, Mass., pp. 37–80.

Shleifer, A. and Vishny, R.W. (1994), 'The Politics of Market Socialism', *Journal of Economic Perspectives*, Vol.8, No.2, Spring, pp. 165–176.

Siegel, S. (1956), *Nonparametric Statistics for the Behavioral Sciences*, Mc-Graw–Hill, New York.

Sik, O. (1967), *Plan and Market Under Socialism*, Czechoslovak Academy of Science, Prague.

Sik, O. (1971), 'The Economic Impact of Stalinism', *Problems of Communism*, Vol.20, No.3, pp. 1–10.

Sik, O. (1972), *Czechoslovakia: The Bureaucratic Economy*, Czechoslovak Academy of Science, Prague.

Simon, R. (1999), 'Russia's Crises', *Capital & Class*, No.68, Summer, pp. 1–7.

Simon, W.H. (1996), 'Inequality and Alienation in the Socialist Capital Market', in E.O Wright (ed.), *Equal Shares. Making Socialism Work. The Real Utopias Project, Volume II*, Verso, London, pp. 45–56.

Singh, I. And Gelb, A. (1994), 'Enterprise Reform and Restructuring in Transition Economies', Transition Economics Division, Policy Research Department, World Bank, Washington, DC.

Sixsmith, M. (1991), *Moscow Coup*, Simon and Schuster Ltd, London.

Slay, B. (2000), 'The Polish Economic Transition: Outcome and Lessons', *Communist and Post–Communist Studies*, Vol.33, No.3, pp. 49–70.

Smith, A. (1986 [1776]), *The Wealth of Nations*, Penguin, London.

Smith, A. (1996), 'From Convergence to Fragmentation: Uneven Regional Development, Industrial Restructuring, and the 'Transition to Capitalism' in Slovakia', *Environment and Planning*, Vol. 28, January, pp. 135–56.

Smith, R. (1993), 'The Chinese Road to Capitalism', *New Left Review*, No.199, May/June, pp. 55–99.

Smyth, R. (1997), 'The Township And Village Enterprises Sector As A Specific Example Of Regionalism–Some General Lessons For Socialist Transformation', *Economic Systems*, Vol.21, No.3, pp. 235–264.

Smyth, R. (1998), 'Property Rights in China's Economic Reforms', *Communist and Post–Communist Studies*, Vol.31, No.3, pp. 235–248.

Smyth, R. (1999), 'Rural Enterprises In Jiangsu Province, China: Recent Institutional Changes And Future Prospects', *Development Policy Review*, Vol.17, No.2, June, pp. 191–213.

Smyth, R. (2000a), 'Should China Be Promoting Large–Scale Enterprises And Enterprise Groups', *World Development*, Vol.28, No.3, pp. 721–37.

Smyth, R. (2000b), 'Old Pension Reform in China's State–Owned Enterprises', *Journal of Ageing and Social Policy*, Vol.11, No.4, pp. 69–85.

Socialism: Theory and Practice Round Table, (1989), 'The Plan Dogma or Market Spontaneity? No, Their Unity And Interaction', *Socialism, Theory, and Practice*, December, p. 19–26.

Stalin, J.V. (1972), *Economic Problems of Socialism in the USSR*, Foreign Language Press, Peking.

Stark, D. (1990), 'Privatization in Hungary: From Plan to Market or from Plan to Clan?', *East European Politics and Societies*, Vol.4, No.3, Fall, pp. 351–392.

Stark, D. (1992), 'Path Dependence and Privatization Strategies in East Central Europe', *East European Politics and Societies*, Vol. 6, No.1, pp. 17–51.

Stark, D. (1996) 'Recombinant Property in East European Capitalism', *American Journal of Sociology*, Vol.101, No. 4, January, pp. 993–1027.

Stauber, L.G. (1977), 'A Proposal for a Democratic Market Economy', *Journal of Comparative Economics*, Vol.1, No.3, September, pp. 235–258.

Stauber, L. G. (1978), 'A Democratic Market Economy: A Response', *Journal of Comparative Economics*, Vol.2, No.4, December, pp. 382–389.

Stiglitz, J.E. (1993), 'Market Socialism and Neoclassical Economics', in P.K. Bardhan and J.E. Roemer (eds), *Market Socialism: The Current Debate*, Oxford University Press, Oxford, pp. 21–41.

Stiglitz, J.E. (2002), *Globalization and Its Discontents*, W. W. Norton & Co., New York.

Stilwell, F. (1993a), 'Economic Rationalism: Sound Foundations for Policy?', in S. Rees, G. Rodley, and F. Stilwell (eds), *Beyond the Market: Alternatives to Economic Rationalism*, Pluto Press Australia Ltd, NSW, pp. 27–37.

Stilwell, F. (1993b), 'From 'Fightback' and 'One Nation' to an Alternative Economic Strategy', in S. Rees, G. Rodley and F. Stilwell (eds), *Beyond the Market: Alternatives to Economic Rationalism*, Pluto Press Australia Ltd, NSW, pp. 189–203.

Stilwell, F. (1996), 'The State: Competing Perspectives', in G. Argyrous and F. Stilwell (eds), (1996), *Economics as a Social Science. Readings in Political Economy*, Pluto Press, Annandale, NSW, pp. 220–3.

Strachey, J. (1976), 'Accumulation, Democracy, and Equality', in I. Howe (ed.), *Essential Works of Socialism*, Yale University Press Ltd., London, pp. 565–584.

Sutela, P. (1992) 'The Role of the External Sector During the Transition', in A. Aslund (ed.), (1992b), *The Post–Soviet Economy. Soviet and Western Perspectives*, St. Martin's Press, New York, pp. 85–101.

Svejnar, J. (1991), 'Microeconomic Issues in the Transition to a Market Economy', *Journal of Economic Perspectives*, Vol.5, No.4, Fall, pp. 123–138.

Svejnar, J. (1996), 'Enterprises and Workers in the Transition: Econometric Evidence', *American Economic Review Papers and Proceedings*, Vol.86, No.2, May, pp. 123–27.

Swaan, W. (1993), 'Book Review of *Reform in Eastern Europe* by O. Blanchard (et. al.)' *Economica*, Vol.60, No.238, May, pp. 239–40.

Szego, A. (1991), 'The Logic of a Shortage Economy: A Critique of Kornai From a Kaleckian Macroeconomic Perspective', *Journal of Post Keynesian Economics*, Vol.13, No.3, Spring, pp. 328–336.

Szekely, I.P. and Newbery, D.M.G. (1993), 'Introduction', in I.P. Szekely and D.M.G. Newbery (eds), *Hungary: An Economy In Transition*, Cambridge University Press, Cambridge, pp. 1–23.

Szelenyi, I. (1991), 'The Intellectuals in Power?', in R. Blackburn (ed.), *After the Fall. The Failure of Communism and the Future of Socialism*, Verso, London, pp. 269–273.

Szelenyi, I. and Kostello, E. (1996), 'The Market Transition Debate', *American Journal of Sociology*, Vol.101, No.4, January, pp. 1082–96.

Szuk, T. (1996), 'Unpleasant Truths about Eastern Europe', *Foreign Policy*, No.102, Spring, pp. 52–65.

Targetti, F. (ed.), (1992), *Privatization in Europe. West and East Experiences*, Dartmouth, Washington DC.

Targetti, F. (1992), 'The Privatization of Industry with Particular Regard to Economies in Transition' in F. Targetti (ed.) *Privatization in Europe: West and East Experiences*, Dartmouth, Aldershot, pp. 1–29.

Taylor, L. (1994), 'The Market Met its Match: Lessons for the Future from the Transition's Initial Years', *Journal of Comparative Economics*, Vol.19, No.1, August, pp. 64–87.

Therborn, G. (1991), 'Vorsprung Durch Rethink', in R. Blackburn (ed.), *After the Fall. The Failure of Communism and the Future of Socialism*, Verso, London, pp. 298–309.

Thomas, V. and Wang, Y. (1997), 'East Asian Lessons from Economic Reforms', in W.T. Woo, S. Parker and J.D. Sachs (eds), *Economies in Transition. Comparing Asia and Europe*, MIT Press, Cambridge, Mass., pp. 217–242.

Thompson, E. (1991), 'The Ends of Cold War: Rejoinder', in R. Blackburn (ed.), *After the Fall. The Failure of Communism and the Future of Socialism*, Verso, London, pp. 100–109.

Thompson, F. (1996), 'Would Roemer's Socialism Equalize Income from Surplus?', in E.O. Wright (ed.), *Equal Shares. Making Socialism Work. The Real Utopias Project, Volume II*, Verso, London, pp. 170–183.

Thurow, L.C. (1996), 'Comparative Advantage, Factor–Price Equalization, Industrial Strategies, and Trade Tactics', in C.J. Whalen (ed.) *Political Economy for the 21st Century*, M.E. Sharpe, Armonk, New York, pp. 213–224.

Thurow, L.C. (1996, [1983]), 'Rebuilding the Foundations of Economics', in L. Thurow (1983), *Dangerous Currents: The State of Economics*, Oxford University Press, Oxford, reprinted in G. Argyrous, and F. Stilwell (eds), (1996a), *Economics as a Social Science. Readings in Political Economy*, Pluto Press, Annandale, NSW, pp. 98–99.

Ticktin, H.H. (1998), 'Soviet Studies and the Collapse of the USSR: In Defense of Marxism', in M. Cox (ed.), *Rethinking the Soviet Collapse. Sovietology, The Death of Communism and the New Russia*, BookEns Ltd., London, pp. 73–94.

Tilly, C. and Albelda, R. (1996), 'Not Markets Alone: Enriching the Discussion of Income Distribution', in C.J. Whalen (ed.) *Political Economy for the 21st Century*, M.E. Sharpe, Armonk, New York, pp. 195–210.

Tittenbrun, J. (1995), 'The Managerial Revolution Revisited: The Case of Privatization in Poland', *Capital & Class*, No.55, Spring, pp. 21–32.

Tobin, J. (1994), 'One or Two Cheers for the 'Invisible Hand'', in F. Roosevelt and D. Belkin (eds), *Why Market Socialism?*, M.E. Sharpe, Armonk, New York, pp. 325–338.

Trainer, T. (1996), 'Abandon Affluence!', in G. Argyous and F. Stilwell (eds), *Economics as a Social Science, Readings in Political Economy*, Pluto Press Australia, N.S.W., pp. 18–22.

Trotsky, L. (1967), *The Revolution Betrayed*, New Park Publications, London.

Unger, R.M. and Cui, Z. (1994), 'China in the Russian Mirror', *New Left Review*, No.208, November/December, p. 78–87.

Urban, M. and Fish, M.S. (1998), 'Does Post–Sovietology Have a Future?', in M. Cox (ed.), *Rethinking the Soviet Collapse. Sovietology, The Death of Communism and the New Russia*, BookEns Ltd., London, pp. 164–180.

Vaclav, K. (1995), 'Privatization Experience: The Czech Case', *Policy*, Vol.11, No.1, Autumn pp. 45–47.

Van Brabant, J.M. (1991a), 'Property Rights Reform, Macroeconomic Performance and Welfare' in H. Blommenstein and M. Marrese (ed.), *Transformation of Planned Economies: Property Rights and Macroeconomic Stability*, OECD, Paris.

Van Brabant, J.M. (1991b), 'Convertibility in Eastern Europe Through a Payments Union', in J. Williamson (ed.), Currency Convertibility in Eastern Europe', Institute for International Economics, Washington, pp. 63–95.

Van Brabant, J.M. (1993), 'Lessons from the Wholesale Transformations in the East', *Comparative Economic Studies*, Vol.35, No.4, Winter, pp. 73–102.

Van Parijs, P. (1991), 'Why Surfers Should be Fed: The Liberal Case for an Unconditional Basic Income', *Philosophy of Public Affairs*, Vol.20, No.2, Spring, pp. 101–132.

Van Parijs, P. (1996), 'Basic Income and the Two Dilemmas of the Welfare State', *The Political Quarterly*, January, pp. 63–66.

Van Parijs, P. (1997), 'Reciprocity and the Justification of an Unconditional Basic income. Reply to Stuart White', *Political Studies*, Vol. 45, No. 2, June, pp. 327–330.

Vanek, J. (1970), *The General Theory of Labor–Managed Market Economies*, Cornell University Press, Ithaca, New York.

Varga, E. (1939), *Two Systems: Socialist Economy and Capitalist Economy*, Lawrence and Wishart, London.

Varhegyi, E. (1993), 'The Modernization of the Hungarian Banking Sector', in I.P. Szekely and D.M.G. Newbery (eds), *Hungary: An Economy In Transition*, Cambridge University Press, Cambridge, pp. 149–162.

Vasiliev, S.A. (1997), 'Economic Reform in Russia: Social, Political, and Institutional Aspects', in A. Aslund and R. Layard (eds), (1993), *Changing the Economic System in Russia*, St. Martin's Press, New York, pp. 72–86, reprinted in A. Aslund, *Russia's Economic Transformation in the 1990s*, Pinter, London, pp. 25–40.

Vickers, J. and Yarrow, G. (1991), 'Economic Perspectives of Privatization', *Journal of Economic Perspectives*, Vol.5, No.2, Spring, pp. 111–132.

Wade, R. (2001), 'Showdown at the World Bank', *New Left Review*, No.7, Second Series, January/February, pp. 124–137.

Wagener, H.J. (2000), 'Has Russia Missed the Boat?', *Journal of Institutional and Theoretical Economics*, Vol.156, No.1, pp. 125–130.

Walder, A.G. (1996), 'Markets and Inequality in Transitional Economies: Toward Testable Theories', *American Journal of Sociology*, Vol.101, No. 4, January, pp. 1060–73.

Walker, M. (1986), *The Waking Giant. The Soviet Union Under Gorbachev*, Abacus, London.

Walters, A. (1992), 'The Transition to a Market Economy', in C. Clague and G. Rausser (ed.), *The Emergence of Market Economies in Eastern Europe*, Blackwell, Cambridge, pp. 99–105.

Wang, Z.K. (1996), 'Integrating Transition Economies into the Global Economy', *Finance and Development*, Vol.33, No.3, September, pp. 21–3.

Ward, B. (1958), 'The Firm in Illyria: Market Syndicalism', *American Economic Review*, Vol.48, No.4, September, pp. 566–89.

Ward, I. (1988), *Comparative Economic Systems: Theory and Practice*, Department of Economics, Monash University Melbourne.

Ward, I. (1990a), 'The Gorbachev Reforms: The Search for Economic Viability', *Australian Journal of Political Economy*, April, No. 26, pp. 47–67.

Ward, I. (1990b), 'The Gorbachev Economic Reform' *Arena*, No.90, pp. 117–128.

Ward, I. (1990c), '*What Economic Systems are we Likely to see in Eastern Europe and the Soviet Union?*', Centre of European Studies Conference, July.

Ward, I. and Kulkari, A. (1987), 'The Rise and the Fall of National Allocative Planning in Australia', *Australian Economic Review*, Second Quarter, pp. 37–48.

Waring, M. (1996), 'A Woman's Reckoning', in G. Argryous and F. Stilwell (eds), *Economics as a Social Science, Readings in Political Economy*, Pluto Press Australia, N.S.W., pp. 184–188.

Waud, R.P., Maxwell, A., Hocking, J., Bonnici and Ward, I. (1996), *Economics*, Longman, Melbourne.

Wei, S. (1997), 'Gradualism versus Big Bang: Speed and Sustainability of Reforms', *Canadian Journal of Economics*, Vol.30, No.4, November, pp. 1234–47.

Weil, R. (1996), *Red Cat, White Cat. China and the Contradictions of 'Market Socialism'*, Monthly Review Press, New York.

Weisskopf, T.E. (1993), 'A Democratic Enterprise–Based Market Socialism', in P.K. Bardhan and J.E. Roemer (eds), *Market Socialism: The Current Debate*, Oxford University press, Oxford, pp. 120–141.

Weisskopf, T.E. (1994), 'Challenges to Market Socialism: A Response to Critics', in F. Roosevelt and D. Belkin (eds), *Why Market Socialism?*, M.E. Sharpe, Armonk, New York, pp. 297–318.

Weisskopf, T.E. (1996), 'The Prospects for Democratic Market Socialism in the East', in E.O. Wright (ed.), *Equal Shares. Making Socialism Work. The Real Utopias Project, Volume II*, Verso, London, pp. 277–289.

Weitzman, M. L. and Xu, C. (1994), 'Chinese Township–Village Enterprises as Vaguely Defined Cooperatives', *Journal of Comparative Economics*, Vol.18, No.2, pp. 121–45.

Weiying, Z. and Yi, G. (1995), '*China's Gradual Reform: A Historical Perspective*', Working Paper Series No: E1995001, China Centre for Economic Research, Peking University. Beijing China.

Whalen, C.J. (ed.) (1996a), *Political Economy for the 21st Century*, M.E. Sharpe, Armonk, New York.

Whalen, C.J. (1996b), ' Preface', in C.J. Whalen (ed.), *Political Economy for the 21st Century*, M.E. Sharpe, Armonk, New York, pp. xv–xvii.

Whalen, C.J. (1996c), 'Beyond Neoclassical Thought: Political Economy for the Twenty–First Century', in C.J. Whalen (ed.), *Political Economy for the 21st Century*, M.E. Sharpe, Armonk, New York, pp. 3–28.

Wheelwright, T. (1993), 'Economic Controls for Social Ends', in S. Rees, G. Rodley and F. Stilwell (eds), *Beyond the Market: Alternatives to Economic Rationalism*, Pluto Press Australia Ltd, NSW, pp. 15–26.

Wheelwright, T. (1996), 'The Crisis in Contemporary Capitalism' in G. Argyrous and F. Stilwell (eds), *Economics as a Social Science. Readings in Political Economy*, Pluto Press, Annandale, NSW, pp. 4–9.

White, S. (1998), 'Rethinking the Transition: 1991 and Beyond', in M. Cox (ed.), *Rethinking the Soviet Collapse. Sovietology, The Death of Communism and the New Russia*, BookEns Ltd., London, pp. 135–149.

White, S. (2000), *Russia's New Politics: The Management of a Postcommunist Society*, Cambridge University Press, Cambridge.

Wilber, C.K. (1996), 'Ethics and Economics', in C.J. Whalen (ed.) *Political Economy for the 21st Century*, M.E. Sharpe, Armonk, New York, pp. 45–64.

Williams, B. (1976), 'Socialism and Freedom', in E.L. Wheelwright and F.J.B. Stilwell (eds), *Readings in Political Economy: Volume 1*, Australian and New Zealand Book Company Pty. Ltd, NSW, pp. 101–105.

Williamson, J. (1991a), 'The Case for a Payments Union', *International Economic Insights*, September/October, p. 11–14

Williamson, J. (1991b), 'The Economic Opening of Eastern Europe', Washington, DC, Institute for International Economics.

Williamson, J. (1992), *Trade and Payments After Soviet Disintegration*, Institute of International Economics, Washington.

Williamson, O. (1985), *The Economic Institutions of Capitalism: Firms, Markets, Relational Contracting*, The Free Press, New York.

Williamson, O.E. (2000), 'Economic Institutions and Development: A View from the Bottom', in M. Olson and S. Kahkonen (eds), *A Not–So–Dismal Science: A Broader View of Economics and Societies*, Oxford University Press, New York, pp. 92–118.

Winieski, J. (1992), 'Privatization in Eastern–Central Europe: Avoiding Major Mistakes', in C. Clague and G. Rausser (eds), *The Emergence of Market Economies in Eastern Europe*, Blackwell, Cambridge, pp. 271–278.

Winter, D. (1990), 'Market Socialism and the Reform of the Capitalist Economy', in J. Le Grand and S. Estrin (eds), *Market Socialism*, Oxford University Press, New York, pp. 139–164.

Winter, D. (1993), 'Discussion of Part Six', in I.P. Szekely and D.M.G. Newbery (eds), *Hungary: An Economy in Transition*, Cambridge University Press, Cambridge, pp. 323–325.

Wittman, D. (1989), 'Why Democracies Produce Efficient Results', *Journal of Political Economy*, Vol.97, No.6, pp. 1395–1424.

Wolf, T.A. (1991), 'The Lessons of Limited Market–Oriented Reform', *Journal of Economic Perspectives*, Vol.5, No.4, Fall, pp. 45–58.

Wollen, P. (1993), 'Our Post–Communism: The Legacy of Karl Kautsky', *New Left Review*, No. 202, November/December, pp. 85–94.

Wonnell, C.T. (1998), 'Roemer and Market Socialism', *Review of Social Economy*, Vol. LVI, No.1, Spring, pp. 37–46.

Woo, W.T. (1994), 'The Art of Reforming Centrally Planned Economies: Comparing China, Poland and Russia', *Journal of Comparative Economics*, Vol.18, No.3, June, pp. 276–308.

Woo, W.T. (1997), 'Improving the Performance of Enterprises in Transition', in W.T. Woo, S. Parker and J.D. Sachs (eds), *Economies in Transition. Comparing Asia and Europe*, MIT Press, Cambridge, Mass., pp. 299–324.

Woo, W.T., Parker, S. and Sachs, J.D. (eds), (1997a), *Economies in Transition. Comparing Asia and Europe*, MIT Press, Cambridge, Massachusetts.

Woo, W.T., Parker, S. and Sachs, J.D. (1997b), 'Preface', in W.T. Woo, S. Parker and J.D. Sachs (eds), *Economies in Transition. Comparing Asia and Europe*, MIT Press, Cambridge, Mass., pp. xi–xiv.

Wood, A. (1994), 'China's Economic System: A Brief Description, with Some Suggestions for Further Reform', in Q. Fan and P. Nolan (eds), *China's Economic Reforms*, St. Martin's Press, Hampshire, pp. 21–45.

World Bank, (1996), *World Development Report: From Plan to Market*, Oxford University Press, Washington DC.

Wray, L.R. (1996), 'Monetary Theory and Policy for the Twenty–First Century', in C.J. Whalen (ed.) *Political Economy for the 21ˢᵗ Century*, M.E. Sharpe, Armonk, New York, pp. 125–148.

Wright, E.O. (1995), 'Coupon Socialism and Socialist Values', *New Left Review*, No.210, March/April, pp. 153–160.

Wright, E.O. (1996a), 'Introduction', in E.O. Wright (ed.), *Equal Shares. Making Socialism Work. The Real Utopias Project, Volume II*, Verso, London, pp. 1–3.

Wright, E.O. (1996b), 'Political Power, Democracy and Coupon Socialism', in E.O. Wright (ed.), *Equal Shares. Making Socialism Work. The Real Utopias Project, Volume II*, Verso, London, pp. 122–136.

Wright, E.O. (1996c), 'Preface: The Real Utopias Project', in E.O. Wright (ed.), *Equal Shares. Making Socialism Work. The Real Utopias Project, Volume II*, Verso, London, pp.ix–x.

Xiao, G. (1991a), '*What Is Special About China's Reforms?*', Transition and Macro Adjustment Division, Policy Research Department, World Bank, Washington, DC.

Xiao, G. (1991b), '*Property Rights Arrangements and Industrial Productivity in China*', Transition and Macro Adjustment Division, Policy Research Department, World Bank, Washington, DC.

Xiaochuan, Z. (1993), '*Minimum Package and Sequencing of Reforming Socialist Economies*', International Symposium of the Theoretical and Practical Issues of the Transition Towards the Market Economy in China, Haikou, 1–3 July.

Xiaoqiang, W. (1992), '*Transcending The Logic Of Private Ownership: Chinese Enterprise Reforms Vs. Privatization*', Department of Applied Economics Working Paper No.9602, Cambridge University.

Xing, L. (1996), 'Democracy and Human Rights: China and the West', *Monthly Review*, Vo.48, No.7, December, pp. 29–40.

Yang, X. (1993), '*Theories of Property Rights and China's Reforms*', Department of Economics, Monash University, Melbourne, Australia.

Yang, X. (1994), '*A Theory of the Socialist Economic System and the Differences Between the Economic Reforms In China and Russia*', Department of Economics, Monash University, Melbourne, Australia.

Yang, X. (2001), '*China's Entry to WTO*', Department of Economics, Monash University, Melbourne, Australia.

Yavlinsky, G. and Braguinsky, S. (1994), 'The Inefficiency of Laissez–Fair in Russia: Hysteresis Effects and the Need for Policy–Led Transformation', *Journal of Comparative Economics*, Vol.19, No.1, August, pp. 88–116.

Yergin, D. (1999), 'Foreword: Russia in the New Century', in T. Gustafson (ed.), *Capitalism Russian – Style*, Cambridge University Press, Cambridge, pp.ix–xiv.

Yifu, J., Cai, F. and Li, Z. (1996), 'The Lessons Of China's Transition To A Market Economy', *Cato Journal*, Vol.16, No.2, Fall, pp. 201–31.

Yu, T. (1993), '*Challenges Faced in Transforming from a Centrally Planned to a Market Economy*', Occasional Paper, No.9306, Chaung–Hua Institution for Economic Research, Taiwan.

Yunker, J.A. (1986), 'Would Democracy Survive Under Market Socialism?', *Polity*, Vol.18, No.4, pp. 678–695.

Yunker, J.A. (1988), 'A New Perspective on Market Socialism', *Journal of Comparative Economic Studies*, Vol.30, No.2, pp. 69–116.

Yunker, J.A. (1994), 'Agency Issues and Managerial Incentives: Contemporary Capitalism Versus Market Socialism', in P. Zarembra (ed.), Research *in Political Economy*, Vol.14, Greenwich, JAI Press, pp. 1–61.

Yunker, J.A. (1997), *Economic Justice: The Market Socialist Vision*, Rowman and Littlefield Publishers Inc, Boston Way.

Yusuf, S. (1994), 'China's Macroeconomic Performance and Management During Transition', *Journal of Economic Perspectives*, Vol.8, No.2, Spring, pp. 71–92.

Zhou, X. (1992), 'The Theoretical and Psychological Obstacles to Market–Oriented Reform in China', in M.J. Kovacs and M. Tardos (eds), *Reform and Transformation in Eastern Europe. Soviet Type Economics on the Threshold of Change*, Routledge, London, pp. 199–214.

Zwass, A. (1999), *Incomplete Revolutions. The Success And Failure Of Capitalist Transition Strategies In Post–Communist Economies*, M.E.Sharpe, Armonk, New York.

Index

alternative models
  analysis 239–49
analytical framework 27–70
  key issues 28
changes
  desired 32
  initiating 32
Chinese approach *see* non-pluralistic
  market socialism
civilized society *see* Post Keynsian
  model
common good
  ideological structure 46
competitive capitalism
  good society 34
conditions, initial *see* initial conditions
consistency
  between structures 7–8
  Stalinist system 9-17
  within structures 9-13
democracy
  political structure 41
desired changes
  transition models 32
economic analysis
  financial system 59–61
  fiscal policy 61
  foreign aid 62
  good society 34
  ideological structure 44–8
  initial conditions 48–50
  institutional structure 57–9
  international trade 62
  Marxist 34
  monetary policy 59–61
  neoclassical 34
  non-pluralistic market socialism
   206
  pluralistic market socialism 170–1
  political structure 41–4
  Post Keynsian model 34, 137–9
  price liberalization-stabilization 52
  privatization 52–7
  shock therapy 74–5

social policy 62–3
speed 37–40
transition models 34
economic cost *see* transition cost
economic structure
  Stalinist system 9-13, 17–22
financial aid cost 70
financial intermediaries
  privatization 54, 55
financial system
  economic analysis 59–61
  neoclassical gradualism 126–7
  non-pluralistic market socialism
   225–7
  pluralistic market socialism 191–3
  Post Keynsian model 156–8
  shock therapy 91–3
fiscal policy
  economic analysis 61–2
  neoclassical gradualism 128–9
  non-pluralistic market socialism
   228–9
  pluralistic market socialism 193–4
  Post Keynsian model 159–60
  shock therapy 93–5
foreign aid
  economic analysis 62
  neoclassical gradualism 129–31
  non-pluralistic market socialism
   229–31
  pluralistic market socialism 194–6
  Post Keynsian model 160–4
  shock therapy 95–8
foreign direct investment
  cost 70, 242
  formalist approach 241–5
  cost indices 243
  economic cost 241
  foreign direct investment cost 242
  ideological cost 241
  international cost 242
  Kendall's Coefficient 243
  political cost 241
  ranking of models 242

total cost 244
good society 32
  competitive capitalism 34–5
  economic analysis 35
  market socialism 36–7
  non-pluralistic market socialism
    207–8
  pluralistic market socialism 171–4
  Post Keynsian model 139–41
  shock therapy 75–6
  social-democratic capitalism 35–6
  transition models 32
gradualism 39–40
ideological cost see transition cost
ideological structure
  common good 46
  economic analysis 44–8
  non-pluralistic market socialism
    213–14
  participation 46–8
  pluralistic market socialism 178–9
  Post Keynsian model 144
  self-interest 45–6
  shock therapy 81
  Stalinist system 15–16, 24
ideology
  consistent 8–9
initial conditions
  economic analysis 48–50
  influence on cost 245–6
  neoclassical gradualism 116
  non- pluralistic market socialism 214
  pluralistic market socialism 179–80
  Post Keynsian model 144–5
  shock therapy 81–2
institutional structure
  economic analysis 57–9
  influence on cost 246–9
  neoclassical gradualism 123–5
  shock therapy 88–91
institutions
  non-pluralistic market socialism 222–5
  pluralistic market socialism 190–1
  Post Keynsian model 152–6
international cost
  formalist approach 242
  transition 70
international trade
  economic analysis 62
  neoclassical gradualism 129–31
  non-pluralistic market socialism
    229–31

pluralistic market socialism 194–6
  Post Keynsian model 160–4
  shock therapy 95–8
Kendall's Coefficient 243
labor-managed firms
  privatization 55–6
  leasing, in privatization 56–7
market socialism
  good society 36–7
models of transition see transition
  models
monetary policy
  economic analysis 59–61
  neoclassical gradualism 126–7
  non-pluralistic market socialism 225–7
  pluralistic market socialism 191–3
  Post Keynsian model 156–8
  shock therapy 91–3
neoclassical analysis 34
neoclassical gradualism 111–36
  financial system 125–7
  fiscal policy 128–9
  foreign aid 129–31
  initial conditions 116
  institutional structure 123–5
  international trade 129–31
  monetary policy 126–7
  political structure 114–6
  price liberalization 117–19
  primary elements 112–16
  privatization 119–23
  secondary elements 117–33
  social policy 131–3
  speed 112–14
  stabilization 117–19
  transition cost 67–70, 134
  transition process 133
non-pluralism 42
non-pluralistic market socialism
    203–35
  conclusion 233–5
  economic analysis 206–8
  financial system 225–7
  fiscal policy 228–9
  foreign aid 229–31
  good society 207–8
  ideological structure 213–4
  initial conditions 214
  institutions 222–5
  international trade 229–31
  monetary policy 225–7
  political structure 42, 210–3

price liberalization 215–8
primary elements 206–14
privatization 218–22
secondary elements 215–32
social policy 231–2
speed 208–10
stabilization 215–8
transition cost 232–3
transition process 232
optimum model
analysis 239–49
participation
ideological structure 46
pluralistic market socialism 169–203
conclusion 199–203
economic analysis 170–1
financial system 191–3
fiscal policy 193
foreign aid 194–6
good society 171–4
ideological structure 178–9
initial conditions 179–80
institutions 190–1
international trade 194–6
monetary policy 191–3
political structure 176–8
price liberalization 180–3
primary elements 170–80
privatization 183–90
secondary elements 180–98
social policy 196–8
speed 174–6
stabilization 180–3
transition cost 199
transition process 198–9
political cost see transition, cost
political pluralism
political structure 41
political structure
democracy 41
economic analysis 41–4
neoclassical gradualism 114–16
non-pluralism 42
non-pluralistic market socialism
210–3
pluralistic market socialism 176–8
political pluralism 41
Post Keynsian model 143–4
shock therapy 78–80
Stalinist system 13–15, 22–4
Post Keynsian model 137–68
conclusion 166–8

economic analysis 137–9
financial system 156–8
fiscal policy 159–60
foreign aid 160–4
good society 139–41
ideological structure 144
initial conditions 144–5
institutions 152–6
international trade 160–4
monetary policy 156–8
political structure 143–4
price liberalization 145–9
primary elements 137–45
privatization 149–52
secondary elements 145–65
social policy 164–5
speed 141–2
stabilization 145–9
transition cost 166
transition process 165–6
Post Keysian analysis 34
preventive therapy see neoclassical
gradualism
price liberalization–stabilization
economic analysis 52
neoclassical gradualism 117–19
non-pluralistic market socialism
215–8
pluralistic market socialism 180–3
Post Keynsian model 145–9
shock therapy 82–4
primary elements see transition models
privatization
economic analysis 52–7
financial intermediaries 54
leasing 56–7
labor-managed firms 55–6
neoclassical gradualism 119–23
non-pluralistic market socialism
218–22
pluralistic market socialism 183–90
Post Keynsian model 149–52
restitution 53
sale of state property 54
shock therapy 84–8
spontaneous 55
voucher distribution 54
restitution
privatization 53
secondary elements see transition models
self-interest
ideological structure 45–6

shock therapy 38–9, 73–110
    conclusion 102–8
    economic analysis 74–5
    financial system 91–3
    fiscal policy 93–5
    foreign aid 95–8
    good society 75–6
    ideological structure 81
    initial conditions 81–2
    institutional structure 88–91
    international trade 95–8
    monetary policy 91–3
    political structure 78–80
    price liberalization–stabilization
        82–4
    primary elements 74–82
    privatization 84–8
    secondary elements 82–100
    social policy 99–100
    speed 38–9, 76–8
    transition cost 100–1
    transition process 100
social policy
    economic analysis 62–3
    neoclassical gradualism 131–3
    non-pluralistic market socialism
        231–2
    pluralistic market socialism 196–8
    Post Keynsian model 164–5
    shock therapy 99–100
social reality
    transition models 32
social welfare
    maximization 67
    transition 67
social-democratic capitalism
    good society 35–6
speed
    economic analysis 37–40
    gradualism 39–40
    neoclassical gradualism 112–14
    non-pluralistic market socialism
        208–10
    pluralistic market socialism 174–6
    Post Keynsian model 141–2
    shock therapy 38–9, 76–8
stabilization
    neoclassical gradualism 117–19
    non-pluralistic market socialism
        215–8

pluralistic market socialism 180–3
Post Keynsian model 145–9
Stalinist system
    collapse 3–25
    consistency 5–9, 16–17
    economic structure 9–13, 17–22
    ideological structure 15–16, 24
    political structure 13–15, 22–4
    viability 5–7, 24–5
state property
    sale 54
total cost
    transition cost 67–70, 100–1, 134, 166,
        200, 239–49
    cost indices of models 243
    cost rankings 242
    economic cost 69
    formalist approach 241–5
    ideological cost 69
    implementation costs 67–70
    international cost 70
    net benefits 67
    political cost 69
    process 63–5, 100, 133, 165, 198–9,
        232
    ranking of models 242
    social welfare 67
transition modeling
    developmental process 33
    process aim 33
transition models
    comparative analysis 27–70
    conclusions re optimality 239–49
    desired changes 32
    economic analysis 34
    good society 34–7
    initiating changes 33
neoclassical gradualist see neoclassical
    gradualism
    primary elements 31–50, 74–82,
        112–16, 137–45, 170–80, 206–14
    secondary elements 51–65, 82–100,
        117–33, 145–65, 180–98, 215–32
    therapy shock see shock therapy
    social reality 32
viability
    Stalinist system 5–7, 24–5
voucher distribution
    privatization 54

Printed in the United States
by Baker & Taylor Publisher Services